CASTE, CATHOLIC CHRISTIANITY AND THE LANGUAGE OF CONVERSION

CASTE, CATHOLIC CHRISTIANITY AND THE LANGUAGE OF CONVERSION

Social Change and Cultural Translation in Tamil Country, 1519-1774

S. JEYASEELA STEPHEN

KALPAZ PUBLICATIONS
DELHI-110052

Caste, Catholic Christianity and the Language of Conversion : Social Change and Cultural Translation in Tamil Country, 1519-1774

Rs. 890

ISBN: 81-7835-686-4

Published in 2008 in India by
Kalpaz Publications
C-30, Satyawati Nagar,
Delhi-110052
E-mail: kalpaz@hotmail.com
Phone : 9212729499

Printed at : Excel Prints. Naraina. New Delhi.

Contents

SECTION IV

List of Abbreviations

Archives and Libraries

AAAM	Archives of the Archdiocese of Madras –Mylapore, Chennai
AAPC	Archives de l'Archevéché de Pondichéry-Cuddalore, Pondicherry
AGC	Archives General of the Capuchin Order, Rome
AGS	Archivo General de Simancas, Valladolid.
AHU	Arquivo Histórico Ultramarino, Lisbon.
AMEP	Archives des Missions Etrangères de Paris
AN	Archives Nationales, Paris.
APF	Archivio Della S. Congregazionae di Propaganda Fide
ARSI	Archivum Romanum Societatis Iesu. Rome.
ASV	Archivio Secreto Vaticano, Vatican City
BA	Biblioteca da Ajuda, Lisbon.
BAV	Biblioteca Apostolica Vaticana
BFP	Bibliothèque Franciscaine Provinciale, Paris
BL	British Library, London.
BNL	Biblioteca Nacional de Lisboã, Lisbon.
BNP	Bibliothèque Nationale, Paris.
HAG	Historical Archives of Goa, Panaji.
IANTT	Instituto Arquivo Nacionais/ Torre do Tombo, Lisbon.
MPJA	Madurai Province Jesuit Archives, Shenbaganur.
NA	Nationaal Archief, The Hague
NAIP	National Archives of India, Pondicherry

Records and Journals

AA	Acta Asiatica
AHSI	Archivum Historicum Societatis Jesu
ALB	The Adyar Library Bulletin
APO-BP	Arquivo Portugues Oriental (ed.) Bragança Pereira.
APO-CR	Archivo Portuguez Oriental (ed.) Cunha Rivara.
ARE	Annual Report on Epigraphy.
BFUP	Bolteim da Filmoteca Ultramarina Portuguesa.
BUB	Bataviaasch Uitgaand Briefboek.
CAA	Cartas de Affonso de Albuquerque.
CC	Corpo Cronológico.
CDI	Caixa da India.
CHJ	Ceylon Historical Journal
CSL	Coleção São Lourenço.
DACB	Diary and Consultation Book.
DI	Documenta Indica.
DR	Dagh Register.
DRI	Documentos Remetidos da India.
EFI	English Factories in India.
EX	Epistolae S. Francisci Xaverii alia que eius Scriptura.
ICHR	Indian Church History Review
IES	Indian Ecclesiastical Studies
IESHR	Indian Economic and Social History Review.
JIH	Journal of Indian History.
JOR	Journal of Oriental Research
LEC	Lettres Edifiantes Curieuses
MDR	Monções do Reino.
NAF	Nouvelle Acquisitions Françäise.
SII	South Indian Inscriptions.
SITI	South Indian Temple Insciptions.
SM	Studia Missionalia
TTDES	Tirumala- Tirupati Devasthanam Epigraphical Series

Preface

When my earlier book "Portuguese in the Tamil Coast: Historical Explorations in Commerce and Culture" (ISBN 81-87382-00-7, Navajyothi, Pondicherry, 1998) was declared out of print within three years of publication, there has been constant pressure on me from the students, scholars and general readers to republish it as a new, revised/ enlarged edition or as it is. First, I thought of bringing it out an updated and revised version of it, particularly because I had continued to do more research in the same field (except trade and commerce) on various new themes such as social and cultural history, also by extending the period of study. At this time I also came across several new writings on micro history, new cultural history and history of mentalites by scholars of different disciplines. In the light of such studies I began to reflect upon writing this new book by including fresh and updated treatment of the subject on society and culture including the history of art and architecture. Hence, this is the end result.

All the archives and libraries which are referred to here have received me with great kindness. I visited Europe in 2000 and again worked in different archives in quest of materials relevant to my study of research. I am deeply indebted to Dr. José Blanco and Dr. João Pedro Garcia for the award of the Grant of the Fundação Calouste Gulbenkian in Lisbõa, Portugal. I also thank Dra. Maria Emilia Freyssenet for her help. I am grateful to Fr. Cornu and Fr. G. Moussay, of the Missions Étrangeres de Paris for the award of a grant to consult the records. I would like to mention Prof. L.F.F.R Thomaz, Lisbõa, Prof. K.S. Mathew, Director, IRISH, Tellicherry,

Dr. George Pattery, the Jesuit Provincial of the Calcutta Province, Dr. João Manuel de Almeida Teles e Cunha, Lisbõa, and Prof. Pierre & Vasundhara Filliozat, Paris, who encouraged me in the making of the book and extended me hospitality, making my stay comfortable and enabling me to work without any distraction. I am thankful to all of them.

In this venture, I am greatly indebted to a good number of friends particularly Late Françoise L' Hernault, the art historian and Pierre Pichard, an eminent French architect at the Ecole Française d' Extreme-Orient who had given me insights through discussion. At the same time my association with INTACH (Pondicherry) which at one time had worked in collaboration with the EFEO helped me immensely. Further, Mr. Ramesh, at the Institut Français, Pondicherry was always willing to extend all possible help as and when I needed. Dr. Murugesan who was deeply interested in the progress of the work gave me a moral boost since he himself had specialized knowledge in the documentation of art and architecture at the EFEO/IFP. In fact, all worked together to provide me with a congenial situation for research. I whole heartedly thank all of them. Lastly, I am indebted to the publisher for bringing out the book with efficiency.

I hope this book will remain as a symbol to all those who in distant shores keep alive the memories of Portugal and this will continue to serve as a source of inspiration to all those interested in the rich and variegated culture of India as well as to those concerned with the wider artistic heritage of Portugal.

Dibrugarh, Assam
8 August 2007

Introduction

In the Sangam literature of the Tamils five *thinais* are mentioned and they represent a caste like or proto-caste stage in the early social formation. The *kanavar, kunuvar* and *vedar* were the people of *Kunrinji*. The *Aayar* and *idaiyar* belonged to the *Mullai*. The *Uzhavar* and *thozhuvar* lived in the *Marutham*. The *Parathavar*, *valayar* and *minanavar* were the people of *Neithal*. The *Kalavar*, *eyinar* and *maravar* were of the *Palai thinai*.[1] Scholars have accepted the above mentioned divisions as the Dravidian origin of caste. Increasing interaction and interdependence among the socio-cultural groups with fundamentally different systems took place at that time in which each community had remained encapsulated retaining its separate identity. During the Sixth Century B.C the Jain and Buddhist movements emerged and they were directed against Brahmanical priesthood (not the Brahmins) and the *varna* hierarchy. Writers have also traced the evidence for caste in the Vedic texts, the origin of caste and the elite in India in the later period besides stratification of the Rig Vedic society. The word *varna* (colour) and *jati* (class) in fact carried altogether different meanings. *Jati* was used since the post-Vedic age to denote a group of persons born as a result of inter-*varna* marriages. Manu in his time was able to mark out as many as 200 *jatis* (class) and *upajatis* (sub-classes).[2] It must be said that the Brahmanical priesthood had received patronage of the Hindu kings from the Third Century A.D. onwards. Ritual and social behavior became important at that point of time. Hence the religious-mystical theory, the biological theory and the socio-historical theory of caste system were slowly propagated and they remained popular. No single individual in India could challenge the *chatur-varna* theory beginning from Gautama Buddha (566-486 BC) to Ram Mohan Roy (AD 1772-1833).

It should be admitted at the outset that there had been regional differences in the social formation in India. I shall address here only the Tamil social formation. *Bhakti* religion in Tamil country did not emerge suddenly in the medieval period. We find in the ancient period the central theme in The *Bhagavad Gita* itself where *Bhakti* has been combined with the *varna* system explained as an expression of *gunas* (inherent qualities) and *karamas* (functions) of human nature. Krishna himself was said to have created the four *varnas* according to the *guna* and *karma*.[3] Further, it had been mentioned in The *Bhagavad Gita* and The *Manusmiriti* that even if one does not want to do a particular action he will be compelled to do it by the inherent nature.[4] Thus *Bhagavad Gita* tried to shift the injustice involved in considering a human being superior to another, just due to an accident of birth, off the shoulders of the divine creator and justified it in the light of the their of *karma*.[5] The *Varnashrama Dharma* was thus reestablished by the philosophy of The *Bhagavad Gita* for strengthening the forces of social determinism under the grab of *Bhakti* movement. In the light of the above details, the views of some scholars like M.G.S. Narayanan and Veluthat Kesavan that *Bhakti* religion was the result of a new wave of Aryan and Hindu influence among the Tamil people and it was a byproduct may be called into question[6] The door of *Bhakti* was opened to all for *moksa* was made conditional. For no one could achieve *moksa* unless he observed the caste duties. The *Bhagavad Gita* upheld the philosophy of social fatalism of divine determinism and left man in the state of theistic spiritualism.

The Kings of Tamil country themselves followed different faiths within the same dynasty. Nandivarman Pallava and Paramesvaravarman were *Saivites*. Narasimhavarman Pallava was a *Vaishnavite*. Among the Pandya rulers also Nedunjadaiyan was a Vaishnavite, while Varguna was a *Saivite*. The Chola rulers were generally staunch *Saivites* without exception but with varying degrees of attachment to that *Bhakti* religion.

Changing one's religion from Hinduism to Buddhism and Jainism and vice-versa was common. Hence it may be said that conversion was present in India much before the advent of Islam and Christianity. Mahendra Varman I, (AD. 590-630) the Pallava king who was a Jain became a *Saivite*. Chola King Anapya identified with Kulottunga II, (AD. 1133-1150) who was a follower of Jainism was converted to *Saivism* by the *Nayanmars*. In Hinduism itself the *Vaishnavites* had converted the *Saivites* and the *Saivites* converted the *Vaishnavites*. Virupaksha II (AD.1467-1478) the Vijayanagara ruler was converted to *Vaishnavism* by Ettur Narasimhacharya.[7] Chinna Bommu Nayaka the ruler of Vellore who was a *Saivite* was converted by Tatacharaya to *Vaishnavism*.[8] Religion and politics came very much inter-linked through the religious conversion of the Kings.

In Tamil Country during the medieval period there were four *samayas* (religious sects) such as the *Saiva*, *Vaishanava*, *Buddha* and *Jaina*. We find the rulers taking the title of *Chatus-Samaya-Samuddharana*[9] (supporter of four faiths). It appears that the Kings for the legitimization of their authority generally had used such titles. In their public role they assumed a liberal disposition allowing freedom as well as at times promoting religious beliefs and practices other than their own. Endowments to *Jaina*, *Buddhist*, *Saiva* and *Vaishanava* institutions[10] may be said to be indications of tolerance of the rulers. It is very difficult to depict the inner feelings of persons and their mentalities in the course of writing history of different periods and changing times. Destroying the Vishnu temples and persecuting the *Vaishnavites* by the Chola ruler who was living in Gangaikonda Cholapuram has been well known. Owing to the persecution by the Chola King Ramanuja Acharya made a flight in AD.1096 from Tamil Country to Mysore in the Kannada region.[11] However, this may be said to mark an act of intolerance within the fold of sectarian Hinduism.

The ideological and ritual differences that crept into sectarian Hinduism had led to divisions and factions. There came intense philosophical and theological debate between the *Saivites* and the *Vaishnavites*. It is said that Vishnu came down upon the earth several times (as many as forty times) with various *avatharas* (incarnations) to save mankind.[12] Siva did not do so at any rate. Harping on this point the *Vaishnavites* revolted against the spiritual monism of Sankaracharya (AD.781-820) during the Eleventh century.

A measure of increasing social exclusiveness of these sects is found in an inscription of AD.1160. It is mentioned that a decision was taken by the *mahasabha* of Tirukkaddiyar and it was resolved that those *mahesvaras* who contrary to their tenets as custodians of the Siva temple and its observances, if mixed freely with *Vaishnavites* would forfeit their property to the temple.[13] Religious rivalry and fanatical attachment to one's own faith had been depicted in the inscriptions. The temples at Tirumayam dedicated to Siva and Vishnu stood adjoining each other but separated only by a wall. The *Saivites* and the *Vaishnavites* had bitterly quarreled between themselves and stopped the worship at both the temples. Appana Dandanayaka, one of the generals of the Hoysala King Vira Somesvara who after his conquest of the region had sent word for both the parties. The points which brought about the quarrel between the *Saivites* and the *Vaishnavites* were gone through by him in detail and he settled the emotionally charged issues and disputes.[14]

Proliferation of castes is an important feature in Tamil history.[15] It is mainly linked with the practice of making land grants to *Brahmins* and the Pallava rulers had patronized it very much.[16] In the Tenth century *Saiva Siddhanta* system of Tamil culture emerged and it was a protest against Brahmin authority and *varna* system. In the Twelfth century the Lingayat movement in Karnataka emerged and it challenged the Brahmanical priesthood and *varna* hierarchy. It succeeded in its goal and had a tremendous impact in Tamil country. Stratification of the Tamil society in medieval Chola times is well known through inscriptions.[17] The *Brahmin* and peasant identity had been examined by Burton Stein.[18] The uprisings of the *Valangai* and *Idangai* groups prevalent at that time besides the conflicts in agrarian society had been also analyzed by Noboru Karashima.[19]

However, scholars opine that the caste cohesion is an important reason why Hinduism could survive even today. It is true that the institution of caste had offered a lot of communal togetherness, social security and certain pride in one's caste identity and I have pointed out them elsewhere as gleaned from the inscriptional data.[20] But when the forces of *Brahmin* domination, authoritarianism and hegemony became very strong in society the people had protested against it . Social inequality of privileges came to be prevalent on wider scale in Hinduism and it had vitiated the whole system. Thus the caste system which did not do much harm to the people in the initial stages or early historical period became an evil force in the early medieval period. *Varnavyavastha* (caste system) which meant both for cooperation and competition towards the progress of the society became ultimately as a result to exhibit superiority and establish inequality. It was at this *Bhakti* religion in Tamil country preached equality because the intrinsic and cardinal virtue of Hinduism came to disappear and the *Bhakti* preachers were unhappy with institution of caste.[21]

Bhakti religion in Tamil country began to introduce an egalitarian approach which disregarded caste. Sankaracharya used dialectics to demolish the Buddhist ideas and to establish that Vedas were the fountain head of knowledge. The preachers of *Bhakti* did not challenge the caste system or the primacy of the *Brahmins*. In temples elaborate rituals and ceremonies had developed. Ramanuja (AD.1017-1137) argued that for the salvation the grace of God was more important than knowledge about him. He argued that the path of *Bhakti* was open to all irrespective of caste. Thus Ramanuja acted as a bridge between those who based on *Bhakti* and total surrender to God and the upper caste movement based on the Vedas.[22]

The spread of *Bhakti* religion in medieval Tamil society undoubtedly brought about changes in people's behaviour but failed to uproot the basic discontentment prevailing in their social life. The kings as part of their duty were preserving and maintaining the *varnasrama dharma* as influenced by the Brahmins. The *Bhakti* religion opened the doors of spiritual religion to women, *sudras,* untouchables and outcastes. Some individuals from the low castes became religious leaders. The *Bhakti* religion fostered equality only in the religious sphere not in secular life. It did not favour social radicalism and the preachers did not live up to the standard of social utility and they failed to understand the social and economic conditions were responsible for groveling continuance. The *Bhakti* preachers did not offer any other alternative programme of social and economic reorganization of society and their appeal was very emotional rather than rational. They did not think of building up organizations of secular type which could carry out some positive social programme for mass awakening. The preachers thus failed to forge a social unity and they did not aim at reforming Hindu Tamil society on radical lines. Their sole interest was religion which included an inquiry into other-worldliness of transcendental and unfathomable nature.

Socio-Historical and Missiological Studies: An Overview

Portuguese were the first to impose the alterations of a newly emerging and evolving colonial order in India. The term Christians is very broad one constituting Roman Catholics, Syrians, Baptists, Presbyterians and Lutherans. Hence delimitation has been imposed; separate identity is spelled out and in this work we shall deal with Roman Catholics. It is a fact that the Tamil society of a given period (chronology) is the web of inter-relationship that exists among various individuals and social groups of Tamil country (the geographical area). Society and culture are closely related but both are distinct. The former is the patterns of association and relations through which persons influence or motivate one another, whereas the latter comprises certain products of these regulations in the form of communicable values, norms and standards. Socio-cultural changes had been intensive because the interaction of the Portuguese missionaries was exhaustive.

Some works have been produced so far on the Catholic Church history of India and their worth is to be assessed because they also deal with caste, conversion and society in a limited way. The work of Felix Alfred Plattner is essentially written to locate the past and place them within the context of the Christian tradition.[23] Aloysius Soares emphasized on the key personalities and key debates at particular points of time and traced the history of the church from the perspective of the present.[24] Thus these two works do not move away from the traditions of Christian way of writing history besides catering to the needs of a few, dealing part of the history of the church and not attempting to cover the history of the Christian people in its entirety.

Rev. M. D'Sa published two volumes of the history of the Catholic Church in India and his treatment is entirely a justification of the Portuguese mission from the padroadonist framework.[25] The attempt of Rev. Alex J.D. D'orsey was from an Anglican point of view and he carried the bias against the Catholic missions of the Sixteenth and Nineteenth centuries and his concern was desperately to establish how the Catholic missionaries had failed in their tasks. He wanted to show more importantly the role of the Anglican Church and how it could play in the spread of Christianity.[26] Thus both the clergymen have chiefly written their works with some sense of narrow-mindedness and we find inherent bias either attempt to glorify or justify the missionary actions.

Moving away from the traditional missionary writings that referred to the concentration of single individuals and their work in establishing Christian communities and in building churches many works have appeared dealing with religious conversions in the broader framework of social and economic history. Their emphasis was on pre-conversion, post-conversion and the problem caused by adhering to Christian beliefs and practices in a non-Christian milieu. This trend found in the history of the Catholic Christianity in India followed the framework of the socio-cultural history.[27] The study of Patrick Roche had looked into the newly found identity of the *Paravas* after their conversion to Roman Catholicism.[28] David Mosse in his work dealt with the social and religious history of a small village in Ramnad and showed that the expectations of the Roman Catholic congregations were decisive factors in shaping missionary strategy. He argued that the Jesuits mission with a very keen sense of the workers of the existing social system adapted itself and shaped its requirements and set up accordingly.[29]

Susan Bayly in her work agreed that the history of conversion movements cannot be studied merely in terms of a succession of events and mentioned that there is a need to place these movements within a broader social frame work. A misconception found in the writing of conversion movements has been the notion of the obliteration of pre-existing beliefs and ties among the new affiliates and in this connection she mentioned that conversion depended upon the capability of the missionaries to setup a viable relationship between the new God with that of the pre-existing one. The adoption of a religion also depended on the pre-existing social conditions and according to her in Pre-colonial South India society was in a state of flux and was still establishing its hierarchies.[30] She showed that Christianity was shaped to fit into the South Indian religious environment and into the social normative system that the shifting religious identity did not signify and sharp break between orthodoxies but rather a form of syncretism.

Bayly and Mosse had laid emphasis on the missionary process as adaptation and mutual dependency rather than as breaks with previous relationships. Both of them belong to the new paradigm with the focus on literary theory inspired by Michel Foucault emphasizing on the written and oral sources as texts while the broader structural analyses of caste and class had been given a secondary role.

It is known that missionary methods were not always unified and there were debates as to whether the means employed were in the interests of Christianity and true to Christianity itself. Ines G. Zupanov in her work had pointed out that the missionary movement was not a homogeneous one in Tamil country.[31] Houtart and Lemercinier attempt to show the conversions from the view of the process itself, besides classifying conversions as individual/group. Their main concern had been to look into the manner in which Catholicism and its institutional paraphernalia replaced Hinduism and served the same functional purposes as the latter.[32]

Henriette Bugge dealt with power and ritual that gave a whole new angle to the study of Catholic Christian missions in the South Arcot region from 1840-1900 and the analysis of religion as a dynamic factor in Indian history was seen in a social and economic context.[33] There are also other works dealing with Catholic Christianity for the Nineteenth and Twentieth centuries where we find marginalization of Christian. It is mentioned that the British rule in India did not privilege Christians but pushed them to the margins of a predominantly Hindu society.[34]

Therefore, there is a greater need for the study of the Catholic Church and the history of the period particularly the Sixteenth, Seventeenth and the Eighteenth centuries under the Portuguese *Padroado* and this study attempts to examine the caste, Catholic Christianity and the religious conversion in Tamil country. It begins with the year 1519, the first arrival of the Portuguese along with an Armenian Merchant to visit the tomb of Apostle St. Thomas in Mylapore from Melaka via Pulicat . The study ends in 1774 after

Pope Clement XIV published his brief *Dominus ac Redemptor* on 21 July 1773 by which all the Jesuit missions were suppressed in Tamil country.

Approach to the Study

Fernand Braudel had used the term 'micro history' pejoratively to refer superficial history of events. Emergence of micro-history is noticed with emphasis among the Annales historians and its practitioners affected by the crisis in Marxist politics and theory (which had a strong political and cultural presence in Italy), as well as more broadly in the so-called 'grand narratives' of progress. Giovanni Levi has mentioned that the intention of micro history was to narrow the historian's analytical focus onto a tightly defined aspect of the past so as to investigate it in greater depth. The two distinct methods of micro history include social and cultural.[35] Thus micro history became the first attempt to overturn the received model of social history which had from the outset been cast in the mould of macro history. Against this backdrop the book deals with the advent of the Portuguese and the Tamil society.

The earliest attempt to yoke history within it under the 'social' had been done by Auguste Comte. He divided sociology (a term coined by him) into 'social statics' and 'social dynamics' the latter being history and understood as the science which discovered the laws of social transformation and development. The approach of the Annales historians who raised the discipline of history to a prominent institutional and intellectual place had become important to understand the society and culture and their approach adapting quantitative methods had been so successful in economic and social history because by assembling the statistics of quantifiable information preserved in series of documents it was possible to trace changes over time. Against this backdrop the first section deals with religious conversions, castes and communities, societal changes, the origin and growth of the Christian institutions such as seminaries, sodalities, colleges, schools, orphanages, hospitals and holy houses of mercy in the Tamil region.

In the age of renaissance the word 'culture' (*cultura*) was associated with the cultivation of literature, painting, eloquence, law, arts and sciences whose fruits were the human and civil virtues necessary for the civil society. In the Seventeenth Century we find the form of culture firmly established and it was employed by Francis Bacon, G.W. Leibiniz, J.F. Buddeus, Christian Thomasius and others who spoke of a cultivation of the soul, mind, intellect or reason. What is very interesting had been the way in which the focus of culture shifted from an individual to a social level and later became a way of indicating levels of civilization and finally we find the emergence of a discipline of cultural history. According to Jacob Burckhardt (1818-1897) the father of cultural history, that culture is one of the three powers alongside the state and religion and that they are supremely heterogeneous to each other and cannot be coordinated. Roger Chartier has taught the historians to look closely at the processes by which ordinary people use the cultural artifacts produced for them. He dealt with relations between culture and social life. He said that culture cannot be seen as simply a manifestation of social arrangements and he argued that the social has its own rules and logic which cannot be reduced to those of culture or language. [36] He objects that symbols do not have the kind of public, observable fixity but mentioned that they are unstable, mobile and equivocal.

The work of Clifford Geertz has tended to become the dominant reference point for historians engaging with anthropology - to the extent of obscuring the degree of conceptual and methodological debate within that discipline.[37] He has pressed strongly the 'text analogy' for reading the meanings of social actions; the 'thick description' of key events which he advocated anthropologists should produce. He had examined public behaviour for what it said rather than what it did. It read the symbolic content of action and interpreted it as sign. The transition from social to cultural history and the accompanying shifts in subject-matter and method are responses not only to the internal developments of history as a discipline, but also to wider political and intellectual trends. The work of the church historians mentioned earlier has not been concerned much to reconstruct and depict vividly the complex agency of individuals outside the social elites of medieval and early-modem society, and their capacity to win a degree of freedom within powerful religious or political systems. Hence against this backdrop the various Catholic Religious Orders such as the Franciscans, the

Jesuits, the Dominicans, the Augustinians and the Capuchins and their steps involved in conversions, the role of the Portuguese Missionaries, response of the native Christian Communities such as the *Paravas*, the Mukkuvars, the *Brahmins, Vellalars, Shedars, Thottiya Nayakkars, Chetti Nayakkars, Paraiyars, Kambalavars, Kammalars, Kallars, Maravars, Shanars* and other castes, caste system and the attitudes of the Tamil Christians and the societal changes are examined along with conversion statistics.

Michel Foucault and New Historicism became very important to understand society and culture. It had an important influence on modern ways of thinking about history and historiography. Foucault's work is indebted to Georg Wilhelm Friedrich Nietzsche,(1770-1831) and he was concerned to discover how the idea of the human subject had evolved, and in what ways that subject could know itself and, more importantly, differentiate itself from others. He therefore undertook research that was historical in nature and was always careful to distance away from the characteristic methodologies of traditional history. He claimed even at one point that he was interested in the past only in so far as it enabled him to write 'the history of the present'. Foucault's influence tends to be in areas addressed to broader issues of method and the philosophy of history, rather than in actual empirical debates. According to him identifying and accounting for the changes that have overtaken the human subject should be the historian's real task. Founded on the Enlightenment principles of order, reason and progress and with the human subject placed firmly at the centre of history, its early practitioners felt that knowledge of the past should be ordered along the same rational, anthropocentric lines as every other field of knowledge.[38] Thus the professional history was earlier incapable of historicizing the evolution of these values but, the modern human subject came to be constituted the discipline's central concern. The idea of history advanced in this fashion according to some over-arching idea or human-centred narrative was anathema to Foucault, and he wanted at this time to define a method of historical analysis freed from the anthropological theme. Everyday life history (*Alltagsgeschicte*) has become so important and against this backdrop, section two of the book attempts to deal with the Christian life and everyday practices of the Tamils including

Christian pilgrimage and cults of saints like that of Francis Xavier at Kottar, João de Britto at Oriyur, St. James at Suranam, feast of Our Lady of Snows at Tuticorin, Our Lady of Health at Velankanni, Our Lady of Refuge at Elakurichi, festivals such as Pongal and Mattu Pongal, enacting mystery plays, satirical plays, miracle plays, passion plays, miscellaneous plays and dramas on the lives of saints at that time.

Until recently sexual matters were rarely discussed in historical writing except allusively. Sigmund Freud in his writings had attributed much to sex but Michel Foucault had influenced historical work on sexuality. According to Foucault sexuality is a thing, a natural fact, fixed and immovable element in the eternal grammar of human subjectivity. Sexuality is a cultural production. It is not a somatic fact but it is a cultural effect.[39] Against this background we trace cases involving adultery and sex, murder and death, slavery, immorality and disorderly conduct, marriages, dowry system, Luso-Tamil cultural relations and social life of the Portuguese *Casados* and *Mestiçoes* in the Indo-Portuguese settlements on the Tamil coast

The approach of Max Weber (1864-1920) towards culture was seen as involving values the very common one used by the sociologists from an analytical view point and they tried to outline which values a certain social structure embodied. Some sociologists have argued that there is more to the notion of culture than values, or alternatively, that it is a mistake to centre a sociological analysis around values in the first place. Some others have been influenced by the anthropological concept of culture, both in its classical sense as artifacts and in its modern sense as meaning structures. The end result of these developments is a mixture of the old and the new meanings of culture and values.

It must be categorically stated that the Marxists showed interest in the history and theorisation of culture primarily for political reasons and their concern was primarily to establish the role of culture in political struggles and in particular the cultural roots of resistance and subordination among the subaltern classes. They explained the character and mechanisms of ideology to evaluate the effects of mass culture which has been a major and distinctive feature of Twentieth-century societies. The starting point for such an analysis has been ascribed to Karl Marx (1818-1883) and to his famous metaphor of base and superstructure[40] Culture had been seen here as part of the superstructure and its character ultimately determined by the structure of the economic base of society. In the crudest versions, Marxist theory shows the culture of a given society that was merely noticed as an automatic reflection of the prevailing political and economic system. Recently Marxist theorizing of culture has been worked out either to modify this model by loosening the ties supposed to bind base to superstructure, or more fruitfully to challenge the very notion that culture is located in a separate superstructure. However, such modifications leave it doubtful how far Karl Marx's original metaphor retains any value.

As the concept of culture has been used in a number of ways, including its everyday meaning as high culture, being a mode of living it includes elements of language, customs, habits, techniques, beliefs, ideas, attitudes, religions, material culture and values, section three of the book aims to analyze and highlight the role of the missionaries, Tamil Prose, Development of Christian devotional literature and printing, Portuguese contribution to Tamil Grammar and Lexicography, religious architecture and the impact of the Portuguese in Tamil Country, ecclesiastical art in Tamilnadu and the role of the missionaries and Armenian traders.

Thus the book focusses on quantitatively based social history over the *longue duree* (lengthy periods, often of a century or more). This work also takes up Lucien Febvre's original interests - the history of *mentalites* (mentalities, belief systems). Hence the writing of the social history of the Tamils has been characterized by ambition to write *histoire totale* (total history) by extending into every aspect of human life by interdisciplinary methodologies.

Notes and References

1. K. Siva Thamby, "Early South Indian Society and Economy: The Tinai Concept", *Social Scientist*, (henceforth SS), Vol. 29, 1974, pp. 20-37.
2. P.V. Kane, *History of Dharmasastra*, Bombay, 1974, Vol. II, Pt. I, pp. 56-60. Suvira Jaiswal, *Caste: Origin, Function and Dimension of Change*, Delhi, 1998. In the *Purusosukta* of Rig Veda there is reference to four

orders of society emanating from the sacrifice of the Brahmins. The Rig Veda refers to *Arya* and *Dasa* as two types of people. The four fold division of caste was purely functional. Besides the *sudras* there were some people below the status of the four divisions. These included untouchables out castes. The Brahmins were the *Dharma Sutra* writers and they assigned duties and occupations.

3. *The Bhagavad Gita*, IV, 13.
4. *The Bhagavad Gita*, XIII, 60; *The Mansumiriti*, I, 28-30; See also, D.P. Vora, *Evolution of Morals in Epics*, Delhi, 1959, p.130.
5. D.P. Vora, *op.cit.,* p.130.
6. M.G.S. Narayanan & Veluthat Kesavan, 'Bhakti Movement in South India' in S.C. Mallik, (ed.,) *Indian Movements: Some Aspects of Dissent, Protest and Reform*, Simla, 1978, pp. 33-54.
7. Anantacharya, *Prapannanritiam*, cited in S. Krishnawamy Ayyengar, *Sources of Vijayanagar History*, reprint, Delhi, 1986, pp.71-73. Prapannamritam is a Vaishnava hagiographical work of the 17th century. See also, Konduri Sarojini Devi, *Religion in Vijayanagara Empire*, New Delhi, 1990.
8. These are discussed in N. Ramesan, *Sri Appaya Diskhita*, Hyderabad, 1972. See also William J. Jackson, *Vijayanagara Visions: Religious Experience and Cultural Creativity in a South Indian Empire,* OUP, Delhi, 2007, pp. 280-283.
9. *Epigraphia Carnatica*, (hereafter E.C) Vol. XII, No. 13.
10. *South Indian Inscriptions*, (hereafter S.I.I) Vol. IV, p. 366; Vol. IV, pp.1011-1014.
11. Alkondaville Govindahaya, *The Life of Ramanujacharaya*, S. Murray & Co, Madras, 1906.
12. T.S Rukmani, *A Critical Study of the Bhagavata Purana*, Madras, 1970, p. 4.
13. *Annual Report on Epigraphy*, (hereafter ARE) 257 of 1925.
14. ARE 387 of 1906; See also ARE 1907, Part II, Para 26, p. 55.
15. Simon Cassie Chetty, *The Castes, Customs, Manners and Literature of the Tamils*, (reprint) Delhi, 1988, see the division and subdivision of castes in chapter II. See also, J. Pandian, *Caste, Nationalism and Ethnicity, An interpretation of Tamil Cultural History and Social Order*, Bombay, 1987.
16. K.K. Pillai, "Were the Pallavas Brahmanas?" *Journal of Oriental Research*, (henceforth JOR), Silver Jubilee Volume, 1975, pp. 242-245.

17. M. Arockia Sami, "The Origin of the Vellalars" *Journal of Indian History*, (henceforth JIH), Vol. XXXIII, 1955, pp.25-29; See also, Vol. XXXIV, 1956, pp. 191-193.
18. Burton Stein, "Brahmana and Peasant in Early South Indian Society", *The Adyar Library Bulletin*, (henceforth ALB), Vol. XXXI-XXXII, Madras, 1967-68, pp. 229-269.
19. Noboru Karashima, "The Uprising of the Valangai and Idangai Groups: Conflict in Agrarian Society" *Toward a New Formation*, Delhi, 1992, pp. 141-158.
20. S. Jeyaseela Stephen. *The Coromandel Coast and its Hinterland: Economy, Society and Political System, 1500-1600*, Manohar, Delhi, 1997, pp. 176-178.
21. S. Jeyaseela Stephen, "Religious Mapping in Medieval South India: Interpretations of the Bhakti Religion and the Historical Debate", Sri Sri Aniruddha Deva Chair Lecture delivered at the Dibrugarh University, Assam on 9 August 2007.
22. S. Jeyaseela Stephen, *Literature, Caste and Society: The Masks and Veils*, Kalpaz Publications, Delhi, 2006, p.24.
23. Felix Alfred Plattner, *The Catholic Church in India: Yesterday and Today*, Bangalore, 1964.
24. Aloysius Soares, *Catholic Church in India: A Historical Sketch*, Bombay, 1964.
25. M. D'Sa, *History of the Catholic Church in India, Vol. 1, AD 52-1652*, Bombay, 1910; *Vol. II, 1652 -1924*, Bombay, 1924.
26. Alex J.D. D'Orsey, *Portuguese Discoveries, Dependencies and Missions in Asia and Africa*, London, 1893, p. xiii
27. G.A. Oddie, "Protestant Missions, Caste and Social Changes in India, 1850-1914", in *IESHR*, Vol.6. 1969, pp.259-291; A. Mathias Mundadan, *History of Christianity in India Vol. 1*, Bangalore, 1986; Joseph Thekkedath, *History of Christianity in India, Vol. II*, Bangalore, 1988, E.R, Hambye, *History of Christianity in India, Vol. III*, Bangalore,1996. Judith Brown mentions that conversions should be understood in the situation of socio-economic changes that were taking place and the attempt of individuals or groups to find meaning in their lives to be able to situate themselves in new locations in society. See, Judith M. Brown in J.M. Brown & Robert Erick Frykenberg, (eds.,) *Christians, Cultural Interactions and India's Religious Traditions*, Michigan, 2002, pp 6-7.

28. Patrick A Roche, *Fishermen of Coromandel*, Delhi, 1984. R.E. Frykenberg mentions that while attempting to study conversion movements we should examine namely the reason for the genesis of the religious communities, the character they come to develop and the cause of it, patterns of growth and even the growth of relative importance/decline of these communities. See, R.E Frykenberg, On the Study of Conversion Movements: A Review Article and a Theoretical Note", in *IESHR*, Vol. 17, No.1, 1988, p. 121.
29. C.D. F Mosse, *Caste, Christianity and Ideology: A Study of Social Organization and Religion in Rural Ramand*, D.Phil. Thesis, University of Oxford, 1986.
30. Susan Bayly, Saints, *Goddesses and Kings: Muslims and Christians in South Indian Society*, Cambridge, 1989, pp. 69-70.
31. Ines G. Zupanaov, *Disputed Mission, Jesuit Experiments and Brahmanical Knowledge in Seventeenth Century India*, Delhi, 2001.
32. Francois Houtart & Genevieve Lemercinier, *Genesis and Institutionalisation of the Indian Catholicism*, Louvain-la Neuve, 1981, pp. 108-110. Gauri Vishwanathan has pointed out to the underlying assumption on conversion debates in recent times, which presupposes a lack of agency amongst the poor and the weaker sections in society in determining their choice and their vulnerability to conversions. See, Gauri Vishwanathan, *Outside the Fold: Conversion, Modernity and Belief*, New Delhi, 2001, p.xiii. She has also written of the need to look at conversion as a process and not as a static category like Houtrat et al. It is believed that conversions mainly privilege the poor because of their economic dependency. Pertinent to this are the questions what about the people of high castes who were not exposed to poverty. It may be said that accepting the new religious beliefs are important than anything else in conversions.
33. Henriette Bugge, *Mission and Tamil Society: Social and Religious Change in South India, 1840-1900,* London, 1994.
34. Hugald Grafe, *Tamilnadu in the 19th and 20th Centuries: History of Christianity in India, Vol.IV, Pt.2*, Bangalore, 1990. See also, Chandra Mallampalli, *Christians and Public Life in Colonial South India, 1863-1937*, London, 2006.
35. Carlo Ginzburg, "Micro History, Two or Three Things that I Know about it", (trs.,) John & Anne C. Tedeschi, *Critical Inquiry*, Vol. No. 20 1993, pp. 10-35; See also, Sigurdur Gylfi Magnusson, "The Significance of History: Social History, and Micro History within the Post-Modernist State of Knowledge", *Journal of Social History*, Vol. No. 36, 2003, pp. 701-735.

36. Roger Chartier, *On the Edge of the Cliffe: History, Language and Practices*, (trs.,) Lydia G. Cochrane, Baltimore, 1997. See also. Jonathan Dewald, "Roger Chartier and the Fate of Cultural History", *French Historical Studies*, 21 (2) 1998, pp. 221-240. The Frankfurt school of cultural criticism though had been eclipsed by the vogue for French theory it continues to be an important background influence. Walter Benjamin associated with the school whose influence on cultural thinking is currently marked seems to have a potential to generate work in cultural history that has not yet been realized.
37. Clifford Geertz, *The Interpretation of Culture: Selected Essays*, New York, 1973. Geertz defined culture as "an historically transmitted pattern of meanings embodied in symbols a system of inherited conceptions expressed in symbolic form by means of which men communicate, perpetuate and develop their knowledge about and attitudes towards life".
38. Foucault in his *"The Order of Things"* (1970, p. xxii) speculated that Western history was made up of a series of distinct epistemes. An episteme denotes the historical conditions that, in a given period, delimit in the totality of experience a field of knowledge, define the mode of being of the objects that appear in that field, provide man's everyday perception with theoretical powers, and define the conditions in which he can sustain a discourse about things that is recognized to be true. See, Michel Foucault, *The Foucault Reader*, (ed.,) Paul Rabinow, New York, 1984. See also, Andre Burguiere, "The Fate of History of Mentalites in the Annales", *Society for Comparative Study of History and Society*, 24, 1982, pp. 424-437.
39. Michel Foucault, *The History of Sexuality*, Vol. I, (trs.,) by Robert Hurlay, New York, 1978. Michel Foucault, *The Use of Pleasure: The History of Sexuality*, Vol. II, (trs.,) by Robert Hurlay, New York, 1985.
40. Karl Marx, *Articles on India*, Bombay, 1945; See also, Anil Sen Gupta, "Karl Marx and India", *Society & Change*, Vol. 6 (1), 1989. Karl Marx wrote in 1859 that "The sum total of the relations of production constitutes the economic structure of society, the real foundation, on which rises a legal and political superstructure, and to which correspond definite forms of social consciousness. The mode of production of material life conditions the social, political and intellectual life process in general". See, Raymond Williams, "Base and Superstructure in Marxist Cultural Theory", *New Left Review*, No. 82, 1973, pp. 3-16.

SECTION-I

1

Tamil Hindu Society and the Advent of the Portuguese

Many scholars have generally treated the study of medieval South Indian society within the framework of a fourfold division.[1] B.A. Saletore explained the traditional Hindu social order as built around the epigraphical term *varna-shrama-dharma* (becoming the inspiration in the struggle of Vijayanagara rulers against the Bahmani rulers).[2] Nilakanta Sastri depicted the Vijayanagara rulers as protectors of Hindu society, defenders of Hindu culture and institutions.[3] He used the epigraphical term *purva mariyadai* to explain the keen attention the rulers gave to building temples and making generous endowments. A. Krishnaswami Pillai continued Nilakanta Sastri's tradition, putting forth the view that rulers followed the noble tradition of *purva mariyadai bhaddati*-preservation of old culture and tradition.[4] T.V. Mahalingam added that respect for *purva mariyadai* was confined to certain customary rights which certain individuals or groups enjoyed for a long time in society under the Vijayanagara rule.[5]

These views of *varna-shrama-dharma* and *purva mariyadai* are, however, not entirely accurate. The kings of Vijayanagara did not only perpetuate the old social order; they encouraged real and fundamental change. The rise of nayakas as revenue collectors in Tamil Country and the dynamics of Vijayanagara political process did affect Tamil society. We shall try to highlight the manner in which society reacted to the new milieu.

Burton Stein's study of Vijayanagara state and society challenged the conquest theory suggested by the South Indian historians like Krishnaswami Iyengar, Venkataramanaya, Nilakanta Sastri and A. Krishnaswami Pillai. He hypothesised at first that Vijayanagara expansion into Tamil country resulted in the establishment of segmentary state and society where the Vijayanagara emperors exercised sovereignty over big and small *nayakattanams.*[6] Later he revised his thought to introduce the patrimonial system where the formal state and all other political forms were brought face to face with a distinct kind of social relations of production, which was neither a feudal nor modern capitalistic system.[7] This view is to some extent acceptable.

The Tamil society could not have been a static society.[8] Stein himself has described some structural changes that took place in Tamil society in the thirteenth century in the process of change. Some studies on aspects of social life have limited themselves to the social institutions such as marriage, sati, women, court life, food and dress, luxuries, games and amusements, religion and education but no one has focused on the structure of society, interrelations between classes and groups and the impact of the process of social change. We shall identify major social parameters and study how the Tamil society was a changing society, with a mixture of classes, groups and economic divisions. The nature of change, its direction and causes which led to this change can be situated in the socio-economic context.

Peasants

In the Tamil society the position of the peasantry declined, the status of weavers rose vis-a-vis merchants and social mobility increased among particular caste groups. Restructuring of peasant society occurred during the sixteenth century on account of the heavy and unjust tax burden imposed on them by rulers.[9] Taxes prevalent had no relation to the yield of a crop[10] and their living conditions were deplorable. Lands in Devikapuram were uncultivated, the peasants having deserted the place[11] for more hospitable neighbouring areas. In Srimushnam *nayakattanam* too peasants deserted.[12] In Tirukoyilur, some peasants, unable to pay taxes, sold their lands dirt cheap and left.[13] The taxes on peasants using the plough were higher than those on *Kaikolars* (weavers) and others not using the plough.[14]

The dispirited peasants realised that their problems arose because they were not organised. They began to form voluntary associations to resist extortion[15] and decided to pay only what they thought were just taxes, in proportion to the yield of the crop. Organised peasant activity involved emigration, sale of land, desertion and non-payment of taxes.[16] The vastness of land encouraged them to migrate rather than revolt.

The resulting temporary dislocation in cultivation served very well in settling the peasants' grievances. Nayaka rulers promptly undertook remedial measures, resettling the migrant peasants, giving them concessions and revising the tax rates. Thyagara nayaka pledged to reduce oppressive taxation on the peasants of Magadai mandalam and asked them to stop migrating.[17] Seshadhri Ayyan resettled the peasants who had migrated from Polur and Tiruvannamalai region.[18] As late as 1592 we find nayakas trying to induce peasants to return to their lands.[19]

But unjust taxation was only one problem of the peasants. Although in the wake of the remedial measures undertaken by nayakas general expansion of agriculture took place in the localities of Tamilnadu, peasants became poor owing to many other reasons, including probably the frequent droughts and famines. Certain social restrictions imposed on cultivating peasants in Villiyanoor[20] lead us to believe that peasants were reduced to a lower status and led a miserable life.

Weavers and Artisans

Weaving communities comprised *Kaikolar*, *Devangar*, *Saliyar* and *Pattunulkar*. *Kaikolars* were ranked the highest on account of their ritual links with temples. *Kaikola Mudalis* were those appointed to high posts and acted as authorities of various temples.[21] They maintained temple lands[22] and were in some cases paid for their services.[23] They decorated the *mantapam*, fanned the deity with *camaras*, blew the conch and trumphets, lighted lamps with oil supplied by the temple kitchen, supplied plantain leaves from the temple garden for packing *prasadam*, and carried the jewellery box of the deity when it was taken out for sacred bath.[24]

A local ruler bestowed on the weavers of Tribhuvanai, Naduvakkarai and Nemalai the right to go about in palanquins and the right to blow the conch shell on all ritual and other social occasions. These privileges were granted on par with other weavers of the Pennar riverine basin.[25] The weavers of Tiruvennainallur, Tiruttalur and Tirukoyilur were also accorded the same privileges. This indicates that regional inequality of social privileges existed among the weavers in South Arcot region.[26]

In the two flourishing textile production centres of Kanchipuram and Vrinchipuram the weaving community enjoyed certain special privileges and honours, probably on account of their professional skills. A recommendation by these privileged weavers to grant similar social privileges to the weavers of Valudilampattu[27] indicates unity among the weaving community.[28] Similarly, the privileges enjoyed by the *Kaikolars* of Kanchipuram were granted to the *Kaikolars* of Brahamadesam, which included permission to build two storeyed houses, to have double doors, and to bedeck the exterior of their homes with garlands of water lilies.[29] Royal charters of special privileges were generally given to the weavers with insignia.[30] Those objecting to the unity of weavers' privileges were punishable and the award of punishment was fixed.[31]

Weavers' unity is demonstrated in the many petitions they made to the local rulers to restore the deprived privileges in many localities.[32] This resulted in consultation among various nayakas and rulers like Konguravar, Karayar and Kachirayar to award equal privileges.[33] Finally the rulers enacted laws to grant social privileges to all weavers on par with those of Kanchipuram.[34] This process of weavers' social transformation was a remarkable feature of the time.

Tamil economy was supported by artisans who produced various commodities at several villages. The inscriptions generally describe their communal life.[35] Their living quarters were called *cheri*.[36] Some sources club five artisan communities into a single group called *Anjujati Panchalattars*. The artisans of Gingee, Padaividu and Tiruvannamalai, where metal, stone and wood works flourished, enjoyed special social privileges probably due to their professional skill. Some social privileges on important ritual occasions, such as accepting the dress put on the deity and receiving its headgear were at first granted to *Anjujati Panchalattar* of Gingee, Padaividu and Tiruvannamalai alone[37] and were later extended to artisans of other regions,[38] which indicates that there was discrimination of social privileges among *Anjujati Panchalattar*.

The clamour among the artisans of various localities for equality of privileges called *pavadai*, *parivattam* and *mugam-tudai*[39] was sought to be sorted out in meetings held in temples.[40] Artisans believed that they were descendants of the five sons of *Visvakarma*, son of Siva and his consort, each son representing a craft.[41] The *Anjujati Panchalattar* therefore assembled at the *mukha mantapa* of the Siva temple or that of his consort for such meetings. Inscriptions at various localities such as Villiyanoor, Tirupati, Kalakhasti and Chandragiri record that these deprived social privileges of artisans were restored to them after the discussion in temples. The unity of the artisan community was an important factor in its success in securing equal social rights among themselves.[42] Any one who objected to the grant of privileges to artisans was fined twelve pons.[43]

The social privileges were, however, not permanent; they could be withdrawn.[44] Thus artisans of Virudhachalam, Nagalapuram and Tirunavalur, who once enjoyed honours like *pavadai* and *parivattam* were deprived of them in 1572 and 1579. The rights had been granted earlier in return for cultivation and service in temples.[45] *Anjujati Panchalattar* was not recognised for their professional skill, but received social rights under the patronage of temples. This state of affairs induced the artisans to canvass the support of traders of the region to regain the privileges.[46] The *Nattavars* of Villiyanoor and Ariyalur consented to restore their privileges.[47] But later on, when restoration of privileges was denied, the artisans emigrated en masse to other villages; faced with this situation, the *Panchalattar* were given assurances of redressal of their grievances.[48] This was a victory of *Anjujati Panchalattar*[49] and indicates that there was social consciousness among artisans at the regional level to fight against exploitation. In this context, it is difficult to estimate the pivotal position of temples and related religious institutions in the social life of Tamil country during Vijayanagara period.[50]

Historians who have studied the social life of artisans of the Vijayanagara period have not highlighted the marked degrees of social inequality in Tamil society.[51] Many sociologists have advanced theories of social stratification to explain why inequality exists in society. Karl Marx's sociological theory, which is the most popular, sees the determinant of inequality and stratification in all societies through a single approach of economic domination' of society by one ruling class. Marxists also explain craft stagnation in production at the secondary sector created by communalistic village bodies. Max Weber's theory differed in many ways from Marx, clearly differentiating between the concepts of class, status and power as distinct axes of inequality which were not reducible into one another or to a more fundamental dimension of inequality. Sociologists of the elitist tradition argue that the existence of elite is necessary and persistent in all human societies. They are much concerned with the circulation of elite and the extent to which new governing individuals or groups replace the older ones. American sociologists of the Functionalist School argue that inequality has not taken root in the attempt by one group to achieve power at the expense of the majority.

All these theoretical discussions on stratification state that inequality embraced a variety of factors within society and may be related to legal, political, social and economic factors. How would they apply to the unique context of Tamil society? Social scientists declare that the features expounded by them are valid for all societies but Tamil society did not display such features. The application of these theories of social stratification to Tamil society would therefore be meaningless.

The Weberian approach, however, offers a particularly valuable framework for examining the situation of Tamilnadu where groups arose in the social and political hierarchy and not directly as part of the bourgeois ruling class. Specialisation in crafts existed in many localities of Tamil country with a wide gap between artisans. While social differentiation of skilled and unskilled artisans led to a continued struggle for the restoration of privileges of the artisans, craftsmen like weavers secured prestige and authority, having closely associated themselves with the functions of the clergy in temples.[52]

Merchants

Scholars have studied the place of merchants in society and their relationship with the state and established authority. We shall discuss the role of merchants as partly inside and partly outside the political system. Merchants had a lower status in society than weavers, who monopolised many titles such as *kandiyadevan*, *kalingarayan*, *patta manangkattan* and *ulakalam venran*. The merchants resented this state of affairs. The betel leaf merchants of Villiyanoor, when they saw the privileges of weavers carved in an inscription, bribed the officials concerned to erase them and instead allot some such titles to merchants.[53] The *Kaikolar* and *Devangar* weavers, when they came to know of this, demanded justice from government officials but to no avail. When they migrated in protest, the local ruler Tirumalaideva Maharaya heard of it and deputed an officer, Vijayarayan to conduct an enquiry. This official ordered the original Kanchipuram copper plate grant to be brought for examination, which was read and compared with a similar copy of privileges inscribed on the walls of the Siva temple at Villiyanoor. He then gave his verdict that the weavers alone were entitled to use the titles.[54] A similar incident occurred in Tiruvamattur in 1567 and the merchants gave an undertaking that they would not claim their lost titles.[55] Apparently, the merchants had to come to terms with the weavers.

In temple affairs, too, the privileges of merchants were less than those of weavers. An inscription notes that the *chetti* merchants of Pattisvaram in Kumbakonam region claimed some privileges in temple offerings in competition with the silk weavers such as receiving betel leaves and arecanut on the occasion of marriage, and making offerings of commodities to the goddess for which the merchants had no precedent. The privilege belonged to *Pattunulkars* alone.[56] Another similar dispute between merchants and weavers of Manampadi was settled in favour of weavers by the officer of Venkatapatidevaraya.[57]

Although merchants participated in the deliberations of the temple assembly, they never enjoyed a privileged status in Tamil society; the weavers, on the other hand, became a dominant social group through ritual links with temples and specialisation in weaving. A marked feature of the social history of the period was the rise of social consciousness among different communities, aiming at social solidarity among them to clamour for privileges and honours. There were no merchants who made political alliances and built up considerable power to redirect the course of political events in the state.

Slaves

Slavery as an institution developed because of socio-economic distress. Poverty, famine, drought, debt, desertion, and problems of taxes pushed people to sell themselves into slavery. Kaikolars owned slaves. The nayakas collected *adimaikasu*, (taxes on the owners of slaves) in Tamil country.[58] *Mudaliars* and *Padayachi* also owned slaves. Three palm leaf manuscripts in possession of the state Department of Archaeology, Tamilnadu, describe in detail the condition of slaves during Krishnadevaraya's reign.[59] They record that one Thiyagaraja Mudaliar sold a slave named Rayan, son of Santhosi, of *Paraiyar* caste, in the presence of an arbitrator for ten *pons*; Ramachandra Nayinar, a resident of Reddikadalangudi village, sold four of his slaves Muthan, Vellichan, his wife Parvathy and a male slave to Subramanya Mudaliyar of Manganallur for fourteen *pons*; Subba Padayachi sold his slaves-Raman, his wife Mukkatai and their children to Appachi Mudaliar of Ganja village for eighty *pons*. These pieces of evidence show that the family as a whole entered into slavery in the Thanjavur region where rice cultivation was intensive.

The deeds recording the sale of slaves were called *al-vilaipirama-isaivu tittu*. The sale was done through an auction and the prices recorded in the presence of an arbitrator. The manuscripts display the signature of slaves, witnesses and that of the writer of the document.[60] A standard clause in the sale deeds was that the slaves were to be the property of the purchaser as long as the mountain, river Cauvery, the earth and grass lasted. The sale of *Paraiyars* had increased in this period. In an instance one family of seven *Paraiyars* were sold for eight and a half *pagodas* in 1593.[61]

Epigraphical evidence throws light on why an entire family entered into slavery. The main reason appears to have been government taxes charged on families, which led poor families to enter into slavery as a whole. A differential tax was charged on joint families vis-a-vis nuclear families. A joint family paid a quarter *panam* and a nuclear family a half *panam* per month as tax.[62] The ninety-eight castes of *Idangai* (left hand)and *Valangai* (right hand) paid one *panam* on each big family, and a half *panam* on small families.[63] On the occasion of marriage the families in the Jambai region had to pay one *panam* as tax.[64] There was also a *talaikattu panam* levied on households;[65] Achyutappa nayaka charged two *panams* per head of family and one *panam* per family in 1590 in Thanjavur region.[66] Possibly also, the expansion of agriculture demanded the employment of slaves for cultivation[67] by individuals and institutions. The social conflicts of this period and the existence of slavery show that there was a wide gap between the privileged and the unprivileged in Tamil society.

Caste

Epigraphs of the period also convey the social ideas relating to the origin of duties and privileges of mixed caste called *Anuloma*.[68] The mythical explanation of caste given in it may be ignored. More to the point are the political and economic circumstances that contributed to changes in the caste system. Members of different *varnas* practised occupations not allowed to them under Hindu Law. Many Brahmins had entered into various careers prohibited to them when traditional employment became unavailable. Thus Brahmins engaged in wet agriculture in the Thanjavur region[69] and as soldiers in the army of Krishnadevaraya and Vitthaladeva Maharaya,[70] the class of farming and soldierly Brahmins emerging unequal in caste rank to the priestly Brahmins.[71] Roberto Nobili the missionary who observed the castes in Tamil country in the beginning of the Seventeenth century mentions that the *Sudras* were subdivided into six classes (a) V*ellalas* (b) *Totti*, *Arupeni* and *Maraveni* (c) carpenter, tailor and masons (d) barber and fullers (e) diggers ditchers and *Pallars* (f) rustics and *Paraiah*s.[72] It may be construed from the above that the changing society of Tamilnadu cannot be studied from the angle of caste. The only usefulness of the *varna* system was that it became a readymade instrument for highlighting the ideals set forth in myths and commentaries written by each caste from time to time. In the following chapter we shall study how the

Portuguese missionaries came to Tamil country in the Sixteenth century and what experiences they gained while making conversions and learnt about the Tamil society when they spread Christianity.

Notes and References

1. B.A. Saletore, *Social and political life in Vijayanagara Empire*, Vol. I, Madras, 1934, pp. 27 and 34.
2. *Ibid.*
3. K.A. Nilakanta Sastri, *A History of South India*, Madras, 1976, p.309.
4. A. Krishnawami Pillai, *The Tamil Country under Vijayanagara*, Annamalai Nagar, 1964, p. 102.
5. T.V. Mahalingam, *Administration and Social Life under Vijayanagar*, Madras, 1940, p. 101.
6. Burton Stein, *Peasant State and Society in Medieval South India*, Delhi, 1980, pp. 439-51.
7. Burton Stein, "Vijayanagar and the Transition into Patrimonial System", Anna Libera Dallapicola, (ed.,) *Vijayanagar City and Empire*, Stuttgart, 1985, p. 75; Karashima opines that social formation of Vijayanagara rule in the Sixteenth Century seems to have displayed some resemblance to Feudalism which characterised Medieval Western Europe and Japan; N. Karashima, "Nayak's rule in North and South Arcot districts in South India during the Sixteenth Century", *Acta Asiatica*, (henceforth AA) 48, Tokyo, 1985, pp.1-26.
8. The Sanskrit composite expression *Varna Shrama Dharma* included three fundamental proposition of Indian Society. *Varna* represented the structural code within which only the Brahman enjoyed an exclusively defined status through performance of rituals. *Shrama* signified whether an individual inherited at birth by the code of *varna* should choose to remain within the structural limits. The term Dharma finally turned the other two propositions into an overarching idea of capacity. K.N. Chaudhuri, *Asia Before Europe: Economy and Civilization of the Indian Ocean from the Rise of Islam to 1750*, Cambridge, 1990, p. 55.
9. A.R.E., 353 of 1912,355 of 1912,395 of 1912 and 396 of 1912.
10. *Ibid.*, 216 of 1917 (1429).
11. *Ibid.*, 199 of 1940-41 and 190 of 1940-41 (1512).
12. *Ibid.*, 246 of 1916 (1513) and 247 of 1916 (1504). Transcript line six of the text runs as follows: "Rekhai erina idinale kudikku nerukkam aki kudiyum kulaindadu".

13. *Ibid.*, 33 of 1921-22 (1505-1506).
14. *Ibid.*, 140 of 1915-16 (1522).
15. *Ibid.*, 92 of 1918.
16. *Ibid.*, 50 of1916.
17. *Ibid.*, 442 of1913.
18. *Ibid.*, 161 of 1941-42.
19. *Ibid.*, 190 of 1938-39.
20. *Ibid.*, 198 of 1936-37 (1575).
21. *Ibid.*, 482 of 1919-20 (1573).
22. *Ibid.*, 356 of 1912 (1533).
23. *Ibid.*, 482 of 1919-20 (1573).
24. T.T.D.E.S., vol. V, No.2, vol. II, Nos. 35,135 and 140 and vol. IV, Nos. 3 and 39.
25. A.R.E., 368 of 1917; 1918, part II, para 70 (1503).
26. *Ibid.*, 422 of 1925-26, 221 of 1928-29 and 162 of 1918-19.
27. *Ibid.*, 291 of 1928-29.
28. *Ibid.*, 368 of 1917.
29. *Ibid.*, 136 of1905, 151 of 1905 and 454 of1916.
30. *Ibid.*, 422 of 1925 and 473 of 1921.
31. *Ibid.*, 368 of1917.
32. *Ibid.*, 162 of1918.
33. *Ibid.*, 291 of 1928-29.
34. *Ibid.*, 41 of 1922.
35. *Ibid.*, 372 of 1912, 59 of 1914-15, (1429) 201 of 1936- 37) and 257 of 1926-27.
36. S.I.T.I., vol. II, p. 637. Epigraphs mention *Kollancheri* and *Kammalacheri* in many places.
37. S.I.I., vol. II, No. 25; A.R.E., 493 of 1937-38.
38. *Ibid.*
39. A.R.E., 273 of 1939-40 and 293 of 1928-29; S.I.I., Vol. III, p. 47.
40. *Ibid.*, 198 of 1937 (1575). They assembled before Tirukamiyyappar temple of Villiyanoor.
41. The five sons are named as tnanu, mayasilipi, thurastra, visvagna and daivagna.
42. N. Karashima, "The Kammalars of Sixteenth Century in South Arcot District in South India", K.V. Ramesh, S.P. Tewari arid M.J. Sharma, *Dr. G.S. Gai Felicitation Volume*, Delhi, 1990, pp. 205-8.
43. A.R.E., 65 of 1922 (C) and 378 of 1922 (B).
44. S.I.I, vol. III, p. 47; A.R.E., 293 of 1928-29 (1574).
45. A.R.E., 293 of 1928-29, 620 of 1904 and 273 of 1939-40; S.I.I., vol. XVII, p. 388.

46. *Ibid.*, 103 of 1906, 198 of1937 and 493 of 1938.
47. *Ibid.*, 198 of 1937 (1575) and 493 of 1938 (1573).
48. *Ibid.*, 80 of 1938-39 (1582).
49. *Ibid.*, 340 of 1925-26 (1533).
50. Peter Granda, *op. cit.*, p. 133.
51. Vijaya Ramaswamy, "Artisans in Vijayanagar Society", *Indian Economic and Social History Review* XXIII (4), 1985, 417-443; N. Karashima, *op. cit.*, pp. 205-8.
52. A.R.E., 356 of 1912-13 (1533) and 482 of 1919-20 (1573).
53. *Ibid.*, 201 of 1936-37 (Achyutadevaraya period).
54. *Ibid.*
55. A.R.E., 41 of 1922 (1546).
56. *Ibid.*, 257 of 1926-27.
57. *Ibid.*, 218 of 1930-31 (1601). See also ARE 1912-13 C.P.13. (1576) Kanchipuram.
58. *Ibid.*, 445 of 1913 (1502).
59. The original texts of the Manuscripts have been published in the Journal *Kalvettu*, No. 17, pp. 1-3. see for texts pp. 3-6.
60. *Ibid.*
61. A.R.E., 296 of 1911.
62. *Ibid.*, 47 of 1888 (Achyutadevaraya period) 246 of 1916.
63. *Ibid.*, 103 of 1906 (1532).
64. *Ibid.*
65. A.R.E., 149 of 1942 and 426 of 1929.
66. *Ibid.*, 426 of 1929.
67. *Ibid.*, 334 of 1954-55 (1568).
68. P.V. Jagadisa Aiyar, *South Indian Shrines*, Madras, 1920, p. 375.
69. E.I., vol. XII, pp. 340-48.
70. A.R.E., 47 of 1906, for details see also A.R.E. 47 of 1904; 52 of 1905, where we find Brahmanas occupation as soldiers.
71. K.N. Chaudhuri, *op.cit.*, p. 56.
72. S. Rajamanickam, (ed.,) *Robert de Nobili on Indian Customs*, Palayamkottai, 1971, pp. 5-6.

2

The Catholic Religious Orders and Glimpses into the Conversion of the Tamils

"Go Ye therefore, and teach all nations baptizing them in the name of the Father, and of the Son, and of the Holy Ghost."

- The Holy Bible (Mathew 28:19)

That the cross and the crown, the throne and the altar, faith and empire, god and mammon often worked in unison as inseparable twins in the history of the Portuguese has been well recognised as an aphorism of pre-modern history.[1] But how trade along with religion contributed towards Portuguese expansion in the East is still shrouded in mysteries buried in unexplored records. The contribution made by the Catholic clergy to bring about such sweeping changes in the social and cultural life of the people in the Tamil Coast calls for further attention by historians. Hence it is important to probe into these aspects. The *Padroado Real* (Crown patronage of the Church) was an important feature of Portuguese history during this period. Let us now examine the role of religion in the expansion of Portuguese influence in the Tamil Coast.

The Advent of the Roman Catholic Church in the Tamil Coast

The Vicar-General of the Military Order of Christ at Tomar in Portugal was the chief ecclesiastical authority appointed by the Pope to take care of the Christian population in India. This arrangement continued till 1514. Later, the jurisdiction was transferred to the Diocese of Funchal in Madeira and it continued till 1533. The Diocese of Goa was created on 31 January 1533 but as the Pope died before signing the bull of erection, his successor Pope Paul III issued the bull "*Aequum Reputamus*" on 3 November 1534 and appointed Dom Francisco de Mello as the first Bishop of Goa.[2] He was consecrated in Lisbon but died in Evora on 27 April 1536 even before sailing to India. Therefore Dom João Alphonsus de Albuquerque was later appointed as Bishop in 1538 and he reached Goa on 25 March 1539. As he was sick at the time of his arrival in Goa, no public reception was given to him on that day. He then took over the pastoral work in the entire East that extended from Sofala to Hormuz and from Diu to Maçāo. The *Padroado Real* however was not a gratuitous favour conceded by the Holy See to the Crown of Portugal but serious obligations were attached to it. Dom Manuel, the king of Portugal had the duty to build and maintain the churches and the convents needed for carrying on the pastoral work.

The overseas Church was placed under the Patronage of the kings of Portugal in their capacity as Grand Masters of the Order of Christ. The king of Portugal had to depute chaplains to attend to the spiritual needs of the faithful. He had to support them with adequate salary. Franciscans were the first to be sent by the king of Portugal to India. In 1517 Fr. Antonio de Louro arrived in Goa with a letter from King of Portugal by which he and his eight companions were allowed to erect a convent of their order. Following Francis of Assisi (1182-1226) the Franciscans missionary order was formed and it came as a religious order in medieval Europe with the ideals such as 'To be united to God in prayer, to be an apostle of the Church and imitate literally the life of Jesus". The king thought the Franciscan spirituality and their way of life found in a practical detachment from littleness and poverty was important for the spread of Gospel in the East.

To expand the missionary activities in the whole of Asia, Pope Nicholas V (1447-1455) permitted the king of Portugal to conquer and subjugate the territories under non-Christians, vide his bull "*Dum Diversas*" issued on 18 June 1452. Later the same Pope declared Portugal to be the rightful owners of the lands conquered, vide his bull "*Romanus Pontifex*" issued on 8 January 1454. The same right was reconfirmed by Pope Calixtus III, vide his bull "*Inter Caetera*" issued on 13 March 1455. Pope Sixtus IV issued the bull "*Aeterni Regis*" on 21 June 1481 and confirmed the exclusive rights over the areas discovered and conquered by Portugal. Pope Alexander VI, vide another bull "*Cum Sicut Majestas*" issued on 26 March 1500 empowered the king of Portugal to nominate the Apostolic Vicars to the mission lands in the Far East. Pope Leo X, gave the king of Portugal the right of choosing an episcopel candidate in the lands already gained or yet to be gained, already acquired or yet to be acquired in the East, vide his bull "*Dum Fidei Constantiam*" issued on 7 June 1514.

It may be recalled that as early as in 1501 Dom Manuel, the king of Portugal had written in his letter to all the rulers in Europe that one Pedro Alvares Cabral had sent him definite information about the tomb of Apostle St. Thomas in Mylapore and had brought some earth from there.[3] In 1507 Francisco de Almeida, the first Portuguese Viceroy of Goa sent a team of four persons from Kochi to Mylapore to get more information about the tomb of St. Thomas.[4] Two of them died soon after, while the remaining two returned with a report to be sent to the king of Portugal.[5] Further we also get some information about what has come to be regarded as the sepulchre of St. Thomas from Fr. Penteado in his account written from Kochi on 6 January 1515.[6] Gaspar Correia who along with Pero Lopes de Sampayo and others had visited the tomb in Mylapore in 1521, described in his account the thrilling experiences he had at the chapel of St. Thomas.[7]

On Tuesday, 2 June 1523 The Portuguese decided to examine the veracity of the claim made in respect of the tomb. Manoel de Frias, the Portuguese Captain of the Coromandel Coast, then residing at Pulicat was entrusted the responsibility of carrying out the assignment.[8] After going to confession, the investigators began to dig up the grave on Saturday, 6 June 1523 in the afternoon. The entire report (now available at the *Archivum Romanum Societatis Jesu*, Rome) was prepared and it was sent to the king of Portugal. Based on the report it was declared by the Portuguese that this was the original tomb of St. Thomas, one of the apostles of Jesus Christ.

In 1525 Fr. Antonio Penteado managed to get himself appointed as Keeper of the Chapel and the tomb of St. Thomas at

Mylapore although according to a fellow missionary, he had not converted even a single native as he was taking care of the Portuguese population that had settled down around the tomb.[9] In 1530 Fr. Vicente de Laguna requested the king of Portugal that he may be placed in charge of the Chapel of St. Thomas in Mylapore.[10]

In 1532 when trouble arose between the *paravas* and the Muslims in the South Eastern Pearl Fishery Coast, the Franciscan missionaries and the Portuguese lost no time to take advantage of the situation. According to contemporary accounts,[11] the trouble is said to have started when a *parava* lady was insulted by a Muslim when she was buying a *paniyaram* (rice cake). The lady reported the matter to her husband who picked up a quarrel with the Muslim. The latter in his anger tore the earlobe of the *parava*. In the estimation of the *paravas* to have one's earlobe torn out was a great insult to the whole community and thus a serious dispute arose between the *paravas* and the Muslims. As a result, the *paravas* refused to undertake pearl fishing for the Muslims. João da Cruz, a horse dealer at this time is reported to have suggested the *paravas* to approach the Portuguese in Kochi for support and help. The Portuguese requested them to become Christians and assured to provide them protection. Hence in the same year, three Franciscan priests went to the Pearl Fishery Coast and converted the *paravas* en masse. That was how the Franciscans were drawn to evangelisation work on the Tamil Coast and started offering holy mass regularly thereafter.[12] The Franciscan missionaries also preached to the Portuguese on Sundays and feast days in the church, heard confessions and attended to works of Christian charity.[13] These Franciscans were the pioneers who were involved in missionary activities in the Pearl Fishery Coast from Punnaikayal to Tuticorin.[14]

The Franciscan Missionaries

According to the missionary reports, the Franciscans were the first to settle down at Mylapore in 1536.[15] They had a convent and a parish in due course of time. At Nagapattinam they had settled down and had a convent and two parishes. Portuguese citizens of Mylapore were not so edified by the Franciscan missionaries who seemed to be more interested to come to Santhome of Mylapore more for reasons of health as the climate was considered to be good. Missionaries, at least a good number of them, were also attracted by the profitable trade that was conducted there.[16]

As there were very few priests even to look after the spiritual needs of the Portuguese in the region there was no one to offer mass for the *paravas* or to teach prayers like the *Pater Noster* (Our Father), *Ave Maria* (Hail Mary), and the *Credo* (The Creed) which every Christian was expected to learn and recite by-heart on all occasions.

However we learn that Fr. António de Padrão, the Franciscan priest who came to Mylapore in 1540 began preaching the Gospel to the Hindus and he built a church for the new converts.[17] Fr. Belchir de Lisboã in a letter dated 21 March 1559 mentioned that the Franciscans were permitted to have their own new residence in Mylapore.[18]

The Franciscan missionaries came to establish their residence at Tuticorin and it was approved at the chapter meeting held in Goa during 1595.[19] Dom Andre de S. Maria, the Bishop of Kochi welcomed them and handed over the residence of Madre de Deus (Mother of God) at Tuticorin to them.[20] Fr. Custos selected the missionaries who had to reside there.[21]

The Jesuits and the Spread of Christianity in the Tamil Coast

The Society of Jesus was instituted by the Papal Bull "*Regimis Militantis Ecclesiae*" issued by Pope Paul III on 27 September 1540. Fr. Francis Xavier, Paul Camerle and Francisco Mansilhas, the three Jesuits arrived in Goa on 6 May 1542 and reached the Pearl Fishery Coast in October 1542. They found that the baptism received by the *paravas* had not brought about any tangible change in their way of life although they had become Christians ten years ago.[22] The Jesuits therefore considered it their bounden duty to give proper religious instructions to the *paravas*. They introduced the routine of teaching the prayers to the girls in the mornings and to the boys in the evenings.[23] A catechist was appointed in each village and another to collect the children for these classes every day.[24] The Portuguese Governor had allotted an yearly revenue of 4,000 gold *panams* towards the salary of these catechists. Further, the Jesuits insisted that all the *parava* Christians should fulfill all their obligations on the Sabbath day. The women were also encouraged to attend the spiritual instructions offered especially on all Saturdays. The services in the church were followed by readings and explanations of the Articles of Faith. The bonded females were also required to attend service on all Sundays after the return of their masters from the church.[25] These religious instructions, at the instance of the famous Jesuit missionary Francis Xavier, (Francisco de Yasu y Xavier) were given to the *paravas* to wean them away from the influences of their earlier life style, beliefs and customs.[26]

In 1560, Fr. Henrique Henriques started the work of consolidation of the faith of the converts by forming Sodalities in Punnaikayal and Tuticorin. He believed in the efficacy of Catholic education, Christian literature and promoting charitable institutions in strengthening the faith of the *parava* converts.[27] Fr. Henriques laid stress on the free will in all matters of conversions. He did not want to interfere in the prevailing caste system both within the church as well as outside. This did not mean that others like Francis Xavier used force. Thus all in all the missionaries were very successful in their endeavours directed towards evangelisation. Padre Ruy Vicente, the Papal Visitor from Rome who wrote about the state of the missions in the Pearl Fishery Coast during 1582 stated that he found among the *parava* Christians the true spirit of the primitive church and among the priests, the spirit of the primitive Christian society.[28]

The missionaries also introduced the system of appointing *pattangattis* from among the *paravas* as chiefs of the villages. Thus Lazaro Vaz and Manuel da Cruz were appointed as *pattangattis* of Punnaikayal and Tuticorin respectively to take care of the Christians in the absence of the missionaries.[29] Fr. Gaspar de Aguilar in Punnaikayal was appointed by the Vicar of Kochi to advice on all matters connected with missionary activities in the region. Lengthy reports in the form of letters were sent frequently to their spiritual and temporal authorities in Portugal describing their activities as well as the problems faced by them, besides the state of affairs in India.[30]

Diocese of Kochi and the Missionaries in the Tamil Coast

According to a letter written from Kollam dated 27 January 1550 the Jesuits went to live in Mylapore only in 1550.[31] Fr. Francis

Xavier also requested that the church of the Apostle St. Thomas in Mylapore be handed over to the Jesuits.[32] Fr. Alphonso Cypriani was the resident Jesuit. He frequently complained that the behaviour of the Portuguese were far from exemplary and as a result men who could otherwise be persuaded to embrace Christianity were deterred from doing so.[33] In spite of the above drawback, the number of native converts in the hinterland of the port of Santhome slowly continued to grow and by the year 1559 there were about 2000 Christians.[34]

Goa became an Archdiocese in 1557 by the Apostolic Constitution "*Etsi Sancta et Immaculata*" while the Dioceses of Kochi and Melaka were erected as suffragan. The Diocese of Kochi was erected on 4 February 1557 by Pope Paul IV through the promulgation of the Papal bull "*Pro Excellenti Praeeminentia*".[35] Jorge de Themudi, the Bishop of Kochi made his first episcopal visitation to the East Coast in 1566 and he spent three and a half months in Mylapore. The Bishop announced the decrees of the Council of Trent (1545-1563) introducing drastic measures for the moral improvement of the Portuguese and the native Christians living in Santhome.[36] Several of the 'sinners' were made to stand at the door of the Church of St. Thomas in Mylapore dressed in rags, with a stick in their hand and a label on their forehead which specified their crime. A fine of 1400 *pardaus* was imposed and collected from them for various offences. The total amount collected was handed over to the Bishop who finally gave it to the *Santa Casa da Misericórdia* (Holy House of Mercy) for a new building for the hospital in Santhome of Mylapore.[37]

The Jesuits in the meanwhile established cordial relationship with the local *nayak* (name not mentioned) who had in 1571 given some property that yielded 1000 *pardaus* for the sustenance of the missionaries.[38] Subsequently the *nayak* authorised the Jesuits in Santhome in 1594 to collect an annual revenue of 300 *pardaus* from the agricultural lands in the village of Ezhumbur (Egmore).[39]

Fr. Alessandro Valignano, the Jesuit who visited Santhome in 1575 reported that the Jesuits were mainly engaged in attending to the needs of the Christians who lived within the settlement.[40] These Jesuits had also baptised about two thousand people who were newly converted from Hinduism between 1571 and 1575.[41]

According to Jesuit sources there were not many conversions during 1579 because of the disturbed political conditions in Santhome.[42] Later, i.e. during the year 1583 many people from the interior places reached Santhome and sold themselves to the Portuguese because of the famine that ravaged the region and this led to a spurt in conversions. Later, i.e. in 1593, eighty persons were baptised in Santhome.[43]

In a letter written in 1598 to the Superior General of the Society of Jesus in Rome, Fr. Pimenta who had come to India as a Visitor requested two more priests to be sent to Mylapore so that one of them could work for the salvation of souls in the region, i.e. from Santhome to Kunimedu and the other in the area from Kunimedu to Devanampattinam. It was reported in 1598 that Fr. Simão de Sa, the Rector of the College of St. John in Santhome was anxious to build a church at Sadurangapattinam (Sadras) which was occasionally visited by Fr. Alexander Leni.[44] The strength of the Jesuits living in Mylapore increased to eight in 1620. Three Jesuit missionaries were at the court of Venkata II, the king of Vijayanagar in Vellore who treated them very benevolently. He favoured them as much as a Christian king would do in Europe since these Jesuit missionaries led an exemplary life.[45]

Some of the missionaries of the Society of Jesus went to Vedalai region in 1549 for preaching the gospel and converted a large number of people of the community of traditional shell burners called *karaiyalars*. Fr. António Criminali was chiefly responsible for these conversions and he became the Superior of the Missions in the Coast when Francis Xavier departed for Japan in 1550. There is a reference to this Christian community living at Periyapattinam as early as in the year 1553.[46] There is also mention in the letter of Fr. Henrique Henriques about another caste called *pachamas* who also took part in pearl fishing being converted to Christianity in 1558.[47] Periyapattinam became an important centre of missionary activities in 1574.[48] Fr. Nicholas Pimenta who came from Rome in 1599 to visit the Jesuit missions mentions that there was a Jesuit residence at Periyapattinam where two priests lived.[49] He also says that the jurisdiction of their mission comprised the areas as far as Thirupachur in the hinterland and extended up to Rameshwaram on the coast.

Records also attest to early missionary activity by Francis Xavier at Devanampattinam. This port town became an important centre for the Franciscan and the Jesuit missionaries as many *paravas* came to settle down there to trade with the Portuguese. One of the leading Christians of Devanampattinam was Manuel Fernandes, a *parava* trader who hailed from Virapandyanpattinam.[50] Fr. Francisco Perez, a Franciscan priest is reported to have attended to the spiritual needs of the Christians at Devanampattinam in 1574 because of the scarcity of missionaries. He used to visit Devanampattinam from Santhome of Mylapore where he resided permanently.[51]

According to Portuguese sources, missionary activities and conversions were more pronounced between 1580 and 1590 at Devanampattinam. Fr. Francisco do Oriente, another Franciscan arrived from Nagapattinam and settled down permanently at Devanampattinam in 1581.[52] He converted many people there and built a church at Devanampattinam.

The Jesuits however raised objections to the conversions of Hindus made by Fr. Francisco do Oriente and complained about it to the Bishop of Kochi, as the evangelisation work had been entrusted to them by him. Fr. Francisco do Oriente is said to have replied that the Franciscans had expanded their scope of missionary work beyond serving the Portuguese population and there should be no rivalry at all in preaching the Gospel. The matter seems to have become so serious that Dom Matheus de Medina, the Bishop of Kochi reported the matter to the king of Portugal, vide his letter written from Kochi dated 16 January 1588.[53]

From a later source it however becomes evident that the king of Portugal had favoured the Jesuits. On learning this, the Bishop of Kochi sent his Vicar to Devanampattinam to convey the message of the king and reported the matter as fait accompli.[54] However an order from the king of Portugal in Lisbon dated 22 February 1589 was received by the Viceroy in Goa directing him to request the Franciscans in Devanampattinam to restrict their missionary activities within the Portuguese speaking community and not to extend their sphere of activities among the natives.[55] In this connection Fr. Gaspar de Lisboã wrote a letter from Goa on 23

November 1589 to the king of Portugal saying that the Bishop of Kochi was not justified in accusing Fr. Francisco do Oriente who was greatly respected and liked by the native people for his commendable missionary work.[56]

Since many Portuguese private traders had in the meanwhile settled down at Porto Novo, some Franciscan missionaries moved down to Devanampattinam to take care of the spiritual needs of the Portuguese traders. However when in 1607 a Jesuit resident priest was appointed to look after the spiritual needs of the Portuguese in Porto Novo, the Franciscans left for Mylapore permanently.[57]

The Portuguese in the settlement of Nagapattinam were taken care of by the Franciscans as mentioned in a record dated 21 February 1550.[58] Later the Jesuits also settled down here and had purchased a place for 500 *ducats* to build their residence there.[59] The missionaries from Nagapattinam visited Tranquebar (Tharangambadi) and converted some Hindus there initially. Later we find that the Jesuits had established their residence in 1602. This is evident from a letter written by Fr. Pimenta to Fr. Acqua Viva.[60] The resident Jesuit priest continued to remain there (1620) even after the Danes settled down in the port.[61]

The King of Portugal wanted the Dominicans to settle down in India and so the missionaries settled down in Mylapore. The order of St. Dominic established in 1216 was a group of itinerant preachers in Portugal traveling on foot teaching the laity the true Christian dogma. St Dominic's attempt was to create space for research, individual thought and contemplation within the Church and not strike down what was happening in the secular world was liked by the King of Portugal. The contribution of St. Thomas Aquinas, a Dominican was the systematic summation of what was already known expressed in a new way, more critically, more subjectively and in a holy way had been popular. Thomas Aquinas had made Aristotle acceptable to the Church for the rational demonstration of the existence of God and the immortality of the soul. The king of Portugal thought the Dominicans could preach Gospel and contribute towards the growth of Christianity. Six Friars under Fr. Diogo Bermudes arrived Goa in 1548 with a royal mandate to grant them a site by the Viceroy of Goa and 5000 *cruzados* to build a convent according to the plan they brought with them. In course of time the Dominicans settled down at Mylapore and Nagappatinam and had convents there.

Similarly The Order of Hermits of St. Augustine (OSA) popularly known as the Augustinians established in 1248 had been asked to begin their mission stations in India. The Augustinian idea mainly drawn from the teachings of Augustine which can be said as "Unity of heart and mind in God, and life in common without personal possessions" was felt important by the king of Portugal for the overseas missions. On 3 September 1572 under Fr. Antonio da Paixao the Augustinians arrived in Goa. In course of time the Augustinians settled down in Mylapore. Even many Bishops of Mylapore diocese were of the Augustinian order.

Mylapore Diocese

Dom Andre, the Bishop of Kochi felt that the jurisdiction of the Diocese of Kochi covered a vast area and suggested its bifurcation, particularly by creating another diocese on the East Coast of India. Dom Filippe II, the king of Portugal who was also convinced of the need requested Pope Paul V to form a new diocese with headquarters at Mylapore.[62] His Majesty's petition was presented to the Pope by Cardinal Eduardo Farnesse. The Mylapore Diocese was erected by Pope Paul V on 9 January A.D. 1606 according to the desire of the king of Portugal by issuing the Papal bull "*Cedula Consistorialis*".[63] An Augustinian Friar Dom Sebastião de S. Pedro was appointed as the first bishop. The Church of St. Thomas was raised to the status of a cathedral. The new diocese of Mylapore covered the area of the Coromandel Coast, Orissa, Bengal, and Pegu and it was placed under the Archdiocese of Goa. The letter of the king of Portugal addressed to the Bishop of Mylapore dated 28 February 1606 mentioned that the salary and expenses of the clergy and the vicars in the several churches in the diocese of Santhome of Mylapore will be sanctioned initially for a period of four years including his expenses towards the pastoral visit.[64] The stipend of the Bishop, fixed at 2000 *xerafins* per annum was also ordered to be paid from the royal treasury of Goa.[65] The vestments and other liturgy articles of the church were to be delivered to him as they were being sent through a ship leaving Lisbon.[66] Further, a resolution was passed in the State Council by the Portuguese Viceroy of Goa in India to buy a house and building immediately for the Bishop of Mylapore to reside. The construction of a new Bishop's house in Mylapore was carried out by the Viceroy of Goa in consultation with the Archbishop of Goa.[67] Money was also sanctioned for various other things required for the Bishop and also for the cathedral, such as furniture, carpets, etc.[68] The king further in his royal order dated 13 March 1606 gave the Bishop of Mylapore a sum off 7,00,000 *reis* annually for the maintenance of the diocese.[69]

Royal Grants and Donations to Churches and Religious Orders

In 1606, the king of Portugal even allotted funds to be made available to the Jesuit priests in Madurai for their evangelisation works.[70] The Viceroy of Goa further ordered on 7 September 1612 that in times of financial difficulties, the Bishop of Mylapore could be paid from the funds available in Goa. Further, the expenses of the clergy in Bengal and Pegu were also ordered to be paid from the same funds.[71]

Various liturgical articles and religious items needed by the churches in Nagapattinam were ordered to be supplied by the Viceroy as the king of Portugal had sent a communication to that effect dated 14 September 1612.[72] The Bishop of Mylapore in a letter dated 20 February 1614 requested the *Santa Casa da Misericórdia* in Nagapattinam to extend whatever help required by the priests to carry on their missionary work there.[73] The Viceroy further asked the Captain of Nagapattinam that the funds allotted by the king of Portugal be disbursed to the missions for their own maintenance as well as for the churches in Nagapattinam.[74]

In order to mobilise the funds required for the execution of the work related to the propagation of faith, the Bishop of Mylapore ordered the *Santa Casa da Misericórdia* of Mylapore on 15 March 1617 to levy fines on those who committed offences and suggested that the funds thus raised could be used for missionary work.[75] Further, we find that the Viceroy of Goa had informed the Bishop of Mylapore on 7 March 1619 to collect marriage fees and to use the amount for the purpose of evangelisation in the diocese of Mylapore.[76]

According to a record dated 15 January 1633, a sum of 3500 *cruzados* was released from the treasury of Goa to the Bishop of Mylapore towards allotment of funds for the evangelisation work of that year.[77] The *orçãmento* (budget) document for the next year (1634) also mentioned the funds sanctioned under the various heads of accounts to the Bishop of Mylapore to be used for the missionary activities.

TABLE 1
Details of funds for the missionary work of the Bishop of Mylapore sanctioned in 1634

Head of account and nature of expenditure	*Amount in Xerafins - Tanga - Reis*
Towards stipend for the Bishop	2666 -3 -20
For the pastoral visit of the Bishop	500 -0 -00
Towards stipend for the Vicars	133 -1 -40
For travel (by sea and land)	133 -1 -40

Source : See note [78]

The financial crisis faced by the *Estado da Índia* in 1646 however constrained the Portuguese administration in Goa to pay only the stipend of the Bishop of Mylapore and the Captain Major (*Capitão-mor*) of the town of Santhome who received annually 2000 cruzados.[79] All other grants under various heads of accounts were temporarily suspended. The Jesuit Annual letter of 1648 mentioned that the Viceroy was compelled to spend huge sums of money for the war with the Dutch and therefore could not afford to send the stipend to the missionaries.[80] We however find that the Viceroy of Goa had ordered that at least stipends to the Bishop of Mylapore and other missionaries of the various churches should be always paid on time. He further requested the Bishop of Mylapore to get in touch with the bursar of the treasury seeking permission to use all the deposits that belonged to Mylapore and Nagapattinam trading factories for pastoral work.[81]

Missionaries in the Pearl Fishery Coast (1584-1662)

The centre of missionary activities was moved from Punnaikayal to Tuticorin in 1584. As Tuticorin developed, Pedro Gonçalves, the Vicar of Kochi built a church in honour of *Nossa Senhora de Nascimento* (Our Lady of Nativity). The Jesuits became powerful on the Pearl Fishery Coast since they had set up many institutions in several places. However they did not obey the orders of the Bishop of Kochi in evangelical matters leading to conflicts between the Franciscans and the Jesuits. This is evident from a letter written by Fr. Valignano to the Jesuit Superior General on 17 December 1585 that Dom Matheus de Medina, the Bishop of Kochi had withdrawn two vicars from Punnaikayal and Tuticorin[82] and had further decided not to send any priest to Punnaikayal and Tuticorin. The Jesuits however continued their missionary activities in the region as evident from the writings of Fr. Nicholas Pimenta who visited the Jesuit residence at Punnaikayal during 1598.[83]

The Portuguese missionaries treated the *paravas* very well and even admitted them into their houses. As these priests mixed freely with the low caste people, the Portuguese fell in the estimation of high caste Tamil Hindus. That the *paravas* and the Portuguese ate meat and drank the fermented juice of the palm tree was another reason for the high caste Hindus to think that both the Portuguese and the *paravas* were one and the same class of people who must have arisen out of the same low breed.[84]

Muthu Veerappa (1606-1623), the *nayak* of Madurai attacked the *parava* villages for not paying revenue from the pearl fishery in December 1612. This made many *parava* Christians to migrate en masse to the other Portuguese trading settlements and they came in large numbers to Santhome.[85] However the *nayak* of Thanjavur was in good terms with the Portuguese and it was favourable for the missionary expansion. A letter of the king of Portugal dated 7 March 1613 addressed to the *nayak* of Thanjavur profusely thanked for the immense help that he had extended to the Portuguese in Santhome during the attack of the king of Vijayanagar. This royal letter was sent to the Viceroy of Goa through the Bishop of Mylapore and it was handed over to the *nayak* of Thanjavur.[86]

The relationship between the Jesuits in Tuticorin and the Bishop of Kochi was not very cordial. These matters were brought to the notice of the king of Portugal. A letter from a Jesuit missionary in 1637 mentioned that although God's purpose in inspiring the Portuguese sea-borne trade in one way had increased the harvest of souls, the missionary work on the other hand always encountered difficulties.[87] The *pattangattis* of the villages in the Pearl Fishery Coast wrote a letter to the king of Portugal on 4 November 1642 requesting to be placed under the control of the Jesuit priests instead of the Portuguese Captains who always oppressed them very much.[88] Sometimes the spiritual care of the *parava* children, men and women was entrusted to the *pattangattis* by the missionaries in the Fishery Coast.[89]

When the Portuguese settlements of Tuticorin, Nagapattinam and Santhome fell into the hands of the Dutch one after another between 1658 and 1662, the missionaries of the various religious orders were not permitted to live in the same settlement by the Dutch. The evangelisation and pastoral work of the *Padroado* missionaries received a set back in the ports of the Tamil Coast. The Dutch missionaries now attempted to draw the *paravas* in Tuticorin towards Protestantism. Philip Baldeaus, the Dutch protestant missionary wrote (1662) that all the *paravas*, out of fear for the protestants remained squatting on the porch and they listened quietly to him. Although a good number of paravas came to listen to his sermons in the streets, none of them became Protestants. In due course of time, the number of listeners to the sermon also went on decreasing.[90] It is further reported by Philip Baldeaus that the native Catholics did not mind walking a couple of miles interior from the coast to be with their *padroado* missionaries and these Tamil Catholics practised their religion very fervently. The *parava* Catholics carried their infants into the hinterland to have them baptised by the *padroado* priests.[91] The Dutch were not as tolerant as 'heathen' rulers towards the Catholic missionaries, that they dared to destroy in 1664 the altar of the Catholic church in Nagapattinam.[92] In spite of all their crude attempts they could not convert the Catholics to their brand of Christianity.

Conversions in the Hinterland, 1600-1662

Francis Xavier, in one of his letters written to Ignatius Loyola said that Christianity in India will survive only in the coastal regions which was within the reach of the Portuguese.[93] In fact the Portuguese missionaries did not penetrate into the interior to preach the Gospel till the end of the Sixteenth century as they confined themselves to the Tamil Coast. Changes and developments took place in the socio-political conditions of the Tamil Country with the rise of three independent nayakdoms in Gingee, Madurai and Thanjavur after the battle of Talikota in 1565. The centre of gravity of missionary activities moved out from the Portuguese port settlements on the Tamil Coast to the courts in the interior. This helped the spread of Christianity in the hinterland on a large scale.

The Holy See also wanted to bring the missionaries of various religious orders like the Franciscans, the Jesuits, the Dominicans and the Augustinians under its direct management and assert the authority of the Church under the Pope. This led to the establishment of the Sacred Congregation for the Propagation of Faith in Rome on Epiphany Day, 6 January 1622 during the reign of Pope Gregory XV (1621-1623). A Congregation composed of thirteen Cardinals and two Prelates and also a Secretary was constituted to whom the Pope committed and recommended the affairs of the propogation of faith. This organ of the church encouraged Christianisation of India and also helped avoid conflicts and tensions in the various missions in the East.

The Portuguese priests noticed that a certain class of people here among the Tamils were treated as untouchables so much so that they were detested by the brahmins and had no communication with each other. The *brahmins* did not also allow the poor untouchables to live in their own villages or allow them to enter their houses, or pass through their streets and utilise their services for anything.[94] This prompted the Portuguese Jesuit missionaries to adopt different methods to handle the conversions of high castes and low castes in the Tamil Country working as two separate groups, i.e. as *sanyasis* (ascetics), and *pandaraswamis* (non-brahmin ritualists).

According to the Jesuit Annual Reports of 1606-1607 sent by Fr. Melchoir Coutinho, very few Hindus in Mylapore were converted to Christianity during the period under report. The Hindus who came to the place for the purpose of business were very carefully dealt with in matters of conversion.[95]

The Jesuits played a major role in the conversion of Hindus in Madurai located in the hinterland. It is recorded that Fr. Gonçalvo Fernandes was sent to Madurai in 1595 where there was a sizeable *parava* population to attend to their spiritual needs. He was asked to convert people of other castes if possible. As he won the confidence of the *nayak* and others he could convert some Hindus in 1596. The Annual Report of the Jesuits from Madurai in 1608 speak of their missionary activities in the interior places during this period. The influence of Roberto Nobili on the growth of the Church in the hinterland of the Tamil country was enormous. He preached the Gospel to the high caste Hindus as in the form of *upanyasams* (religious discourse) partly singing and partly reciting texts as practised by the local religious men. He dressed himself like a *brahmin sanyasi* and also ate vegetarian food. Nobili who put on the garb of a *brahmin sanyasi* denied that he was a Portuguese and affirmed that he was a brahmin from Rome. Many Jesuits followed in the footsteps of Roberto Nobili and behaved like *sanyasis*. The last missionary in this line of *sanyasis* was Fr. Arcolini, a Jesuit who died in 1670.

Fr. Balthasar da Costa was the founder of another group which adopted a different method of preaching the gospel to the low caste people dressed in yellow-ochr garbs. He was followed by João de Britto and others who also donned the garb of a *pandaraswami*.[96] The number of conversions effected among the high caste Christians by the Jesuits in the Madurai Mission touched the figure of 1208 in 1644 while conversions among the low castes touched 2975, the total number of converts in the Tamil country reaching 4183.[97] In 1651, Fr. Manuel Martins, another Jesuit in the region, commended the merits of both the classes of missionaries in the Tamil Country. He also pointed out that a *brahmin sanyasi* could make more converts among the high castes than three or four of those who wore the dress of *pandaraswami* could achieve together.[98] The lower castes found in their conversion to the new religion a way for their own emancipation from the caste ridden traditional Hindu society.

Even later, missionaries like Fr. Beschi used the dress of *pandaraswamis* as mentioned in his letter written on 4 November 1711 from Avoor to Rev. Fr. Tamburini, the Superior General in Rome.[99] He said that he had adopted a style of life so different from the one that he followed in Europe. In the Jesuit Annual Letter of 1731 he said that the dress adopted by the missionaries in the Madurai Mission did not protect them from the inclemency of weather. The diet was light that consisted of only rice, vegetables and milk. The climate with the burning sun and tempestuous winds appeared very bad. Although all of these seemed in the beginning unbearable to the new missionary, as years went by, these burdens became sweet, thanks to divine grace.[100]

In the Marava region, João de Britto (1647-1693) preached the gospel and made many conversions mainly among the low caste Hindus. Many catechists were chosen by him from among the pious Christians in the locality who taught the mysteries of the Holy Faith to the public.[101] João de Britto even succeeded in converting Thadaiyathevar, the *palayakarar* of Siruvali domain who was a cousin of Vijaya Raghunatha Kilavan Sethupathi (1674-1710), the Marava ruler to Catholicism and baptised him on 27 August 1686.[102] Fr. Martin mentioned that 8,000 Hindus were converted to Christianity in the *Marava* Country between 1640-1680. The number of conversions effected in the year 1686 was two times higher than that of the previous year, according to the Jesuit Annual Letter written and sent from Madurai to Fr. Superior General in Rome.[103] The number of conversions among the *maravas* and *agambadaiyars* also increased which fact was mentioned in the letter dated 11 July 1692 of Fr. João de Britto to Fr. João da Costa.[104] The Sethupathi ruler of Ramanathapuram therefore prohibited the preaching of Gospel to the Hindus in his kingdom. The Jesuit missionaries defied his order and continued their activities without much publicity.[105] Fr.João de Britto was held on 8 January 1693 for violating the royal order and making conversions in the *Marava* country. He wrote a letter from the prison to Fr. General on 12 January 1693 describing the political conditions that prevailed in the region and the trial held in the Sethupathi court. However, João de Britto was convicted for violating the order of the *Marava* ruler and preaching the Gospel to the natives. He was beheaded at Oriyur on 4 February 1693. Manucci, the Italian traveller mentioned that a chapel was built at the site and it was on the main route to Rameshwaram. It is learnt from the Jesuit Annual Letter written by Fr. J. Vieyra dated 14

July 1735 that Kattathevar Sethupathi built the first shrine at the site of João de Brittos' execution in 1730.[106]

In the Tirunelveli region, the conversions of Hindus were carried out by a band of ardent missionaries since 1638 who travelled from place to place. In 1644, Kayathar was a flourishing centre of missionary activity as recorded in the Jesuit annual letter. A chapel dedicated to St. James was built in Kayathar that year. Fr. Antão de Proença and Fr. Balthasar da Costa were always on the move visiting different places, such as Tenkasi, Tirunelveli, Kamanayakanpatti and Maaranthai.[107] The number of conversions among the Hindus in the region in 1662 touched the figure of 485 as reported by these Jesuits in 1665. Fr. Manuel Rodrigues continued the missionary work in the same region. He went to Tenkasi to spread the Gospel as mentioned in his letter dated 15 August 1666. Fr. Andre Ferreira joined as his assistant the very next year (1666). He is known to have walked all the way from Madurai to Tenkasi to take up his assignment as reported by him. During the Advent of 1666, Fr. Andre stayed in the house of a Telugu speaking man called Kannappan and offered Christmas Mass for the Christians of Tenkasi. A Jesuit was actually residing in Kamanayakanpatti since 1688. The *palayakarar* of Ettayapuram proclaimed eternal protection and support to the Christians of Kamanayakanpatti in 1690 and this old inscription is found in the church there.[108] As mentioned in the Annual Letters of the Jesuits, conversions took place at Vadakankulam and Gurukalpatti in 1701.[109] In Sendamaram, 351 *maravas* were converted in 1714. This is found recorded in the Jesuit Annual letter of that year. A letter written on 8 September 1716 mentioned that *shanars* in the Vadakankulam area embraced Christianity. Their job was climbing the palmyrahs and it preserved them against laziness. Their widows did not remarry and they practised chastity as a virtue. These *shanars* after their conversion led an exemplary Christian life as recorded by the Jesuit who attended to their spiritual needs.[110]

In the Tiruchirapalli, Thanjavur and Pudukottai regions Fr. Balthasar da Costa and Fr. Manuel Martins converted many Hindus to Christianity between 1629 and 1639. Avoor and Kandalur became the two main centres of Jesuit missionary activity where a number of *kallars* became Christians. Fr. Balthazar da Costa built a chapel at Kandalur where seventy Christians lived in 1640. It is reported in the Jesuit Annual letters that the Christians of Tiruchirapalli region were very pious and attended the services in the church very regularly. They were reported as attending to the reading about the passion of Our Lord on all Fridays and on Mary, the Mother of Jesus on all Saturdays. The Jesuit Annual Letter of 1644 mentioned that 300 *brahmin* coverts lived in Tiruchirapalli. It is reported that a *Kallar* chief whose domain was near Thanjavur embraced Christianity in 1660 as said in the Jesuit Annual Letter of that year.[111]

TABLE 2
New conversions made by the Jesuits of Madurai Mission (1666-1686)

Place	1666	1674-76	1677	1678	1679-81	1682	1683	1684-86
Tiruchirapalli & Kandalur	549	1223	222	185	764	405	-	200
Vadugarpatti	272	1647	401	541	2122	1051	1040	478
Anaikarai palayam	-	240	51	92	70	130	-	-
Mullipadi	220	207	247	297	375	165	1136	75
Madurai	266	184	49	69	-	100	-	95
Nanda vanampatti	-	1198	339	504	1238	520	630	-
Kanavakarai	-	300	-	-	1047	-	660	300
Karanapattu alias Agaram	-	-	390	280	2280	810	1003	404
Kuvattur	-	-	59	335	-	100	500	150

Source: See note[112]

Capuchins in Madras and Pondicherry (1642-1739)

Fr. Ephrem of Nevers, a French Capuchin happened to stop at Madras on his way to Pegu in 1642. He was very much liked by the Portuguese who had migrated from Santhome and settled down in Madras. These Portuguese citizens at first pleaded with the priest to stay on with them in Madras. He was hesitant to do so since he was entrusted with a new mission in Pegu. Eighteen prominent Portuguese citizens of Madras who lived under the protection of the English East India Company made a petition on 8 July 1642 to Andre Cogan, the English Governor of Fort St. George to permit him to reside in Madras.[113] The Governor and Council of Madras on 8 July 1642 also invited him to give his answers and inform the English Company.[114] Finally he accepted the proposal and expressed his willingness. Thereafter the English Governor and Council of Madras permitted Fr. Ephrem to reside in Madras and to attend to the spiritual needs of the Portuguese living there. A church was also ordered to be built at a convenient place by the English Governor.[115]

The Capuchin missionaries of the Province of Tours who were in Madras had been invited by the French to Pondicherry to take care of their spiritual needs.[116] These Capuchins therefore came along with the French who arrived in Pondicherry on 15 January 1674.[117] Fr. Cosmas de Gien was appointed officially to look after the spiritual needs of the French and native Christians in Pondicherry. Fr.Cosmas built a chapel.[118] Some native Christians like Thanappa Mudaliar alias Lazaare de Motha, originally from Poonamallee but converted by the Portuguese in Santhome accompanied the French and settled down in Pondicherry. As the Capuchins mainly took care of the French Catholics, the first conversions took place in Pondicherry on 21 September 1674 when five Indians received baptism and Bellanger de Lespinay, an official of the French East India Company, stood as their godfather.[119] It is reported by François Martin, in the year 1676 that the baptism register maintained by the Capuchins contained the above said entries and the details were also recorded in the registers of the état civil in Pondicherry.[120] From the signatures found in the baptism registers we learn that there were four Capuchin priests in Pondicherry at that time. The baptism register contains an entry on the baptism given to André, the son of Thanappa Mudaliar who was then (1686) the *dubash* of the French East India Company.[121] Three Capuchin missionaries, namely Fr.Jacques of Bourges, Fr. Lawrence of Angouleme and Fr. Francis

Spiritus of Tours arrived at Pondicherry in 1686.[122] There are instances of slaves, both adults and children being baptised in 1688. Illegitimate children were also baptised in 1691 in Pondicherry.[123]

Fr. João de Britto, the Jesuit who was working in the *Marava* country visited Pondicherry in July 1691 and stayed here for some time. On Wednesday, 5 August 1691, he administered baptism in the native church to one Domingo aged between 18 and 20, João Cascaran, aged between 25 and 30, Francisca aged between 18 and 20, besides two slaves named Catherina and Aurelia and a child. On Sunday, August 1691, he blessed the wedding of Isabella, the daughter of Francisco and Maria de Monte with João.[124]

On 8 September 1693, the Dutch in Cuddalore attacked Pondicherry leading to its surrender. Under the terms of surrender, the missionaries were deported to Europe.[125] The Dutch ruled Pondicherry for six years and were obliged to return Pondicherry to the French at the conclusion of the Treaty of Ryswick signed in Europe on 21 September 1697 and the port of Pondicherry was handed over on 13 September 1699. Soon after, the Bishop of Mylapore (November 1699) entrusted the apostolate among the non-Christians of Pondicherry and its surrounding areas exclusively to the Jesuits. The Capuchins were asked to confine their pastoral work among the French, the Portuguese and other Europeans besides the Eurasians and their Indian servants. This arrangement worked out by the Bishop of Mylapore did not satisfy the Capuchins of Pondicherry and so the Capuchin Superior sent a petition to the Propaganda Fide to certify their jurisdiction and settle the matter for good.[126] The Capuchins also petitioned to the king of France through Fr. Seraphim of Paris, the preacher and adviser to His Majesty.[127] The King of France sent a letter from Versailles in March 1702 to the Pope to settle the matter.[128] As in their view, justice was not rendered to them, the Capuchins decided to send a member of their congregation to Rome to castigate the missionary activities of the Jesuits. Fr. Francis of Tours went to Rome and pleaded the case before the Propaganda Fide and returned to Pondicherry with a final decree in favour of the Capuchins. On 28 September 1706 the Bishop of Mylapore, who was himself a Jesuit, was asked to execute the decree but he refused. Therefore on 1 November 1706

Fr. Spiritus read the letter in the church in Pondicherry and the native Christians were happy.[129] After protracted correspondence and discussions the dispute was finally resolved in January 1751.[130] It must be stated that the dispute was centred not so much on the question of spreading Christianity but the honour and reputation of their own respective religious congregations.[131]

After the restoration of Pondicherry to the French, the site earlier occupied by the Capuchins was returned to them by François Martin, the French Governor of Pondicherry on 14 December 1702.[132] The title deed was signed by Hardancourt, the notary and secretary of the French Company in Pondicherry and the extent of the site restored to them covered 48 *toises* (North-South) and 34 *toises* (East-West). The laity is understood to have paid the price for the site as the Capuchins did not have sufficient funds with them at that time. A sum of 119 *pagodas* and twenty two *panams* was paid towards the cost of the site by the laymen. In September 1726, the Bishop of Mylapore visited Pondicherry to administer the sacrament of Confirmation to as many as 4000 Christians. Coja Safar, an Armenian merchant was permitted in February 1732 by the secretary of the French Company to give donations to the Capuchins. The Capuchins then built a residence with a hospital consisting of ten small rooms. In accordance with the deliberations of the Superior Council of Pondicherry dated 7 August 1739, the French Company gave its sanction to the Capuchins to acquire two houses, one owned by Chevalier Faisant and the other by Sieur Bouteville. The Capuchin missionaries purchased these houses after paying them respectively 742 *pagodas* and 300 *pagodas*.[133]

Missionary Work in the Tamil Coast and its Hinterland, 1700-1774

As the missionaries in the Tamil country did their utmost in proclaiming the Gospel, Count de Villa Verde, the Portuguese Viceroy of Goa wrote (in 1698) that the members of these religious congregations who had come out to the missions in India regarded the region where they exercised their vocation as their own country.[134] Almost towards the beginning of the Eighteenth Century, the Muslim rulers in the Carnatic began to harass the missionaries and the catechists who were active in their region. Fr. Martin however saved the life of three catechists at Elakurichi where many natives embraced Christianity in 1702.[135] Similarly at Karuveppampoondi near Kanchipuram where the Jesuit missionary activities flourished, three persons were arrested and made prisoners.[136] In spite of these incidents seventy two persons became Christians between October 1703 and January 1704 through the efforts of the Jesuits.[137] In 1705 the missionaries in Chengam found it difficult to carry on evangelisation work.[138] Fr. Bouchet in his letter written from Pondicherry dated 20 December 1711 to His Holiness the Pope Clement XI, mentioned that he was arrested and thrown into prison. He further added that he had come to live in Pondicherry after the release.[139]

The missionary work in the port of Santhome of Mylapore came to a halt in 1754 even though Mylapore continued to remain as the seat of a bishopric. The place was invaded and the palace of the Bishop was plundered by the Muslims. As a result, Dom Francisco Laynes, the Bishop of Mylapore was forced to leave Santhome on 18 March 1704 and he lived in the parish church of Our Lady of Light located outside Mylapore.[140] The Bishop could return to his house only after the political situation returned to normalcy.[141]

The religious houses of the various congregations in Santhome were once again looted in 1711 by the Muslims. Disturbed by these events, the Archbishop of Goa wrote a letter to the Vicar-General of Santhome in 1711 to find out the actual situation in Mylapore.[142] The residences of the missionaries in Santhome were once again attacked by the Muslims in 1749. This time also, i.e. on 27 September 1749 the Portuguese Viceroy of India wrote a letter to the Bishop of Mylapore inquiring about the political situation in Santhome.[143] The Jesuit Annual Letters (1712-1713) further mentioned that the missionaries had to live in the huts of Christian laymen because of the political disturbances in the Tamil Country. These houses of the poor were more like stables than houses and there was scarcely any room to say the Holy Mass. The missionaries could exercise their pastoral work only during the night and every one was careful to avoid meeting the Christians during the day as the environment was hostile.[144] The civil war situation and famine conditions lasted for five years during which the missionary work suffered very much in the Tamil country.[145]

According to a record in the Overseas Historical Archives in Lisbon, Dom João Ribeiro, the Archbishop of Kodungallur (Cranganore) (1705-1716) had written a letter on 13 June 1710 to the king of Portugal mentioning that the *padroado* supported evangelisation work in the Madurai Mission was flourishing very well.[146] He therefore sent a proposal to the king of Portugal to form a new diocese covering the regions of Madurai and the Carnatic. The proposal however could not be considered favourably because of the shortage of priests at that time.

Although this was the state of affairs in Santhome of Mylapore, missionary work by the French (who were Catholics) in the port of Pondicherry continued smoothly under the *padroado* diocese of Mylapore. The Jesuits have noted down in two registers (now available at the Madurai Province Jesuit Archives) the number of baptisms given to the natives in Pondicherry from the year 1699 to 1743 and from 1744 to 1778. As the number of conversions of the low castes had increased since 1744, a separate register was opened exclusively for them from that year. The pages in the baptism registers maintained till 1743 are not found numbered. They could therefore be only transcripts of the originals as all the entries are in the same handwriting throughout the register. About forty five baptisms are registered on a single page along with the details of age, caste, native place of the persons concerned. The names of the priests who administered the baptism are often not mentioned.

From the year 1744 onwards, the original baptism registers bearing the signature of the priests who performed the baptisms are found. On some pages it carried the signatures of Dupleix, the Governor and his wife as they have stood as god-parents. Baptisms given in the suburbs of Pondicherry town such as Ariyankuppam and Olugarai are maintained in separate registers. The first conversion of a *brahmin* in Pondicherry took place on 8 July 1723 and it was surprisingly a woman who hailed from Koliyanoor near Villupuram. She had adopted the name of Marie and she was aged twenty. It is interesting to know that she was a spinster and a Tamil scholar.

More conversions of Hindus to Catholicism by the Jesuits took place in the hinterland of the Tamil country than in the coastal areas of Tamilnadu during the first half of the Eighteenth Century.

The baptism registers show that the Jesuit missionaries had given baptisms to the new converts at Gingee, Sirkazhi, Ayyampettai, Chingleput, Tiruchirapalli, Thanjavur, Kumbakonam, Kanchipuram and Palayamkottai between 1715-1744. The number of baptism cannot however be taken as a correct indicator of the number of conversions. Hence what is given below is the number of baptisms of only those identified as new converts baptised by Jesuits as recorded in the baptism registers.

TABLE 3

Details of new converts who received baptism from the Jesuits in the various ports of the Tamil Coast between 1717 and 1724

Place name	*1717*	*1718*	*1719*	*1722*	*1723*	*1724*	*Total*
Santhome	3	1	2	8	5	14	33
Pondicherry	52	59	12	23	28	28	202
Nagapattinam	1	-	-	3	2	4	10
Porto Novo	-	-	2	-	1	3	6
Sadras	7	16	5	2	4	3	37
Devanampattinam	-	2	-	-	2	6	10
Tranquebar	-	-	-	-	2	3	5

Source: See note[147].

The largest number of baptisms, i.e. to 202 individuals was given in the French settlement of Pondicherry between 1717 and 1724 and it was then under the control of the diocese of Mylapore.

The French settlement of Pondicherry continued to record the highest number of conversions which touched 574 between 1725 and 1734. The port of Santhome which recorded 291 baptisms came second. The number of converts in Cheyyur, Sadras and Marakkanam showed steady increase as the Jesuit missionaries from Pondicherry visited these places more often during this period.

TABLE 4

Details of new converts who received baptism in the various ports of the Tamil Coast between 1725-1734

Place name	*1725*	*26*	*27*	*28*	*29*	*30*	*31*	*32*	*33*	*34*	*Total*
Madras	12	9	6	5	24	7	22	19	28	14	146
Mylapore	-	-	3	14	3	10	2	7	-	-	39
Santhome	11	35	19	15	14	11	17	27	49	93	291
Pondicherry	37	26	39	40	84	38	61	86	43	120	574
Porto Novo	7	2	4	4	2	11	7	22	6	35	100
Sadras	12	6	11	5	15	2	24	14	8	20	117
Marakkanam	4	1	2	6	7	1	8	11	5	3	48
Cheyyur	10	10	20	7	17	10	27	14	4	26	145
Devanampattinam	2	3	2	6	7	16	19	10	7	29	101
Tranquebar	2	7	3	6	4	5	9	17	16	5	74

Source: See note.[148]

TABLE 5

New converts who received baptism in the hinterland between 1725 and1744

Place names	*1725-34*	*1735-1744*	*Total*
Kanchipuram	-	34	34
Kumbakonam	135	146	281
Palayamkottai	-	19	19
Thanjavur	44	69	113
Tiruchirapalli	25	7	42
Chidambaram	159	-	159

Source: See note.[149]

Evidences suggest that Kumbakonam became the main centre of evangelical work followed by Chidambaram and Thanjavur in the hinterland of Tamil Coast. However, the number of conversions declined very much between 1745 and 1760 owing to disturbed political conditions in the Tamil region during this period.

Karaikal became a centre of Jesuit missionary activity in 1739. The French East India Company agreed to give 2000 French pounds for the maintenance of two priests. One of them worked as chaplain of the French and the other looked after the spiritual needs of the natives.[160] Alamparvai was another coastal centre near Sadurangapattinam where the Capuchins converted some natives in 1748. Funds were also allotted for the catechists who worked in the mission of Alamparvai.[161] Madame Dupleix, the wife of the French Governor of Pondicherry, in her letter written from Pondicherry on 27 February 1751 to the Jesuit Superior General mentioned that she had given the income of two villages called Archamangalam and Kandenour to the Jesuits for the propagation of faith.[162] She requested the Jesuit Superior to send two priests so that one can permanently reside at Archamangalam where she could build a church in honour of the Holy Cross. In her letter dated 1 June 1751 to the Jesuit Superior she mentioned that she had already begun the construction of the church, thanks to the graces bestowed by Lord Almighty on her husband and herself.[163]

The Jesuit missionaries who came to India just after the Reformation period were inspired so much by the spirit of the age and played a very significant role ushering the Tamil Country into the modern age. The Inquisition carried out in Goa by the Portuguese in the Sixteenth Century did not have much of an impact on the Tamil Coast. The Jesuit method of conversion is known to us from the pen of François Martin, the French Governor of Pondicherry.[164] He says " That the natives who passed through the hands of the Jesuits were thoroughly grounded in the mysteries of the religion. We see a great difference between them and those who have been instructed by the missionaries of other orders.... The Jesuits administered baptism only after complete instruction and imparting of a proper knowledge of the principal mysteries of our Faith".

Activities of the Missionaries

Men of various castes were converted in Tamil countryside. We find that Vannans (washer men) at Kanguapatti were converted.[165] Similarly Kammalars (smiths) at Mullipadi were converted.[166] It has been reported by the missionaries that not a single Komatti who was a merchant had been converted till the year as late as 1682. Those Sudras who were converted to Christianity in Tamilnadu were expelled by their fellow Hindu men of their own caste. Kaikola Weavers who became Christians were at first refused to be admitted into the same caste by their Hindu brethren and after conducting the *Mahanadu* (General Assembly) and meeting of their caste of all weavers, the Hindu weavers permitted saying that they belonged to the same caste even if they were converted as Christians.[157]

Learning the native language, i.e., Tamil by missionaries for carrying on their apostolic works are recorded. Fr. Balthazar da Costa was learning Tamil. Fr. Roberto Nobili and Emmanuel Martinz who mastered Tamil had composed books in Tamil. Their book on the Lives of Saints had been used as readings in the church of Sathyamagalam.[158] Fr. Andres Freyre was deputed to Ambalakadu to supervise the printing of books in Tamil written by Roberto Nobili.[159] Late Fr. Rodrigo de Abreu was also deputed to supervise the printing of books of Roberto Nobili.

Social work undertaken by the missionaries had been recorded. Fr. Manuel da Correia had dug a well at Kavanakkarai and he arranged for its cleaning too in order to get good drinking water for the people of that place.[160] Further Fr. Vincent Duarte had purchased cotton in large quantities and he stored it in his house at Kangupatti and he generally gave it to the poor Christian weavers to spin so that they might earn a living. It was reported that his house was set fire by the Hindus and the cotton stored there was completely lost.[161]

Jesuit missionaries had carried with them the various curious objects which they had brought from Europe. It is found that Sathyanathan a new convert was given a fine prism of glass by Fr. Balthazar da Costa. This new Christian who became later a catechist presented the same prism to the forest chieftain in Chengam who admired the variety of colours after observing it.[162] Similarly Fr. Balthazar da Costa had also sent another catechist with a small present of wax candles during his visit to Lingama Nayak, the father-in-law of Madurai nayak. This nayak had highly appreciated the talent of the artist who had skillfully adjusted the wick inside the wax and made the candle appear as white as milk.[163] We also find that Fr. Vincent Duarte who resided at Kongupatti calculated time by means of sand glass and he was very punctual in his meditation by using it.[164] Thus we find that Portuguese Jesuits had introduced prism, sand glass and wax candles. This perhaps could be explained to show the European technological superiority to the natives in Tamil country.

We find also that many Christian objects came to be widely used by the new converts as per the instruction of the Jesuits. It was a custom to give a rosary to the newly baptized and it was also worn by the converts around their necks. Instances show that rosaries were available for sale in Tamilnadu and we find mention that a Christian by name Peter had sold his donkey and bought a rosary. During the divine services in the church, gold plated chalices were generally used and in one instance we find mention that the chalice could not be noticed by the robbers otherwise those who attacked the church would have stolen it. Further curtains were used and it hung before the reredos at the church in Kandalur.[165] Holy Cross was also fixed to the wall in the center of the church and when the church in Madurai was attacked, it was the only piece left by those who raided. Evidence suggests that the churches had several pictures of Catholic saints for encouraging devotion.[166] We find that various holy images were also kept in the church at Pudur. It has been reported by João de Birtto that he had arranged for a canopy made of gilt wood for the sanctuary of the Church in Gingee which the Christian artists had executed it with much skill and art, and it was supported by four columns which rested on six lions and the work was carried out with perfection.[167] Thus Portuguese had introduced several elements of Christian art and it came to be used widely in the churches of Tamilnadu.

Portuguese Jesuits had carried always some medicines with them for their own use if they fell sick. Antidotes against snake bites were generally kept by them for the use of the common people. It is reported that the Tamil physicians knew little about medicine and the medical facilities which were then available to the people had also been very poor at villages such as Ellamangalam.[168] The payment for the native doctors always came first well before the treatment. It was in practice then chiefly owing to the reason that the physician felt by himself that he might go unpaid for his work.

Some of the Portuguese records convey the sentiments of the natives in circumstances like when the missionaries died. When Fr. Francisco Peres, the Jesuit at Nagapattinam died on 12 February 1583 at the age of seventy, it was reported that many Hindus accompanied the cortege that carried his body to the grave and they wept as much as or more than many Christians who were his devout admirers. Some of the people told that they would erect for him a temple because he deserved it. The exemplary life he led, edified so much the people of Nagapattinam, that it prompted them to say so.[169]

Similarly it is reported that when Fr. Henrique Henriques died on 6 February 1600 in Punnaikayal and was buried in Tuticorin, all the Muslims of *Pattinam* (Kayalpattinam) observed a fast. The Hindus also fasted for two days. They closed all their shops for a day as a mark of mourning. It was also said that all the people on the Fishery Coast wanted to touch his body at the time of the burial for they believed him to be a very holy man.[170]

The missionaries also tried to understand the *agamic* features of Hindu temple architecture. They never kept themselves away from the temples too. In one instance we find that the Jesuits who were on the way to China came to Nagapattinam in 1655 and during their stay visited a local temple and admired the icons from outside. At the entrance of the temple they saw the figure of an elephant and a European lying at its feet beautifully carved in stone. The story of this carving was that the European having got so drunk had cast himself down before the temple and died while asleep. The Hindus explained that the elephant of the temple had killed him in punishment of his sin. In memory of this chastisement the sculptor of the temple had made the figure of the European lie at the feet of the elephant.[171]

In a letter dated 30 January 1699 Fr. Martin wrote that the Hindus had no relationship with the Europeans, of whom some by their debauchery and bad examples have spoilt and corrupted the entire Christianity of India. He said that the horror of the Indians for the Europeans had more than one cause. Some missionaries seem to have asked the question "What do men say that I am?"(Mark 8:28) and the answer is also given. According to Fr. Martin the

Europeans had often indulged in great violence in India. The natives had seen terrible examples of all kinds of debauchery and vice; but what shakes them particularly was that the *Firangis* (Portuguese) drink (alcohol) and eat meat, regarded by them as horrible and they treat those who eat meat and drink as vile".[172] Fr. Martin in his letter dated 1 June 1700 had attributed the difficulty in converting the Hindus to the conduct of the Portuguese. He said that the Portuguese never understood in the beginning the differences between the castes. They never troubled themselves to differentiate between the high and low castes. They employed freely the *pariahs* and fishermen. This conduct of the early Portuguese shocked the natives and became very prejudicial to Catholicism; for the Hindus considered there afterwards the people of Europe as a despicable and miserable lot with whom one cannot deal without dishonouring oneself. If the Europeans had taken wise precautions from those very days, as in Madurai for more than a century, it would have been easy to win all these people for Jesus Christ.[173] In this connection it may be said that Fr. Buccerio who was in charge of the Mukkuvars of Kolachel mentions at the end of the Sixteenth century "the fact that the Portuguese officials and the local gentry deemed it an honour to visit (him) did not raise him in the caste hierarchy. Those Christians acted thus because if they did otherwise the Hindus would taunt them with becoming Mukkuvars as barbers of the Portuguese. Now if in old parishes we must to humour non-Christains, put up with these and many other miseries how much more it is necessary to do so in this new mission until the Hindus have learnt to distinguish between caste and religion."[174] Thus we find the individual views of the different missionaries but it is to be noted that the times had changed which is almost a century.

Fr. Jean Venant Bouchet who lived in Pondicherry in his letter had also cautioned the missionaries not to identify themselves with the European colonisers. He stated that "all our attention should tend to hide from these people (Indians) that we are what they call '*Firangis*' (the Portuguese) the smallest doubt that they have in this regard, will be an insurmountable obstacle for the propagation of the (Christian) faith. The idolators reasonably perceive the missionaries as persons who want to destroy the religion of the country. Generally speaking, the Indians, except the Untouchables, hate drunkenness. They never drink liquor that will render them drunken. They actually express against this vice more strongly than our zealous missionaries and this inspires in them partly a great disdain for Europeans".[175]

To conclude, we may say that the Portuguese missionaries at first settled down on the ports where the Portuguese traders had established their settlements. Thus Santhome of Mylapore, Devanampattinam, Nagapattinam, Porto Novo, Punnaikayal and Tuticorin became the main centres of missionary activities in the Sixteenth Century while many sub-stations developed at various places in the Seventeenth Century. Regarding the missionary activities on the Pearl Fishery Coast, it may be said that not many conversions had taken place in the littoral extending from the port of Kilakkarai to Rameshwaram, while at the same time the *paravas* who lived in the coastal villages from Vembar to Ovari on the South Eastern Coast embraced Christianity en masse in 1532. Periyapattinam and Devanampattinam emerged as the most important mission stations towards the end of the Sixteenth Century. Although the Hindu rulers were generally much more tolerant to other religions, they did not stand as mute spectators whenever the Portuguese acted overzealously against the Hindus. The local rulers objected to it and even raided the port settlements. However in the Seventeenth Century the Portuguese missionaries who had taken up residence in the royal courts of Madurai, Chandragiri, etc., converted people and took care of the souls in the hinterland. The conversions made by the missionaries brought about an increase in the Christian population especially in the Portuguese settlements. There was a close relationship between the Portuguese regime and the Catholic religion. Substantial funds were allotted for pastoral work by the king of Portugal as the missionaries received generous financial help.

The Franciscans were successful in running hospitals and charitable institutions. The Jesuits carried out their pastoral work by learning Tamil, running schools, colleges and seminaries, in addition to printing books. Thus the Jesuits took up their apostolate by pioneering into the field of education. The Dominicans, the Augustinians and the Capuchins mainly attended to the spiritual needs of the European Catholics and the Eurasians.

As expansion of the Christianisation of India by the various religious congregations took place, the Holy See strengthened the missionary activity in the East by erecting the Sacred Congregation for the Propagation of Faith. Each mission or parish in the Tamil Country had a large number of sub-stations which covered a vast area. Christo-centric and Mario-centric worship and religious activities developed where many churches were built dedicated to Jesus and Mary. The *padroado* missionaries gradually expanded their work to deepen the spiritual life of the laity in the Tamil Coast and hinterland.

As for conversion, depending on the circumstances the rate of growth was sometimes rapid and sometimes slow. The caste ridden Tamil society was found favourable for carrying out conversions of different groups of Hindus by different groups of missionaries who adopted either the life style of *brahmin sanyasis* or *pandaraswamis* concentrating on the conversion of high castes and low castes respectively. As many members of the higher castes could not be converted, missionaries like Roberto Nobili adopted the method of acculturation. The converts in Tamilnadu were in a large measure from the lower caste people. In due course of time, the Portuguese missionaries themselves adopted some of the Tamil customs and practices which gradually penetrated into Christianity. Social inequality was the bane of Tamil society for centuries and this continued even after their conversion to Christianity. Another problem faced by the early Christian converts was the persecution they faced from the overzealous protestant Dutch missionaries especially at Tuticorin and Nagapattinam after these Portuguese settlements fell into the hands of the Dutch. The *Sanyasis* and the *Pandaraswamis* Jesuits respectively working among the high castes and the low castes came to an end in 1744. With the Bull of Pope Benedict XIV "*Ominum Solicitudinum*" dated 12 September 1744 the Malabar rites had also come to an end.

Notes and References

1. C. R Boxer, "A Note on the Portuguese Missionary Methods in the East, 16th- 18th Century", *Ceylon Historical Journal*, (henceforth CHJ) Vol. X, 1961, pp.77-90.

2. Levi Maria Jordão Paiva, *Bullarium Patronatus Portugallie Regum in Eccelsiis Africae, Asiae et Oceanie, Olisipone*, 1872, tomo. I, p.149, pp.222-224, 31-34, 36-37, 26-27, 59, 98-99, 192, 278-81. See also, C.C. Nazareth, *Mitras Lusitanas no Oriente..op.cit.*, Tomo.I, p. 9; See, Gaspar Correia, *Lendas da India.. op.cit.*, IV, 10.
3. William B. Green Lee, *The Voyage of Pedro Alvares Cabral to Brazil and India*, London, 1938, p. 49.
4. Correia, *op.cit.*, cap. X, p.739. Mathias Mundadan, " The Portuguese Settlement in Mylapore", *Indian Church History Review*, (hereafter ICHR), Vol. III, 1969, pp. 103-114.
5. Correia, *op.cit.*, Vol. I, p. 739. We also find in 1508 that an armada was sent to discover Melaka under the leadership of Diogo Lopes de Sequeira. He was instructed by the King of Portugal to inquire into the matter related to Apostle St. Thomas. See, Regimento de Diogo Lopes de Sequeira, issued from Almeirim on 13 February 1508 in IANTT, CC, I-6-82. It is also published in CAA, II, pp. 403-419.
6. Silva Rego, *História das Missões ...op.cit.*, cap. XI, pp. 411-435, p. 550. In 1517 a team of Portuguese traders along with some Armenians who came from Melaka to Pulicat mention the discovery of the tomb of Apostle St Thomas. See, BNL, *Fundo Geral*, Codice 7638, Doc. 87; See also, BA, Codice 50-VI-21, fl. 206-207v; See also, Silva Rego, *Documentação...op.cit.*, Vol. I, doc. 137, pp. 296.
7. Barros, *op.cit.*, Decada 3, Livro 7, Capitulo 11, pp. 225-226; Correia, *op.cit.*, Vol.II, pp.725-724.
8. Barros, *op.cit.*, Decada 3, Livro 7, Capitulo 11, pp. 227-229; Correia, *op.cit.*, Vol.II, p. 787.
9. Silva Rego, *Documentação...op.cit.*, Vol.II, pp. 197 & 356.
10. Letter of Vicente to the King of Portugal dated 25 December 1530 in Silva Rego, *Documentação...op.cit.*, Vol.II, p.197.
11. ARSI, Goa, 37, fl. 31v-32r.
12. DI, Vol. I, p. 97.
13. Elaine Sancaeu, CSL, Vol. II, p. 382. João Villa de Conde complained to the Viceroy of Goa in his letter 22 April 1547 that many Paravas of the fishery coast resided in the region between Kilakkarai and Vedalai.
14. ARSI, Mss, Goa Collections, No. 38. fl. 307.
15. Couto, *op.cit.*, Decada VI, Livro VII, Capitulo V.
16. Silva Rego, *Documentação...op.cit.*, Vol. II, pp. 357 & 147; DI, Vol. I. p. 81.

17. Fr. Fernando de Soledade, Chronica Serafica da Provincia de Portugal, III. Vols, Lisboã, 1885, Livro 3, Capitulo 21, p. 559.
18. Paulo de Trinidade, *op.cit.*, Vol. III, p. 738.
19. Fernando Felix Lopez, Missóes Franciscans na India Oriental em 1595 Casa Pessoal e Legislação, 1953. See also Achilles Meersmen, The Franciscans in Tamilnad, Schoneck Beckenried, 1962.
20. *Ibid.*
21. *Ibid.*
22. Schurhammer, EX, Vol. I, pp. 147, 161-62; Venantius Fernando, *The Impact of the Portuguese Padroado on the Indian Pearl Fishery Coast*, Doctoral Thesis, Urban University, Rome, 1977, p. 184.
23. DI, Vol. I, pp. 225-26, Letter of Fr. Henriques written from Punnaikayal dated 6 December 1547.
24. DI, Vol. I, p. 283. Letter of Fr. Henriques written from Vembar dated 31 Oct ober 1548. Letter of Francis Xavier written from Kochi dated 31 December 1543 in Henry James Coleridge, *The Life and Letters of St. Francis Xavier*, 2 Vols, London, 1881, pp. 153-155
25. DI, Vol. I, p. 284. Letter of Fr. Henriques written from Vembar dated 31 October 1548.
26. Letter of Francis Xavier written in February from Manapadu in 1548, EX, Vol. I, pp. 422-434.
27. J. Wicki, " The Confraternity of Christianity of Henrique Henriques", *Indian Church History Review*, Vol. 1, March, 1967, p. 4.
28. ARSI, *Litterae Annuae, 1582*, p. 3.
29. HAG, MDR, Livro 19D, Codice 24-26/3-4.
30. Letter of Fr. Francisco Perez to Fr. Miguel de Torres de São Roque dated 1 January 1558 written from Kochi in BA, Codice 49-IV-50.
31. DI, Vol. II, p. 17.
32. DI, Vol. IV, p. 70.
33. DI, Vol. II, pp. 16-17; DI, Vol. III, pp. 298-299; DI, Vol. IV, p. 286.
34. DI, Vol. V, p.181; It was in 1559 that Ramaraya, the King of Vijayanagar attacked the Portuguese settlement of Mylapore for the Portuguese missionaries had caused disturbances to the temples. See, DI, Vol. IV, p.491; Hosten, *Antiquities...op.cit.*, pp. 45-46. The Portuguese residents had to pay a ransom of 50000 pagodas because twenty five citizens were taken as prisoners by Ramaraya. See DI, Vol. IV, pp. 368 & 491, DI, Vol. V, p. 180.
35. *Bullarium Patronatus*, Vol. I, pp.192-195.
36. DI, Vol. VII, pp. 202-204.

37. DI, Vol. VII, pp. 202-203.
38. DI, Vol. VIII, pp. 426-427.
39. ARSI, *Litterae Annuae Provinciae Malabarensis, 1602*; DI, Vol. XVI, pp.344-345 & 750-751.
40. DI, Vol. X, pp. 486-487
41. DI, Vol. XIII, p. 502; DI, Vol. XVI, pp. 344-345
42. Silva Rego, *Documentação...op.cit*., Vol. XII, p. 513.
43. DI, Vol. XVI, pp. 344-345
44. ARSI, Mss Goa, Letter of Fr. Pimenta in 1589; MPJA, *Litterae Annuae Provinciae Malabarensis, 1608-1609*, Vol. VI, fl. 7
45. Christovao Suarez de Figueira, *Historia y Anal Relacion de las Cosas que Hizier on los Padres de la Companhia de Jesus por las Artes de Oriente y Otras en la Propagacion del Santo Evangelico los Anos Passados de 607 y 608*, Madrid, 1913, pp. 113-115.
46. DI, Vol. IV, doc. no.429, p.160.
47. It is found in a letter of Fr.Gomez, Rector of the Jesuit College at Goa, written to the king of Portugal. See Henry Heras, The *Aravidu..Op.cit*., pp.156-157. For details on Panchamas, See, Edgar Thurston, *Castes and Tribes of South India*, 1909, (reprint) Delhi, 1975.
48. IANTT, DRI, Vol. 57, fl. 31.
49. Samuel Purchas, *op.cit*., p.105; DI, Vol. XV, p.706. Fr. Leni wrote that the expenditure of the Pearl fishery included tribute paid to the Hindu rulers during 1611 in Periyapattinam. ARSI, Mss, Goa Collections, No.17, fl. 67v.
50. ARSI, Mss Goa, No. 12, fls. 209 & 216-217. António da Silva Rego, *Documentação...op.cit*., Vol. XII, pp. 286-287; See, IANTT, *Colleção Jesuitica*, Livro 28, fls. 19v-20. While saying mass St. Francis Xavier was found raising above the ground. He is further reported to have preached to the people in Tamil and all the natives were surprised for he spoke pronouncing the words so well.
51. BFUP, Vol. 15, pp. 18.
52. DI, Vol. II, P. 152; Vol. III, p. 227.
53. Letter of Dom Mateus, the Bishop of Kochi to the King of Portugal written from Kochi dated 16 January 1588 in BFUP, Vol.V, fls. 559 & 597. (See also other letters dated 16 January 1585, 23 November 1589).
54. APO-CR, II, p. 213. (22 February 1589)
55. APO-CR, III, p. 213. (22 February 1589) See also HAG, MDR, Livro 3B, Codice 52-55/2 ; BFUP, Vol. I, p. 229.

56. Letter of Frei Gaspar de Lisboã to the King of Portugal dated 23 November 1589 written from Goa. See AGS, Mss *Secretarias Provinciales*, Codice no. 1551, fls. 669-674, fls. 324-324v, 313-313v, 323-323v, 32-312v; See also, BFUP, Vol. V, pp. 960 & 597.
57. Fernão Guerreiro, *Relação ..op.cit.*, Vol. III, p. 77.
58. IANTT, CC, Ia-83-90.
59. DI, Vol. XV, pp. 334-344, 756-759; Purchas, *His Pilgrims... op.cit.*, Vol. X, p. 207.
60. DI, Vol. XV, pp.334-44, 756-759.
61. BM, *Additional Manuscripts*, 9853, fl. 52v-53v. fl. 143; Gurreiro, *op.cit.*, Vol. I, p. 321; Achilles Meersman, "The Catholic Church in Tranquebar and Tanjore", *Indian Church History Review*, Vol. I, 1967, pp. 94-95.
62. BA, Codice *Jesuitas na Asia*, 49-VI-12.
63. Vicecomite de Paiva Manso, Bullarium Patronatus Portugallie Regum in Ecclesiis Africae, Asiae et Oceaniae: Bullas Brevia, Epistolas, Decreta acta que Sancte Sedis ab Alexandre III ad hoc Usque Tempus Amplectens, Tomo II, (1601-1700), Olisipone, 1870, pp. 4-6. J.C. Houpert mentions the month of erection of the Mylapore diocese wrongly as 9 February 1606. See J.C. Houpert, *Church History of India & Ceylon*, Vol. I, Trichy, 1942, p. 199.
64. AGS, *Secretarias Provinciales*, Codice 1494, fl. 65.
65. BNL, Mss *Iluminado*, No. 140, fl. 242B.
66. AGS, *Secretarias Provinciales*, Codice 1494, fl. 65.
67. AGS, *Secretarias Provinciales*, Codice 1494, fl. 65-65v. 60v - 61v.
68. AGS, *Secretaries Provinciales*, Codice 1494, fl. 64v.
69. AGS, *Secretarias Provinciales*, Codice 1494, fl. 71-71v.
70. HAG, MDR, Livro 12, Codice 13/5/1, fl. 26.
71. HAG, MDR, Livro 12, Codice 49/1/2.
72. IANTT, DRI, Livro 6, fl. 57.
73. IANTT, DRI Livro 7, fl. 255.
74. HAG, MDR, Livro 12, Codice 49-12, fl.145.
75. HAG, MDR, Livro 10, fls. 280-281.
76. HAG, MDR, Livro 12, fl. 552.
77. HAG, MDR, Livro 30, fl. 257v.
78. BNL, Codice 1783, fl. 110-111v.
79. *Memoirs*, p. 298.
80. MPJA, *Litterae Annuae, 1648*.

81. HAG, MDR, Vol. 12, Codice 47/3/5, fls. 143-144.

82. DI, Vol. XIV, doc.21.

83. C. Gomez Rodeles & S. Cardon, "Early Jesuit Presence in India" *Journal of the Royal Asiatic Society of Bengal*, Vol. IX, pp.149-168. See also, Samuel Purchas, *His Pilgrims*, Vol.X, Glasgow, 1965, pp. 217-219.

84. Fernão Perreira de Britto, *Vida e Martyrio do Veneravel P. João de Britto*, Coimbra, 1722, see pt. II, chapter III.

85. HAG, MDR, Livro 12, Codice 15/3/4.

86. HAG, MDR, Livro 12, Codice 48/1/3, fls. 143-144.

87. HAG, MDR, Livro 12, Codice 8/12, fl. 14; Letter of Manuel Barradas to Manuel Severim de Faria written from Goa dated 5 November 1637 in Camilo Beccari, (ed.) *Rerum Aethiopicarum Scriptores Occidentales Inediiti a Seculo XVI ad XVII,* Vol. XIII, Roma, 1913, pp. 130-133.

88. IANTT, DRI, Livro 54, fl. 97.

89. On Manuel Fernandes, see Schurhammer, *Francis Xavier...op.cit.*, Vol. II, p. 556. ARSI, Mss Goa, No. 32, fl. 654r. See also *Monumenta Xaveriana,* 2 Vols, Matriti, 1899-1912, Vol. II, pp. 546-547, 555-557.

90. Philip Baldeaus, *A True and Exact Description of the Most Celebrated East India Coasts of Malabar and Coromandel as well as of the Isle of Ceylon, 1672,* (trs.,) London, 1703, p. xxii.

91. Philip Baldeaus, *op.cit.,* p. xix.

92. NA, BUB, VOC 879, fls. 502-503 (9 November 1664); NA, BUB, VOC 882, fl. 135, (29 March 1667); NA, OBP, VOC, 1231 1143, fl.870. (12 May 1665).

93. EX, II, pp. 9-10.

94. Letter of Fr. Balthasar da Costa in 1644 in Jean Castets, *L' Ancienne Mission du Madure des Origines et Ses Histoire*, MPJA, pp. 111-115.

95. Fernão Guerreiro, Relacam Anual das Coisas que Fezeram Os Padres da Companhia de Jesus Nas Partes da India Oriental & em Alguas Outras da Conquista Deste Reyno no Anno de 606 & 607 do Proceso de Conversao & Christandade da Quellas Partes Tirada das Cartas dos Mesmos Padres Que da *la Vierao Pelo Padre Fernao Guerriero da Companhia de Jesu Natural de Almodura de Portugal*, Lisboã, 1909, pp. 105-107.

96. Fernão Perreira de Britto, *op.cit.*, pt II, chap III; See H. Heras, " Two Missionary Methods in the Nation of Ancient Civilization", in *Studia Missionalia,* (hereafter SM), Rome, 6, 1951, pp. 181-184.

97. Annual letter of Fr Andre Lopez 1644, in Fr. L.Besse, *La Mission du Maduré*, Trichnopoly, 1914, pp. 30-32. In the Pearl Fishery Coast the number of Christians were 26218 in 1644. See L. Besse, *op.cit.*, pp. 15-21.

98. Letter of Fr. Martin written during October and December 1651 in J. Bertrand, *La Mission du Maduré d aprés de documents in edits*, 4 Vols, Paris, 1850-1854, Vol. II, pp. 393-94; Letter of Fr. Martin to Fr. de Villette in 1700, *Travels of the Jesuits into various Parts of the World*, 2 Vols, London, 1762, Vol. I, p. 5.
99. MPJA, *Litterae Annuae 1711.*
100. MPJA, *Litterae Annuae 1731.*
101. Fernão Perreira de Britto, *op. cit.*, part II, Chapter IV.
102. MPJA, Letter of Britto to Superior General, 20 July to 29 August, 1686. See also S. Khadirvel, *A History of the Maravas 1700-1802*, Madurai, 1977, p. 42.
103. Travels of the Jesuits, *op.cit.*, Vol. I, pp. 452-453; MPJA, Annual Letter of the Marava Country 1686 to Superior General.
104. MPJA, Letter of João de Britto dated 11 July 1692.
105. MPJA, Letter of João de Britto to João de Costa dated 22 July 1692.
106. Bertrand, *op.cit.*, Vol.III, p. 448. Manucci, *op.cit.*, III. p. 236; MPJA, *Litterae Annuae, 1734.*
107. MPJA, *Litterae Annuae, 1644* ; L.Besse, *La Mission ...op.cit.*, p. 565.
108. MPJA, *Litterae Annuae, 1666.* R. Cald well, *A History of Tinnevelly*, Madras, 1881, p. 236 ; Muttusami Pillei, *op.cit.*, pp. 268-269.
109. MPJA, *Litterae Annuae, 1701.* J. Bertrand, *La Mission... op.cit.*, IV, pp. 344-345.
110. MPJA, *Litterae Annuae, 1714.*
111. Letter of Fr. Balthasar da Costa to the Jesuit Superior General in 1644 cited in Bertrand, *op.cit.*, Vol. II, p. 340. MPJA, Mss. *Jesuit Records Parish Diaries and Historical : Historical Notes - Tinnevelly District* (by Adrian Caussanel, 1925) pp. 140-142. MPJA, *Litterae Annuae*, Vol. II, fls. 35-37, J.S. Chandler, *History of the Jesuit Mission in Madura, South India in the 17th and 18th Century*, Madras, 1909, p. 5.
112. MPJA, *Litterae Annuae, 1666-1686.*
113. Archives of the Archdiocese of Madras-Mylapore (hereafter AAMM) Bundle no. 8, No. 5110; See also AGC, H, 55, XIII,2, fls. 15-16.
114. Ibid., AGC, H, 55, XIII, 2, fl. 15.
115. AGC, H, 55, XIII, 2, fl. 16.
116. Peter Celestine, *Early Capuchin Missions in India*, Sahidabad, 1982, pp. 12- 13; APF, SC, *Indie Orientalie Cina*, Vol. 7, fl. 268; AGC, H, 55, XIII,1.

117. MPJA, *Documents Bertrand*, Vol. I, document no. 3. See also, Joe Sebastian, *The Jesuit Carnatic Mission*, Hyderabad, 2004.
118. AGC, H, 55, XIII, 2; BFP, Mss. 43, Memorabilia 29.
119. Alfred Martineau, *op.cit.*, Vol. II, p. 630.
120. *Ibid.*, p.150.
121. MPJA, Mss, *Baptemés' Indiens Administrés par les RR G.P.Capucins*, 20 March 1677, fl. 1.
122. Archives General of the Capuchin order, (hereafter AGS) Rome, H, 55, (India), XIII, 2, fl. 143; Bibliothéque Franciscaine Provinciale, (hereafter BFP) Paris, Mss. 43, Memorabilia f. 29; Mss 192, fl. 101.
123. *Ibid.*, fl. 3.
124. MPJA, Documents Bertrand, Vol. I, document no. 5. Fr. João de Britto also visited Pondicherry earlier. François Martin in his diary mentions on 3 May 1681 as follows: " Fr. João de Britto with whom I was in regular correspondence visited me in Pondicherry and stayed three days. Then he travelled to Santhome and two days before my departure for Surat returned to Pondicherry".
125. S. Jeyaseela Stephen, "Urbanism and the Chequered Existence of the Indo- French Town of Pondicherry" *Revue Historique de Pondichéry*, Vol. XIX, 1996, p. 35.
126. APF, Acta, Vol.80, fl. 155.
127. AGC, H,55, XIII, 2. fls. 148-151.
128. APF, Acta, Vol. 73, fl. 49.
129. AGC, H, 55, XIII,2, fls. 154-160.
130. ARSI, Mss Gall, 118 fl. 146-149; See also Adrien Launay, *Histoire de la Mission de l' Inde, Pondichéry Maissour, Coimbatour*, Vol. I, Paris, 1898, Appendix. V, p. 460.
131. Abbe Platel, *Memoirs Historique sur les affairs des Jesuites avec le Saint Siege*, Lisboã, 1766, 4 Vols; MPJA, *Documents Bertrand*, Vol. I, Document No.32. This document is dated 1 March 1701, a letter written by Pontchartrain to the French Governor; See also, Joseph Thekkadath, *History of Christianity in India: From the mid 16th Century to the End of 17th Century, 1542-1700*, Bangalore, 1982, p. 9.
132. NAIP, Mss *Registre de Deliberations du Conseil de la Compagnie*, Vol. I, Cart 17, fl. 3.
133. NAIP, Mss, *Eighteenth Century Documents*, no. 430, fls. 2-2v.
134. C.R. Boxer, *The Church, Militant and Iberian Expansion, 1440-1770*, Baltimore, 1978, pp. 69 & 132.

135. MPJA, *Documents Bertrand*, Vol. I, Document No. 40. See, Letter of Fr. Bouchet to Cochet de Saint Valier, dated 7 February 1702.
136. *Ibid.*, Vol. I, Document No. 44, Letter of Fr. Tachard to Jesuit Superior General written from Pondicherry dated 25 October 1703.
137. *Ibid.*, Document No. 46. Letter of Fr. Tachard to Jesuit Superior General dated 12 February 1704.
138. *Ibid.*, Document No. 52 is in Latin. The same content is the next document with no. 53 which is in French. Both are written by Fr. Mauduit to the Jesuit Superior General written from Erudurgam, dated 18 February 1705.
139. *Ibid.*, Vol. II, Document No. 212.
140. AAMM, Document No. 2889 (18 March 1704).
141. *Ibid.*
142. AAMM Mss. 2348.
143. *Ibid.*
144. AAMM, Mss. 2940.
145. MPJA, *Litterae Annuae, 1712-13*. The letter is signed dated 19 August 1713.
146. AHU, India, Mss, *Documentos Avulos,* Maco 8.
147. MPJA, Louis Facheux, Mss, *Lieux d'Origine des Chretiens Baptises a Pondichery par les Jesuites, 1715-1777.*
148. *Ibid.*, 1725-1734.
149. *Ibid.*, 1724-1744; See also, MPJA, Louis Facheux, *Baptemes Administres aPondichery par les Capucins e 1676 a 1693 et par les Jesuites de 1715 a1776,* fls.1-4.
150. MPJA, *Documents Bertrand,* Vol. III, Document No. 354. Letter of Fr. Gargam to Souciet, written from Ariyankuppam dated 21 September 1739.
151. *Ibid.*, Vol. III, Document No. 374.
152. *Ibid..*, Vol. III, Document No. 378.
153. *Ibid..*, Vol. III, Document No. 379.
154. Archives Nationales, Paris, Mss. *Serie,* T. 1169.
155. Letters of the Portuguese Jesuits, *Ibid*, pp. .28-36.
156. *Ibid.*, p.130.
157. *Ibid.*, p. 42.
158. *Ibid.*, p. 37.
159. *Ibid.*, p. 65.
160. *Ibid.*, p.138.

161. *Ibid..*, p. 146.

162. *Ibid..*, p. l5.

163. *Ibid..*, p. 19.

164. *Ibid.*, pp.145-146.

165. *Ibid.*, pp.167-168.

166. *Ibid.*, pp. 246-247.

167. *Ibid.*, p. 260.

168. *Ibid.*, p. l40.

169. Fr. Luis de Conceicao, the guardian of the Franciscan Friary at Nagapattinam wrote on Ash Wednesday in 1583 about this incident. For details see, in Francisco de Sousa, *Oriente Conquistado,* pt II, Conq II, Division II, no. 8.

170. MPJA, *Litterae Annuae Provinciae Goa,* 1600, Letter of Fr. Sebastiao Goncalves; see also *Litterae Annuae* 1601, Fernao Gurreiro, *Relacao anual... op.cit.,* Vol. I, p. 32. see also, J. Wicki, "P. Henriques S.J. (1520-1600) Eni Vorbildicher *Missions Indiens", Studia Missionalia,* XIII, 1963, pp. 113-68. see also, *Life of P. Henriques...op.cit.,* pp. 166-170.

171. Jean L' Hernault, *Relation des Missions des Peres de la Compagnie des Jesus dans les Indes Orientales, Dresse Par en Pere de la Mesme Compagnie,* Paris, 1959, pp. 149-150.

172. Letter of Fr. Martin to Fr. Vilette dated 30 January 1699, in *Lettres Edifiantes et Curieuses* (henceforth *LEC*) tome X, 10, Paris, 1781, pp. 44- 46.

173. Letter of Fr. Martin to Fr. Gobien dated 1 June 1700, in *LEC,* tome X, pp. 66-71.

174. S. Rajmanickam, *His Star in the East*, Chennai, 1999, pp. 150-151.

175. Letter of Fr. Bouchet in *LEC*, tome XIII, MDLCLXXXI, pp. 45, 50, & 87. See also, Letter of Fr. Bourges to Mme. La Comtesse de Sondé dated 21 September 1713, in *LEC,* tome XII, p.77. See also *LEC,* tome X, see the Preface.

3

Castes, Communities, Societal Changes and the Catholic Institutions

With the entry of the Portuguese in the overseas trade of the Tamil Coast during the Sixteenth Century and the attempts of the missionaries to convert the natives in the region to Catholicism, there emerged a Christian community in Tamilnadu. It would be worthwhile to find out how the native Christians in the Tamil country were exposed to a sudden change and gradual change in their customs, manners and daily life. Certainly this new Christian community in the Tamil Coast was introduced to an altogether different civilisation built on the tenets of Christian doctrine. We shall highlight the manner in which societal changes had occurred in the native Christian society.

It may be recalled that during the rule of the Cholas in the medieval period in Tamilnadu, each group of people were placed in a system of local self government and their participation is known through the joint organizations established by them[1] which emerged at the *Nadu* and *Periyanadu* level (with *nattar* and *periyanattar*). Although the functioning of these organizations differed from place to place and region to region, the caste appears to be very strong as evident from the text of the Chola inscriptions[2] which proudly express "*Nammudaya Sathikutkadavaar*" (Our Caste men) in the case of *Vaniyars* and "*Engal sathikumm, Yengal vamsathukkum*" (for our caste and for our inheritors) in another instance, in the case of *Pathinen Vishayathar*. In the subsequent period with the advent of the Vijayanagara rulers in the Tamil region led to the migration of Kannadigas and Telugus in large numbers and the Tamil society was geared up to change with a mixture of classes, groups and economic divisions.[3] The nature of change in the Hindu society at that point of time had been already examined in detail by me with reference to Hindu peasants, weavers and artisans, merchants, slaves, Portuguese society, etc., and it has been pointed out that the Hindu Tamil society could no more be treated in the framework of the fourfold division.[4] Change as dialectics to Tamil Hindu society is noticed in this age of Portuguese expansion in the Tamil Coast. The change in Tamil Hindu society is seen often as triggered and driven forced by class conflicts of the right hand and left hand division with an array of other changes being seen as contingent.[5] As a result of this class conflict we find, that the Tamil Hindu society existed in the new form of class relations. Hence scholars have explained the most widely debated form of change in Tamil Hindu society based on immanence by employing some form of dialectical change in its very nature portraying and containing inner conflicts.

The Hindu Paravas in the Tamil Coast revolted against the Muslims and embraced Christianity under the protection of the Portuguese and this new Tamil Christian society's affairs were resolved through this sudden revolutionary change. Some scholars have limited themselves to the study of conversion of the Paravas stressing the systematic structure or organizational characters of the society and explained the dynamics of societal system.[6] But there is a need to establish a more systematic understanding of the wider groups of Tamil people and also enter into the debate over change laying emphasis on the paramount role played by Catholic clergy, the human agency which had not been dealt in detail until now and the present chapter attempts to examine here.

Change as social action is found, through the efforts of the Portuguese missionaries in the Tamil Coast. The study of this primacy of human agency is done, because such an approach becomes a rich interweave of human perceptions, intentions, actors and events. It is also one of the best types of approaches in respect of the analysis of change in experimental terms. Thus we are able to understand societal changes in its wider understanding through the careful reconstruction of events much more than the role played by the Political rulers of the Vijayanagara kingdom of that time.

We have to admit frankly that the Portuguese missionaries as human agents were paramount but it is equally true that they cannot be divorced from the wider possible structure. This concern helps us maintain the link between the actions of the missionary individuals and the wider structures of Tamil society which has produced large and complex models dealing with change.[7] Among the historians it had provided the basis for the core philosophy of the Annales school of history. Scholars like Fernand Braudel[8] too had developed a history based on different scales of analysis, on the one hand there were structures, ever explosive moments of change which played out at the tempo of individuals and studying through *l'histoire evenmentielle* or the history of event. Around these events there is larger scale of analysis based on the trends and cycles of social and economic life or what are called conjectures. Further at a still larger scale, we have the *long duree* that are structures. In effect, the link between the short term and the long term between event and structure could be portrayed as if the flow of social change was like a lava flow with those parts which had cooled down and solidified which obstruct and deflect the surge of fresh eruptions created by the Portuguese missionaries. Thus the present study attempts to provide a counter view to overtly systematic interpretation of social systems and it is based on the absolute primacy of Portuguese missionaries, the human agency.

Social Changes and the Christian Paravas in the Sixteenth Century

The Portuguese had not taken any efforts for doing missionary work in the Tamil Coast from their arrival in India in AD. 1498 till the year 1534. Only a few missionaries of the Franciscan and Dominican orders arrived on the Tamil Coast to take care of the Portuguese traders. The establishment of the diocese of Goa in 1534 gave them some space so that unified missionary enterprise could be undertaken in the Tamil region.

The Paravas, the fishermen of the Tamil Coast were the first converts by the Portuguese missionaries in 1537. The event of their conversion laid the foundation for the Portuguese pastoral work and their mass conversions also had a great impact in the Coastal politics of Tamilnadu. These new converts retained many of the distinctive features of the earlier social and Hindu religious life. Thus in reality, religious conversion of the Paravas initially had not sought much impact in the practice of Christian religion by the individuals. These details are well recorded in the letters of Francis Xavier. For him thus, Parava conversion to Christianity in the Sixteenth Century Tamilnadu meant that breaking away from all pre-existing beliefs and social ties.[9]

Paravas being Christians and following Hindu traditions, made Francis Xavier to appoint *Pattangattis* and other village officers as a kind of moral policing agency. He had empowered them on the Paravas to levy fines for drunkenness, adultery and other transgressions found common in the Parava society. Francis Xavier in 1544 could not tolerate himself to see the Hindu deities and images being produced in the Christian villages of the Paravas. He was very furious and he threatened the *Pattangattis* of Punnaikayal to be arrested and chained for failing to carry out his orders and to follow the Christian way of living turning a new leaf.[10]

As these Paravas had to be instructed the Christian faith, the Portuguese missionaries learnt Tamil. They left in each place a copy of the "Christian Doctrine" (*Doctrina Christam*) they prepared in Tamil. On every feast day, the missionaries bid the Christians meet in one place for prayer and sing hymns all together to show their signs of faith. For this purpose, the Portuguese missionaries had also appointed men of intelligence and good character who presided over the function in their absence. Further the Portuguese Viceroy had been very kind enough to allot an annual revenue of 4000 gold *panams* for the salary of these native catechists who acted as the intermediaries between the priest and the faithful.[11]

The pastoral work of Francis Xavier was followed by some missionaries like Fr. Henrique Henriques in Tamil country. He selected the most exemplary individuals to spend their life in the service of the Paravas of the various places such as Manappadu, Kombuthurai, Punnaikayal, Ovari, Vaippar, Vembar, Alanthalai, Virapandiyan Pattinam, Tuticorin, etc., It is mentioned in a letter by Henriques in 1552 to Ignatius Loyola that these catechists were sticking to their places of work. He further stated that the Christians would be able to preserve their faith even if there were no longer any Portuguese missionaries in the region.[12]

It was at this time, the Portuguese missionaries noticed some common social evils prevalent in the Tamil society on the coast and they planned to introduce some reforms. First they found that several marriages took place between the relatives on the Tamil Coast. Because of the prevailing eccelsiastical prohibition for such marriages, Fr. Henriques felt the need to request the Holy See to allow such marriages among the Paravas in the third and fourth degrees of consanguinity and affinity. He was of the opinion that it was already much if the Christians could be persuaded to avoid marrying first cousins. To demand more from these Parava Catholics it would be too heavy a burden on them.[13] Thus missionaries were very understanding and initially careful in handling the affairs before introducing any drastic social reforms among the Paravas.

Further in several other matters also, the canon law was not enforced among the Paravas. To cite, we may say that the rule of annual confession was not imposed as late as in the year 1558 for the simple reason that there were not sufficient number of priests to hear the confessions of the people. Those Christians who were guilty of clandestine marriages were punished but only very lightly. The Christian feast days of obligation were made very few. There were also no obligatory of fast during the season of Lent.[14]

Portuguese missionaries do mention several social disorders that existed in Tamil coast in 1575. In the written report of Valignano, the Jesuit visitor, we find the list. He exhorted the priests of Tamil Coast to insist that the Tamil Christians should not indulge in certain objectionable things like the making of the Hindu idols and performing the Hindu ceremonies. Further he declared that the Christians must be prevented from consulting fortune tellers and from making use of the charms of the magicians in the hope of catching more fish. Sorcery (*Suniam*) for example was popularly thought to account for various kinds of misfortune by the Hindus. The sorcerers (*Suniyakarans*) are thought to have access to the secret knowledge and mystical powers which they employed on behalf of paying clients. The persons who are thought to engage the service of such experts for harmful ends had personal grudges against the intended victims or their close kin. Sorcery thus in its aggressive aspect implied a variety of ritual techniques to inflict harm with pernicious medicines such as mystical ink (*mai*) used in this witchcraft. According to the Christian doctrines of belief in the authenticity of such happenings and ceremonies had been suspended. The Tamil Christians were forbidden to do so whereas the Hindus had continued to resort to a variety of deities and ritual specialists to protect them. Thus the Portuguese missionaries discredited these popular superstitions and beliefs in the existence of evil spirits and the efficacy of magic and sorcery and condemned the actions. The Christian doctrine although confirmed the existence of evil forces thereby providing evidence both of satanic influences, the Tamil Christians were asked to seek the power of the Holy Spirit to defeat them. Valignano also emphasized very much that the Christians must be forbidden to offer anything to the devil or to the Hindu idols and they must not be also allowed to swear by them.[15]

It appears that the Christians of the Tamil Coast had never given up some of their earlier practices completely. In 1582, Fr. Henriques punished the villagers in the Pearl Fishery Coast for some grave faults of theirs by depriving them of the mass and the sacraments for some time. The villagers felt it so much that they went to him in a group and begged that they be given other punishment but not that of being deprived of the mass and the sacraments. Not until the year 1599 (20 June 1599 at the Synod of Diamper) did the Portuguese missionaries succeed in cleansing the chapels even in Tamil Coast of what they considered to be remnants of Hindu worship such as the casting of horoscopes, the use of sandal paste in the various ceremonies conducted by the natives.

For the spiritual well being of the Paravas, Fr. Henriques saw that sermons and spiritual talks were delivered to the more devout people of the Tamil Coast. Further, several of these people were organized into Confraternity of Charity. This Confraternity of Charity was founded by Henriques based on the love of God and the love of one's neighbor. It was like a religious society for the married Christians. The aim of the members of the confraternity was to live a good Christian life and help others to do so. The men associated with this organization attended spiritual talks on Fridays and the women on Tuesdays. Henriques formulated the rules in AD. 1578 and stated that the members had to lead an exemplary life striving for personal perfection. It was also a call to help Christian brethren in need especially the dying and the sick who were poor or abandoned. Some hospitals were also established.[16] The enterprising and sacrificing work of the lay helpers had definitely brought the Christian society to the forefront than other Hindu low castes in Tamil society. These men of confraternity with their words and deeds, urged the Christians to lead virtuous lives.[17] It is gleaned from the annual letter of the year 1575 that the confessors testified that many Paravas passed the whole year without committing any mortal sin.[18] Thus individual attention to the Christians had been made by the Portuguese missionaries. The Paravas in the due course of time became small traders, boat builders and sail makers. They became economically also rich with the expansion of the Portuguese seaborne trade.[19]

Mukkuvars

The Mukkuvars were another group of Christians converted to Christianity at Puthenthurai, Kolachel, Muttam, Rajakkamangalam, Kovalam and Manakkudi on the Tamil Coast by the Portuguese as early as in the year 1547.[20] As found in the Portuguese documents of the year 1553, some of these Christian Mukkuvars had become Muslims[21] and the reasons for such conversions are not mentioned at all. Further we also find that after a few years some Christian Mukkuva girls of Thengapattanam had married the Muslims of that place and they had embraced the religion of their husbands. It is reported that even the mothers of these girls became Muslims.[22] It was at this time the Portuguese missionaries took serious steps to avoid such scandals. By the year 1563 we find that some improvement had been noticed in the moral life of these people especially in matters connected with chastity and brotherly love since they used to be quarrelsome previously. It is reported in the missionary letters that the Christians became peaceful and easily pardoned. Further the Hindu religious practices too were slowly getting abandoned.[23] These Christians refused to make offerings to a temple even though the request had been made in secret.[24] In these villages a judge and a policeman had also been appointed. These priests were always available for hearing the more serious cases and deliver judgments so that there was no miscarriage of justice. However the missionaries did not depose the guilty.[25] The reports of the Portuguese missionaries say that by 1578 the Christians showed love for religion by defending their churches against the Hindus.[26] Thus in the Sixteenth Century the Christian castes and communities of the Tamil region were more or less homogenous in terms of socio-economic criteria especially limited to the coastal people of Paravas and Mukkuvars with whom the Portuguese had been preoccupied with.

Some aspects of the activities of the Portuguese missionaries in the Sixteenth century had been projected in the correspondences and communications of the missionaries of the later period. It is recorded that " The Portuguese never understood in the beginning the differences between the castes... They never troubled themselves to differentiate between the high and low castes. They employed freely the pariahs and the fishermen and made use of them to satisfy their various needs. This conduct of the early Portuguese shocked the natives and they became very prejudicial to our religion. For they (Hindus) considered there afterwards the people of Europe as a despicable and miserable lot with whom one cannot deal with dishonoring oneself".[27] In another instance it is stated that "the idolaters reasonably perceive the missionaries as persons who want to destroy the religion of the country".[28]

The Paravas who became Christians declared King of Portugal as their ruler and the charges levelled on the Christian converts were subject to forces that denationalized and westernized. Thus one can see how westernization could be seriously mistaken for Christianity in the Sixteenth century. This made the Jesuits of the Madurai Mission successful in evolving and Indian Christian Culture that is thoroughly Tamilian and distinctively Christian with a minimum of the western influence in the Seventeenth century as we shall later.

The study of missionary history by several scholars in the past has been centered on single individuals and their conversion work in establishing Christian communities, building various chapels and churches.[29] This type of writing tends to view the converts as separating from their surroundings by the act of conversion and any remaining ties to their previous world of beliefs and social connections as evidence of unsuccessful conversions. Of late the study of Christian conversions had been seen in a broader framework of social and economic history. In this connection the works of Susan Bayly[80] and David Mosse[81] for the first time emphasized not on the missionaries or on what the missionaries expected from their converts but rather on what the converts expected from the missionaries and how they used what they have learnt from the missionaries in new and unexpected contexts. Another significant feature of these studies was that they placed missionary process as adaptation and mutual dependency rather than as breaks with previous relationships. We shall examine how adaptation was followed by the Portuguese Jesuits in the process of conversions in Tamilnadu.

Social Changes and High Caste Christians in the Seventeenth Century

The Portuguese missionary presence in the Tamil hinterland at the end of the Sixteenth century was intimately connected with the expansion of the Christian missions. These missionaries who preached Gospel established themselves initially in a limited number of areas and tended to focus on each mission carefully while respecting and refraining from entering the field of labour of the other.

The early Portuguese missionary penetration into the hinterland of the Tamil Coast is noticed when Fr. Gonçalo Fernandez had moved from the port of Tuticorin to Madurai, the capital of the Nayaka ruler in 1595. He had been attending to the spiritual needs of the Paravas who had then migrated to the town of Madurai. In this place, the Portuguese priest had established a public hospital where patients were given free treatment. There was also a school run by the Portuguese missionaries where the Hindu boys are taught to read and write under a Brahmin master.[82] Inspite of this social work, the conversion was very slow. Fr. Gonçalo Fernandez was of the opinion that he could convert the Nayak of Madurai so that the whole kingdom could be brought under Catholicism. On several occasions Fr. Gonçalo Fernandez begged before the Nayak to permit him to explain the tenets of Christianity to him and his court officials, but permission was refused. Whenever the missionary tried his level best to introduce the subject of Christian faith into conversation, the Nayak immediately retired to his inner chambers under some pretext or the other. In one instance the Nayak had also put a question regarding religion to the missionary but a Brahmin who was next to the ruler touched the feet of the ruler hinting to drop the conversation. At another occasion we find that an officer of the court warned the missionary being a Portuguese, he should never speak of the religion with the political authorities. Father Gonçalo retorted that if he could not speak of the religion and make converts, he would leave the town of Madurai. When these words of the missionary were reported to the Nayak, the ruler was offended and sent word to the priest that if his presence in Madurai was to turn his subjects into Portuguese, the sooner he retired to the coast the better.[38] These instances also show that permission to preach Christianity and make conversions were denied to the Portuguese by the Nayak in the beginning of the Seventeenth Century in Madurai. Thus mass conversions of people that had been envisaged with the conversion of Muthu Veerappa Nayak, (1606-1623) the ruler, expected by the Portuguese could not be effected.

The different historical circumstances present at various places in the Tamil region during the Seventeenth Century and the existence of various castes presented a challenge for conversion of Hindus by the Portuguese missionaries. The Jesuits quickly understood that the Hindus have not learnt to distinguish between caste and religion. Hence they adopted a strategy suitable for the conversion work. Brahmins were mainly converted by Jesuit *sanyasis.* The founder of this group was Roberto Nobili. Thus the other high castes were also converted by Jesuit *sanyasis* in the later years. Approach to converts of the various low castes in Tamil country was realized by Balthazar da Costa and the select group of missionaries called *Pandaraswamis.* These two groups of missionaries followed the different food habits, customs, manners and dress. This social and cultural adaptation helped intensive growth of Christianity in the interior regions of Tamilnadu. Let us examine how the dominant voice came from the middle class and lower class Hindus besides some Brahmin converts.

Statistics of the various castes of people who were converted by the Portuguese missionaries in different pockets in the Tamil region had been known very little till date. The diversities existed at the regional and local level will become clear as we begin to cull the statistics and examine the conversions in Socio-cultural approach. Some Church historians have adopted the mission centered approach to conversion and sought to analyze the motivations of individual converts. In this chapter we shall take altogether a different approach using the statistics for the purpose of analysis culled from the Jesuit Annual letters and the available baptism registers of the period.

Brahmins

It is mentioned in Portuguese records that Brahmins occupied the highest place by virtue of their birth and learning. Excepting the relatively few who had entered the service of royal courts and army, they generally devoted themselves to religious and literary pursuits. Most of the Brahmins lived on voluntary gifts which came from all classes of people besides kings. Conversion of Hindu Brahmins in Tamil country by the like Roberto Nobili was felt when he arrived Madurai in December 1606. He had played a great role and Fr. Emmanuel Leitao had assisted him till the year 1609 and he was succeeded in 1610 by Fr. Antonio Vico.[34]

TABLE 6
Details of Brahmin Conversions, 1606-1611

Years	*Numbers*
1606	1
1607	10
1608	14
1609	60
1610	8
1611	16

Source: See note.[35]

Statistics for the later period is not available in the records although the work continued for Brahmin conversions in Tamilnadu. But after the year 1635, conversions had been seldom because the systematic conversion of the Brahmins had been given up. The work was also not spread all over but confined to Madurai and Tiruchirapalli towns. Out of the 120 high caste Christian conversions in Tamil country in that year of 1635 by the Jesuits there were only twelve Brahmins. Thus conversion from the top of social hierarchy, notably the Brahmin converts by the Jesuit *sanyasis* brought many Tamils giving a new religious identity. With the Brahmin conversions the Portuguese accepted the continued use of a number of Hindu practices not essentially religious but rather social and cultural. This included the use of sacred ash and sandal paste on the forehead besides the use of the Brahminical sacred thread on the chest. The Portuguese Jesuits also built separate chapels for Brahmin converts.[36] Although opposition came for such adaptation and when the matter was referred to the Pope in Rome where in 1623 it was decided to support Roberto Nobili and allow a certain number of native rites in Tamil churches.[37] The intention of the conversion of the Tamil Brahmins by the Jesuits was to gain a better place in Tamil Society whereby if the high castes were converted they would bring the traditional privileges. Further if the Brahmins were converted, naturally the others, especially the lower castes would also embrace Christianity.

Vellalars

In due course of time, some high caste people like the *Vellalars* were also converted. When the Nayak transferred his capital from Madurai to Tiruchirapalli, the Portuguese Jesuits also moved into the place. A *Vellala* called Yesu Adiyan was converted in 1627. Salem and Moramangalam also became mission stations of these high castes. Nallathambi Nayak, the cousin of the ruler was converted.[38] 150 *Vellalars* were converted at Sathyamangalam and Fr. Balthazar da Costa was instrumental for these conversion.[39] Fr. Emmanuel Martins had also converted the *Vellalars* of Erode.[40]

In the year 1639, Fr. Emmanuel Martins speaks of the conversions of a *Vellala* which is worth mentioning since it gives the picture of the attitudes of the Hindus about Portuguese missionary conversions. Although born and brought up in the port of Nagapattinam and lived along with the Portuguese residents there, the said *Vellala* never thought of becoming a Christian. When he came to Tiruchirapalli he saw the missionaries following the Tamil customs and habits. He observed to his surprise that the new convert Christians were following Christianity retaining the age old Tamil customs, instead of adopting those of the Portuguese. This made the *Vellala* to decide and become a Christian and he attended catechism. Later he was baptized under the name Francis Xavier. A few months back he came with his brother and brought with him their respective families and all of them attended catechism. Later they became Christians and left for the port of Nagapattinam. This evidence suggests that there was a difference found in the method of conversions in the coastal region whereby one had to be a Portuguese-like and this was not the case in the hinterland of Tamil country where one could still adopt native customs in the Seventeenth Century.[41]

Sheders

Similarly, *sheders* who by profession were weavers converted at Kanavakkarai in 1630. These *sheders* were well-to-do people and they wielded a certain amount of influence in the region. Nevertheless they were excluded from their caste for becoming Christians by their fellow Hindu brethren for twenty five years through the order promulgated by Chicanen, the chief of the *sheder* caste. These *sheders* were re-admitted during a general assembly of their caste by the chief of the caste held at Sathyamangalam. The reason given was that Christianity had been professed by Brahmins and also by others of high castes hence *sheders* were allowed to be Christians.[42] Thus social awareness and social action could be seen among the high castes.

Thottiya Nayakkars and Chetti Nayakkars

In the year 1635 large number of Nayakkars were converted. Out of 120 high caste Christians, two belonged to *Thottiya Nayakkar* caste and seventy were *Chetti Nayakkars.*[43] It was at this time the Portuguese Jesuits strongly felt that they should never attempt to suppress caste within the church at that time of conversion and afterwards too. They built a sense of caste solidarity upon the people in every region where they had undertaken the pastoral work. However the question arose whether caste among the Christians was a civil or a religious institution still connected with Hinduism. These Jesuits examined the caste factor and clearly understood that caste among the converts was primarily a religious institution based on concepts derived from Hinduism.

Whenever the high castes Catholics did not follow or failed to observe the Christian religious practices, the missionaries were very strict with them. It is mentioned that in 1660, the Christians near Sathyamangalam did not attend the Sunday Mass as the villagers were tired and had to walk five miles to go to church. In the following Sunday, the priest threatened them without mass since they had little appreciation for it. On hearing this matter, the Christian people of the entire village went to ask for pardon. The missionary had kept them waiting for long till the evening and finally told that they were forgiven.[44]

Thus it appears that Christianity spread because certain families were converted as a whole. In some cases, the chief of the caste got converted and so the people of the caste embraced Christianity. Whatever may be these guidelines followed, no doubt the Jesuits had thoroughly given religious instruction about the Christian faith before baptism. It was also in principle seen by the Jesuits that the Christians lived a virtuous life. How far these measures had helped the new Christians to accept Christianity and abandon Hindu beliefs is unknown.

The conversion of Brahmins and other high castes was left to the initiatives of the individual Jesuits like Roberto Nobili. As the continuity of the conversion of the Brahmins is not seen widely we may draw the conclusion that leadership is left to a few charismatic Jesuits at a particular point of time. The spirit of converting the Brahmins systematically had also died out in due course of time for want of support from others.

It may be said that even before the arrival of the Portuguese in India, St. Thomas Christians were able to keep up their native (inculturation of Hindu) social customs besides Tamil Christians. However the offensive style of narrating and describing Tamil culture and social practices by the Portuguese Jesuit missionaries made some historians to suspect the missionary records. Roberto Nobili's experiment was a marked departure from the post-tridentine standardization of Catholic missionary practice. The missionary efforts generated a complex controversy surrounding the method of accommodation to Hindu cultural traditions, in particular, caste practices known as the "Malabar Rites". Portuguese missionaries of the Seventeenth Century had taken great care to see that baptism and the acceptance of Christian faith did not mean their Europeanization. The natives were allowed to retain their former social customs and usages which were not incompatible with Christianity. Fr. Balthazar da Costa wrote in his letter dated 14 October 1646 that the Jesuits were compelled to adapt themselves to the times in which they lived and led the natives by conforming to their childish customs.[45]

Social Changes and Low Caste Christians

The psychological reactions of inferiority afflicted upon the depressed classes who were not allowed to live in villages nor touch any person of caste nor enter the temple was understood by the Portuguese Jesuits. They considered their missionary call to render service in the name of Christ to these low castes. The Karma doctrine in Hinduism that the degradation of low castes was due to their misconduct in the previous birth had strengthened the approach to deal with the degraded and worthless people. Thus the low castes who had no opportunity earlier to respond to the stimulation of nature and environment were attracted towards Christian teaching followed by active Christian worship that had been introduced, a privilege which was earlier denied to them by the entry into the temple. Thus "loving God accessible to all" (alien to the established Hindu beliefs) and the sharing privilege in worship through removal of social injustice gave a new force into their lives and it became strong enough to loosen and destroy their inhibitions. In the year 1638 when Fr. Martin attended the provincial congregation in Cochin, he had been requested by Fr. Pedro de Basto to concentrate on the conversion of the *Paraiyars*.[46]

It has been generally pointed out by scholars till date that how mass conversions of low caste Hindus were taking place. It is equally important to study how conversion of a single man by change of religion became one of the most incisive events in his (or her) human life and those who accepted Christianity did not only experience a sweeping change in their own lives but also became carriers of change in the surroundings. There are instances to show in records that they were able to bring more conversions in the process. To cite an example, Nandipandaram of Chengam was converted first and this was followed by his relatives and thirty others who received baptism. Thus a new Christian community was formed in Chengam in the year 1664 as reported by Fr. Proença. Similarly in a village near Tiruchi (name not mentioned) a woman called Sandanammal became a Christian. Her spirit of faith, prudence and charity enabled to convert some members of her own caste.[47] Thus converted Christians also led an exemplary life acting as a catalyst for spread of Christianity in Tamilnadu. The Christian religion capable of bringing such a change was felt by them as a true one and the low castes were compelled to acknowledge it. Thus family as a basis for conversion was felt by the Portuguese Jesuits since they saw the family like caste was a major force of resistance to Christianity.

Paraiyars

The *Paraiyars* were converted at Karur in 1640. Fr. Sebastião Maya mentions about these conversions. Fr. Balthazar da Costa continued the missionary work at Karur and he took care of the *Paraiyars.*[48] Problem arose when the refusal of a *Paraiya* Christian to give his daughter in marriage to a rich Hindu of the same caste. At the request of the latter, Venkataraya Pillai, the brother-in-law of the Nayak in the region arrested Fr. Emmanuel Martin who was believed to be instrumental. The *Paraiyars* were also arrested and thrown into prison. Later they were also driven out of the region of Tiruchi and Karur.[49] In spite of some such troubles, the low caste Hindus were converted by Jesuit *Pandaraswamis* grew in number at this time. By 1644 Tiruchi became the main mission and it had the Christian population 141 *Paraiya* Christians in the villages located within the radius of twenty five miles. According to sources, a large number of *Paraiyars* were employed as soldiers who received a good salary.[50] Thus they enhanced their social status rather than remaining untouchables.

Kambalavars and Kammalars

A group of *Kambalavar* caste people had embraced Christianity in 1633 and these Christians were looked after by Fr. Alvarez.

Further, many *Kammalars* were converted in Mullipadi in 1661. It is said that these *Kammalars* were rather stubborn in their attachment to several Hindu customs.[61] The same caste people at Thottiyam, Kangupatti and Pachur also were converted and these places had also developed as Christian centres by the end of the year 1666 as mentioned by Fr. Proença in his letter.[62]

Kallars

The *Kallars* were converted at Kandalur, located South East of Tiruchi in 1652-1653. Further one of the chief of the *Kallars* called Meykondan was converted in 1656. This facilitated in the conversion of many *Kallars* during 1660 in the Pudukottai region.[63] By 1680, the Jesuits had firmly established at Avur and they took care of these converts.[64] According to the Jesuit Annual Letter of 1676 written by Fr. Freyre, at Nandavanampatti, as the *Kallars* showed themselves close to the Christians, the *Kallar* converts in Thanjavur area also increased to the tune of 1198 in number.[65]

Maravars

The *Maravars* were converted in the Ramnad region by João de Britto. Britto succeeded in converting Thadaiya Thevar, the Palayakkarar of Siruvalli domain who was the cousin of Vijaya Raghunatha Kilavan Sethupathi on 27 August 1686.[66] Fr. Martin mentioned that 8000 Hindus were converted in *Marava* country between 1640 and 1680. The number of conversions effected in the year 1686 was two times higher than the previous year according to the Jesuit Annual Letter written and sent from Madurai to the Jesuit Superior General in Rome.[67] The Sethupathi ruler of Ramanathapuram therefore prohibited the preaching of Gospel to the Hindus in his kingdom. However missionaries defied his order and continued their activities.[68] Fr. Luis de Mello was arrested, imprisoned and he died on 4 February 1691.[69] Later João de Britto was arrested and beheaded on 4 February 1693.

Shanars

The Jesuit letter dated 8 September 1716 claims the conversion of *Shanars* at Vadakkankulam which became the main centre of Christian activity. The same Jesuit letter mentions that the *Shanar* caste in comparison to all other castes is admirably suited to Christianity because these *Shanars* can easily observe the Christian practices since the necessity of climbing palmyrahs as their way of life preserved them against laziness, the fountain of all disorders. The Christian *Shanars* practiced chastity out of virtue. Their widows did not re-marry.[60] Thus we find in the later period that missionaries were experimenting and narrating the caste functions and the suitability to follow Christianity.

In the Tirunelveli region, Kayathar was a flourishing centre of missionary activity in 1644 where a chapel dedicated to St. James was built. Antão de Proença visited Tenkasi, Tirunelveli, and Maranthai and converted Hindus.[61] At Kamanayakkanpatti Christianity flourished because of the protection given by the *Palayakkarar* of Ettayapuram. An old inscription found in the church is an evidence.[62] The church was dedicated to Our Lady of Assumption. The number of conversions in 1662 touched the figure of 485 as reported by the Jesuits in 1665. Further conversions also took place at Sendamaram and in 1701 at Gurukkalpatti.[63] In all these places various low caste Hindus were converted.[64]

Church historians have neglected the role of native co-workers who did commendable work among the low castes. This has resulted in a one-sided picture of the missionary activities on the whole scene of conversion among the low castes in several places that flourished. The local assistance with a local leadership by the native co-workers (catechists) became unavoidable. These men catered to the needs of the scattered congregations even when no missionary was at hand. They prepared the Christians gave religious instruction and Christian teachings to the families in vernacular. They called themselves *upadesi,* teacher of the Holy Scripture and also made arrangements to conduct baptism, marriages, settling disputes etc. Muthu Adiyan (Hilary) the first *Paraiya* convert, Yesu Adiyan, the first *Kammalar* convert and Gnana Muthu, the *Marava* catechist of João de Britto are some such examples who did commendable service.[65]

Conversions in Pondicherry and Social Changes

Pondicherry although being the French settlement, the jurisdiction of the missionaries fell under the *Padroado* diocese of

Santhome of Mylapore. Initially the Capuchins were invited by Francois Martin, the French Governor to take spiritual care of the Europeans. In due course of time, natives were also taken care of by the missionaries. Many Portuguese also lived under the protection of the French, after the fall of Santhome in 1662. João de Britto, the Jesuit visited Pondicherry in August 1691 and he baptized some slaves and children. Further he also blessed the marriage of Isabella, the daughter of Francisco and Maria de Monte with João on 9 August 1691, Sunday.[66] Pondicherry in the eighteenth century became the main centre of Christian activity when large number of high caste and low caste people were converted by the Jesuits. The baptism registers available for the period from 1715 to 1777 preserved at the Madurai Province Jesuit Archives is worth examining.

TABLE 7
Details of conversions according to castes in Pondicherry, 1730-1737

Caste Name	*1730*	*31*	*32*	*33*	*34*	*35*	*36*	*37*
Agambadaiyar	5	7	10	6	10	15	9	-
Andi	-	-	-	-	-	-	2	-
Beri Chetti	1	-	2	-	-	2	2	2
Brahmins	-	-	5	-	-	-	1	6
Idaiyar	-	-	1	1	-	2	1	4
Ilai Vaniyar	-	-	-	-	-	1	2	-
Inchavar	-	-	-	-	-	-	1	-
Kaikolar	-	-	-	-	-	-	4	-
Kammalar	-	-	-	1	3	1	4	-
Karaiyalar	-	-	-	1	-	1	-	-
Kavarai Chetti	1	-	3	-	1	1	2	1
Komatti	-	-	-	-	-	-	1	-
Koravar	-	2	-	-	1	-	2	-
Kosavar	-	-	-	-	-	-	10	-
Mukkuvar	-	1	1	-	-	2	-	-
Muslim	-	-	-	-	-	1	-	-

(Contd.)

(Contd.Table 7)

Caste Name	*1730*	*31*	*32*	*33*	*34*	*35*	*36*	*37*
Nattamaikar	-	-	-	-	1	-	-	-
Palli	-	-	1	4	21	-	-	-
Panichevar	-	-	-	-	-	-	1	-
Pattanavar	-	-	1	-	-	-	-	1
Reddis	-	1	-	-	1	1	1	1
Sakkili	2	-	-	-	-	-	-	-
Sedar	-	-	-	-	-	-	3	-
Vadugar	-	-	-	-	1	-	1	-
Vaduga Idaiyar	-	-	-	-	-	1	2	-
Vanniyar	-	-	-	-	-	16	5	-
Vaniyar Palli	6	9	-	-	-	-	-	-
Vannan	-	1	-	-	-	-	1	-
Vellalar	20	40	61	-	-	6	-	-

The baptism register contains the slaves who were converted at this time and the origin of the caste of the salve also. The illegitimate children who were baptized are also recorded beginning from the year 1733 in the register. In the surroundings of the Pondicherry town there were also many conversions in various places.

TABLE 8

List of Villages and New Conversions, 1715-1724

Village Name	*1715*	*16*	*17*	*18*	*19*	*22*	*23*	*24*	*Total*
Ariyankuppam	-	10	12	7	3	6	4	1	43
Bommaya palayam	-	-	-	1	-	-	-	-	1
Kalapet	-	-	-	-	-	1	-	-	1
Kunimedu	-	-	1	2	-	6	4	1	14
Marakkanam	-	1	4	1	-	-	1	3	10
Murungapakkam	-	-	-	5	4	2	1	3	15

(Contd.)

(Contd. Table 8)

Village Name	*1715*	*16*	*17*	*18*	*19*	*22*	*23*	*24*	*Total*
Nonankuppam	-	-	-	-	-	-	1	-	1
Odiampattu	-	3	-	3	1	1	2	3	13
Olundai	-	-	-	-	-	-	2	-	2
Olugarai	7	8	15	22	7	12	3	7	81
Pondicherry	-	3	52	59	12	23	28	28	205
Suttoukeni	-	-	-	-	-	-	1	-	1
Valudavur	-	-	-	-	-	1	-	-	1
Villiyanoor	-	-	-	-	-	-	-	2	2
Virampatnam	-	-	9	4	-	1	-	-	14

TABLE 9
List of Villages and New Conversions, 1725-1734

Village Name	*1725*	*26*	*27*	*28*	*29*	*30*	*31*	*32*	*33*	*34*	*Total*
Ariyankuppam	10	7	10	3	8	3	10	1	2	8	62
Bommayapalayam	-	1	-	-	6	-	-	1	-	1	9
Kalapet	1	-	4	-	-	-	4	2	2	1	14
Kunimedu	-	-	-	-	4	-	1	1	-	-	6
Marakkanam	4	1	2	6	7	1	8	11	5	3	48
Murungapakkam	8	2	2	2	26	2	6	-	-	2	50
Muttiraipalayam	3	-	-	-	-	-	-	-	-	-	3
Odiampattu	-	7	1	-	-	-	-	4	2	5	19
Olundai	1	8	3	1	1	1	3	2	2	5	26
Olugarai	17	18	10	14	12	2	7	18	16	5	119
Pondicherry	37	26	39	40	84	38	61	86	43	120	574
Saram	-	-	-	-	-	-	1	-	-	-	1
Valudavur	-	1	3	-	-	6	2	2	1	4	19
Villiyanoor	2	-	-	-	11	1	4	2	-	1	21
Virampatnam	-	3	-	3	11	1	1	3	-	-	21

During famines in Pondicherry it was the missionaries who offered help to the needy and came to the aid of those afflicted.[67] Fr. Barbier wrote on 15 January 1723 that during the famine of 1722 more than 200 adults were converted and baptised by him.[68] The famine had provided the priests a new occasion to exercise their zeal.[69] He mentioned that several Hindus had found along with the preservation of their physical life, an assurance of the eternal life of the soul, through the baptisms they received.[70] When there was famine again in the years of 1737, 1743 and 1744 we find that conversion works had continued and a good number were converted to Christianity.[71] Fr. Poissevin wrote that in May 1747 the famine stalked Pondicherry again and this created the occasion for the conversion of several Hindus.[72] However, the conversions during these years were chiefly made possible to a larger extent by the liberal donations of Dupleix, the French Governor of Pondicherry, and his wife to relieve the famine-stricken people.[73] Thus the missionaries and the French Governor had functioned undoubtedly as a strong source of physical and psychological comfort to the needy Hindus, who as a result converted to Christianity in large numbers.

TABLE 10

List of Villages and New Conversions, 1735-1744

Village Name	*1735*	*36*	*37*	*38*	*39*	*40*	*41*	*42*	*43*	*44*	*Total*
Ariyankuppam	4	3	10	6	6	12	16	8	11	-	76
Olugarai	5	13	12	9	11	14	12	-	-	-	76
Olundai	-	8	3	15	4	10	-	-	4	-	44
Pondicherry	64	34	134	75	41	88	92	151	132	119	930
Villiyanoor	-	-	1	1	2	2	3	-	-	-	9

For the subsequent years, particularly between 1745 and 1754 the baptisms registered in olugarai had been fifteen while in Pondicherry it has been one thousand four hundred and seventy four. However between 1755 and 1760 the parishes of Olugarai and Ariyankuppam became insignificant under the Jesuits, while Pondicherry parish alone had baptism of one thousand one hundred and fifty eight persons. In 1752 and 1753 three conversions took place in Nellithoppu. The figures found between 1765 and 1774 at Nellithoppu were 271 which shows that it had suddenly emerged as a centre of Christian activity in that period compared to Olugarai which had thirty five baptisms in the same period. Many *Paraiyars* had been converted in 1754 in the parish of Olugarai jurisdiction under which the villages of Villiyanoor, Nellithoppu and Odiampattu came.[74] The village of Panikkankuppam near Panruti had many Catholics. The missionary from Tranquebar attempted to bring these converts in to Protestantism. Therefore the Jesuit Superior of St. Paul's church in Pondicherry asked Ananda Ranga Pillai to transfer the village from the control of Sadasiva Pillai to his own, so that he could check the conversion activities of the Protestant missionary. Louis Prakasam, the catechist of the church of St Paul had also spoken to Ranga Pillai in this connection.[75] The importance of the Portuguese and other Jesuits activity was a dynamic factor in the church history of Pondicherry. It was one of the significant causes of intellectual ferment and social change.

Caste System and Attitudes of the Tamil Christians

The word caste has derived from the Portuguese word '*casta*' which means lineage. The Portuguese applied the term caste very appropriately having understood the Indian system. In Hinduism caste is referred to *varna* meaning colour. Caste in India at that time referred to a social stratification along lines of descent, that meant an individual born into a given social category remained there for life. Thus caste was inborn and it determined his social status. The rigid system also did not allow an inter-caste marriage. The violation of the rule led to the expulsion from the caste. Many natives who become Christians had been ostracised and boycotted either by the parents or by the family and by their entire caste men. It became very difficult for the converts to find a bride within his caste and establish a family since all marriages were caste endogamous.[76] Thus conversion to Christianity by those belonged to a particular caste where there were no converted Christians implied excommunication.[77] The natives have realised that caste was a big obstacle after conversion to survive in the Tamil Christian society. There was no unity among the various castes of Christians who were also divided into right and left hand castes like the Hindus in Tamil society. The left hand caste that comprised of drummers, pipers, tom-tomers, *chuckilis, Beri Chettis, Vaniyars, Devangars* and *Panchalattars*, (*Kammalars*, *Kollars*, carpenters) represented an inferior status while the right hand caste said to be superior status included *Mudalis, Pillais, Komutti Chettis, Kavarai Chettis, Idaiyars, Agamudaiyars, Vellalars, Kaikolars* and *Padmasalis*. Some of the castes stood for a number of sub-castes and communities bunched together on the basis of commonage of interests.

It is mentioned in Portuguese records that the Hindus of one caste could not partake of any dish which had been prepared by members of another caste nor drink in their house.[78] This practice continued even among the Christians. Kanakaraya Mudaliar adopted it, of course slightly in a different way. It is said that on 30 November 1745, the day of consecration of the Reddiyarpalayam church built by him, he had invited Brahmins, *Vellalars, Komutti Chettis*, goldsmiths, weavers, oil mongers and people of other castes for dinner. At this time the food for the Brahmins was cooked by Brahmin cooks and the meals for the *Vellalars* were prepared in the house of *Agamudaiyars*. Thus all the arrangements were made in strict conformity with the religious scruples of each caste and people who attended received every attention.[79]

While this was the practice followed for eating and arranging a common meal for people of various castes, the same also had applied to worship. The gap between the Christians of low castes and high castes remained wide in spite of the efforts taken by the missionaries to narrow it down. Fr. Andrew Lopez had mentioned in his letter written from Santhome of Mylapore in 1644 that it was impossible for the low castes and the high castes to be united in a place of worship, not even in a private house where they can be together.[80]

Inter caste tension among the Christians also arose in the due course of time. It is said that there existed problem between the *Panchama* Christians of Descano church and the parishioners of other churches in Mylapore.[81] It was chiefly related to the ruinous behaviour of *Panchama* Catholics at St. Thomas Mount on the latter's annual feast. Thus in spite of the papal decrees of 1734 and 1744 denouncing untouchability as alien to Christianity it continued in Tamil country.

The Church was built in Karur by Fr. Balthazar da Costa in such a way that the low castes could hear Mass from a place reserved for them, while the high castes had their separate places. Erection of walls and segregation of Christians in churches became a common feature in the Tamil society. Although social inequality was the bane of Tamil society for centuries together it continued to be present even after conversion to Catholicism. The egalitarian message of Christianity was the logical antithesis of the inequality prevailing in the Hindu world and so the missionaries preached that Hindus of high castes could mix with low castes. Whenever the high castes were encouraged to mix with the low castes, they felt that the missionaries have brought disgrace to them.

Since caste system was tolerated among the Tamil Christians, each caste was allotted a separate place in the church by the missionaries. There was a wall inside the church to segregate the upper caste Christians, Europeans and Eurasians from the low caste Christians. The priest of Karaikal who visited Pondicherry on 16 October 1745 found it objectionable and he instigated the *Paraiya* and *Thotti* Christians living in four *Parai Cherris* to remonstrate to the senior priest.[82] Therefore the wall was removed and the high caste Christians protested. They refused to enter the church for worship. The priest complained to Dupleix the French Governor that the high caste Christians had been rebelling against him. The matter was solved finally when a barrier was put-up on 17 October 1745 to separate the *Paraiyars* from the other Christians.[83]

The missionaries were interested in rebuilding St. Paul's church in Pondicherry which was destroyed by the English in 1761 at the time of siege. When Pondicherry was restored to the French in 1765 the Jesuits contacted the Christians for contribution and a sum of one thousand *pagodas* was offered. At the time of laying the foundation stone for the Church in 1766 the priests realized that there would not be enough room for the *pariah* converts and so they suggested a big structure. The high caste Christians quarrelled with the priests for keeping the proposed church open for the *pariahas* and declared that they would build a church exclusively for themselves. The high caste men came forward even with the suggestion of paying for the priest to serve in that proposed new and separate church. The priests did not permit them to attend the religious services because the high caste men did not listen to the suggestions of the priests. So they stood outside the church showing their protest.

The missionaries applied pressure to the French Governor at that time to get the high caste Christians round. So, M. Boyelleau summoned eleven of the high caste men to his office. They were chiefly of the *Mudaliar* and the *Pillai* castes and the names include Mariadass Mudali, Surappa Mudali, Barlam Mudali, Royappa Mudali the short, Muthaiya Pillai and Thiyagappan. They complained to M. Boyelleau and his councillors that the priests insisted on their mixing freely with the *Pariahs,* something that was not done earlier. Boyelleau insisted that they should listen to the priests. But, they refused and so the governor got wild with them and asked them to go to the temple of *Bhagavathi* if they did not like to obey the missionaries.[84]

It was reported that all the eleven were summoned to the Council on 8 April 1766 and were severely censured and punished with a fine of one hundred *pagodas* each for disobeying the Council. They were placed in custody till they paid the fine. But they did not do it and were therefore put in prison in the *chavadi.*[85] Kandappa Mudali with the *nayinar* went to the *chavadi* on 25 April 1766 under the orders of M. Boyelleau to meet the imprisoned Christians who refused to obey the orders of the French Governor as well as those of the priests with a warning that they would be banished from the town if they did not send their family members to church. Pragasa Mudali met the womenfolk of the imprisoned and asked them to go to the church as suggested by the missionaries and the Governor. They expressed their reluctance to go to the church and mix with the *pariahs.* They added that they did not feel sorry for their husbands being imprisoned since they were not guilty of any crime. The report given by the Christians imprisoned in the *chavadi* was conveyed to the French Governor by Kandappa Mudali. At last they paid the fine on 27 April 1766. But the governor told them that they would be released only if they and their women attended the church. Threatened as they were, they agreed to attend the church at the orders of the Governor. Finally on 28 April 1766 they gave a declaration as insisted by Kandappa Mudali to the effect that they along with their family members would attend the church. Thereafter they were released.[86] However later documents mention that the opposition was such that the Jesuits had to modify their plans to satisfy the desire of the high caste Christians.[87]

The conflict between the missionaries and the high caste Christians in Pondicherry continued on the matter of mixing with the Christians of lower status. We find the unwillingness of the high caste Christians to share the expenditure of the feast of Blessed Virgin Mary on 8 September 1766 in which the *pariahs* were chosen for the choir. This made the *pariahs* themselves to meet all the expenses for the procession and the erection of the tent for the exposition of the Statuette.[88]

A life of a convert may be worth mentioning here. Bimakrishna belonged to the *Vellala* caste was in the service of the Raja of Gingee. While in service he embraced the Catholic faith along with his wife in 1765. His conversion was chiefly possible because of Mr. Arulappan who was an officer in the army of the Raja of Gingee. Bimakrishna received the Christian name of Devasagayam Pillai and his wife was called Mariammal. It is mentioned that they were ostracized by their parents and relatives and so one of the French missionaries in Pondicherry arranged their migration with their sons to Mysore. They settled down there and lived peacefully. In due course of time we find that Devasagayam Pillai was appointed as a commandant and his son Sinna Thamby as an officer in the army of Hyder Ali. Similarly we also find that that Mr. Gnana Muthu was employed as the catechist in Srirangapattinam in 1775 who hailed from Pondicherry. He was also the relative of Devasagayam Pillai Thus we find that many Tamil Catholics from Pondicherry had migrated to the interior places with the help of the missionaries and led an exemplary Christian life.[89]

The high caste converts in Tamil country always wanted to maintain distance away from the low castes and the Untouchables. The missionaries were also obliged to give in as they found no way to bridge the gulf between the two. Within the same Church the communion table and the altar had been common to all although the *pariah* Christians and high castes were separated by pillars and stone benches. Even there were separate doors for entry and exit in the church. The same situation prevailed in many places such as Ariyankuppam, Pinnaipundi and Karuvepampundi in the hinterland of Tamilandu as mentioned in the letter of Fr. Perrin dated 14 November 1778.[90] These were not the creations of the missionaries but they were forced to allow the caste customs then prevalent.

The Catholic priests had given some concessions to the high caste Christians without totally compromising the egalitarian principle of Christianity. It was felt by the high castes that a considerable concession had been granted to the low castes and the untouchables to have the entry into the same church since Hinduism had invariably kept them away from temple entry. The high caste Christians were adamant to renounce their high caste characteristics. Distinct areas were also used for burial and separate cemeteries for the *pariahs* had existed.

Thus there arose a complex situation and the missionaries had the high task of convincing the high caste Christians that separation between them and the *pariahs* would be maintained in the churches. On the other hand the missionaries also had to convince the *pariah* Christians that discrimination would not be allowed in the churches and if at all allowed only to some extent and not permanently. In fact, the fear that segregation might be abandoned some day among the Catholics would have deterred the high caste Hindus from converting newly to Christianity. These things had a great impact on the progress of the missionary work and permanently sealed the future of the conversions.

The missionaries therefore took the serious problem of segregation of the high castes, low castes and the untouchables in churches and brought it to the attention of the Sacred Congregation for the Propagation of Faith in Rome and it was decided in 1778 to tolerate the separation of *pariahs* from high caste Christians in the churches.[91] Under these circumstances conversion of Hindus to Christianity became difficult. Conversions in fact did not mean that the converts were ready to abandon the caste altogether just to be in conformity to Christian values as desired by the missionaries mentioned in the letter of. Fr. Tabraca dated 14 October 1777. [92]

The Jesuits in the Indian overseas missions were expelled by Marquis de Pombal, the Prime Minister to King Joseph I of Portugal vide order dated 3 September 1759. Churches were handed over from the Jesuits to the Franciscans.[93] After two decades the suppression of the Society of Jesus was done by Pope Clement XIV in 1773 and it had completely dismantled the Jesuit power. The priests of the Mission Etrangers de Paris (MEP) under Propaganda Fide came to the forefront since being an organization of secular priests and not members of a religious order. The Jesuit missions were handed over to the Capuchins and MEPS. Pope Benedict XIV in 1774 established the rules concerning the Malabar rites and the extent to which the mission were to accept existing customs in the church. It was stated that Christians were strongly forbidden to participate in the Hindu processions. Harsh demands were also made in the Bull which offended on almost every single point of caste sentiments.[94] With the expansion of Catholic Christianity in Tamil country the problems faced by the missionaries in converting the Hindus became numerous. Initially caste was not a problem at all in conversion in the Sixteenth century but gradually it posed a serious threat to the Tamil Christians converts irrespective of the castes and communities during the Eighteenth century.

Christian Institutions in the Tamil Region: Origin and Growth

Candidates to the priesthood were formed in the *Colegio de Santa Fe* (College of the Holy Faith) started in Goa in 1541 by Fr. Diogo de Borba and later it was handed over to the Jesuits.[95] The first students of the little seminary to be ordained priests were three young men from Tuticorin who accompanied Francis Xavier to the Fishery Coast as his interpreters.[96] The college had six seats reserved for the training the students for priesthood hailing from the Tamil coast.[97] The Four Provincial Councils (1566, 1575, 1582 & 1592) held in Goa had laid down norms regarding the selection and formation of native priests. The Jesuit missionaries were also instrumental in starting many seminaries especially for the education of those opting for a religious vocation in the various Portuguese settlements on the Tamil Coast.

Seminaries

The Portuguese found Punnaikayal as an ideal place for starting the first seminary in the Fishery Coast about which there is a mention in a letter dated 16 September 1577 written by Fr. Valignano to the Jesuit Superior General in Rome.[98] On 11 February 1585 the King of Portugal wrote to the Viceroy in Goa that the Archbishop Dom Frey Vicente da Fonseca wrote to him saying that

India was in great need of ecclesiastical ministers and for the lack of priests many churches in the *Estado da India* were deprived of vicars and confessors. He therefore requested the King to send priests from Portugal. However owing to the scarcity of priests in Europe none could be sent in the expedition of that year, nor will it be an easy affair to persuade missionaries to sail for India in the near future. He therefore wrote to him that he shall consider it a great service to God if the Archbishop could establish a seminary in the city of Goa which could provide the churches of the *Estado da India* with the necessary ministers. The King requested the Viceroy to give the necessary help and assistance to the Archbishop and he recommended the Viceroy to employ all the necessary means for the execution of this design, which is so important and to which the King was bound by duty. [99]

Imparting the Portuguese language and other symbols of culture became important. There were distinct groups identified as needing religious instruction. The lack of knowledge in matters related to Christian faith amongst the growing number of Christians of *mestiço* children as well as neo-converts was cause of much concern. Another group of people are the high castes and the low castes of Christians in Tamil country both in the coast and hinterland. Therefore there was a move towards indigenous involvement in the sense that teaching of Christian tenets should not merely to be entrusted to Portuguese and Europeans but to be opened to the natives. Ideas could be communicated better by the locals in their own tongues. However later, the Jesuits wanted to transfer the seminary from Punnaikayal to Tuticorin in 1587. Tuticorin being situated in the Pandya territory was found to be a safe place, while Punnaikayal was open to attacks by the Vijayanagara rulers as it was in their territory.[100] In 1587 there were twenty-six students in the Tuticorin Seminary. In 1588 there were thirty students of whom twenty-two senior scholastics were engaged in the study of Latin.[101] A building was also raised for the seminary at Tuticorin in 1600.[102] The *paravas* contributed three hundred *cruzados* towards it. This fact was communicated by Fr. Durão in a letter dated 4 December 1587 to the Superior General.[103] In 1614 Fr. Sebastião Goncalves wrote that the seminary had produced many priests who with great edification and spiritual profit worked among the souls entrusted to their care, without forgetting the zeal for the conversion of their native brethren which they had acquired during the years of their training in the seminary.[104] One Thomas de Gamboa, son of Ignatius de Amboa and Theodosia de Gomes born in Mylapore had joined the Society of Jesus and lived in the seminary. He was ordained as a priest on 27 July 1616 and served the mission in the Tamil coast.[105] Fr. Manoel de Elvas was appointed by the Bishop of Kochi in 1626 as the Rector of the seminary in Tuticorin.[106]

Schools and Colleges

Despite the many ups and downs in the political and commercial ventures of the Portuguese in the Pearl Fishery Coast, Punnaikayal developed by leaps and bounds after their arrival. The Portuguese established a Tamil School as early as in 1567 and eight students began their course in language there.[107] Fr. Henrique Henriques was the founder and it was set up with a view to impart knowledge of literary Tamil to the *paravas*. Fr. Valignano agreed to send three priests to start an elementary school to teach reading and writing to the children of the Portuguese in Santhome. A three room building for the school was raised by the citizens themselves. Two priests and a brother lived there.[108] In 1577 there were more than 200 children in the *escola* (school). Two years later at the request of the citizens a class for teaching Latin was also started.[109] Even the *nayak* of Gingee contributed some funds for the school as mentioned in the letter of Simão de Sa, the Rector of Santhome in his letter dated 20 November 1598.[110]

The Jesuit missionaries were initially invited by Muthu Virappa Nayaka (1606-1623) to Madurai where they established a School in 1598 giving no more than secondary education.[111] Fr. Nicholas Pimenta in 1598 mentions the functioning of a school in Madurai as follows: " There is a school attended by Hindu boys who learn to read and write under a *brahmin* master whom God has brought so near to the Kingdom of Heaven, i.e. he is thinking of receiving baptism. Following our custom, we distributed prizes to the children according to the merits of each. This gave great joy to the Hindu parents who became daily more sympathetic". Indeed the Portuguese gained more influence in the court of Tirumalai Nayak (1624-1658) who succeeded Virappa Nayak.

Portuguese official and private commercial activities were centred in the port of Tuticorin at this time and Dom Filippe II, the king of Portugal issued instructions to raise the revenue of the Portuguese Crown from the port of Tuticorin.[112] A Portuguese school and a Tamil school had been opened in Tuticorin. It is recorded that twenty-five children attended the Portuguese school while 155 went to the Tamil school in 1644.[113]

There was another school at Nagapattinam run by the Jesuits and the missionaries were paid stipend for the purpose as mentioned in the royal order dated 21 January 1610.[114] This school was developed by the Jesuits and it was later called as a college. After the Dutch occupation of Nagapattinam one of the objectives of Governor Van Goens immediately implemented had been a systematic liquidation of Jesuit residences and the College of Nagapattinam was razed to the ground in 1660.

In the early Seventeenth Century Tamil Schools functioned at Periyathalai, Manapadu, Alantalai, Virapandyanpattinam, Punnaikayal, Vaippar and Vembar all of which could boast of small Christian communities.[115] There was a Tamil school opened by the Capuchin Fathers in Madras in August 1680.[116] Many *pariahs* who were converted by Portuguese priests and Jesuits had their children who attended the school. There was a Tamil Master appointed to instruct the children there.[117]

There was a school established by the Jesuits in Pondicherry in 1692 where twelve students who were sons of the Portuguese attended classes. Teaching of mathematics formed part of the curriculum.[118] This school was later called as 'college' in 1709 by the Jesuits in Pondicherry which had thirty boarders.[119] That a school for teaching Tamil language was opened by Fr. Beschi at Ellakurichi is mentioned in the Jesuit Annual letter of the year 1731.[120]

Sodalities

In the Jesuit Annual Letter of 1648 mention is made about the formation of a Sodality in Nagapattinam. It is recorded that the members of the Sodality were so well behaved that one would easily mistake them for novices. They traversed through one and the same route from home to school and back. The Sodality of native Christians in Nagapattinam flourished well.[121] The Jesuits in Pondicherry had also established another Sodality of Mary, Mother of Jesus in 1709.[122]

Orphanages

An orphanage was started by the Capuchin missionaries in Pondicherry. A new building was purchased from a widow called Catelouse and the same was approved by the clerk of the Registry on 29 December 1758 on payment of rupees 3250. The title deed of the orphanage was executed with witnesses and Fr. Baslieu stood surety on behalf of the Capuchins and signed it.[123]

Holy Houses of Mercy

Following the institutionalisation of public charity, a Confraternity of the *Santa Casa da Misericórdia* came into existence in Lisbon as early as on 15 August 1498. The Portuguese introduced the same institution in Goa in the year 1513. The Franciscan missionaries in Santhome also showed keen interest to introduce the same institution at Mylapore and they founded a Confraternity in 1538. The Portuguese in Santhome defrayed all the extra expenses involved and came forward to give alms generously for the poor in Santhome inspired by the ideals of the Franciscan Order according to which the seven spiritual works of mercy were: converting sinners, instructing the ignorant, counselling the distressed, comforting the sorrowing, bearing ills patiently, forgiving wrongs, praying for the sick and the dead. The seven corporal works of mercy comprised feeding the hungry, refreshing the thirsty, clothing the naked, sheltering the homeless, tending the sick, visiting the imprisoned and burying the dead. The Holy House of Mercy established at Santhome in 1538 subsisted on private benefactions consisting of alms, endowments, annuities and special grants. The *provedor* was the head of the Confraternity. It had a Governing Board whose members were annually elected. A hospital was established in 1540 at Santhome and it functioned as an integral part of the institution.[124] Francis Xavier in 1545 spent most of his time in this Franciscan hospital during his stay in Mylapore. Every year the *Santa Casa da Misericórdia* at Mylapore extended help to the orphan girls to get married. It also helped the new converts.[125] *Casa da Misericórdia* was also later established at Nagapattinam.

It is mentioned in a letter dated 20 February 1614 from the King of Portugal to Dom Hieronoymo de Azevedo, the Viceroy in Goa that the *Casa da Misericordia* at Mylapore was poorly administered. In a separate letter to the Bishop of Mylapore the King stated that the money left by the dead was used to pay the persons that were serving in it rather than taking care of the orphans for which the sum had to be spent. The revenue that was being allotted and sent as grants by the King was not used for the purpose for which it was sent. The Bishop of Mylapore was asked to assume the responsibility to the deposits. Many of the Brothers had been appointed in the *Casa da Misericordia* who had a sinful life and persons of ill repute. Ruy Lourenço de Tavora took the initiative to curtail some of this mismanagement. The King instructed the Bishop to visit the *Casa da Misericordia* at Nagapattinam to look into the matter.[126]

Hospitals

A hospital was established at Punnaikayal sometime between 1588 and 1592 and the *paravas* generously contributed large sums towards its maintenance.[127] There were also hospitals that functioned in Tuticorin[128] and Cape Comorin.[129] It is said that "Father (Gonçalo Fernandes) runs a public hospital which is very popular since poor patients are given treatment on gratis and all the care they need were given". There was also a public hospital run by the Jesuits in Madurai in 1598. A Holy House of Mercy (*Santa Casa da Misericórdia*) which was founded by the Portuguese at Nagapattinam ran a hospital and buried the dead. Funds for running the *Misericórdia* came from various sources, such as bequests and also the income from the estates of those deceased persons which awaited transmission to their legal heirs. Generous contribution had been made by the Bishop of Kochi too for the maintenance of the hospital.[130] There was a hospital in Mylapore which catered to the needs of the people.[131] A hospital was established in Pondicherry in 1692 where the wounded people at war in Gingee were given treatment.[132] The Jesuit Brother Mazereta, a pharmacist was taking care of the patients in the hospital. He in his letter written from

Pondicherry on 15 February 1710 to the Superior General lamented that he could not prepare medicines owing to lack of space both in the hospital and at the Jesuit residence.[133]

To conclude it may be said that the missionaries had to adopt different strategies and methods to reach the people of the various castes and communities to convert them in Tamil country. They were very successful especially the Jesuits who did commendable work and helped the people really to transform their social life with Christian virtues and values. As the Tamil society was caste ridden it was difficult for some missionaries who wanted to do away with the caste system prevalent among the converts since Christianity did not allow inequality in society. However, some missionaries allowed the natives to follow the caste system and they did their best to educate and impress the people about the tenets of Christianity without touching the caste sentiments to increase the Christian population. The institutions such as seminaries, sodalities, schools, hospitals, orphanages and holy houses of mercy that had been established at various places had definitely catered to the spiritual and material needs of the Christians in Tamil country. Missionaries were not preaching the Christian Faith and trying to improve the religious life of the new Christians but also were taking care of the daily life of the converts at the time of problems like a good shepherd looking after the flock. Such care really helped the Christian converts to have faith in God also faith in the missionaries who preached and asked the natives to lead a good Christian life.

Notes and References

1. *South Indian Inscriptions*, (hereafter SII) volume, VI, No. 439; SII, VII, No.129; SII, vol VIII, Nos. 198. 442.

2 An inscription of 1225 A.D mentions the Vaniyar castes and another epigraph records Pathinen Vishayathar of Thiruvaypadi nattavar. See, *Annual Report on Epigraphy*, (hereafter ARE) 163 of 1938-39 (Thiruvanikka) ARE 92 of 1939-40, (Thiruvithyur in North Arcot District)

3 S. Jeyaseela Stephen, *The Coromandel Coast and Its Hinterland: Economy. Society and Political System,. 1500-1600*, Manohar, New Delhi, 1997. See the chapter on Social Environment, pp. 174-200.

4. *Ibid.*

5. Noboru Karashima, Kammalars of the Sixteenth Century in South Arcot District in South India", in K.V. Ramesh, S.P. Tewari and M.J. Sharma, (eds.,) *Dr. G. S. Gai Felicitation Volume*, Delhi. 1990. The people of other castes like weavers claimed for the equality of privileges in various localities besides the merchants and artisans. See, S. Jeyaseela Stephen, *The Coromandel Coast... op.cit*, pp. 176-180. The privileges became more valuable when they were denied. Some acquired new privileges or enjoyed the restoration of the once denied privileges under the Vijayanagara rule in Tamil country. The communities involved in caste conflicts were labourers and merchants of one kind or the other. This did not affect or include the upper castes.
6. S. Manickam, The politico-economic impact of the religious conversions of the Paravas in the Gulf of Mannar,1537-1552, in *Tamil Civilization*, Vol. No.1, pp. 57-73.
7. For the theoretical discussion of the Marxist, Weberian, Elitist and Functionalist school of thought on change See. S. Jeyaseela Stephen, *The Coromandel coast, op.cit.*, pp. 178-179.
8. Fernand Braudel, 'History and the Social Science" in P. Burker (ed.,) *Economy and Society in the Early Modern Europe*, London, 1958, reprint, 1972, pp. 11-42. see p.14 please see also C. Lyold, *The Structure of History*, Oxford, 1993, pp.17-127.
9. In the opinion of S. Arasaratnam, the converts were known as persons who had excised themselves from the trunk of Indian society. See, S. Arasaratnam, *Christianity, Cultures and Nationalism: The South-Asian Experience*, Jaffna, 1978, p. 11.
10. Georg Schurhammer, *St. Francis Xavier: His life, His Times*, Rome, 1977, Vol. II, pp. 336-337.
11. *Ibid.*, p. 308. See also Henry James Colerdige, (ed.,) *The Life and Letters of St. Francis Xavier*, II. Vols, London, 1881, pp. 153-155.
12. Joseph Wicki, *Documenta Indica*, (hereafter DI) Vols. I-18, Roma, 1944-1988, vol. II, p. 301.
13. *Ibid*, pp. 398-400; DI, Vol. IV, p. 30.
14. *Ibid*, Vol. IV, p. 31. Letter of Henriques to the Jesuit Superior General dated 31 January 1558.
15. *Ibid.*, Vol. XI, p. 16.
16. *Ibid.*, Vol. VII, p.166; Vol. XI. pp. 816-817; Vol. XIV, pp. 128-129. J. Wicki, "P. Henriques S.J" *Studia Missionalia*, Vol. XIII, 1963, pp. 160-164; See also " The Confraternity of Charity of Fr Henriques" ICHR, vol. I, 1967, pp. 3-8.

17. DI, Vol. VII, pp. 166-167; DI, vol. VIII, p. 602.
18. *Ibid.*, Vol. XIII, pp. 182-184.
19. Schurhammer, *op.cit*, Vol. II, p. 53.
20. See, Joseph Thekkadeth, *History of Christianity in India: From the Mid 16th Century to the End of the 17th Century*, Bangalore, 1982, pp. 172; On Manakkudi, See, pp. 186-187.
21. DI, Vol. II, p. 608.
22. *Ibid.*, Vol. III, p. 695.
23. *Ibid.*, Vol. VI, p. 435.
24. *Ibid.*, Vol. VII, pp. 645-46.
25. *Ibid.*, Vol. VIII, p. 159; See, DI, Vol. VII, pp. 647-648.
26. *Ibid.*, Vol. XI, p. 290.
27. If we had taken wise precautions from those very days as in Madurai, for more than a century, it would have been easy to win all these people ... for Jesus Christ". See the letter of Fr. Martin to Le Gobien written from Madurai, dated 1 June 1700 in *Lettres Edifiantes et Curieuses Ecrites des Missions Etrangers par Quelques Missionaires de la Compagnie de Jesus*, (hereafter LEC) tome X, Paris, 1781, pp. 66-71.
28. LEC, Vol.13, MDLCLXXXI, pp. 45 & 50.
29. A. Nevett, *John de Britto and His Times*, Anand, 1980; A. Sauliere, (Revised by S.Rajamanickam) *His Star in the East*, Anand, 1995.
30. Susan Bayly, *Saints Goddesses and Kings: Muslims and Christians in South Indian Society, 1700-1900*, Cambridge, 1989; See also the recent work, *Caste, Society and Politics in India from the Eighteenth Century to the Modern Age*, The New Cambridge History of India: 1. IV.3, London, 1999.
31. David Mosse, *Caste, Christianity and Hindusim: A Study of Social Organisation and Religion in Rural Ramnad*, Unpublished D.Phil dissertation, University of Oxford, 1986.
32. ARSI, Mss. Goa 51, ff.3-6. Letter of N. Pimenta to Aqua Viva, dated 2 December 1599. (in Portuguese)
33. ARSI, Goa 51, ff. 110-115. Letter of Fr. Buccerio to Aqua Viva from Madurai, 3 October 1610. (in Portuguese)
34. Ines G. Zupanov, *Disputed Mission: Jesuit Experiments and Brahmanical Knowledge in Seventeenth Century South India*, Delhi, 1999.
35. Leon Besse, *La Mission du Madure*, Trichnopoly, 1914, p. 200. João de Britto in his letter dated 9 May 1684 mentions that " The Hindus of Madurai firmly believed that in as far as one ranks higher than another in noble birth in so far as does he surpass him in spirit. Hence only those

who are on an equal footing with the Brahmins in nobility of birth can learn and touch the law of God and any other knowledge one who belongs to a lower caste is already ignorant thereby and so cannot come forward as a teacher of others. He may be rich and powerful, but as wise he will never be acknowledged. Nobility of birth and wisdom go together and just as one can be neither high and low born at the same time. So too can neither the low born be also wise".

36. A. Sauliere, *op.cit*, p.32.

37. *Ibid*. See also, Susai Arokiasamy, *Dharma, Hindu & Christian According to Robert de Nobili: Analysis of its Meaning and its use in Hinduism and Christianity*, Documenta Missionalia 19, Roma, 1986.

38. ARSI, Goa 51, fl. 312. Goa 56, ff.91-102; Goa 48, ff.217-27; Letter of Antonio Vico to Mascarenhas, 15 December 1624, (in Portuguese). See also Bertrand, *La Mission du Madure d' apres les documents inedits,* Paris, 4 vols, 1874-54, Vol. II, pp 228-238.

39. Bertrand, *op.cit*, Vol. II, pp. 2-39.

40. *Ibid*.

41. ARSI, Goa 53,ff.115-18, Letter of Emmanuel to the Provincial 2 October 1639 (in Portuguese)

42. Madurai Province Jesuit Archives, (hereafter MPJA) Jean Castes, *Ancienne Mission du Madure*, pp. 326-327.

43. *Ibid*, p. 172.

44. ARSI, Goa 53,ff.288-90; goa 54,ff.173-98; Goa 54a, ff.1390-72, Letter of Antonio di Proenza 9 September 1662. (Italian)

45. ARSI, Goa 53, ff.163-84; ff.185-206. Letter of Balthazar da Costa, dated 14 October 1646; See also MPJA, vol. 436, document 36A. fl.115-123.

46. MPJA, Vol. 436, document 36A, pp. 111-114. Special attention was made by the Jesuits to convert the Paraiyars at that time.

47. Letter of Antonio Proença written during 1665 in Bertrand, *op.cit*, vol. III, pp. 165-66; See also A. Sauliere, *His star... op.cit.*, p. 393.

48. Bertrand, *op.cit*, Vol. II, pp. 310-11.

49. Leon Besse, *La Mission... op.cit*, pp. 8, 203.

50. MPJA, Vol. 432, document no.36A, p. 62.

51. Besse, *op.cit*, pp. 127-134.

52. ARSI, Goa 54a,ff.130-172. Letter of Antonio Proenca dated 9 September 1662, from Tiruchirapalli. (in Italian)

53. J. Chandler, *History of the Jesuit Mission in Madura: South India in the 17th and 18th Centuries*, Madras, 1907, p. 5.

54. Letter of Fr. Martin dated 11 December 1700 cited in John Lockman (ed.,) *Travels of the Jesuits into Various Parts of the World: Compiled from their Letters, Now First Attempted in English*, 2 vols. London, 1743. vol. I, pp. 452-75.
55. MPJA, Letter of Fr. Andre Freyere, 1676, p. 12
56. MPJA, Letter of Joao de Britto to the Superior General 20 July to 9 August 1686, p.102
57. John Lockman, *Travels of the Jesuits... op. cit*, Vol. I, pp. 452-453; MPJA, Annual Letter of the year 1686 written to the Superior General.
58. MPJA, Letter of João de Britto to João da Costa, dated 22 July 1692.
59. Leon Besse, *op.cit*, pp. 230-231.
60. MPJA, Annual letter of the year 1714.
61. MPJA, Annual Letter of the year 1644; See also L. Besse, *La Mission... op.cit*, p. 565.
62. MPJA, Annual Letter of the year 1666; See also R. Caldwell, *A History of Tinnevelly*, Madras, 1881, p. 236. Muttusami Pillei, A Brief Sketch of the Life and Writings of Fr. C. J. Beschi, Veeramamuni," *Madras Journal of Literature and Science*, 11, 27, 1840, pp 250-300; See pp. 268-269.
63. MPJA, Annual Letter of the year 1701; See Bertrand, *La Mission... op. cit*, Vol. IV, pp. 344-345.
64. MPJA, Annual letters of the years 1666, 1676, 1678, 1681, 1683, 1688.
65. Balthazar da Costa wrote in 1643 in his letter to the Provincial of Malabar that "We have appointed some men to manage the villages during our absence and to help in conversion of the Hindus and that they may be able to devote themselves entirely to this great and holy work. We give them monthly a small allowance for their own maintenance and that of their families. We have not discovered this arrangement, for our Jesuit Fathers in Japan and China have availed themselves of the help of such catechists and they had the utmost benefit". See, J. Bertrand, *La Mission... op.cit*, Vol. II, p. 318.
66. MPJA, Documents Bertrand, Vol. I, document No. 5, See also, S. Jeyaseela Stephen, *Portuguese in the Tamil Coast ... op.cit*, p. 294.
67. J.B. P. More, "Hindu-Christian Interaction in Pondicherry, 1700-1900" in *Contributions to Indian Sociology*, New Series 32, 1, 1998, pp.98-121, see p. 103. Some scholars like J.S. Chandler opined that baptisms had been given in a large measure to aged persons, or little children or the sick and the dying. See, J.S. Chandler, *History of the Jesuit Mission in Madura*, pp. 70-71.

68. LEC, tome XIII, Paris, 1781, pp. 296-297. It is said that two hundred adults were baptized.
69. LEC, tome XIII, p 336. A large number of high castes were converted in Pondicherry.
70. Letter of Fr. Barbier from Pinneipundi, in *LEC*, tome XIII, pp. .296-297.
71. AMEP, Mss. Inde, Vol. 993, Letter of Fr. Mathon dated 21 December 1744; See also, letter of Fr. Calmette to Fr. Tournemine from Venkatagiri dated 16 September 1737 in *LEC*, tome XIV, Paris, 1781, p.10 ; Letter of Fr. Poissevin from Krishnapuram dated 4 and 16 December 1743 to Madame Hyacinthe, in *LEC*, ibid., p.173 .
72. Letter of Fr. Poissevin to Fr. d'Irlande dated 11 January 1749 in *LEC*, tome VIII, Lyon, MDCCCXIX.
73. Letter of Fr. Estevan to M. Le Comte de from Pondicherry dated 7 December 1754, in *LEC*, tome VIII, Lyon, MDCCCXIX ; See also, Adrien Launay, *Histoire ..op.cit.,* Vol. I, pp. xxxviii - xxxix.
74. MPJA, Mss, *Lieux d' Origine des Chretiens Baptises a Pondichery par les Jesuits de 1715 a 1777.*
75. Frederick Price & H. Dodwell, *The Private Diary of Ananda Ranga Pillai*, 12 vols, (reprint) New Delhi, 1984-85. (hereafter ARP Diary) Vol. IX, pp. 214-15, Vol. III, p. 407.
76. BNP, *Mss. Nouvelle Acquisition Française*, (hereafter NAF) Letter of M. Hebert, the Governor of Pondichéry dated 15 February 1710; Letter of Fr. Caron, to Mesdames les Sœurs Religieuses Ursulines de la Mission du Carnate dated 20 November 1720, in *LEC*, tome XIII, pp. 210-211; Letter to Fr. Etienne Le Gac dated 10 January 1709, in *LEC*, tome XI, pp. 208, 217-18.
77. Letter of Fr. Bouchet to Fr. Baltus, in *LEC*, tome XI, p.44 ; Letter of Fr. Carre from Pondicherry to Fr. Mourgues, dated 30 January 1709, in *LEC*, tome XI, p. 216.
78. ARSI, Goa 53, ff.185-206. Letter of Balthazar da Costa dated 14 October 1646.
79. ARP Diary, Vol. I, pp. 287, 293-294; See also, " Socio-Economic Role of Dubash Pedro Kanakaraya Mudaliar in the French Colony of Pondicherry, 1711-1746: A Study in Resilience" *Revue Historique de Pondichery*, vol. XVIII, 1995, pp. 15-32.
80. MPJA, Annual Letter of the year 1644.
81. E.R. Hambye, *History of Christianity in India: Eighteenth Century*, Bangalore, 1997. p. 143.

82. *Ananda Ranga Pillai Thinapadi Sethikurippu*, Government of Pondicherry, Pondicherry, 1948, Vol. I, p. 214. See also, Archives of the Mission Etrangers de Paris, (hereafter AMEP) Mss. Inde, Vol. 995, Letter to Mgr. l'Evêque de Ceram dated 6 January 1781, See also, Adrien Launay, *Histoire des Missions de L' Inde: Pondichery, Maissour, Coimbatour*, IV Vols, Paris, 1898, Vol. I, p. xviii.
83. ARP Diary, Vol. I, pp. 284-287.
84. S. Jeyaseela Stephen, *The Diary of RangappaThiruvengadam Pillai, 1761-1768*, Institute for Indo-European Studies, Pondicherry, 2000, pp. 219-220.
85. *Ibid.*, p. 224.
86. *Ibid*, pp. 230-231.
87. AMEP, Mss. Inde, Vol. 995, Letter of Mgr. Brigot aux Directeurs du Séminaire from Pondicherry dated 22 October 1777. See also *Le Progrès*, 25 July 1886.
88. S. Jeyaseela Stephen. *The Diary of Rangappa Thiruvengadam Pillai, op.cit.*, p.250.
89. Adrian Launay, *Histoire...op.cit.*, Vol. I, pp. liv- lv.
90. AMEP, Mss. Inde, Vol. 995, Letter of M. Perrin from Pondicherry dated 14 November 1778.
91. AMEP, Mss. Inde, Vol. 995, Letter of l'Evêque de Tabraca dated 5 March 1780; Letter of l'Evêque de Ceram from Pondicherry dated 23 March 1780. See also *Journal de Brigot*, No.31, 12 January 1779, in Launay, *op.cit.*, Vol. I, p.102.
92. AMEP, Mss. Inde, Vol. 995, Letter of l'Evêque de Tabraca to M. Alari dated 14 October 1777. See also, BNP, Mss. Français 8971, Letter of M. Hebert, Gouverneur de Pondichéry aux plaintes du R.P.Tachard, supérieur des Jésuites de Pondichéry dated 20 August 1708, fl.19.
93. HAG, Mss. Vol. 864, fl. 9v-10v.
94. Adrien Launay, *Histoire des Missions op.cit.*, Vol. I, pp. cvi-cix.
95. Carlos Merces de Melo, *The Recruitment and Formation of the Native Clergy in India*, Lisbon, 1955. p.71.
96. G. Schurhammer, *Epistolae Xaveri, op.cit.*, Vol. I, pp. 127 & 245. Francis Xavier mentions that they had very good knowledge of the Portuguese and an ever better knowledge of their own native language. See, Letter of Francis Xavier to his companions in Rome dated 20 September 1542, in J. Costello, *Letters and Instructions of Francis Xavier, op.cit.*, Doc. 15, p. 50.

97. The college hoped to tutor students from all over the East of the Cape of Good Hope. The students enrolled were between the age group of thirteen and fifteen so as to ensure that the children had good command over their native language. The training at the college was exhaustive and it included grammar, science, logic, arts, philosophy and theology. Seats were reserved for a certain number of students from each region. Pearl fishery coast and Coromandel had six seats for boys. There were ten seats for Konkans, six for Malabar, six for Canarins, six for Malays, six for Bengalis, six for Burmese, six for Chinese, six for Gujaratis, six for Mozambians and eight for Ethiopians, See, Silva Rego, Documentação, Vol. III, Doc. 75. p. 355.
98. Joseph Wicki, *op.cit.,* Vol. X, pp. 889-891, Vol. XIII, pp. 285-286.
99. Arquvio Portuguez Oriental, *op.cit.,* fasc III, doc 9.
100. Josef Wicki, D.I., Vol. XIII, pp.184-186.
101. ARSI, Mss Goa, 55, (Malabarica) fl. 15v; see also Mss. Goa, Vol. I3-II, f. 372, ff.458-61;DI, Vol. XIII, pp. 184-186.
102. MPJA, *Litterae Annuae,* 1600.
103. D.I.XIV, Doc. No.104 & 105, See also Madurai Province Jesuit Archives (hereafter MPJA), Shembaganur, India, *Litterae Annuae,* 1600, p. 3.
104. Sebastião Gonçalves, *Historia dos Religiosos da Companhia de Jesus nos Reinos da India Oriental,* 1614, c. 6.
105. *Monumenta Xaveriana,* Vol. II, pp. 945-949. He was the twenty-seventh witness.
106. C.C. Nazareth, *Mitras Lusitanas no Oriente,* Lisboa, 1913, Vol. II, p. 73, *Boletim da Filmoteca Ultramarina Portuguesa,* (hereafter BFUP) Vol.12, 1959, p. 442.
107. ARSI, Goa, 56, pp 529-530, See, Andre Lopez, *Breve Relação das Christanda; Silva Rego, Documentação,* Vol. X, 111, 313, 318 & 319. Joseph Wicki, *op.cit.,* Vol. X, pp.760, 816, 888-889. Josef Franz Schuttle, *Valignano's Mission Principles for Japan,* (Tr.) John J. Coynem, The Institute of Jesuit Sources, St. Louis, 1985, Vol.1, p.117.
108. DI, Vol. XVI, pp. 344-345.
109. DI, Vol. X, p. 486; DI, Vol. XIII, pp. 46-47, DI, Vol. XII, pp. 237, 539 & 720.
110. ARSI, Mss *Goa,* Vol. 14, 370[r-v].
111. King of Portugal appointed Fr. Francisco Barreto to go to Madurai and make conversions. IANTT, *Chancelaria de D. João IV,* Liv,17. fl.16v. The Jesuits established a college at Madurai. See, IANTT, *Chancelaria de Dom FilippeII,* Liv, 35, fl.46.

112. Tuticorin emerged as a *casado* settlement with married Portuguese settlers asearly as 1587. ARSI, Mss *Goa,* No.33, fl.326. For the Royal order of the king Filippe II, see *Chancelaria de Dom Filippe II,* Liv.3, fl. 103. (4th February 1610).
113. MPJA, *Litterae Annuae,* written by Fr. Andrew Lopez in Fr. L. Besse, op.cit.,pp. 15-21; J. Bertrand, *La Mission...op.cit.,* pp. 456-458.
114. IANTT, DRI, Livro 3, fl. 67.
115. *Ibid.*
116. Nicolau Manucci, *op.cit.,* Vol.IV, pp. 277-278.
117. Friar Domingo Navarette, *The Travels of Friar Domingo Navarrete, 1618-1688,* (ed.,) J.S. Cummins, II, Vols, London, 1960.
118. MPJA, *Documents Bertrand,* Vol. I, document no. 14; See the letter of François Martin dated 30 September 1692.
119. *Ibid.,* document, no.68. Letter of Fr. Tachard to the Jesuit General written from Pondicherry dated 14 February 1709.
120. MPJA, *Litterae Annuae,* 1731.
121. MPJA, *Litterae Annuae,* 1648.
122. *Ibid., Documents Bertrand,* Vol.1, document 68.
123. NAIP, Mss, *Eighteenth Century Documents,* no. 430, fl. 2-2".
124. *Ibid;* See also *Monumenta Xaveriana, op.cit.,* Vol.11, pp. 486-488.
125. DI, Vol. VI, p. 92. DI, Vol. VII, p. 204.
126. Bulhão Pato, *Documentos Remetidos...op.cit.,* Vol. IV, p. 95; Vol. III, pp. 65-67.
127. Joseph Wicki, *op.cit., XV,* doc.84, pp.109-111; See also, Silva Rego, *Documentação,* Vol. V, pp.15-16, 206.
128. Silva Rego, *Documentação,* Vol. X, p. 320.
129. Silva Rego, *Documentação,* Vol. IX, pp 148- 149, 408.
130. Antonio da *Silva Rego, Documentação...op.cit.,* Vol. X, p. 320; Jose Wicki, *op.cit.,* Vol. XV, p.708,
131. On St. Rita hospital see, Silva Rego, *Documentação,* Vol. XI, 220-224-225, 310 326.See also Manucci, Vol. IV, p. 68.
132. MPJA, *Documents Bertrand,* Vol. I, document no. 14.
133. *Ibid.,* document no. 75.

SECTION-II

4

The Christian Life and Everyday Practices of the Tamils

Historically speaking, the Hindu pilgrimage tradition in Tamil country was established very strongly in the medieval period. It was connected with the cults according to *Saivisim* and *Vaishnavism*. The philosophical roots of the Tamil pilgrimage tradition had been connected with *Advaita* and *Dvaiata*. However, the proto-typical pilgrimage of the Christians being the pilgrimage which on authority of documentary or widespread traditional evidence established was centered around Mylapore where St. Thomas one of the apostles of Jesus Christ, the preacher of the Gospel lie buried in a tomb. Thus St. Thomas was the main and the first type even before the advent of the Portuguese. It is recorded by John Marignolli that (as early as in AD 1350 when he resided) Mylapore was a pilgrimage centre.[1] Marco Polo, the Venetian traveller also speaks of Mylapore and the veneration of the pilgrims to Apostle St. Thomas and the trust with which the devotees carried away earth from the spot where the saint was buried.[2]

Pilgrimage in Christian Culture: St. Thomas Cult

The Christian pilgrimage centres originated among the Catholics through Pilgrimage to Jerusalem and other places in the Holy Land. Pilgrimages also became common in the days of medieval period when the Christians took their tone from the theological and philosophical emphasis of the epoch like Assisi, Loretto etc., in Europe. The Portuguese who arrived in India, they heard about the tomb of St. Thomas in Mylapore. It may be recalled that as early as in 1501 Dom Manuel, the King of Portugal had written in his letter to all the rulers in Europe that Pedro Alvarez Cabral had brought him definite information about the tomb of Apostle St. Thomas and had brought some earth from there.[3] Further the most interesting thing done by the Portuguese was the excavation of the tomb of St. Thomas and the strengthening of this place as a pilgrimage centre which was then probably used by the Syrian Christians who paid visits there.

Down the centuries, Hindus have been drawn to mountains and rivers for worshipping. Holy men had sung in praise of many places and several *sthalapuranas* were composed in Tamil extolling greatness, power and sanctity. Therefore pilgrimage in the Christian tradition in Tamilnadu was also developed by the Portuguese to those sacred spots connected with the martyrdom of St. Thomas. Little Mount (near modern Saidapet) where St. Thomas said to have taken asylum in a cave was developed as a sacred place. The other is the Great Mount where St. Thomas was executed (located near the modern Chennai airport). The Portuguese traders were encouraged to settle down in these places supporting St. Thomas Cult.

As Hindus believed that God presides in a mysterious invisible way and bestowing grace on all who approach it in a particular place, the Portuguese missionaries began to touch the innermost spiritual feeling and experiences of the people encouraging visits to St. Thomas Mount. The Portuguese also transformed the ways of living, beliefs and the practices connected within the form of a tradition of St. Thomas that still ruled the daily life of the Tamils found in the region and religion. Places of worship were of major importance to Christians and therefore they erected new chapels built in Portuguese style at Little Mount and the Great Mount.[4] These holy places served as the centre of cultural and social activities which encompassed Mylapore.

It is mentioned in a document of December 1563 that a large number of people generally came from Kerala and they visited the tomb of St Thomas in Mylapore.[5] A report sent to Rome in the year 1601 says that every year in the month of December (3 December, on the feast of St. Thomas) about 100 St. Thomas Christians in Kerala formed a group including women and children and they used to come on pilgrimage to Mylapore and visited the tomb of Apostle.[6] Even as late as in the year 1635 Portuguese sources do mention that the people of Kerala visited Mylapore on Pilgrimage.[7]

Mylapore lost its importance as a trading port after AD. 1662 when it was captured by the Sultan of Golconda, but it still continued to be significant from the religious point of view. The seat of Bishop for the Mylapore diocese was housed and it was the centre of religious authority. It may be said that the cult of St Thomas continued and it is evinced through the excavations conducted at the tomb of St. Thomas on 29 April 1729 by the order of the (Jesuit) Bishop J. Pinheiro. When the sepulchre of St. Thomas was opened, it revealed a twin statue of St. Thomas.[8]

Similarly St. Thomas Mount also continued to be a holy place of visit. Fr. Loliere who lived in Pondicherry when he was appointed to the Bishopric of Siam in June 1739 and when the message was conveyed to him by an order sent through an English ship, he proceeded to St. Thomas Mount. He was consecrated there in view of his appointment as a bishop and he returned to Pondicherry from St. Thomas Mount.[9]

Introducing Christian Cults of Saints

The Hindus of Tamil country had several pilgrimage centres. The Tamil Muslims also had the obligatory pilgrimage to Mecca (the Hajj) besides the journey (ziyarat) to the nearby saint who holds a place like Nagore or Kayalpattinam within the local religious culture. Therefore the Jesuits were interested in developing some such Christian places of pilgrimage. As there was only St. Thomas cult existed in Tamilnadu, the Portuguese began to popularize other cults among the Christians. It is noticed that as early as 1582, the missionaries had introduced the Christian calendar with a detailed list of the feasts of the saints and other festivals to be celebrated by the Catholics in the Tamil region. Fr. Henrique Henriques wrote a book in Tamil dealing with the Lives of Saints of both sexes and it was published by in 1586. He had translated and compiled the lives of forty nine saints from three Portuguese books.[10] The publication was generously sponsored by the Paravas who paid 400 *cruzados* in one installment.[11] The book contains readings for the great feasts of the liturgical year besides feasts of Our Lady and of the Apostles which were then held as feasts of obligation. The founders of various religious congregations like St. Vincent, St. Ignatius Loyola, St. Benedict, St. Dominic, St. Augustine and St. Francis of Assisi.[12] Those saints who removed evil such as St. Sebastian (plague disease) St. Vrrus (throat infection) St. Christopher (safe journey) St. Appoloammal (tooth ache) and St. Lucia (eye ache) are also given. It is said in the preface of the book (*Flos Sanctorum*) in Tamil that the purpose of it was to help, know and understand the truth of Christian religion.

Cult of St. Francis Xavier at Kottar

The Portuguese preached that Christian saints rose up from the common people and these saints were the representatives of people in the real sense of the term. Hence they impressed upon the devotion to Francis Xavier who was a great missionary in Tamilnadu so that the Christians could benefit a good deal from the saint. As canonization of St. Francis Xavier was in progress at the Sacred Congregation of Rites, in Rome, the Jesuits collected information through the official inquiries held at Mylapore, Devanampattinam, Nagapattinam, Punnaikayal and Tuticorin besides other places such as Goa, Cochin, Quilon in India. The official canonization in the year 1622 by Gregory XV (1621-1623) helped the Jesuits very much to encourage the cult of Xavier since many were converted by him in Tamil Coast. According to the Portuguese records, there was a church erected at Kottar (near Nagercoil) and it was dedicated to Holy Trinity, in a garden given by the ruler in the year 1603. The Christians of the neighborhood of Kottar especially, from Manakkudi, Pallam and Rachimadam helped in the construction of the church. Fr. Andrew Buccerio placed in this church a picture of St. Francis Xavier, since these Christians had great devotion to him. In due course of time we find the Christians often speaking of favors received from God through the intercession of Francis Xavier. Thus Kottar became a great pilgrimage centre. It is reported that Hindus also went there to pray.[13] The Church at Kottar by the year 1644 was built of stone. It is mentioned that the parish also had the substations of Martandanallur, Alur and Kalkulam.[14] There were 658 catholics in the parish of Kottar in 1716.[15] The church in Kottar was enlarged in 1865. An altar was made of wood and gold in 1876 through the funds sponsored by Joachim Fernandez. Devotion to Francis Xavier was encouraged by Jesuits in Kandalur especially by Fr. Balthazar da Costa. It was stated that he had requested the married couples who were without any issue for long to get child through praying to Francis Xavier. These couples returned to the Church carrying a child later.[16]

Cult of João de Britto at Oriyur

According to Portuguese records, Fr. Luis de Mello who was at Kalpalayam in May 1688 discovered that he cannot conveniently visit Kandalur and so he thought that the old chapel and house of Fr. Balthazar da Costa built at Oriyur was a convenient place for his apostolic work. Although it had been annexed by a Hindu yogi at that time, he negotiated to get back the place back and succeeded in expelling the yogi. On 8 July 1688 he celebrated with the Christians of that place, the feast of St. Elizabeth of Portugal. Thus Fr. Luis de Mello took possession of the chapel and the house at Oriyur. Further in his letter dated 30 May 1689 he wrote that the site was still under his custody.[17]

Later João de Britto, the Jesuit who preached Gospel and did a lot missionary work in the Marava Country was executed at Oriyur on Ash Wednesday 4 February 1693. With his death at Oriyur, the cult of João de Britto was also developed by the Portuguese. It is mentioned in the records of the same year that João de Britto, the martyr was identified as a miraculous healer. The conversion of the Marava ruler of Siruvalli appears in the documents as an episode of Tamil tradition of divine curing when he was afflicted with an agonizing ailment, and submitted himself to João de Britto. He heard the saint's voice reading out a passage from the Gospel and he was cured.[18]

Once again like St. Francis Xavier, we find the Jesuit propaganda for canonization of João de Britto as a saint. Francisco Laynez, the Bishop of Mylapore (who earlier was a colleague of João de Britto) in his letter dated 2 February 1712 to Pope wrote that the fame of João de Britto was universal and no one among the Hindus doubt the cause of his martyrdom. So much so that soon after his death they proclaimed him a martyr everywhere. In order that the relics of his should not fall into the hands of the Hindus, some of the Christians risked their lives and dared to bring it from the place of execution at night. In the diocese of Mylapore all the Christians unanimously desired João de Britto to be placed among the martyrs of the Church. The most praiseworthy desire of the people was to see that he is honoured by public cult.[19] According to Nicolau Manucci, the Italian traveller, Oriyur the place of martyrdom in 1693 became an important one and the chapel was located along the main pilgrim route to Rameshwaram.[20] The place gained more importance when Sethupathi Katta Thevar built the first big church in the year 1730 at the site of João de Britto's execution.[21]

Thus death and blood sacrifice had come into the feature of St. Thomas cult and João de Britto cult in Tamilnadu. The earth representing the blood of both the martyrs became a source of healing and fertility. Thus Christianity took roots in one way as a tradition of devotion focussed in individual cult shrines encouraged by the Portuguese missionaries. As long as the new Christians had earlier remained Hindus they were not admitted to any act of public cult and they could not also assemble in temples. Now that they were permitted to enter the churches, the Christian cults were felt important by them.

Cult of St. James at Suranam

As the Portuguese were not satisfied with the existing cults of St. Thomas, Francis Xavier and João de Britto in Tamilnadu, they had introduced the cult of St. James at (Xurrana) Suranam. The place developed with Christian population during the end of the Seventeenth Century. According to the local legend, four *Pallar* brothers had brought a miraculous cutting of a banyan tree to the village. These *Pallars* were converted to Christianity after the healing of their crippled sister. Thus the cult of St. James the Greater developed focusing on a sacred banyan tree. On every Fridays, Hindus and Christians crowded at the place and they came to fulfill some vows in return for favours asked or to ask for new ones. Since 1730 it is mentioned in the Jesuit Annual Letters of the Madurai Missions.[22] In the Annual Letter of Fr. M. Orti in 1734, by Fr. J. Khrening in 1745 and also by Fr. Felix in 1749, we find the description of tremendous prodigies at the shrine brought about by the tree and its leaves but most prominent among them was the saint's punishment of those who made false oaths.[23] Under the patronage of the native rulers the Jesuits had attempted to make popular the cult of St. James. The ruler at first had granted a piece of land to construct a chapel but later he had withdrawn it for reasons unknown. The Jesuits then erected a church dedicated to St. James in 1731 under the protection of Nallukottai Udaiyan Thevar, the Raja of Sivaganga who himself was the beneficiary of a miraculous cure.[24] The Jesuit missionaries who resided at Sarukani and took care of the *Idaiyar* converts where the Church was dedicated to Sacred Heart of Jesus came to preside over the annual festival of St. James. The festival attracted large crowds in 1740s and there was a considerable income to the church. A new church was erected for a miraculous cure with the statue of St. James by 1760s.[25] Surranam is mentioned in the records of Portuguese Franciscan, Fr. Nicolao de S. Rita as late as in the year 1779.[26]

Development of Christian places of Pilgrimage in Tamilnadu by the Portuguese shows that they had given relative importance to cults of various saints particularly of Portuguese origin. While ranking these sacred places, Santhome of Mylapore became the premier station. Some aspects of this religious travel had been highlighted in the Portuguese sources and the chief purpose of visit was considered to be for the spiritual merit. We find two basic patterns of pilgrim circulation while the first belong to the age old existed centre of visiting Mylapore while the second belonged to the new cult centres developed and emerged in certain areas. Thus pilgrimage by Christians was undertaken as an act of religious devotion. It is not clear in the evidences whether the egalitarian element was present in all these cults at that time. It is possible, perhaps because of this tendency, the popularity of the cults of St. Thomas, Francis Xavier, João de Britto and St. James had been sustained even today in Tamilnadu. These local pilgrimages were so near to the heart of the Christians that they were easily integrated into the larger scheme of conquest ensuring spiritual blessings.

Introducing Christian Feasts

The converts have learnt to worship God as revealed in Christ. Hence it was necessary by the missionaries to establish habits of worship. The study of Christian cult in South India has been the keen subject of discussions and pertinent analysis in the recent studies. But the attempts to combine the area of cultural and social approaches have been few and far between and much neglected in the scholarly debate. Hence an attempt is made to understand the Tamils who became Christians through the efforts of the Portuguese missionaries in celebrating the feasts and festivals and the changes the Portuguese brought in them.

As instruction followed by worship seems to achieve a lot, the Portuguese missionaries introduced the calendar of feasts. According to Christian Calendar, the Church festivals represented a special time and the need for celebrating these Christian festivals was an interlude which helped in the gathering and mixing of all categories of Christian people that are compartmentalized then in Tamil society. Fr. Henriques was the first one to introduce Christian calendar and announce the feast of all saints. He had introduced the Tamil calendar to mark the festivals and feasts of the saints as found correspondingly in the Gregorian calendar. The dates of movable Christian feasts of Ash Wednesday, Easter etc., besides other Christian feasts held from the year 1587 to 1614 were given in the book vide pages 666-667 printed by him.[27] Thus it is construed that the Portuguese missionaries in the Tamil Coast felt the need to organize the Christians to display their faith by celebrating various festivals.

With the rise of Bhakti religion in Tamil country after the Seventh Century, various Mother goddess (*Sakti*, the cosmic Power) worship emerged and they reached the height of importance in the Fourteenth century. This strong worship perhaps noticed by the Portuguese in the Sixteenth century helped them to introduce devotion Mary, the Mother of Jesus Christ although it was popular among the medieval Christians much earlier. The Jesuits also introduced the cult of new saints.[28]

Feast of Our Lady of Snows at Tuticorin

In 1555 Portuguese missionaries brought a statue of the Virgin Mary from Manila and it was installed in the chapel at Punnaikayal which they had built for the Parava converts. It was called *Nossa Senhora das Nevis* (Our Lady of Snows). This wooden image was moved to Tuticorin in 1582 and it was installed in the Church of

Nossa Senhora da Piedade (Our Lady of Mercy). The festival of Our Lady was begun at that time and this new cult became popular and encouraged all the Paravas to be together at that time. Marian devotion was introduced by the Jesuits with the installation of the statuette was celebrated with great pomp.[29] The first Mass in this church was celebrated on 5 August. The feast of Our Lady of Snows attracted all the Parava Catholics of the Coast.[30] The Paravas of the Coast assembled in crowds at Tuticorin for this feast as a caste festival. The consolidation of their faith was shown there at that time. Like any Hindu festival it was also celebrated for nine days (with novena). It is said that the car procession used to take place at nightfall and it was marked by numerous lights and fireworks.[31]

A description of this festival in 1600 AD captures the part-Iberian and part-Tamil flavor that emerged. On the day of the feast of Our Lady of Snows, there were eleven saparams (floats) in the processions. The Jesuit Provincial carried the Blessed Sacrament under a magnificent dais preceded by the priests in cope and chasuble, when the seminarians were dressed in the Portuguese fashion. The festivities lasted for another two days. It was the custom that on the patron feast day, the Jesuit College gave a dinner to the principal Christians of the Coast. The Jesuit Rector and an elderly Priest dined with them. During that year (AD 1600) the dinner was arranged in the new seminary built by the Paravas themselves. There was a large *mesai* (table) where sat more than 100 persons. The Paravas were much flattered by that mark of honour.[32]

After the Dutch occupation of Tuticorin in 1658 the festival was not allowed by the VOC officials. It was only on the 5 August 1709 the festivities of Our Lady of Snows were resumed again with the pomp reminiscent of Portuguese times.[33] Later we also find that in 1714, the renovation of the Church of Our Lady of Snows was completed and the Jesuit letters mention that Dutch Commandant of the fort and other Dutchmen though protestants had attended the ceremony in which the rosary was recited, the *Magnificat* was sung and the baptisms were adminsistered.[34]

Feast of Our Lady of Health at Velankanni

The Portuguese who lived in Nagapattinam had built a church in 1642 dedicated to Our Lady of Health (*Nossa Senhora da Saude*) in Velankanni.[36] It is stated in the Portuguese records that this place was located outside the Portuguese settlement of Nagapattinam. Even after the capture of Nagapattinam port by the Dutch on 23 July 1658, they did not dare to send away the missionaries (Franciscans) who were in-charge of Velankanni for the Dutch feared for the Nayak of Thanjavur.[36] Fr. Antonio do Rosario and Fr. Nicolao de S. Rita in 1779 mention about the devotion to Mary at Velankanni.[37] It had been a pilgrimage centre of the Catholics in the region[38]. However it was not as attractive as that of Tuticorin.

Feast of Our Lady of Refuge at Ellakuruchi

It is reported that in 1715 Fr. Emmanuel Machado was doing apostolic work among the Vellalars of Konapatti and at also Elakurichi. By 1729 Elakurichi had a large Christian population and Fr. Beschi who undertook the work there had arranged for the celebration of the annual festival in the church. Lot of people assembled for the festival. Confessions were heard by priests who came from near by places. In the Jesuit Annual Letter written by Fr. Vincente Guerreio in 1730 it is said that there was a terrible famine that afflicted Ariyalur and Thanjavur region. Many people died of starvation and some Catholics left Catholicism and they were attracted by the abundant alms given by the Lutheran Missionaries. It was at this time Fr. Beschi, who was in the region felt the need to develop Marian devotion.[39] To stop the apostasy he had to recourse to Our Lady of Refuge and he established a great feast in her honour. The Christians flocked to Ellakurichi and prayed there. They also received sacraments and from that time onwards there were no apostasies.[40] The Jesuit Annual Letter dated 27 June 1736 mentions that the Raja of the place had confirmed the perpetual donation of the site on which the church and presbytery were built and a vast plot of land around it.[41] In order that the donation should be known to posterity he had caused it to be erected near the church an enormous stone upon which it was engraved in Tamil about the said donation and he bound himself and his successors by an inviolable oath.

It is important to note that the statues of Our Lady of Snows at Tuticorin, Our Lady of Health in Velanakanni and Our Lady of

Refuge at Elakurichi have the model of a typical Tamil woman with saree and jewels. Thus Tamil culture had been made visible to the devotion of Blessed Virgin Mary.

Feasts of Other Saints

On 5 October 1704 Manucci observed the procession of the Most Holy Rosary held in Santhome. The Sapparam (a sort of hand barrow bearing a niche) of the image of Virgin Mary was carried at that time in a procession.[42] Further the Feast of the Holy Eucharist was celebrated on 24 May.[43] The feast of St. Thomas was celebrated on 21 December with a High Mass.[44]

Fr. Beschi had introduced devotion towards the Portuguese St. Quittery in 1731. He had composed a poem *Quitteriammal Ammani* in honour of the saint and he made it popular.[45] The Christians had acknowledged to have received some favours from the hands of St. Quittery. It is known that several churches in Tamilnadu had statutes and pictures of saints. It is attested in the evidence that fire spread to the altar and the images and pictures of saints were burnt on 31 January 1748 in Pondicherry.[46]

Christian Festivals

Portuguese missionaries had noticed the various Hindu festivals such as social, domestic and private which were the most attractive part of life in Tamil country. Fr. Antonio Dias gives a vivid picture of the *Chitrai* festival celebrated in the town of Madurai.[47] João de Britto had mentioned the *Mahamaham* festival celebrated in Kumbakonam.[48] The numerous Hindu festivals celebrated frequently in the year perhaps made the missionaries to introduce at least some Christian festivals so that new converts may feel comfortable while practising Christianity.

The feast of Epiphany was celebrated by Christians on the day of *Pongal*, the harvest festival of the Tamils.[49] Easter was celebrated with piety.[50] The feast of the eve of Nativity of John was also celebrated on 23 June in Pondicherry. The Tamils called this as *Peru Nal* (the great day). They built a bonfire on the esplanade to the South of the fort St. Louis and Westward to the entrance of the church of the Capuchins in Pondicherry. The Governor and the priests set fire to it at first and the others then followed. Three volleys were fired by the detachment of troops in attendance and these were succeeded by a salute of twenty four guns from the fort and ships at the harbour in Pondicherry.[51] Further other festivals included Christmas, Ascension and All Saints day that were celebrated by the Christians in Pondicherry.[52]

The Portuguese missionaries introduced *Ther* (chariot) processions during the celebration of the festivals. Fr. Martin reports in 1700 AD that chief of the village, his whole family and the rest of the people who assisted in the car procession fell prostrate thrice before the statue of Risen Christ. They worshipped in the most fervent Christian manner very happily.[53]

It is mentioned that the feast day processions in Pondicherry were undertaken with the spread of Christianity and it had been unheard of to have nocturnal processions till (the year 1701) then. But the Jesuits had begun to introduce this novelty, making no scruple from their arrival to imitate the Hindus in this manner. A description of one such procession held in the night between the 14th and 15th of August 1701 on the feast of the Assumption of the Holy Virgin Mary is interesting to note. The procession began a little after nine o' clock in the night without any preceding form of devotion. It had more the style of a play, as have all the processions and marriages of the Hindus and Muslims. It was not at all like a devout Christian function. Christian piety changed into cries, into torch illuminations, into rockets and other fire works made with powder of sulphur and camphor. A crucifix was carried in the first place and it was so smothered in flowers that it was not visible to be seen. This type of function was not held in the previous year and it did not appear at all. It was probably introduced by the recent (new) Christians. The statue of the Virgin Mary was in procession surrounded by parasols. Several persons fanned it and drove of the flies with hand-kerchieves. A number of Christians and Hindus followed, just as they follow in a marriage and in no order. The Christians joined because they had no real devoutness. The Hindus joined the Christian procession because they held the image of Mary with child Jesus to be that of *Bhagavathi* and of Ram. As the Hindus of Pondicherry celebrated the festival of their goddess *Bhagavathi* in the month of *Avani* which corresponds to the full moon of

September, the date on which the feast of Assumption of Our Lady was celebrated. The Jesuits were not satisfied with imitating the Hindus in their processions. They have gone farther, for they have forced the Christians to make use of certain ashes and this product was much revered by Hindus. The missionaries insisted upon the Christians to make use of these holy ashes. Thus Hindus were encouraged to see these Christians displaying these ashes just in the way the Hindus did themselves. Thus the Hindus were really made to believe that the Christian festival was to be of their religion and to hold the same opinion as themselves.[54] Thus cultural change is noticed in this festival here by incorporation or aggregation of Hindu customs in Christianity.

When the Dutch occupied Tuticorin on 1 February 1658, they took possession of the Catholic churches. Thereafter the festival of Our Lady of Snows could not be celebrated. Fr. Emmanuel Perreira, the Jesuit in 1712 obtained permission from the Dutch resident captain at Tuticorin to build a new church and celebrate the festival of Our Lady of Snows, since the church had been made into a protestant house of worship.[55] The Paravas who formerly gave donations to the church out of the sale of pearls for the conduct of festivals could not do so because the pearl fisheries were controlled by the Dutch authorities. For the Jesuit missionaries too, the property in Asolna in Goa was the only source from which the revenue was provided, ceased to yield anything owing to the Maratha incursions.[56] Therefore the financial crisis had made them not to celebrate the festivals in grand scale. Sometimes a well-to-do family on the Coast met the expenses of the feast. It is recorded that in 1708 A.D. at Manpadu De Mello family met the cost of entire expenditure on the festival day preceding the feast of Our Lady of Assumption.[57]

Tamil Christian Culture

Christian religion cannot be separated from Tamil Culture was noticed by the missionaries. Hence their rethinking on Tamil society and Christianity made them to celebrate harvest festival called the *Pongal* and *Mattu Pongal* etc. However Change from the Hindu label to Christian label was given when certain Christian elements were introduced turning it into a Christian ceremony.

Pongal

Ponghel as found in a document of 1608-1609, the harvest festival of the Tamils celebrated in Madurai had been described by the Jesuit missionaries. The festival is reported to be lasted for three days. On the final day, the Tamils boiled rice with milk in the open air shouting Pongal! Pongal! Pongal!. If the rice boiled and spilled over, it was considered a sign of good luck. Friends visited each other and enquired as to know whether boiling was over. They were happy to know when the reply came yes. The boiled rice was taken and offered to the Hindu Gods. It is stated in the document that the new convert Christians were requested by the missionaries to celebrate Pongal at the foot of the Cross which they planted for the purpose. The new rice cooked was also blessed by the Jesuit missionary.[68] This is a clear case where cultural change occurs by replacement and substitution.

Mattu Pongal

Mattu Pongal celebrated in Pondicherry in 1702 was also described by the Jesuit missionaries. It was the festival of cow and on this day all the cows were taken generally in a procession. The afternoon is chosen as the most auspicious time for beginning the ceremonies. Those among the Hindus who owned many of these cattle were the special observers of the feast. Those who possess only a few cows unite and collected them from several households. When the hour came, the cows were decorated and their horns were painted red. Vermilion was applied to their heads just as was done to men at that time. Then the rituals began and the cows were worshipped as if they were idols. Round the necks of the cows were thrown garlands of flowers. The cows were bathed with saffron water and a certain herb called *arugam pullu*. Finally the animals were incensed just as they did to their idols. The gifts consisted of figs, coconuts, jaggery, ginger and rice cooked in milk. When this ceremony was over, all the things included in the offerings were hung around the cow's necks and thus decked out. The cows were paraded through the town in procession to the sound of drums and trumphets. It is in honor of the solemn function of this great festival, the *Brahmins* erected an altar upon it, they exhibited several idols. Beneath it they placed grains, vegetables and different sorts of merchandise besides some jewels. Before it they passed the whole night in prayer chanting and then they inspected the things previously placed below the altar. There should be nothing missing or spoiled and it was believed to indicate that in the particular year such an article will be scarce and dear. It was also upon this day that they prognosticate whether there will be a murrain among cattle or a pestilence among men. On all these points the Christians as well as Hindus visited and consulted them in the morning. Finally in the evening a solemn procession was held in which *Parameswari*, *Arumugam*, *Vinayagar* and other idols were carried. The truth was that the Christians did not follow these details. Only on the previous day, Some Christians delivered their cows to an ordinary cowherd making him some payment in return for which he charged himself with the performance of these rites in the mode he thought the best. Other Christians contented themselves with the reddening of the cow's horns and heads and wetting them with saffron water. Then the cows were loosed and took part in the procession. But what was the most remarkable one in the procession was the travelling throne of the Gods. The Jesuits paraded the statue of the Blessed Virgin Mary in the same manner as that of the Hindus who did carry their idols. The procession of the cows was closed by several matchlock men and some umbrella holders.[59] This also shows that devotion to Blessed Virgin Mary was done by the Jesuits to translate the faith of Hindu Goddesses. Thus interweaving the Hindu-Christian traditions was already under way in Tamil society at large and the cultural changes seem to have occurred by substitution and replacement of certain rituals.

All Catholics were asked to strictly adhere to the decisions taken in the Ecumenical Council of Trent (1545-1563) which were adopted by the Portuguese missionaries. Further, the First Provincial Council held in Goa in 1567 also emphasised the need for carrying on a relentless war against the Hindu religious and social practices followed by the converted Christians in India. The *padroado* missionaries felt that the Hindu practices were harmful for the spiritual health and growth of the new converts. Hence worship of idols, bearing sandal marks on the body, wearing the sacred thread were not allowed. The Fifth and the last Provincial Council held in the year 1606 in Goa also banned the Hindu customs followed by those converted to Christianity. The acceptance of Catholicism by the natives was then considered as a denial of their age old cultural heritage.

On the other hand, after seventeen years there was a reversal of the trend when Roberto Nobili, the Jesuit in Madurai encouraged the Tamil Christians to celebrate *Pongal*, the harvest festival along with the Hindus adding a cross at the centre of the *kolam* (flour decoration on the floor) done at the entrance of the houses. He also encouraged the Christians to wear the sacred ash on the forehead as the Hindus did, although Catholicism permitted the use of sacred ash only on Ash Wednesday as a sign of penance.[60] Pope Gregory XV, on 13 January 1623 approved Roberto Nobili's methods, vide, *Romanae Sedi Antistites* in preaching the Gospel to the Tamils.

Public Theatres and Religious Themes in Tamil Society

Placing the Tamil Christian plays that were composed and introduced by the Jesuit missionaries in the context of religion and society during the early modem period is an important feature to understand the nuances of culture. Ever since the advent of the Jesuits in 1542 to anchor the conversion of the Paravas and to secure souls in Tamilnadu, they did commendable work in the field of literature and arts. Various strategies, techniques and methods had been adopted in their process of evangelization while working with the various castes in the Tamil coastal region. These Jesuits for the first time were expelled in 1605 from the Pearl Fishery Coast for a period of sixteen years by the Portuguese authorities of Goa due to suspicion over the declining pearl fishery revenues and the disturbances caused by them for interfering in the affairs of the Paravas.[61] By this time many Jesuits had moved to the Tamil hinterland to continue their apostolic work and the return of some Jesuits in the 1620s led also to more social activities among the Paravas. Therefore in the 1630s we again find that the Portuguese authorities of Goa had made a final attempt to secure direct control over the Pearl Fishery Coast. The Jesuits who had already moved to the hinterland preached the Gospel among the various castes and adopted many of the local Tamil customs and manners.[62]

The writers of history on Jesuits so far had paid relatively little attention to matters related to art and literature in Tamilnadu at this period and it is still small in quantity. Hence the mixing and mingling of religion, culture, society have to be merited great attention and an attempt is made in the present chapter to make a detailed study of the various kinds of plays and dramas composed and introduced by the Jesuits. The history of every day life that pertains to the realm of "embedded history" in contrast to externalized history is a very significant one in this context also, because this embedded history has an emphasis on the local or regional situation. Although local narratives, myths and epics were employed for specific purposes to make us realize the importance of the oral tradition and narratives, we shall chiefly use the letters of the Portuguese Jesuits, the diaries of the Pondicherry merchants written in Tamil besides the travelogues to examine and understand the public theatres and religious themes and the Jesuit impact and influence. It must be borne in mind that Tamils had a rich tradition of enacting plays and dramas in the medieval period as gleaned from many inscriptions.[63] The Jesuits wanted to enact dramas and plays on Christian themes and so they composed and successfully staged the various types of plays

Passion Plays

Mass of the people converted knew very little about their own religious belief and that ignorance concerning their religion could be eradicated through popular plays and dramas which also led many to take the new Christian religion. The missionaries also showed more interest in the spiritual than economic conditions of their congregation. Thus the idea of receiving material help from the Portuguese missionaries was totally absent in Tamil country. The clergy also became aware of the role of the local customs, traditions of theatre and therefore plays and dramas were enacted by the native Christians under the instructions of the missionaries during the season of Lent, Holy Week and also after Easter inspiring the Christians and Non-Christians. At Kottar near Nagercoil it is said in a record that the Christians of the place staged there the Gospel story in the year 1644 which was enjoyed by thousands of spectators during the Lent.[64] During Easter plays were enacted at Gingee and the feast of Easter was celebrated with fire works.[65]

Plays on the Lives of Saints

Similarly the *Kallar* Christians of Kandalur had staged the life of the Saints Barlam and Josaphat being translated into elegant Tamil in verse by the catechist namely Hilary in the year 1653 during Easter. The villagers of the neighbourhood who witnessed were so much taken up by the play that many of them wanted to become Christians. They were taught catechism and were prepared for baptism.[66] A large gathering of Christians and Hindus witnessed plays which had been composed by the Jesuits on the lives of saints at Kavanakarai.[67] After the beatification of St. Francis Xavier plays were written on the saint and they were also enacted.[68]

Miracle Plays

Jesuits had composed several dramas and plays in Tamil and we find that an emphasis is made on the miracle plays at that time. It is reported in the letter of Fr. Andres Freyre to Giovanni Palo Oliva, the Jesuit Superior General in Rome dated 10 July 1678 written from Viranam that a large concourse of Christians and Hindus had witnessed the plays which had been composed by the Jesuits.[69] These were amusing as they contained many miracles.

A miraculous story of Our Lady, Virgin Mary was composed by the Jesuits and it was enacted in the year 1705 in Pondicherry during the month of July. This play was staged and all the French officials had watched it. Even the natives were present and they participated in it to a noisy accompaniment of drums and trumpets besides the discharge of fireworks. The Jesuits had not given over their performance of extravagant comedy. In the play, they represented a knight of good family who married a rich and noble lady. By gambling and other dissipation he came in a few years to the end of his wealth, and fell into extreme-poverty. Oppressed by his needs, and finding no one would lend him any money, he had recourse to the Devil. The Satan lent him money on condition that, should he not find the wherewithal to satisfy the debt, he must make over his wife in payment. The term fixed having passed the Devil appeared to demand his money, but the knight having nothing from which to pay the debt, contended for a long time with his creditor. Finally he agreed to produce his wife at a place appointed by the Devil. In order not to break his word the husband enticed his wife away from the house on a pretext of taking a walk in some gardens. On the way they passed close to a church, when the wife craved leave from the husband to enter and offer a prayer to Our Lady, the Virgin Mary, for whom she felt great veneration. While the woman was at the foot of the altar engaged in prayer, it came to pass that the Virgin Mary descended from the altar and said to her: "Stop where you are, for your husband is taking you away deceitfully. I will take your place". The Virgin issued from the church, joined the knight, and they continued the journey. Upon arriving at the place fixed upon, the knight said to the Devil: "Here is my wife in the place of cash". The Devil approached to seize the woman, but received, a great shock of terror and with a backward leap cried: "This is not your wife as you promised me; it is the Virgin Mary, whom I am impotent to lay hands on". The knight assured him it was his wife; but in the meanwhile the Virgin had disappeared. The character was played by a native man dressed in woman's clothes. The devil's and the knight's parts were taken by two other men, who now commenced to shoe-beat each other. Thus the comic play came to an end.[70] In this miracle play we find two parts. The first part contained mainly secular and comic incidents dealing with the sinners who are shown in their lustful or bad life and in the second part we find that they are converted usually by a miracle worked by Our Lady Virgin Mary. Hence the motive for conversion comes from these miraculous plays. It may be said here-that such conversions could certainly be 'a feigned one. This play introduced by the Jesuits was witnessed by the Tamil population to noisy accompaniments of drums, trumpets and the discharge of fire works. This play shows that religious themes were covered in the play such as devotion to Virgin Mary, morality, self discipline in family life, practising Christian virtues, self cantonment in life, etc.

Satirical Plays

Further we find that the Jesuits were keen on composing and staging fine comedies often the subject-matter being Hindu belief systems and gods. This took place at Kottur and it is mentioned in the letter dated 25 January 1682 written by Fr. Andres Freyre to the Jesuit Superior General in Rome.[71] The Christians were asked to subscribe towards the expenditure of the play and also to be present. Staging a fine comedy in honour of Hindu Gods also took place at Kottur.[72]

A satirical play was composed by Fr. Charles Francois Dolu and it was enacted in front of the Jesuit residence in Pondicherry in the year 1701 during the month of February. For several days before the performance, the Christians had run about the streets of the town announcing that on such a day there would be a play. The Brahmins and Hindus of various other castes were invited to be present for the play by the friends of the Jesuits. The play was witnessed by Monsieur Deslandes, the Director of the French East India Company besides Hindus and Brahmins. In this play they represented the most respected and the most venerable gods of Hindus like *Brahma*, *Vishnu*, *Rudra*, *Rishavan*, *Velavar*, *Parvathy* and *Sivagami*. After stating some truth, the actors who were Tamil Christians declaimed against these gods and against those men who acknowledged and adored them. This was done by the Christians chiefly out of zeal but it was indiscreet and out of place. The Hindus plucked out the performers beards and kicked them. Following this up, after more ill treatment and buffeting, they knocked them down pitching them under the stage into a sort of fire intended to represent hell.[73] The Brahmins and other Hindus present at the play reported the matter to the King of Thanjavur. They also narrated the other things done at various times by missionaries against the Hindu customs. The Jesuits in their satirical plays often made unfriendly comments about Hindu deities in vernacular. This was not very pleasing for the French officials and for the natives, and on hindsight one might say, surely not in the spirit of inter-religious dialogue that we witness today.

On such occasions of Christian feasts celebrated, when Tamil Christians who staged a drama, it is reported that there arose also problems in which when the Hindu Gods were held up in ridicule. The letter of Fr. Antonio de Barros dated 4 August 1702 speaks of the trouble partly due to the indiscretion of the Christians. The Hindus who were present in large numbers to watch the drama were furious when their gods were mocked and so they reported the matter to the King who immediately ordered the arrest of all the Christians in his kingdom and those arrested were thrown in the prison. Fr. José Caravalho was one among them. The prisoners were treated with utmost cruelty in order to force them to give up their faith. A number of them remained firm. Although Fr. José Caravalho was not beaten with rods, yet he fell seriously sick and he died on 14 March 1701.[74]

Mystery Plays

Mystery plays and passion plays that were composed by the Jesuits were enacted during the festival of Easter. It is mentioned in the letter written by Fr. João de Britto that passion plays were-enacted at Gingee in the year 1681. The feast of Easter was celebrated with fire works when the plays were enacted.[75] These mystery plays dealing with the salvific acts of God as recorded in the Bible had been enacted to make the Christians to be well instructed in religion.

A *kuravanji* (dance-drama) on St. David as mentioned in the Bible composed by a Tamil called *vidwan* Malaiyappan was performed on 11 August. 1762 at Poraiyar in the car street of the village which was located near Tharangambadi, (Tranquebar) the Danish settlement. The drama was held with good make-up and it commenced at eleven o' clock in the night and it lasted till half past four in the early morning. Necessary announcements regarding the drama had been made in all the neighbouring places such as Erukattancheri. In the *agraharam*, fifty or sixty Brahmins were given dinner on this day. Other Hindu invitees for the dinner included Bhoomiyappa Mudaliar, the son of Periyanna Mudaliar, son of Appu Mudaliar, Venkatachala Pillai the son of Thiruvengadatha Pillai's brother, Thiruvamabala Nayinar who was brought up by Swami Periyanna Nayinar. Some Christians like Barlam and Savari Muthu had also dinner. Everyone watched the *kuravanji* and all the performers were offered turbans.[76] Thus we find that the dramatic method had been found to be very effective for teaching the Holy Scripture. The Return of the Prodigal Son mentioned in the Bible also formed theme of a drama that was staged to emphasize the teachings of Christ and follow the tenets of Christianity.[77]

Miscellaneous Plays

Veneration to Blessed Virgin Mary had been encouraged by the missionaries-through enacting plays during the feast days. On 5 October 1762, just before the feast of Our Lady of Rosary, a play was enacted at night in the village of Sathangudi that fell within the jurisdiction of the Danish settlement of Tharangambadi.[78] Further we find that during May, the Marian month, a drama was enacted in Pondicherry on 12 May 1795. A Christian by name Savari, who belonged to Nellithopu, located in the vicinity of Pondicherry had played the role of king in the drama. This Savari who returned home after the drama had suddenly fell down and died on-the-spot.[79]

To conclude we may say that the Jesuit plays reflected various complexities of the times, strongly apologetic and uncharitably polemic. Jesuit dramas had a fundamental Catholic religious basis. The Jesuits had used theatre for religious instruction and propaganda. The occasion of the performances had been generally festivals. The places of performances had been either Jesuit residence, or churches. Jesuit plays in due course of time came to be also conducted in public places owing to the encouragement. As dramas and religion had been linked in Hinduism very much, the Jesuits also used it as an effective tool for religious and social education. Sacred stories were enacted. Drama perhaps was not at the beginning was used as a means of communication and as an art in this early period of expansion of Christianity. It is to be noted that the Jesuits understood the power of theatre for propaganda. The Jesuit clergy supplied the scripts for the play. Jesuits wanted the Christians to live according to the Christian culture, distinct from the Hindu surrounding. The play-wrights had been initially Jesuit missionaries. Later it appears that Tamils had also composed plays. The audience generally composed of both the Hindus of high and low castes and the Tamil Catholic Christians. Funding had been undertaken by the people themselves and some wealthy men of the town were patrons of the plays who financed it. Laity participated in acting and staging the play by doing rehearsal. Since the Tamil texts of the plays are not available we are unable to explore the language of the drama whether it was simple or literary, used mainly to convey ideas or it dazzled the audience. The mystery plays, the miracle plays and the satirical plays had been the three main types of plays introduced at this time. These plays were both comic and tragic in nature. The main object was to entertain and also to provide religious instruction. Plays were enacted according to Tamil theatrical traditions. Jesuits deeply versed in the doctrine of the Church skilled in the rhetorical arts of preaching could touch the hearts of those who heard. Thus doctrinal and devotional character was well guarded. We do not know whether the same plays were repeated every year with a few changes here and there. Thus Tamil Christian plays have also brought humour and some times violence. Jesuits presence in Tamil Country and their activities have made a deep and lasting impact on Tami plays and they displayed considerable natural skill in creating imaginary characters and situations caught from life. Thus the Jesuits had turned their hands to set designing, choregraphy and stage engineering while producing plays. We may even say that the theatrical activity had some effect on Jesuit evangelization but it also brought tension among various communities. Tamil prose was supplanting poetry and this is a very important feature introduced by the Jesuits in this period. It appears that the Christian plays were reportedly extremely successful in Tamil Country as the Tamils were great lovers of poetry and declamation and nothing has made a more forceful impression than the plays. In the Jesuit estimation these plays covered two didactic purposes. One was the training that it gave the actors in oratory and the other it was a means through which the Christian doctrine could be put forth effectively. The Jesuit plays has thus portrayed the conflicts which were intrinsic to most kinds of Baroque art, the themes of virtue and vice, God and man, time and eternity.

To conclude it may be said that changes in social characteristics and standards took place in Tamilnadu among the *Paravas*, *Mukkuvars* and *Paraiyar* converts who have embraced Christianity in mass movements more rapidly since their age old social integration was destroyed by individual conversion. It had been found that the way Christian rituals celebrated had either merged with or supplanted the existing rituals. These rituals mirrored the religious and social relationship between the Christian mission and congregation. The products of societal change noticed could be said to be of varied nature such as change by expansion or contraction, change by replacement or substitution, change by incorporation or aggregation, change by addictive or accretionary change besides involuntary change. These changes were made possible and they were brought out because the Portuguese Padroado and Jesuits as a group or community had a clear policy regarding evangelisation, inculturation and social apostate in Tamil country.

All these changes possessed a morphology or trend. However three types of the morphology of change are found are such as change as smooth and continuous trend, change as a non-linear trend with catastrophic switches and revolutionary movements besides continuity or discontinuity. The influence of Hinduism in the Christian way of life by the *Paravas* was seen by missionaries initially since proper Christian teachings had not been given. In the Sixteenth Century perhaps baptism allowed the change of name was disliked by the Tamil Hindus. Portuguese links only with the maritime communities in Tamilnadu perhaps hindered the growth of expansion of the mission stations interior and other castes in the Sixteenth century. The number of Brahmin converts although increased, was much less, when compared to other castes. The simple reason was that the *Brahmins* could not obtain any social advancement by becoming Christians. The lower caste converts found it possible to elevate their social status by embracing Christianity. By becoming Christians they could freely enter the church and learn the Holy Scripture which was forbidden fruit to them, a monopoly enjoyed by the Brahmins for down the ages. The Portuguese Jesuit Mission among the Tamils was exclusively for the benefit of men and their family in their spread of Gospel and Christianity. The Jesuits moved from one place to another in search of various castes Hindus in Tamilnadu for conversion and they saw that no elements in the native culture and Hindu religion which they could emulate and much less consider superior to their own Portuguese culture.

Notes and References

1. John Marignolli, *The Travels of John Marignolli in the East*, London, 1895.
2. Marcopolo, *The Travels of Marco Polo*, London, 1958.

3. William B. Green Lee, *The Voyage of Pedro Alvares Cabral to Brazil and India*, London, 1938, p. 49.
4. S. Jeyaseela Stephen, *Portuguese ... op.cit*. pp. 305-306.
5. DI, VI, pp. 91-92.
6. Giuseppe Beltrami, *La Chiesa Caldea Nel Secolo dell Minore*, Rome, 1933, p. 261.
7. Joseph Thekkedath, *The Troubled Days of Francis Garcia S.J: Archbishop of Cranganore, 1641-1659*, Rome, 1972, pp. 51-52.
8. S. Jeyaseela Stephen, *Portuguese ... op.cit*, p. 303.
9. ARP Diary, Vol. I, p.117. Governor Dumas and others congratulated the bishop. See ARP Diary, vol. I, pp. 95-96. Further when Bishop Loliere embarked in a ship on 16 March 1740 a salute of fifteen guns was fired from the shore.
10. S. Jeyaseela Stephen, *Portuguese op.cit,* pp. 343-345.
11. DI, Vol. XI, p. 292.
12. S. Rajamanickam, *Adiyar Varalaru*, (Flos Sanctorum) Tuticorin, 1967. The details are found in original Mss. vide pp. 11, 33, 37, 40, 47 & 48.
13. Fernão Guerrio, (ed). A. Veigas, *Relação Anual das Coisas que Fizeram Os padres da Companhia de Jesus nas Suas Missões India*, 3 vols, Coimbra, 1930, See, Vol. I, pp. 328-34. II, p. 343.
14. Leon Besse, *op.cit*, pp 8-14, MPJA, Annual Letter of the year 1644 by Fr. Andre Lopez; MPJA, L. Besse, History of the Malabar Province, (typescripts) Vol. II, pp. 397, 478. Susan Bayly argues that the cult tradition surrounding St. Francis Xavier resembled the tradition of the Muslim holy man (pir) and the Hindu ascetic Guru with a heavy emphasis on the saint's physical ordeals, his asceticism and his overcoming of spiritual obstacles. Susan Bayly, *Saints... op.cit*, pp. 329-330.
15. LEC, Vol. X, pp. 77-78, 82-92, Letter of Fr. Martin to Fr. Le Gobien dated 1 June 1700.
16. MPJA, Annual Letter of the year 1666 by Fr. Andre Freyre to Fr. J.P. Oliva, See also his letter written from Kandalour dated 14 July 1667.
17. MPJA, *Annual Letters of the Madurai Mission*, (typescript) Loyola College, Madras, 1910. See Appendix.C.
18. MPJA, Annual Letter of the year 1692.
19. Archives of the Archdiocese of Madras-Mylapore, Santhome, Mss 2889, document no.4, fl. 6.
20. Nicoao Manucci, *Storia. op.cit*, Vol. III, p. 236.

21. MPJA, Annual Letter of the Madurai Mission for the year 1734 written by Fr. Vieyra dated 14 July 1735. The annual letter of 1735 speaks of pilgrimage that royal members of the Maravas made to Oriyur. They prayed on the spot of martyrdom and with carried with their own hand the bricks for building a church there. Fr. Rossi had built a rotund in 1770. The altar was built on the very spot where the blessed martyr was beheaded. Beatification of João de Britto was done by Pope Pius IX on 13 May 1852.
22. MPJA, Annual Letter of the year 1734 written by J. Vieyra.
23. David Mosse, "Catholic Saints and the Hindu Village Pantheon in Rural Tamilnadu", *Man*, 29, 1994, pp. 301-302.
24. MPJA, Annual Letter of the year 1731 written by Beschi; Annual Letter of the year 1730 by Fr. Joseph Vieyra 1730.
25. MPJA, Mss, Resume du Diarium Marave, p. 148.
26. Achilles Meersman, *Franciscans in Tamilnadu*, Schoneck- Beckenried, 1962, p. 88.
27. S. Rajamanickam, *Adiyar Varalaru*, (Flos Sanctorum) Tuticorin, 1967.
28. In AD. 1622 in St Peter' Church in Rome five saints were canonized in a single ceremony. Four of them namely Ignatius of Loyola, Teresa of Avila, Francis Xavier and Philip Neri were made saints within fifty years of their death which was unusually soon in Roman Catholic procedure of that times.
29. MPJA, Annual Letter of the year 1582, p. 3.
30. DI, Vol. XII, pp. 717-718. The car festival in Tuticorin Church began to take place once in thirteen years during the month of August at the time of the feast of our Lady of Snows. The festival celebrated in 1720 and 1806 have been mentioned. See, Susan Bayly, *Saints, Goddesses and Kings, op.cit.*, p. 341 & 343.
31. DI, Vol. XI, p. 817.
32. MPJA, Annual Letter of the Year 1600, p. 3.
33. MPJA, Annual Letter of the Year 1710, p. 9.
34. MPJA, Annual Letter of the Year 1714, p. 11.
35. Panduranga Pissurlencar, *Assentos do Conselho do Estado, (1618-1750)*, 5 vols, Goa, 1953-57, See, vol. III, pp. 655-656.
36. Achilles Meersman, "The Origin and Cult of Our Lady of Vailankanni" in *Indian Eccelsiatical Studies*, (henceforth IES) vol. I, 1962, pp. 66-67.
37. *Ibid.*

38. S. Jeyaseela Stephen, *The Diary of Rangappa Thiruvengadam Pillai, 1760-1766*, (in original Tamil, Critical introduction and edited with Historical Notes) 2 vols, Pondicherry Institute of Linguistics and Culture, Pondicherry, 2000, See the entry dated 8 October 1763.
39. MPJA, Annual Letter of the year 1730 dated 2 August 1730.
40. The letter written by Fr. Joseph Vieyra dated 18 June 1731 speaks of the abundant fruits obtained in this manner.
41. MPJA, Annual Letter of the year 1736. It is mentioned that Rangappa Mazhavarayar of Ariyalur donated 175 acres of land to the church in 1735. The document is in an inscription in Tamil still found in the Church.
42. Niccolau, Manucci, *op.cit.,* Vol. IV, p. 60.
43. Lotika Varadarajan, *Memoirs op.cit.*, Vol. I, p. 385.
44. *Ibid.,* Vol. I, p. 138.
45. C.J. Beschi, *Kitteriammal Ammanai*, Madras, 1849.
46. ARP Diary, Vol. IV, p. 344.
47. MPJA, Annual Letter of the year 1708 written by Antonio Dias dated 20 July 1709.
48. MPJA, Annual Letter written of the year 1683 written from Madurai dated 5 September 1684.
49. ARP Diary, Vol. III, p. 232.
50. ARP Diary, Vol. XI, p. 26.
51. ARP Diary, Vol. I, p.174; Vol. IV, p. 107.
52. Edmond Gaudart, *Proces-verabux des deliberations du Conseil Superieur de Pondichery*, Pondichery, 1913, tome I, p. 154, 4 February 1715. Bibliothèque Nationale. Paris, (hereafter BNP), Mss Français 6231, fl. 55; *Mss, Nouvelle Acquisition Française*, 9225, fl. 293.
53. Letter of Fr. Martin, John Lockman, *Travels of the Jesuits... op.cit*, Vol. II, pp. 288-289.
54. Nicolau Manucci, *op.cit,* Vol. III, pp. 333-334.
55. MPJA, Letter of Fr. Emmanuel Perreira, to Fr. Tamburini, the Superior General dated 1 November 1714 p. 253; See also the Annual Letter of the Year 1712, pp. 220-21.
56. Bertrand, *Excerptae Catalogis Provincae Malabaricae*, Trichy, 1910-11, pp. 43-44.
57. MPJA, Annual Letter of the year 1708, p. 190.
58. ARSI, Goa 54a, ff. 17-75, See also the letter of Roberto Nobili to Laerzio dated 15 June 1609 in Bertrand, *op.cit*, vol. II, p. 29; Further see the letter of Laerzio to Aqua Viva written from Cochin dated 20 November 1609. (in Italian)

59. Nicolau Manucci, vol. III, pp. 353-356.

60. S. Rajamanickam, *op.cit.*, p. 87.

61. S. Jeyaseela Stephen, *Portuguese in the Tamil Coast: Historical Explorations in Commerce and Culture, 1507-1749*, Navajyothi Publishing House, Pondicherry, 1998, for details see chapter eight, Evangelization by the Padroado Missionaries, pp.276-323.

62. S. Jeyaseela Stephen, "Societal Changes: Portuguese and the Native Christians in Tamil Country, Cir AD 1537-1759", in K.S. Mathew, Teotonio Rosario Desouza and Pius Malekandathil, (eds.,) *Portuguese and the Socio-Cultural Changes in India, 1500-1800*, Tellicherry, 2002, pp.479-513.

63. According to Tolkappiyal songs played an important role in ancient dramas. "Nataka vazhakkinum ulakiyal vazhakinum patal sanra pulaneri vazhakkam" (whether it be the tradition of drama or whether it be the tradition of the world, it is all a sense of songs by tradition). See, Tolkappiyal, Porul, Akarathiyial. According to Madurai Kanchi natakams did take place during the festival times in the nights. Perungathai mentions *"vayir kuttum cerippatalum koilnataka kulukkalum varukena"* (Welcome to the koil drama troupe to those who play kuthu and to those who sing songs of villages) and thus it distinguishes between kuthu (skit) and natakam (drama). The Tamil Kings had favoured Natakams and these were also liked by people much better than kuthus (skits). An inscription of A.D 960 of King Adithiya Chola II period mentions that there was a man called Kirtti Maraikatan alias Tiruvellarai Cakkai in Tiruvidaimaruthur and he staged a play called 'Ariyakuthu' which was attended by the officers and the public who assigned the artist a land and in return for his services rendered to play also a Kuthu for three days on Thaippusam festival. Subsequently on Vaikasi festival also he agreed to play a kuthu for three days and thus in total seven plays were enacted. He was also given a salary of sixteen kalams of paddy. See, *South Indian Inscriptions*, Vol. V, p. 529. An inscription of Uttama Chola (974-985) mentions that Kantatol Kantapaiyan alias Attaman Aiyar constructed the drama shed in Tiruvadigai temple. He had also arranged for feeding the temple lamps by donating sixty-two goats. In A.D. 994 Tirumula Nayanar drama was enacted at the Emperumal temple in Tiruvaduturai. A gift of land called Nirutha bogam was granted to Kumaran Sri Kandan for playing Ariyakkattu seven times there. Inscription mentions that there was a drama stage called Nanavitha Natakasalai (stage for all

kinds of dramas). There are inscriptional evidences to show that two dramas had existed in book form about Raja Raja Chola (1012-1044) alias Arul Mozhi Varman. One of them was called Raja Raja Vijayam and the other was Raja Raja Varam. The first book was the biography of Raja Raja which was read out to the public by Narayanan alias Suvarnan. He was awarded gifts for this. The Raja Raja Varam dealt with the life, heroism and virtues of Raja Raja. South Indian inscriptions, Vol. II, p. 67. During the reign of Rajendra Chola I in A.D. 1041 in Kamarasavalli Caturvedi the public had donated a gift of a land to Sakai Mahayan Vikrama Cholan for playing three times the Cakkaikkuthu on Tiruvathirai day in the month of Vaikasi In an inscription of A.D.1088 of Kulotunga Chola I, we find that in the Mahadevar temple at Viranarayanapuram Virutarasa Payankara Achariyan known as Vikramaditan was appointed to see that Tamil kuthu was staged five times during the Chittirai festival. Inscription further states that he was given a land as Uttakkani by the local public and the temple authorities. The inscription of Vyakrapunjeswarar Temple of Pudukottai region speaks of the donation of land for the performance of Santhikkuthu in A.D. 1132 (King Vikrama Chola period) and mentions that Santhikkuthu was performed in front of the threshold of the Veikai Vayilamar temple in Cikakula Valanadu. This performance was carried out by Ezhunattu Nangai. For this she was assigned the land and the tank of Tippaiyar. During the festival days she played nine kuthus. If the land went dry, she was also given food for the services rendered. The Peruvayil Nattumega committee had therefore issued standing orders and the text runs as follows: *"cittirait tirunalukku cantik kuttu atukaikku cantik kuttatukira elunattu nankaikku uitta nilamavatuu . . . Ival in nilan kontu ittiru nalukku atakkyava kuttu onpatum atuvalakavum vilaiyata antu atina kuttukku korru vitu vataka"*. See *Inscriptions of Pudukottai State*, No. 128. Another inscription of A.D. 1168 records that King Rajendra Kulottunga Chola had installed Catura Vitaiika Nayakan statutte in the temple and the Tiruvathirai festival was celebrated the Vaikasi month, and on that occasion six Santhi Kuthus were performed by two women. The artists were given land which was purchased from Tiruvenkai Vasal committee members and it was exempted from taxation and the boundaries were also clearly marked. The women also received six kalams of paddy whether the land was in a position to yield paddy or not is stated in the inscription. Another inscription of A. D. 1226 of King Maravarman

Sundara Pandya I mentions about Sankti Kuthan Onrayiram and he was given land by those who inspected the temple. They gave the land in his favour with kudivaram (tenancy) rights. See, *Inscriptions of Pudukottai State*, No. 139. The inscription of Vikrama Pandya in A.D. 1249 mentions that there was a nataka shed in Atrur in the Tirunelveli region and in the temple of that place a natakam was staged during the Avani Tirunal. For this one Priyataran was presented with two ma of land and it was given by Kulatarayan alias Kunramolic Singa Piran. See, *Annual Report on Epigraphy*, 445 of 1924.

64. Leon Besse, *op.cit*, pp. 8-14. See also his work, *History of the Malabar Province*, 2 vols, Madras, 1946, vol. II, pp. 397-478.

65. S. Jeyaseela Stephen, *Letters of the Portuguese Jesuits, op.cit.*, p.207

66. Leon Besse, *op.cit*, p. 13.

67. Leon Besse. *History of the Malabar... op.cit*, vol. II, pp. 507-510; See also, *La Mission du Madure*, vol. IV, p. 149.

68. The Jesuit Annual letter of 1621 also had an interesting depiction of play that was enacted on the occasion of the celebrations of the beatification of Xavier. On the fourth day of the celebrations a tragic-comedy entitled "Heaven Feasting Xavier" was gone through. The First Act was that of the zones - Torrid, Frigid, and Temperate, reciting in their manner and with marvelous precision the praises of the Beato. The Second Act represented the ten Circles of the Zones – the Equator, the Zodiac, the Meridian, the Horizon, the Equinoctial Colure, the Solstitial Colure, the Tropic of Cancer, the Tropic of Capricorn, the Arctic Circle and the Antarctic Circle. The Planets i.e., the Moon, Mercury, Venus, the Sun, Mars, Jupiter, and Saturn described their orderly revolutions in the Third Act. The Fourth displayed the starry heavens in both hemispheres the constellations and their fabulous monsters. Finally in the Fifth Act, the starry heavens opened their portals, and the heaven of crystal, the prime mover the empyrean dazzled the beholders. The last scene showed the Saint borne on a triumphal chariot, with a host of angels and blessed denizens forming his court. One of the most successful scenes - an entr'acte, we may suppose represented a snow-white swan singing the birth of the Saint and predicting his future greatness. A lyre discoursed sweet music meanwhile, and nine palms - waved their applause so swiftly and joyfully so as to confuse the eye. The comic side was not forgotten. Two centaurs were seen going on a hunting expedition, and what was funny about them was that they aimed in one direction, and the game

fell dead in another. Thus the plays were extremely elaborate and all in all would have been extremely interesting. See, Rev. H. Hosten, "Jesuit Annual letters from Goa and Cochin in 1621" in *The Examiner*, 10 February 1912, pp 107-108. It was not uncommon in fact for a play to last for many days. A play was performed at the time of the celebrations of the canonization of St. Francis Xavier in 1624 in Goa which lasted for four days. See, Georg Schurhammer, "Festas em Goa no Ano 1624" in *Boletim do Instituto Vasco da Gama,* Vol.69, 1952, p. 36.

69. S. Jeyaseela Stephen. *Letters of the Portuguese Jesuits from Tamil Countryside, 1666-1688,* Pondicherry, 2001, p.137.
70. Niccolao Manucci, *Storia do Mogor,* (trs.) William Irvine, reprint, New Delhi, 1989, Vol. IV, pp.198-199; pp. 211-212.
71. Jeyaseela Stephen, *Letters, op.cit.*, p. 205.
72. *Ibid.*
73. Fr. Charles Francois Dolu, a member of the Society of Jesus had left for India in 1688 and was made curator of Pondicherry Mission in 1699. He returned to Europe in 1710 and died on 6 January 1740. See, C. Sommervogel, *Bibliographie de la Compagnie de Jesus,* Vol. III, p.123.
74. See, Niccolao Manucci, *op.cit.,* Vol. III, pp. 324-325. A Brahmin teacher succeeded in enacting a different version of the drama before the king. He prepared a public procession in which was carried with all the state and pomp of which these people were capable a representation of the saviour, around him stood their five Gods in the position of slaves and servants. One of them presented Jesus with a tray or basket containing betel, another a platter of arecanut, another some prepared lime, and other something else. But the representative of the saviour refused their offers and ill treated them and kicked them after the fashion of the actors in the Jesuit drama held in Pondicherry. The procession was made to defile before the King. Surprised at a thing so unusual the King asked with angry and threatening countenance what was the unusual ceremonial and there upon the Brahmin, the author of the piece took up his parable and explained as the Christians dealt with and looked at the Hindu Gods, saying that the Hindus had carried out to carry their complaints. See, Nicolau Manucci, *op.cit.*, vol. III, pp. 325-328.
75. S. Jeyaseela Stephen, *Letters, op.cit.*, p.207.
76. S. Jeyaseela Stephen, *The Diary of Rangappa Thiruvengadam Pillai,1761-1768*, Translated from Original Tamil, Pondicherry, 2001, pp.27-28.

77. Commenting on the play of the prodigal son Fr. Irmão Jeronimo Roiz in his letter wrote to his Confrades in Portugal as follows: "This year upon the arrival of the feast (of Our Lady) everybody came together to the college. Master Bishop, the friars of St. Francis and St, Dominic and many noble people came. A boy said a prayer and after it a tragic comedy of beautiful characters in a richly set theatre dealt with the history of the prodigal son was staged. It was a play to be seen, and some people who heard it would cry principally when the prodigal son would return, elegant and bright, naked and ragged, mourning his loss. And at some parts boys would sing very well to a harp, having also flutes and bagpipes. And at the end of the play which lasted nearly two hours, some went singing, taking the father to the prodigal son, with great grandeur, playing also the flutes; and this gave great encouragement to the students to go ahead in their studies; and for the circumstances, in order they would order their sons to learn. See, Silva Rego, *Documentação...* Vol. X, Document No.3, pp. 17-18.

78. S. Jeyaseela Stephen, *The Diary of Rangappa Thiruvengadam Pillai, 1761-1768*, p.34.

79. S. Jeyaseela Stephen, *Muthu Vijaya Thiruvengadam Pillai Naatkurippu, 1794-1795,* (The Diary of Muthu Vijaya Thiruvengadam Pillai) Pondicherry, 1999, p.259. See the entry dated 14 May 1795.

5
Luso–Tamil Cultural Relations

The social and cultural history of India during the Sixteenth and Seventeenth centuries is inextricably interwoven with the Portuguese overseas expansion. The importance attached to maritime trade with India by the Kings of Portugal attracted many Portuguese and other European merchants to come from Portugal. They traded at various ports and in due course of time settled down there by marrying the Indian women. This mixed blood group of the Eurasians had been known as *mestições* in Portuguese records who followed a mixture of Indian and Portuguese manners and customs. In addition to this class, there were others known as *casados* married to women of Portuguese origin mentioned in documents. They conducted trade and commerce in Indian ports and lived with their own families retaining the same old Portuguese ceremonies, customs and manners. Another category was the soldiers known as *soldados* in Portuguese sources, who came to India and employed in the royal service of the King of Portugal and they were placed directly under the Portuguese Viceroy's administrative control in Goa and other Portuguese settlements. Those Portuguese nobles who came to serve in India were called *fidalgos* in the records. Mention of Portuguese exiles and renegades do also find place in various official papers. Thus we find the Portuguese society in India of that period had been a mixture of different groups and various elements had been taken into account for the broad social classification.[1] Against this backdrop it would be relevant to examine the intermingling of Indo-Portuguese customs, manners, ceremonies and superstitions, a study which is sadly so far neglected by historians, sociologists and anthropologists.

Life of the Portuguese soldiers in India had been described in records. Concerning the soldiers who were bachelors it is said that they went out in the summer to swim in the tanks and spent very long time lying on the water. They were very stately dressed and went very gravely along the streets within the town with their slaves or men hired for the purpose who wore a hat against the heat of the sun and rain water drop. There were many Indians who were daily hired for these purposes and paid wages by the Portuguese who had no slaves. These soldiers dwelt in groups at least ten or twelve in a house, where they had among them a slave or one or two hired Indians, who did domestic work and served them besides washing their shirts. The house of the soldiers was provided with four or five stools with a table for their use, and every man had a separate bed. Their food was prepared mainly with meat, fish and rice boiled in water. Thus they were happy and well pleased. They had one or two good suits made of silk which they wore for functions. When one soldier went abroad, the others stayed at home. They sat at home wearing their shirts and a pair of linen clothes for the reason of the great heat in India. Soldiers lent their apparel to others who had occasion to go twenty times in one day out of the house. The soldiers also likewise put off their clothes, as often as they came back home again. These soldiers were helped by a captain who gave money to buy dress for them. In the summer season, the soldiers were attracted during the day time to sail in the fleets to sea, but by night they had to be back on duty.[2] All soldiers received their maintenance allowance from the treasury of Portuguese Viceroy in India. Some of these Portuguese soldiers had developed illegal contacts with women, and also with some wives of the Indian Christians. They therefore bestowed liberal rewards and gifts to satisfy and fulfill their unchaste and filthy desire, which they knew very well how to accomplish, and secretly bring to pass.[3]

While turning our attention next towards the *casados*, some ceremonies followed by them may be worth mentioning here. When a new born child was to be christened, the Portuguese *casados* led to the church with horses in a group. There came the priest after whom followed two altar boys on foot while one was holding a great silver guilted vessel full of bread baked like cracklings, which in Portugal called *Rosquilhos*, (rusks) and the other altar boy had a big wax candle, well made and gilded in a big plate with some coins of gold and silver, as an offering. At the time of baptism, the third altar boy had a silver guilted vessel containing salt in one of his hands, and a lamp of the same stuff in his other hand, in addition to very rich and costly towels on the shoulders. The priest then baptised the child which was covered with roses. After administering the baptism, two palanquins covered with a costly mantle was brought to the church in which the midwife with the child left the spot. Thus the ceremony of baptism ended in the church. It was again in the same manner as the Portuguese came were brought back home. There they had the music and several persons ran and leaped with their horses before the window of the house where all the people who came and sat for the celebration. This was the manner and customs of the Portuguese at the time of baptism of the new born child in India since they followed the same custom in Portugal too. [4]

Regarding the Portuguese marriage rituals in India, it is mentioned that when they had any weddings, all the friends and neighbours came together. Every man appeared on horseback, and any one who did not have a horse at least borrowed one for coming to the function. All of them wore very costly dresses. Every man had his hat. They rode altogether on horse back in good order to the church with their servants. The sons, parents and friends went in procession followed at last by the bridegroom who came in between two boys, after him followed the bride between two girls. Each went in their Palanquin which was made of very costly things and well decorated. After that came the slaves, both men and women in troupes. In the same order of procession the couples were also brought back from the church to the house. The priest blessed the couples during the Holy Mass and the wedding ceremony took place there. While the marriage party passed through the streets, the neighbours leaned upon to look out of the windows of their houses for a glance at the couples. They sprinkled rose-water upon the bride and bridegroom, besides various other sweet smelling scents in liquid form. They also threw flowers like roses, and some items like sugar-candy and corn. In the mean time their slaves played upon their trumphet in the most pleasant and melodious manner to hear, till they reached the house where the bridegroom resided. With great reverence and courtesy, the Portuguese bowed down their bodies and they took leave of the company of the new couples. The bride and the bridegroom went up and sat near a window, and then began the horsemen that led them to the church who came in honour of the married couple, one after another and ran twice or thrice before the people in the house, continuously while the music was being played. This being ended, they all passed before the window where the bride and bridegroom sat. The bride and bridegroom drank a cup of wine, juice or water with all those who were present for the marriage. After some salutations and congratulations to the newly married couple, they ate food and departed. Then the bride and bridegroom alone remained along with three or four of their nearest friends and relatives who had their dinner with them including meat. Thus there used to be merry making for a long time in the marriage function. The newly wedded couples were left free only two hours before the sun-set for having an intimate dialogue. Then the couples were allowed to go to bed.[5] Thus the *casados* retained their traditional Portuguese customs and rituals while celebrating the marriages in India.

With reference to Portuguese dress, habits and behaviour pattern, it is recorded that the Portuguese were always very clean in their dress and maintained their houses well. Both men and women wore clean linen, for that matter they changed shirts and smocks everyday. Their slaves and servants were also clean like that in their wears. They did this chiefly because of the climate and the great heat prevailed during the day in India.[6] With regard to their behaviour it is mentioned that while walking in the streets, the Portuguese went very softly and slowly, forwards in stepping. They walked with great pride and vainglorious way with a slave who carried a great hat or umbrella over their heads, to keep the sun and rain away from them. During the rainy season the Portuguese also commonly took a boy with them in the street who had a scarlet or some other cloth with him, to cast over the rain water falling upon them.[7] Whenever the Portuguese met each other in the streets, they allowed a good space before they came together. They stopped their movement and pushed their foot and saluted each other with their hats by removing it from the head and holding it in their hands, almost touching the ground. Likewise when they came into the church their slaves ran at first and prepared the stools ready for sitting and these slaves only stood by their side. The slaves always bowed down with their bodies and did great reverence to the Portuguese masters.[8]

Whenever a Portuguese went to visit a neighbour, relative or friend in his house, although he may be one of the principal gentleman of the place, or an ordinary soldier, or any other simple man, it was the usual custom followed by them that the owner of the house came near the door of his house, with his hat in his hand, and with great courtesy to receive him who came to pay visit. Then he took the guest up to the hall or chamber of the house, where he planned to meet and speak to him. He offered the guest a chair to sit down, and there he himself sat along with him. Then he enquired the reason of his visit and asked him as to what he would like to eat and drink. Having understood finally when the guest would like to take leave of the house, he would bring him down again up to the door of the house.[9] Thus cordial hospitality was prevalent among the Portuguese nobles including the *casados*.

Mestiçõ women in India were very little seen in the public and mostly they spent their time within the house. This is prevailed chiefly because of the typical Indian domestic orientation in which these women had lived for centuries together in India although these native women were married to Portuguese merchants and soldiers. These mestiçõ women went out seldom, unless it be to church, or to visit their friends. Whenever they went out, they were well provided so as to not to be seen, for they were carried in a Palanquin covered with a mat or other cloth.[10] When these *mestiçõ* women went to church, or visited any friend, they used to put on very costly dress with bracelets of gold, and rings upon their fingers and arms, all beset with costly gems and pearls, and at their ear hung laces full of jewels. Their clothes were of damask, velvet, and cloth of gold, for silk was the worst thing they wore. Within the house they went bare headed with a waist-coat, from their shoulders covered up to their navels, and being so fine that one might see all their body through it, and downwards they had a painted cloth wrapped three or four times about their bodies. These clothes were very good, some of them being very costly wrought with loom work, and diverse figures and flowers of all colours. All the rest of the body was naked without any hose, but only footed in a pair of clogs or slippers. This was their manner of dress in the house, both the old and young, rich and poor, because they went out very little. What all the *mestiçõ* wanted was that the slaves both men and women to take them inside the house or to the church.[11]

Regarding food, eating and drinking habits, it is said that the Portuguese *mestiçõ* women ate no bread or very little, nor even their slaves. They refused to eat bread not because it was costly but because they are so used to eat only rice, that they desire nothing. They take rice with water and also with some salt fish, or with a kind of fruit called *Manga*, (raw mangoes) soaked in salt and vinegar or with some other composition of fish, meat and generally curry poured upon it. The Indians ate food only with their hands, for they ate nothing with spoons. If they see any man eating with spoon they laughed at him. When they want to drink water they took certain pots made of black earth, very fine and thin, much like those that the Portuguese in Lisbon used for flower pots, having in the neck thereof a partition full of holes with a spout.[12] When the Indians drank water, they used to hold the pot on high, and touch it not with their mouth, but the water runs from the spout falls into their mouth, never spilling a drop, and this they do for the sake of cleanliness, because no other person should put it to his mouth. When anybody came newly from Portugal, and then if he began to drink water in the Indian style, they spilled water all over the chest and the Indians at this time took great pleasure and laughed at them for not knowing how to behave in such a manner.[13]

Regarding the husband-wife relations in the Indo-Portuguese families, it is mentioned that the men were very jealous of their wives, for they will never liked to bring any man into their house, however a special friend he may be, it is impossible to see the wife or the daughters of the man. Unless the situation warranted for some important conversation or if the guest was a married man who came with his wife to the house it was possible to meet the wife and daughters. Whenever the Indo-Portuguese families went out together to some place to sport and solace, they were always well guarded by their slaves, both men and women for their purpose of safety and service. If any man came to the door to ask for the master of the house, wife and their daughters immediately ran to hide themselves, and leave the slave who stood at the door to answer the guest. No man had been allowed to meet within their house, even the wife and daughters how near the kinsman so ever he may be. Being once fifteen years of age, not even their own brothers and sons visit the women folk within the house, because they have certain separate chambers and places in their house where they lived. The women always sent cooked food, meat and other provisions from the kitchen to the dinning hall and they did not attend or serve them while eating. This prohibition of men-women meeting in the house existed because it had been the practice in India to marry uncle's son to aunt's daughter and the cousin brother with his cousin sister.[14]

There were superstitions followed by Indians found mention in the records. In Santhome of Mylapore there was a Portuguese gentleman called João Carvalho, who had been endowed by nature with such length of arm that his hands reached below his knees. The Hindus of the place whenever they met him they immediately prostrated themselves before him and worshipped him as they did to their Hindu idols, because it has been written in the Hindu prophecies that a person with long arms should be venerated like an idol. João Carvalho became so popular in the town that the Portuguese missionaries and officials summoned him to appear before the Inquisition. After giving valid and very sound reasons he was released on the condition imposed that whenever any Hindu prostrated himself on the ground in front of him, he was asked at once to prostrate himself likewise. This made poor João Carvalho not to go out of his house during the day, for fear of undergoing this penance.[15]

Similarly we also find another superstition that whenever a robbery or theft took place the Hindus went to sorcerers to recover what had been lost. These sorcerers took a brass bowl, and put into it some grains of uncooked rice and some flowers. Then they recited some incantations over it and took another bowl of the same metal and began to beat with a short stick. They said some words softly and the first bowl with the flowers began to move itself very slowly. Finally it arrived at the place where the thing lost was lying. The thief, seeing the crowd and hearing the sound of the basin ran away abandoning everything. The owner, after detailing the marks of his property, carried it away, while the rest of the fugitive's goods were seized by the police.[16]

Tamil Social and Religious Practices

The method and practice of fortune-telling in Tamilnadu is described by the Jesuits. It is mentioned that a basket is placed on the head of the person who consulted the gypsy. She after uttering incantations removed the basket with a blow on the head.[17] Further it was in practice that to show that if the individuals had not committed the fault of which, when they are accused of, the individuals had to take in their hands a red-hot-iron bar or to plunge their hand in boiling butter to testify the truth.[18] The practice of Sati which was in vogue was also described. Regarding a second marriage by a Hindu in Kandalur, it is stated that the permission of the first wife was required, only on the grounds that there was no issue of child after the first marriage.[19] People affected with small-pox were thrown out of their village and it was a custom followed in *Marava* region.

Regarding religious practices we find that entering the Hindu temples with sandals on foot was considered as a sign of contempt. Prostrating at full length by oneself on the ground was a sign of greeting. Visit to pilgrim centers for the cure of diseases and giving alms to the poor were widely prevalent. Devotees branded their shoulders with the sign of their God *Perumal* with a red-hot-iron. *Mahamagam* festival in Kumbakonam was celebrated once in twelve years and it is mentioned in the year 1683 in the Jesuit Annual Letter.[20] Sun worship was prevalent among the Hindus. Similarly *Sakthi* was also worshipped. Various types of sacrifices offered by the Hindus are mentioned in these letters. The Christians knelt down and prayed while the Hindus prostrated on the floor or stood. Tamils also had the usual practice of taking bath during solar eclipse.

Tamil Customs and Manners

With the advent of the Portuguese, the names and surnames came to be adopted by the *paravas*. The Luso-Tamil families in the Pearl Fishery Coast took the surnames such as Correia, Miranda,

Machado, Dias, etc., and these families had definite Christian cultural traits. It is certain that some of the habits of the *paravas* originated due to the cosmopolitan atmosphere that prevailed in the area.

It has been reported by the Jesuits that Tamils asked all sorts of questions and wished to know everything from them which was a common defect in the country.[21] Tamils also generally went out and moved frequently even in heavy rain as noticed in Gingee region. They stream across the rivers too when floods occurred and it was commented by a Jesuit missionary that the Europeans feared wetting their feet when it rained and they generally stayed at home. Killing a Brahmin was crime. Brahmins received chord in a function held as an insignia of his priesthood. It has been mentioned that a Brahmin at Tiruvannamalai begged the Jesuit missionaries to contribute towards the function and it was a practice to collect and raise funds through this means. Selling of oxen for slaughter by the Portuguese was prohibited and complaints were lodged against the Christians of Tharangambadi and Nagapattinam.[22] It had been noticed by the Jesuits that making quarrels and taking poison was a common feature in Tamilnadu. Astrology played an important role in the Tamil society. A great comet which appeared in Europe in December in 1680 was also noticed in Tamilnadu. It was of the same size, and that was longer than a quarter of a sphere. It was the opinion of that time that the comet had been a threat to punish the entire world.

Tamil Christian Marriages

According to Tamil customs, If at all a man wanted to marry for the second time for valid reasons, such as having no issue by the first marriage, the husband had to get the permission of the first wife with whom he was actually living.[23] Thus monogamy is followed in the society. Therefore polygamy and concubinage was not allowed. The new Christians also followed the same like the Hindus in the case of marriage and the Jesuits helped them to develop their knowledge on Holy Family and explained their attitude towards family life.

Marriages were celebrated according to the Tamil customs and manners by the Christians. It was but insisted that the *tali* given to a married Christian woman on her wedding day might contain a picture of saint or image of Our Lady or Cross but not a picture of a Hindu God *Pillaiyar*, the idol presiding the wedlock. similarly several ceremonies used at wedding such as the twig of the *arasu*, the circlets drawn against the evil eye or against ill luck, the number and quality of the dishes were ordered to be omitted by the Christians. Regarding the chord made of 108 threads, and dyed in saffron with which the *tali* was tied around the neck both the colour and the number were condemned as superstitious.[24]

Records point out several Tamil Christian social customs that were followed in Pondicherry. The captain of the peons got married to the daughter of Manuel at Ariyankuppam (located in the environs of Pondicherry) in August 1701 where it had been noted that Hindu practices were followed. The bride and the groom first went to the church where the Christian ceremonies were conducted. In front of the house a *pandal* was erected facing the East, where the Hindu ceremonies were conducted which was adorned with plenty of mango leaves where a branch of pipal tree was planted and the pit was filled with a gallon of cow's milk and water. The branch was smeared with sandal paste, red lead and saffron and flowers hung on the plant. As Hindus believed that Vishnu lived in the pipal tree and his spouse in the form of wind came as gently as possible to remain united with him, the idea of that inseparable relation between the god and goddess was wished for the newly wed Christian couples. Although at the foot of the pipal tree, an altar was prepared and the catechist acted as the master of the ceremonies, a coconut was broken to ward of the evil. The catechist took the *tali* placed in the altar incensed the statue of Mary and handed it over to the bridegroom who tied it around the neck of the spouse. A number of other Tamil customs like using rice, water and coconut water were performed by the catechist with the approval of the catholic priest. Thus Christians continued to follow native customs and Hindu practices side by side with Christian ceremonies.[25]

Tamil Christian Social Customs in Pondicherry

There is a need to study how the Jesuits helped the Tamil Christians to celebrate the feasts of saints, and visit places of Christian pilgrimage and introduced cultural changes with conversions. Christian *Paraiyars* were not allowed to partake in Hindu festivals especially to sing, play music and drum or dance at the Hindu feasts. Further all Christians were not allowed to read books on Hindu religion without special permission. Christian women during the period of menses should not be forbidden to confess and much less to come to the church. Christians were forbidden the white or saffron marks usually made on the forehead or other parts of the body. Some superstitions like the breaking of coconuts to invite prosperity or to keep off misfortune was to be discontinued by the Christians.[26]

The child marriages were strictly forbidden. Those children already married under age were to live with their parents until they came of age. Christian marriages had to be celebrated according to tridentine prescriptions. The missionaries had always stood up against child marriages because it was Hindu inheritance. Further the custom of holding a public feast when a girl reached puberty was ordered to be discontinued. This was because Hindu rituals took place when a girl reached puberty in Christian congregations.[27]

Funeral

Although the rite of burning the dead body was generally followed by Hindus, the Christians adopted the burial ceremonies. The funeral of the Christians also included some Hindu customs. When Andre, the broker of French East India Company died in 1701 a few betel leaves were put into his mouth. The dead body was washed and wrapped in a cotton cloth and placed on a throne of canes beautifully decorated with mirrors and betel leaves and with banana plants at the four corners of the throne. Men carried it in the shoulders to the sound of trumphets and fireworks. The burial procession was almost like a marriage procession. On the thirtieth day after the death, there was another similar procession when a throne decked with mirrors was prepared with a cross on the top. A half coconut filled with cow's ghee with a burning wick was kept in rice flour. The burning wick symbolized fire of heaven. Candles were lit at the corners of the tomb and they had *Rituale Romanum* with the hymn "*Libera me Domine, de morte eterna, in die illa tremenda; Quando coeli movendi sunt et terra*".[28]

The complaint on the Jesuits came from the missionaries of the Franciscan order and it was that they allowed the native converts to practice Hindu customs (*suis alumnis varia gentilismum redolentia permiseurant*). They wrote to the Pope and the papal legate and plenipotentiary, Mgr. Maillaird de Tournon came to Pondicherry in 1704 to investigate into the matter. In principle he had to settle the matters of the Malabar Rites once and for all, but his presence in India had a wider significance. By establishing uniform rules for the rites acceptable in Roman Catholic churches in South India, de Tournon hoped to close widening gap between the Portuguese missions and the missionaries under the *Congregatio de Propaganda Fide*. Mgr. Tournon decided to accept only a few of the rites which had been developed by the Jesuits, but on the other hand not to accept the criticism voiced by the Capuchins. Thus tension arose because of different views and attitudes chiefly between the principles of consolidation and Indianization, clash between the missionary orders of broad-mindedness Vs narrow-mindedness besides Westernization Vs Indianization.

The Archbishop of Goa was informed of what was happening in Pondicherry and on 20 December 1704 he wrote to Rome that he had delayed the execution of the decree because he did not want to ruin of the Christian missions. Fr. Francisco Laynez arrived Rome on 8 November 1706 and he was received by the Pope. He made his written remarks on the decree of Tournon and some of these were dangerous to meddle with the deep rooted caste prejudices and customs of the Tamils. However He had prepared his "*Defenso Indicarum Missionum*" which was printed by the Carmel press in 1707. Later the same was published in Mylapore when he was appointed as the bishop of Mylapore. Thus several social changes were introduced by the Portuguese missionaries and these had taken place for suiting to the needs of the Tamils and also to the convenience. The famous Papal decree "*Compertum exploratum que*" dated 24 August 1734 had the decree of Tournon modified. Pope Benedict XIV issued a bull in 1744 in which he confirmed the decision made by Tournon.[29]

Finally, it may be said that sati was never committed by the Christians as they practised monogamy. It may not be out of place here to speak of sati that was practised by the Hindu nobility in

Tamilnadu as seen by the Portuguese missionaries. Sati committed in Tiruchi is described by Fr. Balthazar da Costa in his letter.[30] Missionaries also throw light on the various methods of committing Sati. In the first method the woman is buried alive when the earth reaches her neck and she was strangled which was noticed by Fr. Balthazar da Costa mentioned in his letter written from Thanjavur on 8 September 1653. In another case Fr. Emmanuel Martins describes in his letter written from Moramangalam on 14 October 1626 to Fr. Mendonca living in Madurai where it is stated that women were stretched on the funeral pyre by the side of the corpse of their husbands and burnt alive to ashes.[31] The missionaries were silent witnesses to this social institution of sati found in royal courts and they could not do anything since it did not fall within their jurisdiction in spreading the message of Gospel in Tamilnadu.

The Portuguese official and missionary control in the Tamil Coast was not so strong and effective as in Goa. The Tamil Christians were therefore permitted to follow certain meaningful customs of the Hindus more especially by the Jesuits as if to compensate for the excesses of the Inquisition in Goa. This facilitated large scale conversions in the Tamil society by the Portuguese Jesuit missionaries. It is reported that the newly converted Catholics planted the branch of the tree in a pit dug where one gallon of milk was poured at the time of wedding. The branches were marked with sandal and saffron.[32] The Hindu belief behind it was that Lord Vishnu and Goddess *Bhagavathi* were thus united and became inseparable. However an altar with a crucifix was also made for prayers in the house. The *thali,* with a pendant crafted with Christian motifs was allowed to be used by the bridegroom to tie the nuptial knot around the neck of the bride. In fact on 23 June 1704, a pastoral letter was issued by the Bishop of Mylapore permitting Christian brides to wear *thali* with a cross or image of Mary, Mother of Jesus.[33] The matter was settled after consulting four *Brahmins* who were brought from the countryside by Fr. Spiritus of Tours and Thomas of Poitiers in Pondicherry to give advice on the *thali.*[34]

The adaptation of the local Hindu customs in the liturgy was introduced by Fr. Spiritus at Pondicherry who lived in the early Seventeenth Century. Thus Hindu converts were allowed to retain many of their former customs and practices. Many abuses were said to have crept into this practice and several complaints were lodged with the Holy See who decided to send an Apostolic visitor to make an on-the-spot study of the problem.[85] The Apostolic Vicar, Cardinal Charles Maillard de Tournon (1668-1711), who arrived at Pondicherry on 6 November 1703 made a detailed study.[86] On 8 July 1704, the famous Decree of Sixteen Articles banning some of the Hindu practices followed by the native Christians was issued.[87] The decree was finally published on 23 June 1704 by de Tournon, the Papal Legate in Pondicherry contained the following: (A) In the administration of Baptism no sacramental rituals (i.e. the application of saliva, placing the salt in the mouth of the child and the insufflation or breathing) to be omitted. (B) The baptismal names are to be taken from the Roman Martyrology and not from the Hindu Gods. (C) Similarly the sign of the Cross and the indications of sacred objects are not to be translated in a faulty manner, but are to be used either in Latin or in some Indian language, provided the translations or the explanations thereof are exact. (D) Children should be baptized as early as possible. Those parents who delayed their children's baptism were to be penalised. (E) Child marriages were strictly forbidden. Those children who were already married should not live together until they come of age. Marriages had to be celebrated according to the Tridentine prescriptions. (F) The Christians should not wear *thali* bearing the image of *Pillayar*, the idol inscribed in the pendant. They may wear the thali bearing the Cross or the image of Our Lady. (G) Regarding the chord, made of 108 threads and dyed in saffron with which the *thali* was tied round the neck, both the colour and the number of threads were condemned as superstitious. (H) Several ceremonies connected with weddings (such as planting of the Pipal tree, the circlets drawn against the evil eye or against ill luck, the number and quality of the dishes to be served on the occasion) to be examined, corrected or omitted. (I) The breaking of a coconut to invoke prosperity and to ward off misfortunes to be discontinued. (J) During the menses, women should not be forbidden to perform the sacrament of confession much less to attend the service in the church. (K) The custom of holding a public feast when a girl attains puberty should be discontinued. (L) As the physicians even visit the pariahs when they are sick, so too the missionaries should not scruple to visit them and administer the sacraments to them even in their huts. (M) Christian musicians should not be allowed to play music or perform dances during Hindu festivals. (N) The use of ashes prepared from the cowdung was forbidden. Similarly the use of sacred ashes or saffron powder on the forehead or other parts of the body was forbidden. (O) The Tridentine prescriptions should be followed as regards baths. (P) The reading of texts of 'false' religions, superstitions and obscenity was forbidden.

Another custom of the Catholics was that the dead body was placed on a decorated chariot in the Hindu manner and taken on a procession with musicians in attendance. Some of those who joined the funeral procession, accompanied the dead body by dancing. All this was typical of the traditional Hindu practice. However the Jesuit priest followed walking in the funeral procession along with the altar boys carrying the cross and candles in front.[38]

It may be said that the Portuguese *casados* had retained and followed all their own customs followed in Portugal. Those Indians married to Portuguese i.e., the *mestiçōes* only began to adopt and mix the Indian and Portuguese manners and customs but they also did not give up the Indian customs in total. There had been an intermingling of customs, manners and ceremonies followed in the Indo-Portuguese families. Some superstitions followed in India were recorded by the Portuguese since they were surprised to see it. It may be said that the Christian and Hindu rituals were not allowed to be mixed for the Portuguese missionaries in India were very strict.

Notes and References

1. On Portuguese society in general, See M.N. Pearson, "The people and politics of Portuguese India during Sixteenth century" in Daniel Alder and Waren Dean, (eds.,) *Essays Concerning the Socio-Economic History of Brazil and Portuguese India*, Gainesville, University Press of Florida, 1977, pp.2-4. See also for details on the Portuguese society of the Coromandel Coast, S. Jeyaseela Stephen, *The Coromandel Coast and its Hinterland; Economy, Society and Political System, 1500-1600*, Manohar, New Delhi, 1997, pp.182-186. See also his another work, *Portuguese in the Tamil Coast: Historical Explorations in Commerce and Culture,*

1507-1749, Navajyothi Publications, Pondicherry 1998, See other related articles, S. Jeyaseela Stephen, "Societal changes: Portuguese and the native Christians in Tamil Country (cir 1537-1759)" in (ed.,) K.S. Mathew, T.R. De Sousa & Pius Malekandathil, *The Portuguese and Socio-Economic Changes in India, 1500-1800*, Tellicherry, 2001, pp. 479-513. See also, "Social Life of the Portuguese and the Luso-Tamils in Mylapore and Nagapattinam during the 16th & 17th centuries, *Bharta Vidya*, Vol. II, 2003, pp.7-14.

2. John Van Linschoten, *The Voyages of John Van Linschoten to the East Indies*, 2 Vols, London, 1885, Vol. I, pp. 199-201. Francis Xavier remarked that "all the soldiers are at sea with the fleet and the merchants keep sailing from one place to another selling their wares, for all here, since they are not lords of the land but only of the sea live on trade" See the letter to Ignatius of Loyola written from Goa on 20 September 1542 in Joseph Costelloe, *The Letters and Instructions of Francis Xavier*, Anand, 1993, document no. 17, p. 59.
3. *Ibid.*, Vol. I, p. 201.
4. *Ibid.*, Vol. I. pp.198-199.
5. *Ibid.*, Vol. I, pp. 196-198.
6. *Ibid.*, Vol. I, p. 193.
7. *Ibid.*, Vol. I, p. 193.
8. *Ibid.*, Vol. I, p. 194.
9. *Ibid.*, Vol. I. p. 195.
10. *Ibid.*, Vol. I, p. 205.
11. *Ibid.*, Vol. I, p. 206.
12. *Ibid.*, Vol. I, pp. 206-207.
13. *Ibid.*, Vol. p. 207.
14. *Ibid.*, Vol. I, pp. 208-209.
15. Nicolao Manucci, (ed.,) William Irvine, *Storia do Mogur,1653-1708*, 4 Vols, reprint, New Delhi, 1981, Vol. III, p.140.
16. Nicolau Manucci, *op.cit.*, Vol. III, p. 213.
17. S. Jeyaseela Stephen, *Letters of the Portuguese Jesuits, op.cit.*, p.7.
18. *Ibid.*, p. 43 & p.198
19. *Ibid.*, p. 85.
20. *Ibid*, p. 305.
21. *Ibid.*, p.71.
22. *Ibid.*, pp. 291-292.
23. MPJA, Letter of Andre Freyre written from Kolei dated 6 May 1677.

24. Archivio della S. Congregazionae Propaganda Fide, (hereafter APF) Rome, Mss Acta, Vol. 88, fl. 123-124.
25. Nicolau Manucci, *op.cit.*, Vol. II, pp. 338-342.
26. APF, Mss Acta 88, fl. 123-124.
27. *Ibid.*
28. *Ibid*, Vol. II, pp. 350-353. Manucci remarks that as for the Christians who lived in the region under the Padroado control they had been absolutely forbidden by the Holy Inquisition to follow Hindu manners and native customs. See, Manucci, Vol. III, pp. 356.
29. S. Jeyaseela Stephen, *Portuguese in the op. cit.*, p. 362.
30. ARSI, Mss. Goa, 53, ff.163-184. 185-206.
31. ARSI, Mss. Goa 48, ff. 228-240.
32. Nicolao Manucci, *op.cit.*, Vol. III, pp. 321-325. See also MPJA, *Documents Bertrand,* Vol. II, document 219. It deals with matters relating the custom of pipal tree and tali.
33. D. Ferroli, *The Jesuits in Malabar,* Bangalore, 1951, Vol.II, pp. 430-431.
34. MPJA, *Documents Bertrand,* Vol. II, document no. 238.
35. Nicolao Manucci, *op.cit.*, Vol. III, pp. 333-334, 326-327.
36. Bertrand, *Memoirs Historiques Sur les Missions,* Paris, 1862, Vol. III, pp. 249-367. See, Archives de 1' Archeveche Pondichery-Cuddalore, (hereafter AAPC) Armorie, 1-6 chemise, I.B. (18 Siecle, 1704-1799).
37. APF, *Mss. Acta,* Vol. 88, fl. 124. See also, MPJA, *Documents Bertrand,* Vol. 1, documents 47 and 48.
38. APF, SC, *Indie Orientali e Cina,* Vol. 8, fls. 220-227.

6

Social Life of the Portuguese Casados and Mestições on the Tamil Coast

The arrival of the Portuguese in India and their direct overseas trade conducted from the ports of Cochin and Goa with Lisbon in Portugal during the sixteenth century had brought enormous changes in the maritime trading pattern of the West Coast. Their presence on the East Coast of India had mainly introduced various dimensions of cultural changes since they had much social interaction with the natives during the sixteenth and seventeenth centuries.[1] It is worth mentioning at the outset here, about the social changes found among the native fishermen, the Paravas who were converted to Christianity by the Portuguese in Tamilnadu. Some of these Paravas had moved slowly from their original profession of pearl fishing and began to emerge as coastal traders along with the Portuguese *casados* and private merchants who encouraged them to conduct business in salt, chank, shells, rice, etc. along the ports of the Eastern Coast of India. We find that there existed two groups of the Tamil fishermen who came to be called. as *Mesaikarars* (those who used table) and *kottukarars* (those who used over-coat) at that time.[2] With the conversion of the people of various other castes in the Tamil hinterland by the Portuguese missionaries, significant socio-cultural changes had also been brought about at that time and I have traced so far only the societal changes found among the Indian Christian converts both in the

Tamil Coast and hinterland.[3] We shall examine how Tamil social life during this period could have perhaps influenced the Portuguese. It is also to be seen how the Portuguese were exposed to the social institutions such as marriage, religion, etc., in the Tamil coast. It is worth analysing also here how the Luso-Tamil community or the so called Indo-Portuguese society flourished on the Tamil Coast with many mixed marriages, and when did actually the process of social change began to occur and the inter-relations between the Luso- Tamil groups began to play a significant role and had great impact in the society of India of that time.

It is a fact that Portuguese men alone were allowed to sail in their ships to India by the Kings of Portugal till the middle of the sixteenth century. It is to be noted here that the second Portuguese Viceroy Affonso de Albuquerque had therefore encouraged mixed marriages after the capture of Goa in 1510 to increase the Portuguese population in India. Portuguese women were permitted to undertake voyages to India only after a very late period.[4] Many Portuguese soldiers and traders under such circumstances happened to marry Indian women and settled down in the various ports of India. They had lived with their families in the several trading settlements on the Tamil coast such as Vedalai, Tuticorin, Nagapattinam, Devanampattinam and Santhome of Mylapore. In a record we find that here were fifty families in 1537. The strength of the Portuguese *casados* (married men) increased to sixty in 1538 and one hundred in 1544.[5] In the end of 1540s there were 6007 Portuguese in India and 600 lived in the Tamil Coast.[6] These Portuguese *mestiçoes* (children born of Portuguese men and Indian, women) and the *casados* (Portuguese married settlers) families had some salient and peculiar features since it had different language, culture and above all religion.[7] The Indo-Portuguese society was a mixed one that adopted various native customs and manners besides certain Portuguese traits. .

Social Life of the Portuguese in the Tamil Coast

Many documents mention that some Portuguese who came to India as criminals and they were sent away from Portugal to serve as soldiers. These social rejects of the West, many of them deserted their military service in Goa and came to Tamil coast to trade and conduct free life. They married native women and lived in the Tamil coast. Jesuit missionary letters written in 1559 and 1563 note that the Portuguese merchants at Santhome engaged in unlawful trading practices, their chief interest being to make money, they were corrupt and their moral standards were poor.[8] The unruly activities of these Portuguese had necessitated the king of Portugal to appoint an *ouvidor* (judge) who lived at Santhome.[9] Criminal activities of the various Portuguese men could be traced back to their background as criminals and deserters in Portugal. The Portuguese missionaries and officials could not also control them at that time.[10]

There were many oppressions and injustices at Santhome of Mylapore. Portuguese slew one another. They dug and fortified trenches in the streets, furnishing them with cannon. They spent much money in maintaining soldiers. If anyone passed carelessly down the street, they shot at him with their matchlocks. They obtained rewards for their evil deeds. They paid no respect even to the clergy and the religious, shooting down men during the religious processions. Owing to the rising of such activities in the town, the convents and churches were barricaded. Friars were forced to go in person to fetch water.[11]

It is mentioned that, besides laming of an innocent person who was passing in the street, orders were issued to fire gun at the servant. This order was given when the person was praying to God while having a rosary in hand. The servant fired and reported to his master that the passerby was lamed. He looked through the window, repeating the Lord's Prayer "Our Father in Heaven". He saw the injured man who was making all efforts in the hope of saving his life. He stopped saying the Lord's Prayer but gave a second order to fire another bullet to finish the killing man.[12] Thus we find the atrocities committed by these Portuguese in the town of Mylapore.

It is interesting to know some of the other happenings of that period too. There was a Portuguese priest who came from Manila to Mylapore, a good theologian whose name was Luis Perriera. He had brought with him some money for the purpose of helping his parents who lived in Daman on the West coast. About the same time there was a newly-arrived Portuguese man by name Martim de Lemos who had left Portugal, because of being a highway robber and a lawbreaker there. In Mylapore, he had no financial resources, and so he begged help from those who lived there. The reply the Portuguese in Mylapore gave was that he might search for his expenses wherever and whatever he could on his own.[13] Finding that he could carry out his plot easily and securely, one day at seven 0' clock in the morning, Lemos went into the house of Fr. Luis Perriera. He pointed a pistol at his breast and ordered four *kaffirs* to blind him. Breaking open the boxes, he robbed all that was in them and left immediately for the English settlement of Madras. At this time the Portuguese officials of the town were in the churchyard of the *Madre de Deus* (Mother of God) Church, on the way to Holy Mass. The urgent report of this incident was brought saying that Martin de Lemos was robbing the priest. Some of them wanted to run to the spot, but Antonio Palha, one of those men who governed the town of Mylapore said, "Your Honours are excused from taking that trouble, for I will see to it. He and the rest went leisurely to their own houses, giving free time for the robber to carry out his attempt and get away in safety".

Thus we find that even priests were not spared from being robbed away for there was a lot of greed for money and there was no morality among the Portuguese of that period.

Social Life of the Luso-Tamil Families

An event that took place in the Portuguese settlement of Nagapattinam may be worth mentioning here. There was a man called João Soares Cove, married to a very pretty woman. He went on a journey and left his wife at home in Nagapattinam. There was another man, rich and influential named Christovão Pexeto, who was married already and this man fell in love with the wife of João Soares Cove. He sent her a message that he wished to be her friend. As an honourable woman she declined to accept, remained at home, and never came out, because of fear of this Christovão Pexeto. Paying neither respect nor heed to the Portuguese citizen of Nagapattinam, he entered the woman's house in open day and used force, went there as if it were his own house, carried away the woman in his palanquin and traversed the town. He mocked at the Portuguese judge and the inhabitants and showed that he was afraid of no one.[14]

When João Soares Cove returned from his journey and landed on the seashore at Nagapattinam, his friends told him of what had passed. Seeing that he had neither strength nor force to obtain satisfaction for the affront, he never entered the house, but started at once for Goa to report the Portuguese Viceroy. There he presented himself before Dom Filippe Mascarenhas, the then Portuguese Viceroy of India, made complaint of the injury done to him by Christovão Pexeto. On becoming aware of that man's insolent conduct, the viceroy gave a letter enjoining on the Judge and the Assembly of the Elder men (*os Eleitos de Negapatão*) of Nagapattinam that in one way or the other they must deprive the disturber and punish him. Christovão Pexeto knowing this, withdrew from the town, and settled in the' country of a Hindu ruler, not far away from the place of Nagapattinam. Finding that they could not carry out their orders, the Judge and residents sent a present to the Hindu prince and a letter requesting him to make Christovão Pexeto to them alive. They also paid money to the Hindu ruler to make over the insolent fellow in chains into the hands of the Portuguese citizens of Nagapattinam. Christovão Pexeto was captured and sent to Nagapattinam. On reaching the town, Pexeto instead of showing repentence and asking pardon from him, called João Soares Cove, a cuckold and other unseemly names. His wrath rising higher and higher, João Soares Cove, the injured man flung himself on his enemy with a pointed knife and stabbed him to the heart. Instead of commending his soul to God in these his last throes, Pexeto continued his abuse until he expired. João Soares Cove filled his two hands with the blood flowing from the wound and drank it, then smeared his body, face and head with the blood, finally mutilating the dead man. The wife of João Soares Cove by this time knowing the incident had fled to Tharangambadi (Tranquebar) the Danish settlement. Her servant boy helped her to reach that place. João Soares Cove on reaching home, found out that his wife had gone, and that the servant too was not there, he left the town and hid near the road. When the servant was returning from Nagapattinam, he killed him. For several days he went about all bloody, solely to prove that he had wreaked vengeance for his wrongs.[16] Thus we have an instance of love and murder found in the Luso-Tamil society.

Another event that took place in Santhome of Mylapore may also be noted here and we may understand better the social life of the Luso-Tamils. There was a lady called Justa Padrao in Mylapore who slept in a bed of which the head was adorned with little bells "of gold and silver' and these served at times to amuse her. She was so rich that she had her own room swept with brooms of gold and other places with brooms of silver. It is to be mentioned that brooms in India had handles of fine twigs and are not like those of Europe. When this lady left the house, whether to go church or pay a visit, two women servants always preceded her with golden censers to incense her. She had other special censers of silver to lend to the church on solemn occasions. From the little that had been said, the reader could conceive in what grandeur the greater part of well these Portuguese women had lived. The woman spoken above when she came to die was so miserably off that she had not even a piece of cloth to make a shroud, and at her burial she was wrapped in a reed mat which was the practice among the Tamils.[16] Thus luxury and grandeur was practised by these Luso-Tamil women and finally misery and death followed them.

In the same town of Santhome of Mylapore, there was a man called Antonio de Viveros, who lived by the sale of poisons, raising false accusations against married women in the hope that the husbands might buy poison from him. He drew huge profits from the business and if the husband had no money with which to pay, he would give poison even on credit. It was noted that twenty- nine married women had died of poison sold by this man to their husbands, among them were friars and priests too. A few days before the Sultan of Golconda captured the town of Mylapore in the year1664, Antonio de Viveros had died. As he had many relations, all of them assembled in his house. There were also at that time many neighbours and acquaintances, who came to see, if it ware true. They were afraid he might be shamming to be dead, and they all rejoiced when confirmed that he was really dead.[17] Such a crowd had filled his public room of the house, that through their weight, the house being an old one had collapsed. Most of those people present around it were wounded while some of them were killed, others had their legs or arms broken or injured. Many had died smothered, for the godown beneath the sitting room was full of *chunambo* (lime in Tamil) which did greater damage, blinding some and stifling others. Great uproar and lamentation ensued and the greater part of the town of Mylapore said with tears, "it was not enough for Antonio de Viveros to kill so many as he did in life, but he must have needs to destroy as many more at his death". Instead of commending his soul to God, the People wished it at the devil".[18] Thus people of the worst character and behaviour, men of ill will had lived in the Portuguese settlements of the Tamil Coast.

Magic, spell and sorcery had been also prevalent in the Portuguese settlements of the Tamil coast. It is mentioned that a young friar in Mylapore had a woman-servant who cooked for him. This woman threw such spell over him that he could not exist without her for a moment. Anyone who went to visit the friar was an annoyance. He sent them away as soon as possible and the few words he uttered would be all in praise of the servant woman. This friar fell ill of diahorrea, and was already almost at the point of death. In place of fixing his mind on God to secure salvation for his soul, his whole concern was for the servant. At this time there arrived some friars from Goa, and seeing him thus forsaken, knew that he was bewitched. They seized the servant woman and by force of torture made her relieve the friar of the spell she had thrown over him. After this happening, the friar could not bear to see her or hear her name. It did not take long to cure him of his disease.[19]

Another incident may also reveal how magic was performed at night by magicians. There was a Portuguese called Thome Borges de Villa Lobo, an inhabitant of Mylapore. To recover after an illness, he moved with his family to the foot of a hill located three leagues from Santhome. After some days had passed he left relieved of his illness. But one night, failing to get sleep, he went out to walk about the town by moonlight. Hearing in a house the sound of dancing and tinkling of bells, his curiosity led him to look through a peep-hole in the door. There he saw two small boys, well clothed, with bells on their feet, wearing jewels and holding bows and arrows in their hands. Opposite them was a magician seated on the floor, holding a rod with which he struck the ground. To the sound of these strokes the children danced. From time to time the magician uttered a cry, and by the reason of the gyrations made by the boys in dancing, their eyes became flaming coals of fire, their faces heavy and fearful to see. When this condition arrived, they swooned and fell to the ground as if dead. The wife of Thome Borges de Villa Lobo awoke later and saw the door open. Her husband was absent from the room. She went to look for him, and found him lying senseless at the magician's door. Hastening home, she brought her brothers and servants, and in dead silence they removed him to his house. There they began to lament. The land-lady of the house hearing the cry and weeping came to them. She was told what had happened to the husband, found lying in front of such-and -such a door. The old lady showed amazement, so that all present were more disturbed than before, Upon seeing this, the old lady consoled them, saying that she knew a cure. Leaving home she had recourse to the magician, who appeared in about an hour. Entering the house, he said there had been too great temerity in seeking to see things that did not concern one. All the relations entreated him to tell them some cure. He gave the man certain fumigations, and placed medicine upon his eyes. After one hour had passed, Thome Borges de Villa Lobo began to move. When the morning came he was able to tell what happened to him last night.[20]

Nicolao Manucci, the Italian traveller visited Mylapore in 1688 and at that time there came to Manucci a sum of three thousand and seven hundred *patacas* which he had deposited with Fr. Salvador Gallo, priest of the Theatine Order in Goa. The said Fr. Salvador had handed over the money to Manucci's attorney, João Lopes de Figureido, a Portuguese born in India to be delivered to Manucci at Mylapore. When João Lopes arrived at the Port of Mylapore the persons who were governing the town had seized him and confiscated everything that he bought with him, taking possession also of his ship, under the false declaration that he was the debtor of certain Jews called Bertalomoeu Rodrigues, Domingo do Porto and Alvaro da Fonseca. Thus the officials and magistrates of Santhome of Mylapore called upon him to pay a debt due from a man of Figureido's faction called Francisco de Lima, owed to the above Jews.[21] Finding this great wrong being done, and that Manucci should also lose money, he had recourse to some of the magistrates in Mylapore. He laid before them the receipt of João Lopes de Figureido, the letters of Fr. Salvador Gallo and attestations by Dom Rodrigo da Costa, the Portuguese Governor of Goa who had also written a separate letter to the leading men of Santhome recommending him to their favour, because their Indian dominions were under great obligations to him. Thus he had done his very best to carry through Manucci's business.[22] All his efforts did Manucci any good. Once again he presented fresh testimony received from Goa from Augustinho Ribeiro and Pascoal Gomes also the letters patent with which the King of Portugal had honoured Manucci. These men had been present when the said Fr. Gallo delivered the said money to João Lopes de Figureido. He was under obligation to pay him in the local currency, and to take the sealed receipts. João Lopes also demanded leave to pay Manucci. He only owed money to him and nothing to anyone else. There was no record produced to show how he was a debtor. In the end the said João Lopes was ruined and destroyed. As for Manucci's claim which they could not deny, after much useless arguments, they resolved to pay Manucci two thousand *patacas*. This they declared as a favour they were doing. The balance they agreed not to pay. One man so decided because Manucci would not marry one of his relations. Others said that if Manucci settled among them in Santhome of Mylapore Manucci should not lose his money. Another said that there was no ground to complain, that the two thousand *patacas* sufficed, as Manucci had a sufficient income to live upon his life. The rest uttered similar irrelevant opinions and Manucci was sent about his business.[23] With regard to the wrongs done to João Lopes, we find that there were two reasons for it. The first was envy at seeing him a man born in India with some fortune and the owner of a ship, a thing they did not possess. The second reason was because three of the said magistrates had asked the wife of João Lopes in marriage, she being a rich woman and as she had refused them all, this produced the hate and envy which impelled them to ruin the man.[24]

In the year A.D. 1700, there came the Governor of Santhome, a representative of the Mughal emperor Aurangzeb. He was told of the injustice and robbery done to Manucci by the Portuguese of Santhome and he received the suit. The men were summoned to the presence of the Mughal Governor and he asked them about the debt due to Manucci. When they answered boldly that they knew nothing and did not owe any money to Manucci and offered to swear upon the Holy Bible. As the Mughal Governor did not know

Portuguese language, he applied to Thomas Pitt, the then Governor of Madras sending him the papers and affidavits of Manucci for inspection. He asked him to decide according to right. The said English Governor sent the papers to be translated into English. There was a delay of two months in getting this done. At the end of this, he sent for the Portuguese and asked them in a friendly way to give Manucci some satisfaction because it seemed to him that Nicolao Manucci was the most reasonable man and they ought to come to an agreement with him. In a most haughty and contumacious manner they replied that they owed Manucci nothing and they would not pay him anything. A few days afterwards, Thomas Pitt, assembled the whole council, the magistrates, and the learned men of different nations. They all sat together and deliberated. The Portuguese were called in, and in their presence in a loud voice, the governor read Manucci's document when those present decided unanimously that Manucci had been right. It was decreed that the debtors must pay Manucci. The Portuguese were thus unmasked before all the Europeans and the Muslims.[25] Thus greed for money was there in the society and justice was only delayed but not denied.

Another event happened during the month of March in the year 1690 at Santhome of Mylapore. Manucci had advanced five hundred Patacas to a Genoese merchant called Jorg Bianco for trading with Pegu in Burma. He sent the principal sum with the agreed profit to be paid to Manucci in Santhome. Manoel da Silva de Menezes was then the Portuguese judge of Mylapore took possession of Manucci's money and gave his usual arguments. In spite of all Manucci's efforts he could not obtain payment of what is his own. In the end Manucci made use of certain friars who interceded for him with Thomas de Maya, the Portuguese captain who was then holding office and he did what he could out of friendship for Manucci. He ordered Manucci to be paid but behold the way Manoel da Silva wanted to satisfy Manucci. He brought some twenty scores of cloth for thirty *Patacas*, the score he wanted to pay him in his cloth, entering every score in Manucci's account at eighty *Patacas*. Since Manucci declined to accept, Manucci received a little cash, losing part of his principle amount and all the profit.[26] Thus corruption was much prevalent to the core in Mylapore.

It is observed that many of the Portuguese soldiers had developed a spirit of freedom, deserting their military service in the West Coast and they migrated to the Coromandel Coast in large numbers. The absence of a strong political leadership in the social organization of these Portuguese settlements helped them to live and move as they liked. The Portuguese captain of the settlement was initially handling the problems of law and order and later we find that the King of Portugal was compelled to introduce a regular administration of justice. Blood feud and seeking vengeance was very common. Portuguese women followed a life of luxury and plenty. Some social rejects of the West who were sent out from Portugal as criminals to India and their presence was always destructive to the Indo-Portuguese society as they did not change their way of life. Superstitions occupied also a prominent place and this perhaps was picked up from the Hindu practice. Many Portuguese acculturated and fitted into the Tamil environment and they formed a part of the Indian society. The Portuguese had also followed some evil practices such as robbery, theft, murder in the Tamil Coast. They were not free from love, hate, extravagance and attachment to their material life of the period. This social group had also been accepted by the natives since they contributed to the Indian economy by conducting overseas trade. Some changes such as emergence of new trading groups in the overseas trade of Tamilnadu, with a new settlement pattern in the ports, governed by the Indian rulers and the Indian settlements very near the Portuguese enclaves were administered by the rulers of Vijayanagar Empire. Change of religion took place among those women who got married to Portuguese. Social evils such as sorcery, adultery, slavery, robbery continued in the Luso-Tamil society.

Crime, Social Ramifications and the Portuguese Diaspora on the Coromandel Coast, 1538-1695

Society in India came into contact with various other civilizations of the world societies such as the Romans, Arabs, Persians, Jews, Armenians and the Chinese through maritime trade in the ancient and the medieval period. The Portuguese, the Dutch, the Danes, the English and the French had extensive cultural contacts with the Indians between AD 1500 and 1800 and as a result of this Indo-European interaction, we find very many small groups of people through mixed marriages living in coastal India identified as Luso-Indians, Anglo-Indians and Franco-Indians who formed part of the Indian society in minority. Their social life is not yet adequately explored and it is necessary to relate the boundaries of the Indian society to these various social groups that emerged with diverse features at that time. The social history of India between AD 1500 and 1800 is an interesting but intricate task for the historian. Writings on this topic will also definitely help in knowing them better as these people had a place in history and the historians are not concerned so far with the manner in which this Indo-European society changed with the passage of time, although the particular literature on society of the period is available.[27] Hence there is a need to examine the Portuguese society in the Eastern Coast of India and study the changes in social institutions like marriage, family and caste. Some important questions are raised in this context. Were the Indo-Portuguese community been accepted by the natives as a social group? Did these people have any distinct cultural traits? Did they adopt any indigenous customs and manners? How far they were accommodative or assimilated into the Indian social environment? Did the families of the Indo-Portuguese have many traditional functions to perform besides existing as the basic unit in the then society? Was there joint family system and eradication or decline among the Indo-Portuguese? Did there arise a situation in which there existed no effective or meaningful interaction among the various members? In the newly emerged nuclear families at that time did several social problems arise? How did the Indo-Portuguese men and women actually live at that time? We shall cull the information from the travelogues and Portuguese documents and try to examine and interpret them very well in order to understand the Indo-Portuguese community and society during the Sixteenth and Seventeenth Centuries.

The stratification of the Portuguese society into various identifiable social groups is possible on the basis of certain characteristics such as military, commercial and religious which are very important elements of the Portuguese presence in India. The various sections of population include *soldados, casados, mercadores* and *fidalgos* and they brought Portuguese (Iberian) culture of Europe with them. These men in the beginning had hesitation to blend Portuguese habits with Hindu influences. They never had a thought to mix rightly or wrongly and colour was a barrier in each step forward. We find that Portuguese women were not allowed to undertake voyages from Portugal to India because of the hazards of travel and as well as moral problems involved during the voyage which normally took six to eight months. An extremely small number of Portuguese women used to sail annually in the company of their husbands such as Garcia d' Orta who brought his wife to India. It is mentioned that on the Cape route there were at least 2000 Portuguese going to Asia each year.[28] The life of these men in India must have become a problem without families in India or with families in Portugal. Hence mixed marriages were slowly encouraged by Affonso de Albuquerque, the (second) Portuguese Viceroy in India after the conquest of Goa in 1510. This policy of miscegenation introduced by Albuquerque encouraged Portuguese to marry local women and he assumed that the progeny of such marriages would remain loyal to the Portuguese Crown. Many Portuguese sailors, soldiers and merchants in the Bay of Bengal took the Indian women and lusitanized them to serve their interests. Thus the population of the Portuguese in the Eastern Coast of India increased and the women who got married to Portuguese men had to get converted to Christianity where they experienced a relatively upward mobility.

On the Tamil Coast, those Portuguese merchants who came to trade had settled down at the various flourishing ports by marrying the Tamil women and this mixed population known as *mesticos* had increased from time to time. It is recorded that the population of Nagapattinam settlement owing to Portuguese social interaction in 1577 was with sixty *casados,* 200 Eurasians and 300 Indian Christians.[29] According to Antonio Bocarro's report in 1635 there were 140 white *casados* 360 black *casados* called *topasses* (artillery men) 700 Indian Christians at Nagapattinam.[30] The Portuguese Viceroy in his letter dated 22 March 1663 requested the Danes at Tranquebar to give shelter to the Portuguese who came from Nagapattinam owing to Dutch occupation of the settlement.[31]

Further, the population of the Portuguese settlement of Santhome of Mylapore had increased steadily from sixty families in 1538 to 100 in 1543. The Portuguese population in 1545 was around 500.[32] Francis Xavier in one of his letters dated 10 November 1545 mentioned that there were more than 100 married Christians in Santhome.[33] After a year (1546) there were 500 Portuguese in Santhome with their slaves.[34] By the end of the year 1559 the population rose to 2000 including the Portuguese and natives.[35] In 1563 as many as 4000 Christians lived there besides sixty war veterans with their families.[36] In 1635 there were 120 white *casados* (Portuguese families) and 200 black *casados* (Tamil Christians).[37] According to a Jesuit report in 1644 we find that 1700 Christians lived there.[38] In 1661 sixty Portuguese settlers migrated from Nagapattinam to Santhome of Mylapore.[39] There were 200 *topasses* and 600 Portuguese *mestiçōs* in 1669 who continued to live there.[40] Thus we find large mixed population and it is very difficult to define the social organization of these groups. Of the Eurasians, certainly there could be broad distinction such as *fidalgos,* (nobles) *soldados* (soldiers) *casados*, (married settlers) and *mestiçōs* (half- blood).

Jesuit letters written in 1559 and 1563 mention several corrupt acts and unlawful behaviour of the Portuguese in the Tamil Coast.[41] There were few missionaries in the early period to attend to the spiritual needs of the Portuguese and the Indo-Portuguese community. Further, it is to be noted that only in the later period when the number of missionaries increased in the coast they took active steps to give really a new shape to the lifestyle of the converted Indians by administering the sacraments. They also noted in their letters and reports about the Portuguese and Indo-Portuguese community which had various social problems that have special and anti-social dimensions. We cannot close our eyes to these hard realities and these issues in criminology have not attracted the attention of sociologists or historians in Europe and Asia and so we shall deal with them here.

Pen-Picture of Murders and death

Portuguese records throw light on several instances of murder. Symão de Britto who lived in Santhome of Mylapore was stabbed by one *mestiçõ*, a relative of Francisco de Freitas. The Portuguese captain of Mylapore therefore arrested the culprit and confined him in a church. An enquiry was later held when Symão de Britto, the injured had died.[42] Similarly there was a man in Santhome of Mylapore married to a rich and influential lady of good connections.

He misbehaved with the servant girl in his house and she became conceived. The landlady found the occasion that she needed to deal with her husband and the servant properly. Hence she managed to kill the maid servant with the help of some paid agents. After mutilating the body, she ordered it to be buried in the garden at the backyard of the house. The flesh removed from the body was taken into the kitchen and a dish was prepared under the direct supervision of the lady. When her husband came home for dinner the dish was served to him and told that she had herself specially prepared it for him. The husband ate and praised very much for its exquisite taste. Then the woman lifted the dish and flung the contents in his face, saying that it was not enough to have enjoyed the maid servant while she was alive; even in death she was of good savour. Her anger overflowing, she gave her husband plentiful abuse, and quitting the house went to live with her relatives. She did not consent to meet husband for the rest of her life.[43]

Evidences suggest that the Portuguese merchants were very brutal to their slaves both male and female. Learning from the reports sent from India to Portugal, the King of Portugal issued a royal order on 26 January 1559 stating the Portuguese merchants should not be brutal to their slaves both male and female and prohibited them from mutilating or slaying slaves.[44] However, instances of murder and death we find in the Portuguese settlements. An instance is worth mentioning. There was a slave girl in the house of Cosmo Lourenço Madeira, a Portuguese in Santhome of Mylapore. His wife name was Dona Escolastica, the daughter of João Pereira de Faria who had imprisoned the slave for having stolen something in the house. By reason of severe punishment meted out by her and deprivation of food that slave died and was buried in the dunghill. No one in the town dared to ask any question about the death of the slave. If the native rulers of the region had known they would have definitely chastised the husband and wife.[45] Thus instances of cruelty were found common among the Portuguese and it continued. The earlier said two crimes committed were with a definite purpose of assault and murder.

Records do mention that the Portuguese soldiers had committed many murders.[46] Antonio Miranda who lived in Santhome of Mylapore had wounded a Dane at a tavern in Madras and he killed an English soldier who had come there to quell the tavern brawl. During his imprisonment Antonio Miranda, the soldier revealed that in the previous year he had killed another person at Santhome of Mylapore and it was found out that the English soldier whom he killed was the seventh murder that he had committed.[47] Further, we find that Manoel Branden Lima a Portuguese soldier of Madras was arrested on the charge of murdering a fellow Portuguese. A jury comprising of six Englishmen and six Portuguese conducted the case. Finally he was found guilty and on 25 September 1678 he was sentenced to death.[48]

Disclosing the Dimensions of Adultery and Sex

Portuguese in the Tamil Coast seems to have acculturated and fitted into the Indian environment. There appears to have been copious sexual interactions and hence reproduction between Portuguese men and Indian women had taken place as gleaned from the increasing population details mentioned earlier. The result was the creation of a very large *mestiçõ* population in the Tamil ports. We also find damsels (*donzellas*) born in India and wives whose husbands were away on duty. The fundamental questions about civil liberties and the power of the Portuguese *Estado da India* can be raised since plenty of crimes are noted. Crime as a social phenomenon is an important area of scientific research, debate and historical study because it helps us to understand the human behaviour in general. Cause behind the rise in crimes against sex, women and youth is important to note and the behaviour in violation of the legal code, the activity that offends the social code and different aspects of behavior that violates crime law is mentioned in various documents.

A report mentions that the Portuguese and *mestiçõ* women were very luxurious and unchaste, for there were very few among them, although they were married. They had besides their husbands, one or two soldiers, with whom they took their pleasure, and they used all the slights and practices. They devised plans by sending out their slaves by night, and at extraordinary times, over walls, hedges, and ditches, how narrow lie so ever, they were kept and looked unto. They had likewise an herb called *Deutroa*, which bore a seed, where of bruising out the sap, they put it into a cup or other vessel, and gave it to their husbands, either in meat or drink. When presented therewith, the man was as if he were half out of his wits, and without feeling, or else drunk, doing nothing but laughed. Sometime it took him to sleeping, whereby he was like a dead man, so that in his presence they did what they wanted. The women took their pleasure with their friend's and the husband never knew of it. In this manner they continued for long hours, but when they washed the feet of the husband for long with cold water he revived his senses and knew nothing thereof, but thought he had slept.[49]

It is mentioned that in 1594 Lopo Alvares da Moura, a rich merchant had abducted the wife of another settler in Santhome of Mylapore as he was interested in sex. Therefore he was punished by the Portuguese captain of the town. Earlier the merchant's house was attacked by the women's relatives.[50] Another incident happened in 1695 and it is said that there was a Portuguese called Antonio Pinto, married to Isabel Rapoza who lived in the town of Santhome of Mylapore. He went the evil way with another married woman called Antonia de Torres, who allowed this Portuguese man at any time to enter her house publicly. Isabel Rapoza who often heard about this affair kept silence. One day when she heard of this, not being able to cool down her passion, found an opportunity in the after noon. She came out of her house followed by four strong and stout slaves. She proceeded to the house of her adversary, dragged her to the streets, attacked physically and the bones were broken by a good thumping, and the face had disfigured also by shoe-beating. The aggrieved wife retired with all dignity to her own house. The wretched Antonia de Torres went off to Madras to be healed. Thus Antonio da Torres and Antonio Pinto were branded with infamy all over the town. The man by way of restoring his credit assigned a reason that his wife was impotent and left for Madras to live with Antonia da Torres.[51]

Further, another incident happened. There was a wealthy and honoured Portuguese called João Perreira de Faria married to Dona Maria de Souza who migrated from Nagapattinam upon the loss of the town from the hands of the Portuguese to the Dutch in 1658 and settled in Madras. One of the slave-girls of the house was much favoured by him and he had given such an authority to her in order to gratify his own desires in an illicit direction. The maid servant wanted to kill the mistress by magic arts. For this purpose she stole some money from her master and resorted to a young Hindu servant to take measures to put an end to her mistress's life. Her idea was to become the head of the house when the landlady was dead and at that time she would reward the Hindu servant. The youth who accepted the task tried to do what the slave-girl wanted, and not succeeding, had to finally recourse to a magician. This man directed him to bring some hair, nail-clippings, and a piece of defiled cloth belonging to the land-lady. The youth reported to the slave-girl, and she sent what was required. When some days had passed, the youth brought one pin, the point of which reached nearly to the stomach, and another pin which was stuck into the navel coming half-way down the legs as given by the magician. The slave girl was told that at midnight she must go entirely naked into the middle of the house-garden, holding up in one hand a doll, and in the other a piece of burning wood. Orders as to what she was to do were added. She was warned that while acting as above, there would appear a black cat, but she must not be afraid. The wretched woman did as instructed. Going to the centre of the court-yard, she set fire to the doll's feet and hands. At that moment there appeared to her the awe-inspiring cat, with eyes which looked like two flames of fire. On seeing such an apparition the slave-girl was in terror. At this time, there also arose in the house loud cries and commotion. Being frightened, the girl went into her mistress's chamber as if she wanted to help, carrying with her the doll, which she hid in the sacking of the lady's bedstead. In her hurry and agitation, she did not thrust it well in, and it remained half-hanging out. The land-lady of the house was in mortal anguish, complained that she felt on fire from her head to stomach, and from the navel down to her lower limbs, besides her hands and feet burning with insufferable heat and agony. They called in the doctors, who could not determine what ailment it was, and the remedies given her did not take effect. For several days the land-lady suffered in the same way.[52]

After a few days, then it chanced that a child of three years old, playing about in the house, went under the bed and saw a doll half-projecting. It pulled it out with a cry of delight, and played with it showing it to the nurse. When the woman saw it she recognized at once what it was, and showed it on the spot to her mistress and the rest of those present, said that it was a piece of magic and through which she had suffered. Upon making sure of this, she called in a Hindu magician, who as soon as entered the house went to João Pereira de Faria, and told him that he was the cause of his wife's sufferings. He was ashamed, and hung his head. Upon seeing the image, the magician told the wife that in short time she would be restored to health, but the people of the house must not be alarmed when they saw her lie without senses or any movement. For his work, the magician retired into a room and very slowly drew out the pins, and unstitched the image bit by bit. Finally he opened up the abdomen, from where he found the nail-clippings, the hair and the cloth spoken of above, with other mixed items put in earlier by the magician. When the image had been entirely pulled to pieces, he threw it into a vessel of milk and after making his incantations, he threw that vessel also into the sea. After twelve hours Dona Maria de Souza came back to her senses and lost all her pains, but she was so weak that it took nearly three months for her to recover strength. The magician immediately fixed upon the slave-girl who had done the mischief and on confessing it, she was punished and banished for the rest of her life. The originator of the trouble was João Perreira de Souza, the master of the house, who had enjoyed sex illegally with the servant.[63] The above said three crimes were committed chiefly because of sexual and economic motives.

Voices from Dowry

According to official Portuguese reports many orphan girls were sent from Portugal to be married in India, the daughters of the Portuguese soldiers and sailors killed in various expeditions held in Europe and Africa. The King of Portugal had taken special interest relating to the affairs of such women in Portugal and so he passed an order in 1623 which stated that these young girls should be given in marriage between fifteen and twenty years. The King also passed another order in 1627 that any Portuguese granted to orphan girls as the marriage settle was to be fixed for a term of three years. Further, the King of Portugal issued a royal order dated 27 June 1684 wherein he allowed widows to remarry unmindful of the caste to which they belonged before. It also sanctioned punishment to the parents and close relatives who forbade a widow for remarrying through the penalty of confiscation of property.[54]

In the beginning of the Sixteenth Century, Portuguese became rich through overseas trade and so they lived in great pomp and show in India. But this was no longer the case in the Seventeenth Century with the decline of Portuguese trade, arrival of the Dutch and the Luso-Dutch rivalry which brought misery. They had barely enough for food. At this time they married any girl after obtaining almost everything on loan that is needed for the wedding. The day after the marriage and feast, everybody came and carried away whatever had been lent out. The greater part of the house also stood empty and the bride was without jewels. As for dowry, the bridegroom did not even receive really the half of what was promised to him.[55]

Though ritual and ceremonial elements were usually present in marriages the material valuation was always dominant. It happened in Nagapattinam that a young man from Portugal came to get married with a recommendation letter to a resident who had a daughter. After reading the contents of the letter, the father of the girl stated the dowry that he intended to give. The young man had also agreed to the amount. When a few days had elapsed, a married man told that young man that he should not marry anyone from that house and family but he himself offered his own daughter instead of the previous one with a larger dowry. The young man accepted this proposal also and spoke no more to the first man. The latter, on learning the facts was very much annoyed. The girl, seeing that the new arrival was governed by his interests, fond of her money and not of her, advised her father to promise him the double of what the other had offered. The self-seeker, being an ambitious fellow, came back to the house, and in a few days their marriage was arranged. On the day of the marriage they went to church for the wedding ceremony. The priest asked the groom if he was willing to marry this lady. He replied most confidently in the affirmative. The same question was put to the bride, and she, in place of saying 'Yes,' lifted her hand and gave him a smart smack on the face and said: 'With this big rogue, I have no intention of marrying. He wanted the money, and he is not worthy of being my husband'. The man, put to shame, hurried out of the church. When this happened, at that time, there was present at the same wedding a rich youth. Seeing this noble action of the bride, he took a fancy to her, and asked if she would marry him. He added that he would accept her without any money benefit. The bride lifted her eyes and had a look at him. Then she accepted him as husband, and the feast was held for him. To no one's imagination this had happened.[56] Thus we find an example that happiness depends on the choice of a girl upon whom one's heart and eyes are set, and not on any other which ultimately helps the husband and wife to be deeply smitten in love. The decision of the girl to marry one in whom she finds a heaven of happiness is shown in this case.

In the year 1694, in Madras, there was an incident related to dowry and love which is interesting. There was a young man born of humble parentage but lofty thoughts. His name was João da Cunha. He became enamoured of a young girl, and, as it seemed to him, fortune could not favour him better than by making her his wife. As the father of the girl never gave it a thought nor could the young girl imagine such a thing, he did not have the courage to declare his concealed feeling. He came to the house every day, nursing a mystic passion, and anything required to be done at the house was carried out by him with exactitude. But time and again he said that many marriage proposals were made to him, though he would not accept any one of these proposed brides, except one whom he strongly desired. Seeing the little progress he was making, he went one day to the father of the girl and said: 'This morning they bribed me to make a marriage by offering a dowry of (Rs.2000) one thousand *patacas*'. He added that the person was of some position and of good fame and the name of the girl was Catharina da Silva. He asked for advice from the father of the girl. The man replied that it was quite certain that God had come to his help and he must accept the proposal. They talked with such secrecy that the whole household heard of it so loud. Everybody congratulated him. He went on to say that he never meant to marry, if the girl were not to his liking. Some days elapsed, and they were continuously asking him, only way of joke, when the wedding was to be. The man was put out, and not wishing to be counted a liar, made out a paper for the banns, showed it to them, and said he was going to the Priest to have the marriage banns published. He delivered the paper to the vicar, who published the banns on two Sundays. The bridegroom, his sisters, and all his parents received everybody's congratulations. Everyone asked about the bride, and he said that she was away from Madras and lying ill. Under this pretext he borrowed jewels from his relatives and from the young girl's parents.

The following Saturday he went to confession, and during the mass on Sunday, when about to receive the host, he fell to the earth in a swoon just as if he were dead, and thus remained nearly two hours before recovering his senses (a just chastisement for his evil deeds). At night he left secretly, and made off to Santhome of Mylapore, and then sent word to his relatives that he was now married, that his wife was ill, and growing always worse. After a few more days passed, he moved to St. Thomas Mount and there he hired a house, and lived with great secrecy being shut up in one room, and said that, it was his suffering wife, whom he had brought to St. Thomas Mount to recover health. From Madras his relatives asked whether they might come and see his wife. He replied not to trouble and he would send necessary transport when the proper time arrived, for his wife was delirious, and it was not good for them to see her in that state.

One day the inhabitants of St. Thomas Mount, with the two hermits went to visit him. He gave a welcome, to which he in a very despondent tone answered: 'Cursed be the hour when I married, and cursed be the dowry paid me, for greed of money made me take a wife troubled with a thousand ailments, so that I was forced to transport her to this St. Thomas Mount to get her well, and I expect that here she will find a sepulchre'. They asked him as to what was the matter with her, to which he said not a word, but burst into tears and lamentation. At this time a woman servant arrived and he brought her with him on purpose. She said that the lady was very weak and it was two days since she had eaten anything. He told the maid to see if his wife could take some broth or medicated drink. The woman went inside before everybody with the bowl of food, and said such words from within that those outside imagined the wife to be really very ill. After a few days, he made a figure of straw and enshrouded it so that it looked like a real corpse, and set up many candles which he had brought for the purpose. Then he sent a message to the Priest to have the bell tolled for his wife Catherina da Silva, she being dead. In great haste he dispatched an advice to his relatives in Madras that his wife had died, and they must all come to attend her funeral. The vicar descended to the house very angrily and said that they had not sent word to him, so that confession and extreme-unction could have been administered. The man answered that she had already been confessed at Santhome of Mylapore. The excess of grief he displayed over the bundle of straw very much affected the attention of everybody present, and the whole night long the two hermits sat on vigil over the dead body, in company with the people of St. Thomas Mount and some other devout persons. From time to time, an old woman whose name was Bernarda, bribed beforehand with a small sum, asked João da Cunha, 'What of the lady Catharina da Silva? The day before yesterday I saw her with these very eyes alive, and today she is already dead! During this time the servant woman cried: 'O my mistress! How could you yield yourself to this wretch who had so long followed you? When I supposed that I was to see you happy, you were going to your death'. João da Cunha frequently fell upon the corpse of straw, and emitted such cries that all present were moved to compassion. Fearing a fit, the hermits and the other guests present there wanted to carry him away and place him on a bed. The cheat, suspecting that those surrounding him might go and inspect the pretended corpse, wrested himself out of the arms of the hermits, and once more threw himself upon the sack of straw and renewed his exclamations. Very early in the next day morning his relatives arrived, and they wailed greatly. With a considerable number of persons following the cortege, the burial took place at the foot of the hill of St. Thomas Mount, and each man retired to his own home. On that day he distributed much alms, and ordered very many Holy Masses to be said. But as the secret lay among some poor women, it soon began to be said that what had been interred was a straw figure. The rumour spread, and it came to the ears of the Bishop of Mylapore. He sent orders to open the tomb, and they lighted upon the straw figure, buried there eight days before. But a month afterwards João da Cunha came to pray pardon for his offences, and he was then given absolution. Thus we find in this incident that all activities had been undertaken because he could not get the old man's daughter in marriage and also to embezzle ornaments and cash.[57] *Stridhana* (women's personal property in the legal Indian literature) was prevalent very common and it was restricted to jewels and other such moveable goods. Property of land was considered as an inappropriate possession for women in the Indian context. It seems that the Portuguese had not picked up the practice of dowry from the Hindus since grants had been made available for marriages of the orphan girls as dowry by the King of Portugal himself.

Women and the Social Universe of Superstitions

The social and economic affairs of the Portuguese settlements in the Tamil Coast were looked after by the Portuguese captains appointed by the King of Portugal. All matters relating to military were decided by the Portuguese Governor in Goa. Law and order problems were handled by the judges appointed in the settlement. In the Indian port settlements near the Portuguese settlements all matters were governed by the *adhikari* appointed by the *Nayaka* ruler.[58] The Portuguese established inquisition in 1560 in Goa to prevent recourse by the converts to non-Christian customs and its range of prohibitions covered a number of socio-cultural practices but it was absent on the East Coast of India. Therefore social evils such as superstitions, sorcery and magic were widely prevalent among the Portuguese and converts in the Coromandel Coast.

A rich Portuguese woman who lived in Madras had a married daughter who was pregnant. The mother wanted to know whether it would be an easy delivery or not. To this intent she asked for an old woman who lived as a diviner to get her to pray. The woman placed herself for prayer near the door to the street at nine o'clock at night. This she did for two nights. The third night while praying she heard a voice saying: 'We shall die and leave no remembrance.' On hearing this, the woman was disconsolate, and said nothing to the widow, so as not to lose the payment promised to her. She produced other reasons to pacify her, and the mother, to maintain her own credit, went about saying what would happen to the pregnant daughter. After some time, it was learnt that the latter had died in child bed.[59]

Similarly, a Portuguese woman who lived in Madras being married to a merchant, being delayed in his voyage, and no news came of him she wanted to know about him. So she went to the old woman directing her to pray, and ask that in a dream she might see what had become of her husband. While asleep she saw the ship wrecked, when several persons died of drowning, including the husband. The news was disclosed to the wife, who mourned and was unable to keep the secret (ordinarily there are few secrets kept by women). She communicated it to her neighbours and thus the news passed through the whole town. At length it came to the ears of the vicar, who made efforts to abolish such an abuse by preaching and admonishment. None the less the practice persisted, faith was still placed in the old woman and the advice of the vicar was disregarded. Some months had passed and news came of the husband's death that he had been drowned. The old woman earned much money through her sooth-sayings and lived as a diviner.[60]

In another case, we find that a rich Portuguese widow in Madras who became anxious to know whom she would marry and so she had sent word for the old woman. She gave a reward to the old woman and commanded her to perform rites in her presence. For this purpose, the old woman sent word to fetch for her a clear glass phial. When it was brought, breaking some eggs she poured them into and prayed into the mouth of this bottle. Slowly the eggs formed into a human shape with some letters showing the name of the person who was to become the widow's spouse. After some time, there appeared a man who bore the name announced by the phial. When the widow saw him, she declared that he resembled the man whom she had seen and so later she married him. In the entire region there was no old woman like her who bore such fame and name after this incident.[61]

In Santhome of Mylapore, there was a lady who sent word for one of the women diviners and requested her to pray in her house in favour of a certain intention which she recommended to her. For the purpose a special chamber was set aside. After ten o'clock at night the old woman took her seat at a window, and engaged in prayer. Fancying she would hear a voice, according to her intention, there appeared instead in the middle of the room a face surrounded by white. On seeing it the old woman became speechless and was in a state of terror, sitting motionless, while the face remained stationary for some time. Finding that no question was put, it went out again by the same window. The old woman then fell down. The people of the house, hearing the fall, ran into the room, where they found the woman extended on the ground in a swoon. They raised her up, and with the help of medicine she came to senses by herself in the next morning. But she was unable to move one of her legs. Asking her what had happened she explained that as the face passed out of the window, she felt it touch her on that leg. On inspection, they found the leg withered into a mere stick, and its flesh all shrivelled. Remedies were applied, but were not effective, and for the few years she survived and it remained in the same condition. She repented herself of her deeds, for no one could fully understand an evil that has not actually experienced.[62] It is often found how people foolishly behaved without applying their mind and reasoning in their daily life and such events make this study particularly rewarding.

In Santhome of Mylapore there was a lady who asked an old woman of a confraternity to inform her on some questions she wanted to be answered. In the depth of night, when the old woman was performing her ritual in the lady's house, there appeared an awe-inspiring monster that seized the old woman by the hair and forced her out of the house, leaving her in the street half dead from the blows it applied. At the same time a ball of fire fell upon the house and all it contained was burnt. The inhabitants escaped with great difficulty. The old woman found herself in the street, and on recovering her senses she repented herself, and decided never again to perform such rites. It took her a considerable time to recover health, and for the few years she lived she seemed to be in a state of right, and trembled at the recollection of what had happened to her. It was a merited punishment for meddling in things that did not concern her. Even by this example people have not mended their ways, for they continued to act as before without any compunction and many of these old women died in misery.[63]

There was an old blind Portuguese woman in Madras called Androza and she lived with the reputation of a saint, many women resorting to her to discover matters similar to those already stated. They bestowed liberal alms on her, by which she lived comfortably.

Through her fame for holiness, the whole village of fisher-folk had recourse to her, presenting to her good fish and some money. They enjoyed hearing her conversation and did not go to church. The vicar noticed their absence, while the alms that they usually brought to church at the time of mass and their other offerings were also missing. On his taking up the question, he discovered the pretensions of the blind Androza, who had imposed this superstition upon the whole village. She was admonished and expelled from the town. After these events Androza moved to St. Thomas Mount (*Monte Grande*) where she continued her practices and lived on the alms given to her by the devout.[64]

Men and the World

A Portuguese called Manoel Macedo de Azevedo lived in Santhome of Mylapore and this man dreamt several nights running inside his house, a treasure being buried in a godown, close to a pillar on which the house rested. To find out whether the dream was true or not he called in a sorcerer, to whom he set forth what he had dreamt. The sorcerer asked for three days to inquire and see if things were as he had dreamt. To find out by experiment whether the sorcerer knew how to divine what had been buried, the Portuguese placed some money and jewels in the earth at four places in his garden. When the three days had passed, the sorcerer came back, and going into the garden, drew forth a small paper from his pocket, and took from it certain black powder and anointed his eyes. Then the Portuguese led the sorcerer to the places where he had buried the things already referred to. The sorcerer halted, and described minutely what had been interred. The Portuguese then believed in the sorcerer through the proof that he had put him to, and took him to the middle of the godown of which he had dreamt. The sorcerer came, stood there and displayed great astonishment, saying that in that spot was a large caldron full of gold; but it was down seven cubits deep near the water-level. The caldron had two rings, and each ring was placed on the horn of an ox which upheld the caldron. On hearing this, the Portuguese was delighted, and wanted to order the pot to be excavated. The sorcerer advised him that it was inexpedient to touch it without having performed a sacrifice. In obedience to his counsel, goats and cocks were sacrificed.

Then men were set to work to dig while the master stood by. As soon as they had dug down about four cubits and when the work was still in progress, an announcement was made that the Portuguese captain had come to call on him. Therefore the work was suspended, the labourers were turned out, and the door was locked. Then the master went to greet the captain at his gate, and conducted him to the garden. While they were in conversation, the house fell down owing to the removal of the foundations of the pillar. Thereby the man saw how the good God had been to him, and the net in which the Devil had tried to catch him. Repenting himself, he abandoned his attempt. All the people in the town heard of this case, and to the unholy rites the sorcerer had performed. The Portuguese man was compelled to appear before the inquisition in Goa to defend himself but he came out free.[65] The Portuguese seems to have followed the local tradition, customs and manners of the natives in the Tamil coast and it is also possible to say that that superstitions were prevalent in Portugal and this enabled the Portuguese to follow the same in India too.

There were many notorious men and criminals who lived in the Tamil Coast. In a letter of 1612 we find a complaint sent to the King of Portugal about Antonio de Sousa who had thrown dead things in drinking water wells from which water was drawn.[66] It is to be borne in mind that the sequences of action of men and women in society were essentially historical phenomena involving persistence and change in time. A scientific study of society must therefore necessarily include a historical method and the absence of this would mean an insufficient understanding of the nature of the facts being studies, a falsification and superficial treatment of them and so the great possibility of error would occur in the findings.

Slavery, Immorality and Disorderly Conduct

Slaves were owned by the Portuguese for domestic purposes in the Tamil Coast. But there was no active slave trade as such conducted by the Portuguese between 1507 and 1662.[67] In the later period we find some stray evidences. According to a report, there was a married Tamil who came from Madurai to Nagapattinam exploring the possibility of finding some means of livelihood and employment to support his family. Having found some job at

Nagapattinam he asked leave of absence after a month from the person with whom he was serving to go to Madurai and fetch his wife and children. After obtaining leave and necessary permission he reached Madurai. There he learnt the news that the neighbour in Nagapattinam to whom he had confided his family had abducted them, telling his wife that the husband had sent word. When the man returned to Nagapattinam he learnt that his wife and sons were already taken to Tranquebar, and were sold treacherously to the Portuguese priest for thirty *pagodas*. His family members were not even aware of it. In the end he came to Tranquebar, and made efforts to recover them. The vicar resisted and reported the matter to the Danish Governor. Further, the man himself was captured so that he could make no further attempts for his own release. Later, when he was delivered away from the prison, the poor man lodged a complaint to the Bishop of Mylapore, but a hearing was refused out of regard for the said priest. He submitted a petition then and prayed that he might at least have permission to re-marry, since the said priest had already bought his wife and sons. In the mean while, he learnt that his family members were sold again for sixty *pagodas* and were ready to sail from Madras to Manila. At this time, the whole of his caste members assembled and undertook to pay the sale price of his wife and sons within one month notice, since this Tamil was a poor man. Even this did not avail. The English Governor of Madras had since earlier decided that resold slaves should not be embarked in the ships leaving for Manila, thereupon the priest was forced to take away the wife and sons. The priest had again managed to send them for re-sale elsewhere into the hands of the Hindu traders. The husband in desperation changed his faith and returned to Hinduism, since he was unable to secure justice from the Portuguese.[68] Thus we find crimes committed against public decency, morality and disorderly conduct and these crimes were against natural justice and breach of trust.

It is not possible to list or to describe all the important aspects of Portuguese society. The Portuguese had introduced a regular administration of justice through *relação* (highcourt) and *ouvidor* (judge) to guard and control the society in the settlements of the Tamil Coast. The assembly of the elders (*Os Eleitos de Negapatão*) had controlled the social affairs of the people according to Tamil customs.[69] The crimes committed by individuals taken here for examination show that the presence of criminals was destructive to the society. The social life of the mestiços by tracing instances of slavery, adultery, murder, dowry and marriage in the society and an analysis throws new light on the mixed culture by outlining the distinct characteristics. Pleasing tales (*manoranjan Itihas*) had been widely prevalent in Indian literature but travellers like Nicolau Manucci had indulged this talent narrating upon the mysterious activities of the Portuguese in Tamil Country is noteworthy. Whether the ridiculous event he relates proceed from that common partiality which he had from a judgment formed upon as an Italian or some external ceremonies and superstitious activities of the Portuguese is very difficult to determine. But his travel account has thrown disgrace upon a system of Portuguese living which they did at that time. Portuguese had followed a life of licentiousness amidst luxury and plenty in the Sixteenth Century. They were also not free from practising the extravagance and vain glory in the daily material life than a very high spirituality as the medieval Christianity and missionaries expected from them. The Indo-Portuguese were also subjected to some of the evil practices such as robbery, adultery, theft and murder. The absence of a strong political leadership in the social organization helped the Portuguese in the Eastern Coast of India to behave as they liked.

It is enjoyable to talk about women and we are able to view a range of life styles concerning Portuguese women. The varied possibilities of identity are not open to Portuguese women in the familial, professional, religious and royal contexts. Conventional historiography that perceives women as silent voices of history because they had little or nothing to do is not applicable in this context. Events and moments are made the central theme and the Portuguese men and women who once walked on the stage of history in flesh and blood are depicted in the historical stage. The Indo-Portuguese community was not a homogenous social group and it was considerably stratified in terms of race and status. The *castizos* or the Portuguese of purer blood were less in the Coromandel Coast and the descendants of mixed parentage or the *mestiços* were more in number. The wayward life style and lawlessness were found common and it created unusual social pressures. It may be concluded that the crimes committed by Portuguese and Indo-Portuguese community could be classified generally into three groups on the basis of their motives, i.e., economic, sexual and miscellaneous. These crimes could also be further classified according to different purposes such as (a) against women (assault and murder) (b) against property (theft and robbery) (c) against public decency or morality (disorderly conduct) (d) against public justice (embezzlement and breach of trust). Blood feud was another practice in society in which the family of a murdered person sought vengeance on the murderer or murderer's family. In sum, it is to be mentioned here that good and bad people had existed in that age and society. Various social problems and crimes mentioned in this chapter had a harmful impact on social interests and detrimental to the well-being of the society of the Sixteenth and Seventeenth centuries in Portuguese India.

Notes and References

1. S. Jeyaseela Stephen, *Portuguese in the Tamil Coast: Historical Explorations in Commerce and Culture, 1507-1749*, Navajyothi Publishing House, Pondicherry, 1998.
2. P. Roche, *Fishermen of the Coromandel : A Social Study of the Paravas of the Coromandel,* New Delhi, 1984.
3. S. Jeyaseela Stephen, "Societal Changes: Portuguese and the Native Christians in Tamil Country Cir.1537-1759" in K. S. Mathew, T. R. De Souza & Pius Malekandathil, (eds.,) *The Portuguese and the Socio-Cultural Changes in India, 1500-1800*, Tellicherry, 2001, pp. 479-513.
4. K.S. Mathew, "Indian Ocean and Cultural Interaction" *Indica*, Vol.35, No. 2, 1998, pp. 97-133.
5. IANTI, *Mss.* CC, Vol. III-part 9-document no. 94. See also for details, S. Jeyaseela Stephen, *The Coromandel Coast and its Hinterland, Economy, Society and Political System, 1500-1600*, New Delhi, 1997, pp. 182-183.
6. IANTT, *Mss Casa Forte*, No. 48. See also, S. Jeyaseela Stephen, *The Coromandel Coast, op.cit.*, pp. 182-183.
7. S. Jeyaseela Stephen, *The Coromandel Coast., op.cit.*, p. 186
8. *Ibid.*
9. *Ibid.*
10. BNL, Mss. Codice, 1976; fls.136-140v.

11. Niccola Manucci, *op.cit.*, Vol. III, p. 119.
12. *Ibid.*
13. *Ibid*, Vol. III p.123.
14. *Ibid*, Vol. III, p.112.
15. *Ibid*, Vol. III, pp.112-113.
16. *Ibid*, Vol. III, pp. 118-119.
17. *Ibid*, Vol. III, p.119.
18. *Ibid.*, Vol. III, pp. 119-120.
19. *Ibid*, Vol. III, p. 190.
20. *Ibid*, Vol. III, pp. 190-191.
21. *Ibid*, Vol. III, pp. 120-121.
22. *Ibid.*, Vol. III, p.121.
23. *Ibid.*
24. *Ibid*, Vol. III, p. 122.
25. *Ibid.*
26. *Ibid.*, Vol. III, pp. 122-123.
27. For details see, Dejanirah Silva Couto, "Some Observed Portuguese Renegades in Asia in the 16th Century" in *Vasco da Gama and the Linking of Europe and Asia* (eds.,) Anthony Disney & Emily Botham, New Delhi, 2000, pp. 178-201; Maria Augusta Lima Cruz, "Exiles and Renegades in Early 16th Century: Portuguese in India", *Indian Economic and Social History Review*, Vol. 23, No. 3, 1986, pp. 49-62; Jurrien Van Goor, "European Exiles, Renegades and Outlaws and the Maritime Economy of Asia, 1500-1750" in Anthony Disney, *Historiography of Europeans in Africa and Asia, 1450-1800*, London, 1998; K.S. Mathew, "Indian Ocean and Cultural Interaction" *Indica*, Vol. 35, No. 2, 1998, pp. 97-132.
28. See, Vitorino Maghalaes Godhino, *Os Descobrimentos e a Mundial*, Lisboa, 1981-84.
29. George Winius "The Shadow Empire of Goa in the 16th Century" *Itinerario*, Vol. VII, No. 2, 1983, p. 92.
30. Antonio Bocarro, "Livro das Plantas de Todas as Fortalezas, Cidades e Povações do Estado da India Oriental" in A.B. de Bragança Perreira (ed.,) *Arquivo Portugues Oriental*, Bastora Goa, 1937-38, pt. II, p. 8.
31. *BFUP*, Vol. 11, pp. 176-179. The Dutch reported the Golconda authorities that the English Council in Madras would not refuse shelter to fellow Christians during the war in 1661. See. William Foster, *The English Factories in India*, 1618-1669, 13 Vols, Oxford, 1906-1927, (henceforth EFI), 1661-1664, p. 145 n.

32. Antonio da Silva Rego, *Documentação Para a Historia das Missões do Padroado Portugues do Oriente, 1499-1582*, 12 Vols, Lisboa, 1947-1958, Vol. II, pp. 252-54; Vol. III 165; See for the statistics of Portuguese residents in Coromandel, IANTT, Mss. *Corpo Cronologico*, III-9-94 (1521) . See also Elaine *Sanceau, Colleção São Lourenço*, (henceforth CSI), Lisboa, 1973-83, Vol. III, pp. 64-65.
33. Jose Wicki, *Documenta Indica*, 18 Vols, Rome, 1948-88. see Vol. II, 16; Antonio da Silva Rego, *Documentação, op.cit.*, Vol. III, p.165; *Monumenta Xaveriana*, 2 vols, Matriti, 1899-1912, Vol. II, p 549.
34. Georg Schurhammer, *St. Francis Xavier: His Life, His Times*, 2 Vols, Rome, 1977, Vol. II, p. 549.
35. DI, *op.cit.*, Vol. V, p. 181.
36. ANTT, *Gavetas*, 11-8-19-7; See also *D.I, op.cit.*, Vol. V. p. 743.
37. Antonio Bocarro, *Livro das Plantas, op.cit.*, pt. II, p. 8.
38. S. Jeyaseela Stephen, *Portuguese in the Tamil Coast: Historical Explorations in Commerce and Culture*, Pondicherry, 1998, p.243 & 252.
39. Antonio Bocarro, *op.cit.*, pt. II. p.8.
40. *Dagh Register Gehouden int Casteel Batavia van het Passerende Daer teer Plaetse als over Geheel Nederlants Indie (1624-1682)*, 27 Vols. The Hague & Batavia, 1887-1931, (henceforth DR) 1661, p. 42.
41. Cunha Rivara, *Archivo Portuguez Oriental*, (henceforth APO-CR) 6 fasciculos in 9 Vols, Goa, 1857-76. See Decree 18, p. 20 and Decree, 40, p.30.
42. D.I, *op.cit.*, Vol. VI, pp. 89-93. S. Jeyaseela Stephen, *The Coromandel Coast and its Hinterland: Economy, Society and Political System, 1500-1600*, New Delhi, 1997, see pp. 182-186.
43. Niccolao Manucci, op.cit., Vol. III, p. 112.
44. *APO - CR, op.cit.*, fasciculo 4, Decree 12, pp.12-16.
45. Niccolao Manucci, *op.cit.*, Vol. III, p. 113.
46. EFI, 1642-1645, *op.cit.*, p. 44.
47. *Ibid.*, p. 59.
48. Records of Fort St., George, *Diary and Consultation Book. 1672*, Madras, 1918, pp.165-66, See also p. 110.
49. John Van Linschoten, *The Voyages of John Van Linschoten to the East Indies*, 2 Vols., London, 1885, Vol. I, pp. 209-210.
50. Annual letter of Francisco Cabral at Goa dated 17 December 1594 in *Documenta Indica*, Vol. XVI, pp. 750-751.

51. Niccolao Manucci, *op.cit.,* Vol. III, pp. 112-113.

52. *Ibid.*, Vol. III, pp. 206-207.

53. *Ibid,* Vol. III, pp. 207-209.

54. See, Vitorino Maghalaes Godhino, *Os Descobrimentos e a Mundial*, Lisboa, 1981-84.

55. Niccolao Manucci, *op.cit.,* Vol. III, p. 118. He says that "I will relate these stories by various old inhabitants, natives of the place of Santhome of Mylapore. Formerly it was richer than all the other towns held by the Portuguese in India, owing to its great trade with China Java Melaka etc., The merchants gained more than a thousand percent but this was before the Dutch came to India. They received goods and paid for them by the *para* which is a measure used in Europe to measure corn and vegetable. Nowadays (1653-1708) they measure in those measure rice lime and other products. The coins for which these goods were exchanged are called pagodas which are still current. These coins which are of gold and weigh a *drachem* are small and circular, stamped only on one side with symbol of some idol. The ancients must have thought little of gold from the way they used it in painting and adorning various unnecessary places such as beams doorways, windows in their houses, and for various purposes such as on chests, chests of drawers, benches, chairs etc., adding nails and fastenings of gold and silver or putting gold feet and other ornaments to their bedsteads of aloes wood or sandal wood, also to the chairs and benches of the same woods".

56. Niccolao Manucci, *op.cit.,* Vol. III, pp. 177-178.

57. *Ibid.,* Vol. III, pp. 187-191.

58. S. Jeyaseela Stephen, *Portuguese in the Tamil Coast, op.cit.*, p. 244.

59. Niccolao Manucci, *op.cit.,* Vol. III, p. 210.

60. *Ibid.,* Vol. III, p. 210 & 254.

61. *Ibid.,* Vol. III, pp. 210-211.

62. *Ibid.,* Vol. III, p. 211.

63. *Ibid.,* Vol. III, pp. 212-213.

64. *Ibid.,* Vol. III, pp. 212 & 255.

65. *Ibid.,* Vol. III, pp. 213-214, p. 256.

66. R.A. Bulhão Pato, *Documentos Remettidos da India ou Livros das Monções,* 5 Vols, Lisboa, 1880-1935, (henceforth DRI) Vol. II, p. 226.

67. S. Jeyaseela Stephen, *Portuguese in the Tamil Coast, op.cit.*, p.158.

68. Niccolao Manucci, *op.cit.,* Vol. III, pp.128-129. See, for details of the nine forms of slavery during the Dutch and French expansion in the Bay of

Bengal, S. Jeyaseela Stephen, "Slavery and Society: Experiences of the Dutch and the French Trading Companies in Coastal Andhra, AD 1600-1800", in (ed.,) R. Soma Reddy, *Social Evils in Andhradesa: 17th and 18th Centuries*, Department of History, Osmania University Publications, Hyderabad, 1999, pp.75-96.

69. S. Jeyaseela Stephen, *Portuguese in the Tamil Coast, op.cit.*, pp. 237.

SECTION-III

7

Role of the Tamil Printing Press: Development of Christian Devotional Literature and Prose

Right from the *Sangam* age, Tamil was written in verse form only. Tolkappiyam, the earliest extant Tamil grammar reveals that prose was not much in existence. In the great epic of *Silapadikaram*, verses are interspersed with prose.[1] There were commentators called urai aciriyar who wrote particularly commentaries on grammar. *Iraiyanar kalaviyal urai* (the commentary on Iraiyanar akapporul) marked the first stage in the development of Tamil prose. This is a grammatical treatise *akapporul* and lord Siva himself is said to be its author. Nakkirar of the Third Tamil *Sangam* was perhaps the first commentator of this work. In the history of Tamil literature, the development of prose was slow. Simplicity and vividness, the two essential features of prose was thus totally absent. Moreover learning the language of Tamil was the preserve of only the upper castes as Sanskrit was the preserve of the *brahmins*. The missionaries were the first to feel the need to develop Tamil prose as it had not well developed till then compared to the Portuguese language. They also recognised the rich literature and deeper diction that the Tamil language was noted for. The missionaries differentiated the two kinds of Tamil language, namely literary Tamil (cultivated dialect) and colloquial Tamil (uncultivated dialect).

The missionaries were always impelled by an urge to convey the Christian religious message to the people of the Tamil Coast.

We find that religious books in Portuguese were imported initially. In 1521 Dom Duarte de Menezes, the Portuguese Governor had entrusted the Factor of Goa with fifty *cartilhas* (primers) five *flos sanctorum* (lives of saints) and four *Avamjelorium* (gospels) to be given to the *mocos* and *orfaos*, so that they could learn and read.[2] Later we find that a list of books that were delivered for the Franciscans through the Governor by order of the King of Portugal in 1518.[3] Most of these religious works were written between the Twelfth and the Fifteenth Centuries. The Missionaries were anxious to convey the printed Portuguese matter in simple Tamil, making it easy to be understood even by the uninitiated. Their sermons and the good tidings of the Gospel had to be conveyed clearly and effectively to all men, women and children who were quite unlettered. Therefore naturally the missionaries had to develop Tamil prose.

Krisittiyani Vanakkam, 1579

Krisittiyani Vanakkam (*Doctrina Christam*) running to 122 pages was the second printed Tamil book (the first Tamil book in prose) written by Fr. Henriques. The author signed his name in Tamil as Andriku Padriyar. It is a collection of Tamil prayers and doctrinal explanations to help *parava* Christians grasp the tenets of the faith. As he had no previous model to imitate while writing Tamil prose, he may be called as the pioneer of Tamil prose. He could be the earliest modern prose writer in Tamil as far as we know.

Krisittiyani Vanakkam was printed on Saturday, 14 Karthigai (November) 1579 (*quatorze de Nouêmbro do Anno de* MDLXXIX) at the *Collegio da Madre de Deos* of the Jesuits in Kochi. The actual size of the book was 10 cms X 14 cms. An examination of the original points out that three pages were blank. This included the back side of the first leaf and both the pages of the last leaf. There is an introduction in the second leaf in Tamil on the front page and in Portuguese on its reverse. It is mentioned that Fr. Henriques had translated this work into Tamil based on the Christian doctrine that was originally written in Portuguese by Marcos George published in 1566.

There are twelve chapters in the book and it ends with the words of the Holy Scripture "There is no salvation except through this name (Jesus)". The original discovered by Fr. Robert Streit in 1928 was available in *Bibliothéque de la Sorbonne*, Paris although it is now said to have been lost. Mr. Graham Shaw discovered another copy of *Krisittiyani Vanakam* at the original manuscript department in the Bodleian Library, London in 1979 and it exists even today.[4] A copy of Kristiyyani Vanakkam is also available at the Jesuit Library at Enghien, Belgium.

Confessionario, 1580

The letter of Fr. Luís Frois mentioned that Fr. Francisco Rodrigues and Fr. António de Quadros had ordered the *Confessionario* (The Manual for Confession) to be prepared in Portuguese for the use of the converts in Goa in 1578. They wanted it to be printed and circulated during the Lent. A devotee came forward to supply paper free of cost for printing and so it was chiefly done for the love of god to be placed into the hands of Christians in Goa. When the same was sent to the Portuguese settlements on the Tamil Coast for distribution, the priests of the Society of Jesus residing there in Punnaikayal translated it into good Tamil.[5] *Confessionario* is the third Tamil book printed on 31 *Vaikasi*, Saturday, 28 May 1580. The original is now available at the Bodleian Library, London, U.K. It was discovered by Mr. Graham Shaw in 1979, although Thomas James had recorded its existence in A.D. 1620. The size of it was 9 X 13.5 cms and the total number of pages was 107. The logo of the Jesuits IHS (Iesus Humanis Salvador) is found there. An examination of the Tamil text in the book shows that works from other languages such as Latin, Portuguese and Sanskrit had been profusely used. It is known that this *confessionario* written by Fr. Henriques has found mention in another book called *Flos Sanctorum*, vide pages 559 and 648.

Flos Sanctorum, 1586

The missionaries brought from Portugal the famous *Flos Sanctorum* originally published in 1513 in the Portuguese language. It may be recalled here that Nicholas Lancillotto, a Jesuit had written a letter from Kollam as early as on 6 January 1551 to Ignatius

Loyola that Fr. Henriques had begun translating the Lives of the Saints in Tamil. Before the publication of this Tamil book, the author had shown the full text to a few natives who were well versed in Tamil and had received valuable suggestions and comments and carried out the corrections as suggested. This book had therefore far less grammatical errors and was very neatly written although its printing was delayed very much.[6]

After taking a long time for translation, this book was printed in Tamil in 1586 at Punnaikayal on the Pearl Fishery Coast. The book was of moderate size (20.5 cms X 14 X 3.5 cms) and handy enough to be carried. An original copy discovered by Fr. Xavier Thaninayagam in 1954 is now available in the Vatican Library although the preface and the table of contents are missing in the book.[7] The original title page is also lost. This book, containing (342 folios) 668 printed pages, may be described as the magnum opus of Fr. Henriques. The author has admitted that he had translated the lives of all saints found in three Portuguese books and that it took more than three years to complete. The publication of this Tamil book was generously sponsored by the *paravas* who paid 400 *cruzados* on one occasion to Fr. Henriques.[8]

In the year 1564, the second printing press was brought to India by Batimande, a missionary from Spain. It was this machine that was used for printing the first Tamil book *Doctrina Christam en lingua Malauar Tamul* (*Thambiran Vanakkam*).[9] The testimony of Fr. Sebastião Gonçalves regarding Tamil publications is worthy of consideration here. He mentioned in the Annual Letter of the Jesuits in 1600 that all those books he got printed in Tamil were made by the Jesuits alone. He further mentioned that there was no need any more to get either the matrices or the letters for printing the books at Venice in Italy. He revealed that these printed books could be found not only in the hands of the Christians on the Pearl Fishery Coast but also with Hindus in the interior places of the hinterland. The Tamils were greatly astonished about the way in which good Tamil types were made and books printed in their language. The Tamil *pandits* and *brahmins* were highly impressed by the novelty and mysteries of printing. The spiritual writings thus began to appear in prose and not in verse at the instance of the Portuguese missionaries.[10]

Tamil Works of Fr. Henrique Henriques

When Fr. Henriques died in Punnaikayal on 6 February 1600, the Annual Jesuit Letter of that year gave the list of his printed works: (a) Lives of the Saints (b) *Doctrina Christam* (c) *Christuvin Varalaru* (Life of Christ till the Ascension) (d) A Manual for Confession.[11] Further, the Annual Jesuit Letter of the year 1602 mentioned a few more books written by Fr. Henriques but which remained unpublished. These included (a) Tamil Grammar (b) Tamil-Portuguese Dictionary (c) *Christuvathin Ethiralikalukku* (Refuting the fables of the gentiles and defending the Christian religion: *Alia contrafabuals ethinicorum pro defensione divinae legis*) and (d) *Adiyarkallin Sagodaratuvam* (Brotherhood of saints).

Tamil Writings of Fr. Roberto Nobili

The Jesuit Superior of the Malabar Province in 1606 evinced interest to appoint Fr. Roberto Nobili in Madurai to enable him to learn Tamil. He mentions in his report that "In the month of March 1606 when I went to visit that residence (Madurai) I left there Fr. Roberto Nobili with Fr. Gonçalves Fernandes so that he might learn the language of the country which is pure and more refined (than on the coast) and to see whether he could find some means of opening a door for the conversion of these Gentiles". Thus Fr. Roberto Nobili (1577-1656) came to Madurai in 1606 to begin his missionary work and evinced deep interest in philosophy and he rapidly gained mastery over Tamil and Sanskrit (Although he was an Italian he should be regarded as a missionary of the Portuguese establishment for he served under the Portuguese *padroado*). He had mentioned that Tamil was a beautiful language which was so elegant and abounding in words but the most difficult language to learn. He had further stated that he gave all his free time to the study of Tamil which he learnt in six months and had he not been sick, he would have learnt it even more quickly.

In a letter Nobili wrote to Gregory Boncompagni, his companion during his days as a youth, he described the first steps taken by him for adapting his life as an Indian ascetic to win the admiration of the Tamils and converse with them.[12] He became more convinced that in order to overcome the mistrustful attitude of the Hindus towards the Portuguese and come closer to the Tamils, it was necessary to get to know deeply their beliefs and traditions and also accept partly their culture by going so far as to live according to their way of life. The uncompromising orthodoxy of his colleagues however inflicted on him the charge of heresy and he was forced to justify himself by writing his Apologia.

It is interesting to know in the words of his contemporaries, how Roberto Nobili had learnt Tamil and acquired mastery over the Tamil language. On 20 November 1609, Fr Laerzio, the Jesuit Provincial wrote to the Superior General in Rome as follows.[13] "Father Nobili had learnt Tamil like the *brahmins* who are the most proficient in that language. He has also read many of their works and learnt by-heart certain portions as well as many verses of their most famous poets".

Fr. Buccerio in his report sent in 1610 to the Superior General mentioned:[14] "His (Nobili) knowledge of Tamil is particularly amazing that one would think it is his native language. It is wonderful how he had been able to master it so well within these few years". Fr. António Vico in his letter dated 25 October 1610 wrote to the Jesuit Superior General in Rome that he was fully convinced about the capacity of Fr. Roberto Nobili to undertake evangelical work in Madurai. He confessed that all he had imagined vanished before his eyes. He called Nobili as the ideally perfect missionary. Further he highlighted the knowledge of Nobili to defend the faith with Hindus.[15] "Shall I speak to you of his knowledge that exposes the most abstruse question of theology as if they were child's play? With that subtle talent he (Nobili) knows how to interest and charm others while making himself understood by the ignorant. He astonishes people with the fertile eloquence by the richness of expressions and also in respect of the variety and different idioms".

In the Annual Jesuit letter of 1656, Fr. Proença mentioned thus[16]: "There is no mystery in our religion which is not explained in the book of Fr. Roberto. There is nothing left difficult that he has not solved so that a missionary needs no other books of theology than those he has written".

Roberto Nobili has written the following works in Tamil prose.[17]

1. *Attuma Nirunayam* (Disquisition on the Soul), Madras, 1889; Tuticorin, 1967.

2. *Gnanopadesam* (Spiritual Instruction), (Mss in *Pontificia Biblioteca Missionaria di Propaganda Fide*, Rome) Madras, 1891. Trichnopoly, 1906; Tuticorin, Vol. I-IV, 1963-68.
3. *Punar Janma Atchepam* (On Transmigration or Refutation of Rebirth), (Mss in Madurai Province Jesuit Archives, fls, 1-83) Tuticorin, 1963.
4. *Dhushana Dhikkaram* (Refutation of Blasphemies or Defence of Christianity), (Mss in Madurai Province Jesuit Archives, fls, 1-470) Tuticorin, 1964.
5. *Devamatha Sarithiram* (Life of Mother of God) Tuticorin, 1964.
6. *Sesunathar Sarithiram* (Life of Lord Jesus Christ), Tuticorin, 1964.
7. *Nithiya Jeevana Sallapam* (Dialogue on Eternal Life), (Mss in Saraswathi Mahal Library, Thanjavur, India, Mss Tamil, no. 536, fls. 1-88) Tuticorin, 1964.
8. *Agnaana Nivaaranam* (Dispelling of Ignorance), Trichnopoly, 1891.
9. *Kadavul Nirnayam* (Theodicy)
10. *Bedhaga Paritchai* (Examination of Errors)
11. *Gnaana Deepikai* (Spiritual Beacon)
12. *Visuvasa Sallaapam* (Dialogue on Faith)
13. *Mandira Maalai* (A Garland of Prayers)
14. *Chinna Kuripidam* (Penny Catechism)

Items from serial numbers one to eight have been printed while from nine to fourteen are not available till date. In a letter dated 6 January 1656, Fr. Roberto Nobili wrote the following lines. "It was my desire that whatever I wrote in Tamil, Telugu and Sanskrit was to be in tune with the doctrine of Our Mother Roman Catholic Church. I pray to Her to correct me if I have written knowingly or unknowingly something wrong, or hurt the feelings of others or if I have omitted anything; I make this request earnestly to all those who make editions or translations of all my writings".

Translations of Fr. Balthazar da Costa from Tamil into Portuguese

Among the works of Fr. Roberto Nobili, two works entitled Gnanopadesam and *Chinna kuripidam* were translated from Tamil into Portuguese in 1661 by Fr. Balthazar da Costa (1610-1673). The work *Gnanopadesam* was dedicated to Dom Affonso (1656-1667), the King of Portugal vide his correspondence dated 12 February 1661 written from Madurai. Balthazar da Costa says: "I have undertaken the task of translating it into Portuguese. It seemed to me that I should be doing thereby some service to all the Missionaries of the East, as this task would be a help to them. If each one translated it into the languages of the pastoral region where he resides it would help the people".

Fr. Jean Castests discovered the Portuguese translation of *Gnanopadesam* in the Goa Archives in 1923. He got typed out a copy and it is now available at the Madurai Province Jesuit Archives (fls. 1-800). The first page of the book *Gnanopadesam* contains the following.[18] "*Gnanopadesam* / in which are explained / with perfect method / all the Catholic truths / necessary for salvation ; / in which are also most clearly refuted / all the heathen sects of the East / A work truly suited to convert the heathens / composed in Tamil / by the venerable Fr. Roberto Nobili of the Society of Jesus / founder of the Madurai Mission / Translated into Portuguese / By Fr. Balthazar da Costa / of the same Society and Mission / for the use of Missionaries in India / dedicated / to the Most High & Most Puissant Lord / Dom Affonso VI, King of Portugal etc / 1661".

Tamil Works of Fr. Jean Venant Bouchet

Fr. Jean Venant Bouchet (1655-1732) was another Jesuit who preached the Gospel at Avur. He composed the following three works in Tamil:[19]

1. *Thivviya Mathrikai* (The Divine Model), Pondicherry, 1870; Tuticorin, 1966.
2. *Gnaana Sanchivi* (Spiritual Medicine) (Mss in the Madurai Province Jesuit Archives) Tuticorin, 1965.
3. Gnaana Natchathira Maalai, (Spiritual Star of Garland), Tuticorin, 1966.

Tamil Writings of Fr. Giuseppe Constantino Beschi

Fr. Giuseppe Constantino Beschi (1680-1764), another Italian by birth also worked for the salvation of souls under the Portuguese *padroado* in the Tamil Country. He is called Veeramaamunivar and had contributed much towards both Tamil prose and poetry which are now acclaimed as classics of Tamil literature. He is also considered the founder of Tamil Philology on account of his work entitled "*Grammatica Latino- Tamulica*". His *Dictionarium Tamulicum Latinum* is also another important contribution. His works also include witty and piquant short stories. His restoration of the *pulli* or dots to consonants and the introduction of double loop symbol for certain consonants are well known. He popularised the cult of Quitteri, the Portuguese saint by narrating the life of the saint and writing the ballad Kittheriamman Ammanai.[20] His writings covered a wide range of subjects which included asceticism, apologetics, grammar, lexicography, linguistics, poetics, theology and humour.

The following is a detailed list of works composed by Fr. Beschi:[21]

1. *Gnaana Kannaadi*, (Spiritual Mirror) 1727.
2. *Gnaana Unarthuthal*, (Spiritual consciousness) 1727.
3. *Tonnul Vilakkam*, (Explanation of Old Texts) 1730; Pondicherry, 1838.
4. Grammatica Latino-Tamulica, in qua de Vulgari Tamulicae Linguae Idiomate Kodun-Tamil dicto fusius tractatur, (Tamil-Latin Grammar) (Mss in Pontificia Biblioteca Missionaria di Propaganda Fide, Rome) Danish Mission Press, Tranquebar, 1838; Pondicherry, 1843.
5. *Vethiyar Ozhukkam*, (Moral Code for Catechists) 1727; Pondicherry, 1847.
6. *Veda Vilakkam*, (Explanation of Religion) 1728; Pondicherry, 1842.
7. Paramaartha Guruvin Kathai, (Story of Paramartha Guru) (Mss entitled "Aventures du Gourou Paramarta" in Biblioteca Instituti Historici Societatis Jesu, Rome) Pondicherry, 1845; Fabula de Ethnicorum Magistro Paramartaguru dicto... Tamulica Scripta et a Bispo Auctore in Latinum Versa, London, 1822.
8. *Kittheriamman Ammanai*, 1732; Madras, 1849; Madurai, 1947.
9. *Thembavani*, composed in 1726, (Garland of Flowers) 1729; Pondicherry, 3 Vols, 1851-1853.

10. Vulgars Tamulicae Linguae Dictionarium Tamulicum-Latinum: (in British Museum Library, Add 26110) Additis in Praefatione aliquot Regulis Necessario Praelegendis, Trichnopoly, 1882.
11. Chathur agaraathi (Quadruple dictionnaire Tamoul de Beschi, Contenant le Dictionaire des Mots, Celui des Synonymes, Celui des Classifications et Celui des Rimes) (Mss in Pontificia Biblioteca Missionaria di Propaganda Fide, Rome,) composed in 1732, published in Madras, 1824, Pondicherry, 1872.
12. *Annai azhungal anthaathi*, (Poem on Our Lady of Affliction) Thanjavur, 1865.
13. *Thirukaavalur kalambagam*, (Poem of Thirukavalur) Thanjavur, 1843.
14. *Adaikala maalai* (Garland of Protection).
15. *Karunaambara padigam* (Poem on Mercy).
16. *Vannam*, (The colour) Thanjavur, 1843.
17. *Thirukkadayur Nirubam* (Epistle of Thirukkadayur).
18. *Thirukural Urai* (Commentary on Thirukural).
19. *Lutherinathiyalppu*, (Refutation of Lutheranism) Pondicherry, 1842, 1847, 1868.
20. *Bedhaga Marutthal*, (Refuting Errors) Pondicherry, 1868.
21. Portuguese-Latin-Tamil Dictionary (Mss in the Madurai Province Jesuit Archives, Old Manuscripts No. 225/5 fls. 1-103; British Library, London, 3101, Mss, Tamil B.3.)

Some efforts to translate the Bible into Tamil had also been undertaken by the Jesuits in the Tamil country. Bartholomeu Ziegan Balg, the Protestant missionary in Tranquebar who came to know about the old Tamil Bible with the Roman Catholic missionaries at Nagapattinam, requested them to send it to him in exchange for a copy of the New Testament published by him on 21 March 1711. The Bible under the possession of the Jesuits contained the Old Testament given in the form of question and answers.[22]

Fr. Coeurdoux, the Jesuit who lived at this time mentions in his letter written from Karaikal dated 26 September 1741 that the Lutherans had translated the Bible into Tamil but its language, style and structure were not good and so it does not bring honour to the Holy Scripture. The defective translation carried out by the Lutherans had been mainly owing to their ignorance of the Tamil language.[23]

There was a shift from the religious writings found common by the missionaries like Henrique Henriques in the Sixteenth Century to an increasing number of secular writings in the Seventeenth and Eighteenth Centuries by Roberto Nobili and Giuseppe Constantino Beschi. However these missionaries mainly expounded the tenets of Catholic doctrine to the Tamil public. Indeed their contribution towards the development of Tamil language and literature was extraordinary.

Palm leaf manuscripts in Tamil were sent by the Jesuits from Pondicherry to the Royal Library of the king of France in Paris. This is mentioned in the letter written by Fr. Jean Calmettee dated 26 August 1730 from a place called Ballabaram.[24] Similarly mention was also made of the plam leaf manuscripts of the four Vedas sent to the Library of the king of France in the letter written from Pondicherry by Fr Le Gac to Fr. Souicet dated 28 September 1732.[25] Thus the missionaries were keen to pass on the rich heritage of the Tamils to Europe.

Contribution to Tamil Printing

A proper understanding of the impact of Portuguese influence on the Tamil language and literature is absent in the writings of Tamil scholars especially for the simple reason that they have not been able to tap the historical primary sources in the Portuguese language.[26] The interaction of the Portuguese with the Tamils has been much more clearly and elaborately recorded in the Portuguese sources rather than in the native Tamil records of the period if at all there is any. Here in this chapter an attempt has been made to unravel this part of the hitherto little known aspect of how the Portuguese, particularly their missionaries played a catalystic role in ushering the Tamil language into the modern era.

With the extension of the Portuguese trading activities from the Malabar region to the Tamil coastal region and more particularly among the *parava* fishing community of the Pearl Fishery Coast living within the orbit of Portuguese influence, more out of necessity than out of any other reason, the early Portuguese settlers came into contact with an altogether different oriental language and cultural entity. They observed that the traders of the Tamil Coast spoke a language called 'Tamul' as they called it, which was different from Malayalam spoken in Malabar, though both the languages had many similarities. They clearly understood the difference between these two Indian languages as between the Portuguese and Castillian in their own country.[27]

It is gleaned from Portuguese archival records that the Portuguese traders took great efforts to speak Tamil for the sake of carrying on their business transactions smoothly with the natives. Manuel Gomes, a Portuguese trader who was fluent in Tamil, is said to have prepared a Portuguese version of a complaint dated 10 September 1527 proposed to be lodged by the Tamil speaking *mudaliar* merchants to the king of Portugal. This Tamil petition addressed to the king of Portugal was translated into Portuguese language on behalf of the Tamil merchants and all the signatures were affixed in Tamil.[28]

Prayers in Tamil were not available as late as 1545. In the meanwhile however the responsibility of writing the prayers in Tamil was assigned to a priest by name Francisco Coelho, who seems to have had a much better knowledge of Tamil than all the other priests among the Franciscans and the Jesuits on the Tamil Coast including Fr. António Criminali who is understood to have learnt by that time to write and read Tamil. Although initially Tamil was very difficult for the missionaries, in due course of time they understood well and spoke it fluently.[29]

Diogo do Couto, (1542-1616) the Sixteenth Century chronicler who lived in Goa in 1598 has also written about the famous Tamil work of Thirukkural. Perhaps he was the first European who had made known Thirukkural to the Western world. He says: "There is a book among them by a man who is held by them to have been very wise, called Valuver, a native of the town of Meliapore (Mylapore) who lived at the same time as the Apostle St. Thomas, which contains one thousand three hundred and thirty verses, in which he speaks of the knowledge of one sole creator, of the reverence that is due to him, of the importance of penitence, humility, abstinence and of the disdain for idols; and for these reasons and for others that are written there, it is learnt that he was taught by the Apostle St. Thomas himself".[30] In the early Sixteenth Century the Portuguese had thus aspired to know more about the then extant Tamil classical works.

Francis Xavier, the Jesuit priest who came to Goa in 1542 was perhaps the first missionary with whom the *paravas* came into intimate contact. He came to Tuticorin at the end of October 1542 and remained there with the *paravas* for a short period of four months.[31] He reported in his letter that he could not understand the mother tongue of the natives. With the little knowledge he had of Tamil, he could not undertake the translation of the Christian liturgical pieces such as *Pater noster* (Our Father), *Ave Maria* (Hail Mary) and the *Credo* (Creed). Further in his letter written on 27 March 1544 from Manapad we understand that he had picked up Tamil slowly whereby he could have an idea of the imperfect state of his first version of Tamil prayers. His eagerness to achieve a more accurate and correct version of the Tamil prayers is also recorded in that letter.[32] As Francis Xavier found it difficult to get the prayers in Tamil translated by himself, he encouraged his fellow missionaries to learn Tamil. Thanks to his vision and encouragement, those missionaries who came to the Pearl Fishery Coast tried their best to master the Tamil language. In a letter written on 31 October 1548, Fr. Henrique Henriques informs Ignatius Loyola, the Superior General of the Jesuits that Fr. António Criminali began to read and write Tamil which was very difficult. He mastered the language by spending time, understanding it well and spoke also fluently.[33]

According to records, Francis Xavier is said to have nominated Fr. Henrique Henriques (1520-1600) to take care of the spiritual needs of the *paravas* on the Pearl Fishery Coast which duty he faithfully performed. In a letter written to Ignatius Loyola he described Fr. Henrique Henriques who was posted at Kanyakumari as a very virtuous and edifying person. His keenness to speak and write Tamil was so great that the native Christians loved him so much on account of the sermons he preached and the talks he gave in Tamil. Having witnessed the zeal of the *paravas*, Francis Xavier once said that they would never give up the Christian religion they had embraced even if the Portuguese were to leave the Tamil Coast.[34] Fr. João Villa de Conde, a Franciscan monk from the Province of Piedade who was stationed at Punnaikayal also took much trouble to get the prayers translated into Tamil. A Tamil scholar well versed both in Portuguese and Tamil was sent by Fr. João from Colombo to help Fr. Henriques to accomplish his assignment.

First Tamil Book Printed in Portugal

The first little book in Tamil containing 38 pages was published in Lisbon on 2 February 1554. An original copy of this tract (discovered by Fr. Xavier Thaninayagam in 1954) is even now preserved safely at the Belem Museum in Lisbon.[35] The text of the book in Latin script was a Tamil word by word transliteration, printed in red colour. Below that was given the Portuguese version in small letters printed in black colour. The title of the book runs as follows: " *Cartilha che conte brevemete ho q todo christão deve aprender pera sua saluacam, a qual el rey dom Joham terceiro deste nome nosso senhor mandou imprimir e lingua Tamul e Portugues co ha declaracam do Tamul por Cima de Vermelho*" (Primer which contains in brief all that a Christian should know for his salvation and which Our Lord, the King Dom John III, had ordered to be printed in the Tamil language and in Portuguese with the Tamil meaning printed above in red).

This book was printed two years before the introduction of printing in India (1556) by the Portuguese. This Tamil book was mainly intended to be used by the Portuguese missionaries in Portugal who were preparing to come to the Tamil Coast for apostolic work. This was the first book used by the missionaries for the propagation of the Christian faith among the natives in the Tamil Coast. All of this confirms the great efforts made by the Portuguese missionaries to master the Tamil language and their dedication and commitment to learn Tamil before they could leave Lisbon for India.

This elementary book was the first one prepared by the missionaries for the study of Tamil alphabets. The prologue was written by three Luso-Tamils then living in Lisbon and their names are mentioned in the book as Vicente de Nazareth, Jorge Carvalho and Thome da Cruz. It is learnt that these three men were responsible for the entire work and it was supervised by Fr. João Villa de Conde.[36]

The Cartilha, otherwise called the primer, contained abridged versions of the Christian doctrines. The book also contained the common prayers like *Pater Noster*, *Ave Maria*, *Credo*, besides *Salve Regina* and the Ten Commandments of the Old Testament. The book had several native words and was written in the colloquial language. Nevertheless it has the distinction of being the first printed Tamil book, even though the script was not Tamil.[87]

How this original copy of the printed cartilha found its way to the Belem Museum is itself an interesting story. This museum was originally part of the Library of the Carthusian monastery. This religious house was founded by Theotonio de Bragança in 1598, who was a distinguished Jesuit scholar born in Coimbra in 1536, educated in Rome and Paris. He later became the Archbishop of Evora. He possessed this cartilha and gifted it to the monastery before his death in 1602. It was preserved there until it was disbanded in 1902. This is evident from a handwritten note on the cartilha. In 1909 this cartilha seems to have passed into the hands of an individual (name unknown) who eventually brought it to Belem Museum.

First Printing Press in India to Print Books in Tamil

Printing was first introduced in Portugal as early as in 1495 only three years before the Portuguese landed in India.[88] In the beginning, a superficial knowledge of the local language was found adequate to carry on their trade dealings with the native merchants. There were not much social contacts with the local people. Prices of all commodities, their weight and measurements were determined by longstanding customs, conventions which did not demand knowledge of the local language. Simple arithmetical calculations were carried out through simple additions, deductions, multiplications and divisions. The more pressing task of evangelisation among the locals required a much deeper knowledge of the Tamil language.

Members of the upper caste *brahmin* community were well versed in Sanskrit and Tamil. The scholars or *pandits* were also masters of prosody. Prose writing was something which was not found necessary. Every system of knowledge such as medicine, rituals, science, religious lores, etc., was written in the form of poetry or verses of which men and women in the field had very little knowledge. In these circumstances it was the missionaries who felt the need not only to learn the language but also to acquire some mastery over it, especially to explain some of the very obtuse interpretations and tenets of Christianity. Moreover the message of Christianity could not be carried far and wide through word of mouth. There was need to spread the knowledge of their religion through some tangible means. They could have used the palm leaves for inscribing their teachings. but as they were already familiar with the printing of books, they resorted to the same tool to spread the religion among the locals here. This state of affairs seems to have continued for more than forty years. Thus there was a great desire to introduce printing in India.

In a letter dated 20 November 1545 addressed to his Superiors in Rome, Joannes de Beira, a Jesuit who lived in Casa de Santa Fe in Goa suggested that the Christian doctrines could be published in all the languages of the Orient.[39] Francis Xavier, the most successful evangelist in the Pearl Fishery Coast expressed the same view in 1549 that the Christian literature should be printed in the Eastern languages.[40] However it took more than ten years for a printing press to be sent in a ship that left Lisbon on 29 March 1556 to reach Goa on 6 September 1556.[41] The first printed work was the "Catechism" of Francis Xavier which summarised the doctrines of Christianity to be taught by the missionaries. A letter written by Fr. Luís Frois on 30 November 1556 tells that the "*Doctrina Christa Ordenada a Maneira de Dialogo Para Ensinar os Meninos*" composed by Francis Xavier for the benefit of the children could be printed only five years after the death of Francis Xavier[42] and this work was done by the Jesuit scholastic João Gonçalves living in Goa.[43]

Fr. Henrique Henriques became the Jesuit Superior of the Missions on the Tamil Coast in 1549 and headed it for more than a quarter century. Fr. Henriques, as the Superior of the Mission felt the need to print the liturgical books in Tamil. When he accompanied the Jesuit Visitor Fr. Alessandro Valignano to Goa to attend the meeting of the Jesuit Superiors in December 1575 they discussed together about it. In the Chapter Meeting held there, this agenda was placed and a decision was taken to print books on catechism, confession, Christian doctrine and the lives of saints in Tamil. At the same time Fr. Henriques was relieved of his administrative responsibility and asked to undertake the composition of those books. Henriques also humbly accepted the assignment and applied his mind, time and talent to write these books. Further the Jesuit Visitor Valignano had also directed the Jesuit scholastic (Juan de Bastamante) João Gonçalves to make Tamil types to be used for printing books and he succeeded in 1577 in making Tamil types for printing.[44] In a letter dated 24 December 1576 we find that Pedro Luíz, a *brahmin* convert from the Tamil Coast was chiefly sent to Goa to acquaint João Gonçalves with the knowledge of typesetting the Tamil letters.[45]

Thambiran Vanakkam, 1578

The credit for preparing the first Tamil metal types goes to João Gonçalves who was then in Goa. Fr. Francisco de Sousa wrote: " He (João Gonçalves) was the first who made in India the types of Malabar (Tamil) letters with which the first books were printed".[46] Thambiran Vanakkam (*Doctrina Christam en lingua Malauar Tamul*) was printed with these Tamil types at the *Collegio do Saluador* of the Jesuits in Kollam on Monday 20 October 1578, (20 Aippasi, 1578). Further Francisco de Sousa wrote: "This (*Doctrina Christam*) was the first printed book which India saw being born in its own land".[47] This printed Tamil book was chiefly based on Francis Xavier's *Doctrina Christam* in Portuguese that had already been printed in Goa in 1556. This small text can thus claim to be the first book printed in an Indian language. It contain sixteen pages of 10 x 14 cms size. With the assistance of Fr. Manuel de São Pedro, Fr. Henriques had translated the prayers found in the book. We have a reference at the end of the book which says that the Tamil letters used in printing was made as per the model that was in use. Fr. Fonseca in Rome who received this book which was sent from India has affixed his signature on it sometime in November 1579. The book ends with the phrase *Soli Deo Honor & Gloria, Amen* (All Praise and Glory to God, Amen).

Fr. Henrique Henriques began to translate *Doctrina Christam* into Tamil on 20 February 1557. Fr. Manoel de São Pedro who was then in Sri Lanka came to Punnaikayal in 1562 to assist Fr.

Henriques in this venture. The work was in progress even when Fr. João Villa de Conde paid a visit to Punnaikayal during October 1567. He expressed his admiration at the monumental work that was in progress then. Henriques continued to make corrections in the Tamil prayers with the help of natives even as late as in 1569. This catechism book which was planned much earlier was actually ready only in the year 1570. It took another eight years to reach the final shape. This book called in Tamil *Thambiran Vanakkam* was a collection of prayers and it had no preface. The first page even carried the picture of Palm Sunday. An original copy donated by Curt. H. Resinger in 1951 is now available in the Harvard University Library, USA.[48]

The missionaries seem to have continued their efforts to improve the Tamil types. In 1578, Fr. João de Faria devised an improved version of the Tamil types in Kollam. In a reference dated in the year 1582 the following passage is found: " Died at Goa, the Rev. João de Faria who built the arches of St Paul and who was the first to start the press at the Fishery Coast for the great glory of God engraving and casting alphabets of the Tamil language".[49] This Fr. João Faria appears to have learnt the art of making types from Gonçalves in Kollam.

As both the Tamil types prepared by Gonçalves and Faria were found to be identical, both were used in printing the book. It was clearly stated on page sixteen of the *Doctrina Christam* that the Tamil types used in the first line were prepared in Goa in 1577 and those used in the subsequent lines were prepared in Kollam in the year 1578.

Regarding the style adopted for printing the books, we find that the *pulli* (dot) was not used on top of the consonants. Further, the long and short consonants called *kuril* and *nedil* were also not indicated. The long consonants (*nedil*) were sometimes found joined in printing. Alphabets such as aa, noo, too had no double loop symbol in printing. Moreover there was little gap between words. A careful scrutiny of *Thambiran Vanakkam* (The Christian Doctrine) shows that many Portuguese words were used. To show that they were not Tamil words, double dagger signs were used before and after the word.

Style and Structure of Tamil Printed books

A comparison of the Sixteenth Century Tamil language style and structure found in the texts of the epigraphs and in the Tamil books printed by the Portuguese can be quite revealing. We may compare the works of the Portuguese in Tamil and understand the improvements introduced in the language style. In this case we may compare the *cartilha* published in Lisbon under the supervision of Fr. João Villa de Conde and Flos Sanctorum published in 1586 by Fr. Henriques in India. At the very outset it becomes evident that the language style of *cartilha* is inferior and the work of Fr. Henriques was definitely an improvement in terms of language, vocabulary and style.

The names of ecclesiastical authorities, liturgical ceremonies and Christian festivals came to be used in Tamil as they were found in the Portuguese language. For example *Bispo, Padre, Vigario, Apostolo, Compadre, Comadre, Missão*, and Catholic. Significantly the names of Jesus, Mary and Joseph were pronounced in Tamil as *Esu, Mari* and *Soosai* almost exactly as in the Portuguese.

A detailed examination of the *cartilha* is taken up here to understand the style and language of Tamil. Although the *manipravalam* style was very common in the Sixteenth Century, we find in the printed Tamil text several Portuguese words used verbatim as given below:

Table 11

Page	*Line*	*Word*	*Meaning*
5	4	Iesu christo	- Jesus Christ
5	5	Cruz	- Cross
28	1	Sacramentos	- Sacraments
29	6	Comunhao	- Communion
29	5	Padrigalodu	- Among the priests

Further, we find that Fr. Henrique Henriques who wrote and published the *Krisittiyani Vanakkam* in 1579 had used Latin and Portuguese terms in Tamil characters while explaining the Christian mysteries of faith.[50] The following table gives a sample of words:

Table 12

Portuguese / Latin word	*Tamil word*	*English meaning*
Gratia	kiraasai	grace
Missa	meesai	holy mass
Averea	Averaesai	avarice
Castidade	Kasithithathe	chastity
Baptismo	Vavatheesvumu	baptism

There were a number of names, verbs and ideas in the new religion of Christianity for which there were no Tamil equivalents. As they had to be made well known to the people at large, many Portuguese words came into usage. Thus new Christian names were coined for use in the *cartilha* when it was printed:

Table 13

Page	*Line*	*Names adopted*	*Equivalent English Names*
16	6	Pedro	Peter
17	1	Andre	Andrew
17	7	Poncio pilato	Poncius Pilot
18	1	Thome	Thomas
16	8	Bertholeomeu	Bartholomeu
19	1-2	Matheus	Mathew
19	3	Simon	Simon
19	5	Judas	Judas
19	6-7	Mathias	Mathias
16	5	Sisser	Ceaser

There were however several errors in the printed Tamil text as mentioned below:[61]

Table 14

Page	*Line*	*Word*	*Correction*
6	1	Aralayathal	Adayalathal
9	6	Vicetapattavale	Visheshapatttavale
14	4	Vixessapatta	Visheshapatta

The Tamil language thus underwent some changes like other languages of the world and it did not remain the same throughout its history. According to the rules of Portuguese grammar, the 'o' inflexion is used for masculine nouns and expressions and the 'a' inflexion for feminine nouns. Some of the expressions borrowed from the Portuguese language could be cited as examples. While addressing persons, *ele* is used for men and *elah* for women. It is grammatically correct in Portuguese to address a third person as *ele* for men and *elah* for women. This is not the practice in Tamil but used in the spoken language of Tamils in the Tirunelveli coast who must have derived it from the Portuguese. We come across even today certain titles still in use in Tamil language. For instance while addressing a person in Nagapattinam-Pondicherry area, the word *dom / don* is used. This practice has also been derived by the natives from the Portuguese.

The study of the evolution of Tamil language had been the field of investigation for some scholars. They opine that the literary language did not always reflect the changes in the spoken Tamil.[52] A comparison made between the literary language with that of the inscriptional records shows that two distinct varieties were used in the Sixteenth Century itself. The spoken variety was mainly found in the prose developed by the Portuguese. The spoken Tamil is also found in inscriptions since they were used to convey simple messages to the public. The literary variety was for poetic works alone. While the spoken language had changed gradually, the language of the poetic compositions remained unchanged. The language of the inscriptions do not provide us a complete picture of the spoken language because the linguistic forms and contents of the inscriptions comprised a limited stereotype range of ideas and thoughts. However the language of Tamil inscriptions in the Sixteenth Century represented an admixture of spoken Tamil with occasional literary flourishes.

The Tamil language was in close contact with the Sanskrit language for a long period of time. Thus there was a much greater possibility for Tamil to come under the influence of Sanskrit. The influence of Sanskrit has been found even in the *Sangam* period. Regarding the style of the Tamil language, the bilingual admixture of Tamil and Sanskrit called *manipravalam* continued in the Sixteenth Century as evident from the Tamil publications of the

Portuguese. Sanskrit words were introduced and profusely used in Tamil by the Vaishnavites in the Tamil country in the medieval period and *Veera Choliyum*, an eleventh century Tamil grammar speaks at length about this *manipravalam* style.[58] If Sanskrit had been kept at a distance not allowing to interfere with the Tamil linguistic system it could not have influenced Tamil very much. The following are some of the Sanskrit words found in the Tamil printed works during this period:

Table 15

Page	*Line*	*Sanskrit words used in Tamil texts*	*Tamil*	*Meanings*
5	3	racxica	ratcikka	to redeem
6	3	puthiran	makan	son
7	7	namaskaram	namaskaram	wishing
8	2	rajyam	arasu	kingdom
9	6	strigalil	penkalil	women
11	1	carvamum	ellamum	all
11	5	cannihastri	kanni	virgin
15	3	logathillude	ulagathilae	in the world
15	5	thosham	tosam	sin
20	1-2	manushan	manidhan	man
25	1-2	snehichu	nesithu	loving
31	2	ahangaram	angaram	pride

The colloquial words were faithfully used by the Portuguese in the written form. They did not adopt the equivalent Tamil literary form when they printed the Tamil books. Some of the differences between the spoken and written forms of Tamil as found in the text of catechism used by the Portuguese may be noted below:

Table 16

Page	*Line*	*In colloquial*	*In Tamil*	*Meaning*
7	2	mulichen	vilizchen	awake
8	4	appan	thanthai	father

(Contd.)

(Contd. Table 16)

Page	*Line*	*In colloquial*	*In Tamil*	*Meaning*
8	5	curucra	kodukira	give
8	1	iriquarray	irukira	seated
9	3	racxichi	ratchitittu	redeemed
28	3	pacradu	parkirathu	looking
21	7	kudukkirvan	kodukkiravan	giving
16	5	iiriquiran	iriukiran	sitting
33	5	codukkuradu	kodukirathu	giving
37	6	irriquiren	irukiren	sitting
37	6	pillachen	pilathithen	alive
39	1	cholichi	cholli	said
16	2	usur kondan	usuru	resurrection
25	7	ettavathu	ettavathu	eighth

Tamil in the Sixteenth Century was a diglossic language since it indicated the coexistence of two varieties of language style with two distinct sets of phonological, lexical and syntactic features. People used Tamil complementarily in specified domains of its use. The formal variety was mostly the written forms of Tamil while the other variety, considered as the informal one, was the spoken one. Portuguese language had a continuous influence only on the Tamil dialect of the low or the informal variety in the age of expansion of the Portuguese on the Tamil Coast.

The influence of Roberto Nobili minimised the use of foreign words and inspired the coining of new Tamil words in the Seventeenth Century. This is considered to be a new development in Tamil. In 1621, Fr. Roberto Nobili coined equivalent Tamil names for Christian names.[64] The following is representative of a few such names:

Table 17

Christian name	*Tamil equivalent*
Peter	Malayappan
Fidelis	Visuvasam

(Contd.)

(Contd. Table 17)

Christian name	*Tamil equivalent*
Constantius	Dairiyam
Hilary	Muthudaiyan
Joachim	Devarambar
Lazarus	Thanappan
Elizabeth	Devannammal
John	Arulappan

Methods of Learning Tamil by Fr. Henrique Henriques and Fr. Antão Proença

Fr. Henriques himself had described his early efforts to learn the Tamil language and we have references about his Tamil learning. While writing to Ignatius of Loyola, as early as in February 1548, he confessed that he did not know more than two words in Tamil and it was at this time that Francis Xavier had just returned from Moluccas. Further he mentioned that it was only under the orders of Francis Xavier that he began to learn, speak and read Tamil as soon as he settled down in the Pearl Fishery Coast. It was so very difficult that he despaired of ever being able to master it. He even gave up learning the Tamil language for some time. On account of this difficulty, he always preferred to use an interpreter. A native who was sent by Fr. João Villa de Conde, helped him for some time. The situation however became critical for Fr. Henrique Henriques once when the interpreter left him. This incident forced Fr. Henriques to learn Tamil through his own effort, sitting by day and night making the learning of Tamil as his one and only occupation. However, visiting other mission stations entrusted to his pastoral care also facilitated the process of learning Tamil. He realised at that time and said in his letter that God was very much pleased to help him greatly to learn the Tamil language.[56]

In another letter written subsequently, Fr. Henriques has given a detailed account of the procedure adopted by him to learn Tamil. He said that he had discovered a new method, just as in Latin to learn the conjugations. By conjugating the Tamil verbs he learnt the present tense, past tense, the futures, the infinitives, subjunctives, etc. He later learnt also the various cases of nominatives, vocatives, accusatives, genitives, datives and ablatives. Finally he was in a position to know easily which was to be put first. He reported that through this way much labour and time was spent to learn where and when the noun, the pronoun or the verb had to be used according to the principles of Tamil grammar. This systematic working method helped him learn Tamil within a short time so that when he wrote in their language, the Tamils were greatly astonished at his mastery.

In a subsequent letter Fr. Henriques mentioned that he did not use any interpreter for the past four months as he had learnt to read and write good Tamil. Although he spoke and preached to the *paravas* in Tamil, he found its pronunciation very difficult. He said that his spoken language was very different with Portuguese accent and at times not all the people present in the church understood him. Therefore whenever he gave some instructions in the church, he asked someone to repeat the same words in Tamil so that all those who had assembled there could follow his language.

Henriques has noted that the nouns in Tamils were classified as rational and irrational according to the neutral gender. All the inanimate substances and irrational beings were classified as neuter in Tamil. The vowels were grouped into two, as long and short, while the consonants were known as plosives, nasals and laterals.

As the missionaries decided to learn Tamil they all took the help of natives to learn the language. In a letter addressed to Ignatius Loyola, it was mentioned that the missionaries at Punnaikayal on the Pearl Fishery Coast received help from a native boy for the study of Tamil who lived in the house of the missionaries.[56] It was a great help to learn the language as the boy was intelligent. He quickly identified the errors in the spoken language of the missionaries. In order to improve their own spoken language they decided to speak only Tamil among themselves and imposed punishment on those who did not adhere to this rule.[57] Fr. Henriques was of the firm opinion that any one who really tried hard, could learn the Tamil language within eighteen months if he used the grammar properly as his own experience had shown.[58]

Fr. Antão Proença, the Jesuit in 1679 has left behind a much more scholarly account of his understanding of the Tamil language and its linguistic nuances of pronunciation, vowels and consonants. He started learning Tamil in 1647 and published his Tamil-Portuguese Dictionary in 1679. He pointed out that the Tamils designated vowels by a beautiful metaphor as *uyir* or the life of a word and consonants as mey or the body. The fusion brought about between the vowel and the consonant was called as *uyirmey* or an animated body. The vowels were named on the basis of the place and manner of articulation like gutturals, palatals and labials. The missionary had given the form, value and pronunciation of the Tamil characters of vowels.[59]

The explanation of these vowels presented no difficulty because they corresponded to the same in Portuguese. The Tamils however had their peculiarity and differentiated between the long and short vowels 'a' and 'i' and 'u'. With 'e' and 'o', the same figure was used for the long and short vowels. The Tamil language also had the dipthong 'ay' formed from the short 'a' and 'i', although the sound tends more toward the 'e' than 'a' and the characters (ay) and (au) were seldom used because there were only a few words which begin with these diphthongs. The sound 'au' is made up of the short 'a' and 'u' but it was not common as the first dipthong even in the medial position when the diphthong occurred in writing, the Tamils used another form, as was also the case with (ai) in the initial position.[60]

Fr. Antão Proença further mentioned that the letter 'ka' corresponded to the Portuguese q or c. It was sometimes used as g especially when it was written singly in the middle of the word.[61] The pronunciation of the letter (gna) was in itself very difficult. In order to explain the letter he used the word *manga* and pronounced it up to the letter n. It was not produced with the tip of the tongue, but by touching the palate with the base of the tongue near the throat, keeping the tongue in that position without striking or pronouncing the g. He said that if they strike that position of the tongue with 'a' or with any other vowel they would produce the full value of the (gna) letter. He further added that this letter was rarely found preceding a vowel but always occurred before 'ka'.[62]

The letter 'sa' was pronounced as 'ch' but in writing sometimes it served as 'sa' and also sometimes as 'x' and at other times as 'j', for want of characters which *Grandha* and Telugu had. Although some Tamil purists did not want or did not know how to pronounce it as 's' or 'j' they pronounced 'x' not exactly but as a mixture of 'x' and 's' and 'j'. All these four different sounds were, as he said, natural to the Portuguese language and it presented no difficulty for the Portuguese people.[63] The letter 'gna' corresponded to the Portuguese sound 'nh' in the words unha or castanha. When in the middle of a word, it occurred without a vowel, it was found before 'sa' or before and other 'gna'. Antão Proença further explained that the letter 'da' was completely foreign to Portuguese pronunciation but it was absolutely necessary to understand its natural sound. He said that the sound was made by striking with the tip of the tongue turned up slightly towards a spot where the plain and smooth surface of the palate begins. Whenever this word was found doubled (da da) the force with which it was struck also doubled and it became like the sound of Portuguese 't'.[64] The letter (zha) which the Portuguese called thick 'l' and (zha) curved 'l' and (ra) corresponded to the Portuguese double 'r' as in the words torre, morra, etc. He noted that the letter da was never written at the beginning of a word.[65] Fr. Antão Proença ended his explanation pointing out that the school children pronounced the vowels such as 'a' 'aa' 'i' 'ii' as 'ana' 'avana' 'ina' and 'iana' respectively.[66]

The order of the consonant letters were also so perplexing to him and contrary to the Portuguese language with its variety of n's, r's and l's.[67] The variety of the letters of the Tamils who, for want of enough letters, had several pronunciations for the one and the same letter as one might see in the letter 'sa' which served for `cha', `xa' and at other times for `sa' or `ja' also baffled him.[68] The word suram could be read in four ways, i.e. *churam, xuram, juram and suram.* The first two pronunciations meant nothing. The third meant `fever' and the fourth `voice'.[69] The same was also found in the letters 'sa', 'ka', 'pa' for the word kayam may be read as *cayam or gayam*, the first meaning `body' and the second `wound'. The word thandu might be read as *tandu* or *dandu*, the first meaning `stalk' and the second `army'. The word pathai may be read as *padey* or *badey* while the first meant the `road', the second `torment'. Antão Proença further noted that in order to teach easily to distinguish these various ways of pronouncing the letter, a new method should be used.[70] He really meant that the difficulty in pronunciation arose only because the letter sa alone had four different pronunciations. He desired to insert four kinds of marks with dots, lines, or other signs to distinguish the normal letter.[71]

These Tamil books printed in India were sent to Europe soon after their printing for the information of the Superior General of the Society of Jesus in Rome and to the king of Portugal. It is fortunate that these originals are still preserved there even today and we are able to unravel at least some of the forgotten facts of Portuguese history.

Portuguese Usages in Tamil

Portuguese was the earliest occidental language with which Tamil had come into close contact during the second millennium. In the initial stages Portuguese words were straightaway adopted for use without any change. The earliest borrowings were of course from Sanskrit, but since the Sixteenth Century borrowings were from Portuguese. Several Portuguese loan words are still in usage

although in a very corrupt form. The loan words were pronounced with innumerable variations. The following are the typically Portuguese words very much popular:[72]

Table 18

Portuguese word	*Tamil word*	*Meaning*
biscothu	biscottu	biscuit
cartas	kaduthasi	letter
khradi	khrathi	altar
mestre	mestri	supervisor
capitao	capitan	captain
mesa	mesai	table
pottan	pothan	button
ayah	ayah	aged women
padre	padriyar	priest

(Contd.)

(Contd.Table 18)

Portuguese word	*Tamil word*	*Meaning*
bataliao	pattalam	army
sepoy	chippai	soldier
tuppaki	thupaaki	gun
receu	rasidu	receipt
chave	savi	key
arratal	rattal	weight
armaraio	alamari	almirah
banaboo	pirambu	bamboo
bolao	balloon	baloon
kamis	kamisu	shorts
cha	chai	tea
chocolate	chocolate	chocolate
copo	coppai	cup
contrato	contract	contract
funil	punal	funnel
janela	jannel	window
jaqueta	jakattu	jacket
sofa	sofa	sofa
verandah	verandah	corridor
sapato	sapattu	shoe
khalsa	kalsat	pant
saco	sakku	gunny bag
escola	escool	school
leileo	aelam	auction
cravado	karvadu	salt fish

Many lexical items were transliterated into Tamil based on Portuguese pronunciation, such as president, *procurdor, compagnie, secretaire*, etc. It may be said that some of the words crept into common usage in the course of commercial and religious dialogues. The adoption of Portuguese items of dress, food and other habits brought still more Portuguese words into Tamil. Similarly a few words of Tamil origin crept into the vocabulary of the Portuguese language such as *manga* which stood for mango.

To conclude we may say that the Portuguese missionaries recognised the richness of Tamil literature, the merits and demerits of its diction. They pointed out the two kinds of literary Tamil (cultivated dialect) and colloquial Tamil (uncultivated dialect) that were prevalent during the period. The significant contributions made by the Portuguese to Tamil prose in the age of discoveries cannot be underestimated. Tamil prose of religious works played a prominent part in the development of Tamil literature through translation from Portuguese. The missionaries seem to have quite easily realised the fact that the Tamil language belonged to an independent Dravidian language family. The far-sighted missionaries learnt Tamil after the conversion of the fishermen on the Pearl Fishery Coast. It may be said that the old Indo-Portuguese saying that the nib of a Jesuit's pen is more to be feared than the point of an Arab's sword may be regarded only as an adversarial remark by those who may be termed as their opponents.

The Jesuits were altogether successful in their task and they were careful to see that the converts were fully instructed of the mysteries of Christian religion in Tamil. Portuguese traders and the missionaries had understood the importance of Tamil and they learnt the language to carry on successfully their commercial and pastoral activities. The influence of the Portuguese was more pronounced in the Pearl Fishery Coast especially in the present day Tirunelveli and Kanyakumari Districts owing to conversion of a very large number of Tamil fishermen. The Portuguese missionaries were responsible to a very large extent in pulling down the barriers of caste although they could not do much to instill the spirit of Christian brotherhood. Knowledge which was the preserve of the *brahmins* until the arrival of the Portuguese was brought closer to the non-*brahmins* through the books printed by the Portuguese. The age old myth that the Brahmins were the sole repositories of knowledge and wisdom as ordained by the divine was effectively exploded by these Portuguese missionaries.

Notes and References

1. T.P. Meenakshi Sundaram, *A History of Tamil Literature*, Annamalai Nagar, 1965; See also, N. Subrahmanyam, *Silapadikaram : The Anklet*

Story, Delhi, 1977, Padikam Line 87. The text runs as follows *"uraiyitai itta pattutai ceyyul"*.

2. Silva Rego *Documentação, op.cit.*, Vol. I, Doc. No. 194, pp. 419-421.
3. Ibid., Vol. I, Doc. No. 143, pp. 336-338.
4. Bodleian Library, London, Mss. Vet. Tam. F.1.
5. DI, *op.cit.*, Vol. III. p. 711.
6. DI, Vol. X, pp. 269, 372 & 801.
7. Joseph Wicki, *IV Centenario da Primeira Imprensa de Goa*, Lisboâ, 1956, p. 11.
8. DI, Vol. XI, p.292. See also, G. Schurhammer "The first printing in Indic Characters" *Orientalia*, 1963, pp. 317-27, pp. 144-146.
9. HLB, Vol. VI, No. 2, 1952, p.10.; With the help of the same printing press the books of Henriques called Krisitiyyani Vanakkam was later published in 1579 and Flos Sanctorum (Lives of Saints) in 1586.
10. Flos Sanctorum, *op.cit.*, p. XII; See V. Fernando, *op.cit.*, pp. 179-203. Henrique Henriques, Tambiran Vanakkam, Kollam, 1579, pp. 6-7. J. Wicki, "The Confraternity of the Charity of Fr. Henriques", *Indian Church History Review,* Vol. I, 1967, pp. 3-8.
11. ARSI, Mss. Litterae Annuae: Mission Madure, Goa, Vol. 53; Litterae Annuae: Provinciae Malabarensis, 1603-1680: Goa, Vol. 55; Catalogi Trien Cochinet Malabar, Goa, Vol. 29; See also, Joseph Wicki, *Life of Henriques...op.cit.,* pp.157-160.
12. BAV, Bon Compagai Section E6, Mss, Lettre di Roberto Nobili, Missionaria Gesuita nel Madure nellee Indie orientali dal anno 1606, fls. 1-12.
13. MPJA, *Litterae Annuae,* dated 20 November 1609.
14. MPJA, Litterae Annuae, 1610.
15. ARSI, Letter of Antonio Vico dated 25 October 1610.
16. MPJA, Litterae Annuae, 1656.
17. S. Rajamanickam, *The First Oriental Scholar,* Tirunelveli, 1972.
18. The introduction found in the *Gnanopadesam* was translated into English and published along with Nobili's Tamil Catechism part I, in 1966 by the Tamil Literary Society, Tuticorin.
19. These works have been published by Tamil Literary Society, Tuticorin in 1965-66.
20. Ignatius Hirudayam, *Christianity and Tamil Culture,* Madras, 1977, p. 30 *Anthathi* is a poem in which the last letter, syllable or first of the last line of one stanza is identical with first letter, syllable or first of the succeeding stanza. The *Ammanai* is a class of poems each verse of which has *ammanai* as its refrain. *Padigam is* a poem in praise of a

deity consisting generally of ten stanzas. *Kalambagam* is a kind of poem composed of different kinds of stanzas.

21. V.M. Gnanapragasam, *Contributions of Fr. Beshi to Tamil,* Ph.D. Dissertation, University of Madras, 1965. A. Muttusami Pillei, " A brief sketch of the life and writings of Fr. J. Beschi or Veeramamuni " *Madras Journal of Literature and Science",* (hereafter MJLS, 11 : 27, 1840, pp. 250-300)
22. Henry Victor, "Tamil Translation of the Bible by the Danish Halle Mission of the 18th Century", *Indian Church History Review* Vol. XVI, No, 1, June, 1982, pp. 72-85. see p. 75.
23. MPJA, *Documents Bertrand,* Vol. III, document, no. 362.
24. MPJA, *Documents Bertrand,* Vol. III, document no.309.
25. MPJA, *Ibid.,* Vol. III, document 320; see also letter of Fr. Calmette to Fr. Souciet dated 25 December 1753 in Vol.111, 346 Bis.
26. T.P. Meenakshi Sundaram & M. Shanmugam Pillai, "Portuguese influence revealed by the Tamil words ", *Journal of the Annamalai University,* Vol. 16 (3), 1951, pp. 11-25. See also, Xavier Thani Nayagam, "Tamil Manuscripts in European Libraries", *Tamil Culture,* October, 1934. See also, Duverdier Gerald, "Rare Tamil copies in European countries", 1981. J. Gnana Selvam Muthuraj, "A survey of the Tamil Christian Writings in European Libraries", *Journal of the Royal Asiatic Society of Great Britain and Ireland,* London, No. 2, 1985, pp. 181-190.
27. Duarte Barbosa, *The Book of Durate Barbosa,* 2 vols, New Delhi, 1989. See also, Tomé Pires, *The Suma Oriental of Tomé Pires and the Book of Rodrigues,* 2 Vols, New Delhi, 1990.
28. IANTT, CC I-37-84. The text has been published *in Revue Historique de Pondichéry,* Vol. XVIII, 1995, Document no.2. pp. 113-114.
29. Letter of Fr. Henrique Henriques to Fr. Ignatius of Loyola, the Jesuits Superior General dated 31 October 1548 in DI, *op.cit.,* Vol.II, p. 279.
30. Couto, *op.cit.,* V/2, pp. 39-40.
31. George Schurhammer, *St. Francis Xavier: His Life, His Times,* Vols. II & III, Rome, 1977-78.
32. See the letter of Francis Xavier dated 27 March 1544, written from Manapadu, in Hugues Dider, *Correspondance 1532-1552: Lettres et Documents,* Paris, 1987.
33. DI, Vol. I, p. 279.
34. DI, Vol. II, pp. 300-301.
35. Fernando de Alemdia, (ed.) *Cartilha em Tamul e Português: Impresa em 1554* (Ministerio da Edução Nacional, Direção-Geral do Superior do Ensino

Superior e da Belas - Artes), Lisboã, 1970. See also, Warren W.H. "Early Tamil Printing" *Memoirs of the Madras Library Association*, Madras, 1941.

36. Jean Filliozat, *Un Catechisme Tamoul du XVIe Siecle en Lettres Latines*, Pondicherry, 1967. See also, Xavier Thaninayagam, "The first printed books in Tamil" *Tamil Culture*, Vol. VII, No.3, July, 1958, pp. 288-308. more specifically see, pp 291-292. See also *Tamil Culture*, Vol. XI, No. 2. 1964.

37. S. Maria Rajamani, A Critical Study of the Foreign Catholic Missionary Contributions to Tamil Language and Literature in the XVIth Century , Ph.D. Thesis, Madurai Kamaraj University, 1972. S. Raja Manickam, *Adiyar Varalaru*, St. Xavier's College, Palayamcottah, 1967, P. LXIX, pp. 175-176. See also, V. Fernando, *"The Impact of the Portuguese Padroado on the Indian Pearl Fishery Coast"*, Unpublished Dissertation, Rome, pp. 200-201.

38. See Rerum Aethiopicarum Scriptures Occidentales Inediti a Seculo XVI and XIX, Rome, 1903-1910.

39. DI, Vol. I, p. 58.

40. George Schurhammer and Joseph Wicki, *Epistolae S. Francisci Xaverii*, Rome, 1945, Vol. II, p. 211.

41. DI, Vol. III. p. 508.

42. Sousa, *Oriente Conquistado a Jesus Christo*, Bombay, 1881, Con I-1-23, p. 18; DI, op.cit., Vol. III, p. 514.

43. Rodeles, C.G. "Early printing in India", *Journal of the Royal Asiatic Society of Bengal*, Vol. IX, April, 1913, p. 155.

44. Flos Sanctorum, op.cit., p. LXX.

45. Geroge Schurhammer and G.W. Cottrell, "The First printing in Indic characters", *Harvard Library Bulletin* (hereafter HLB), Vol. VI, No.2. Spring 1952, pp. 149.

46. Sousa, *op.cit.,* Con I-2-33, p. 81.

47. Sousa, *op.cit.,* Con I-2-12, p. 67.

48. DI, *op.cit.,* Vol. VII, pp. 426-427. In light of the above, the contention of Schurhammer that Malayalam types were first prepared by Gonçalves may not hold ground.

49. Sousa, *op.cit.*, Con II-2-3, p. 157.

50. S. Rajamanickam, *Oriental... op.cit.*, p. 87.

51. Henrique Henriques, *Krisithiayani Vanakkam*, 1579, Chapter 2.

52. S.V. Shanmugam, *The Language of the Tamil Inscriptions from the Middle of the 14th Century up to 17th Century*, Annamalai University, Ph.D. Dissertation; See also, L.S. Ramaiah, *Tamil Language and Linguistics*, 2 vols, Madras, 1995.
53. K.R. Govindaraja Mudaliar, *Vira Coliyum: Mulamum Peruntevanar Iyattrriya Uraiyum* , Madras, 1942, p. 180. The text runs as follows " idaiye vadaveluthu, eithil viraviyal eendi edugai neadiyethumilla *maniparavalam*".
54. S.Rajamanickam, *op.cit.*, pp. 55 & 190.
55. DI, Vol. I, p. 279.
56. DI, Vol. I, p. 279.
57. Joseph Wicki, "Life of P. Henrique Henriques S.J. (1520-1600)" *Studia Missionalia*, Vol. XIII, 1963, pp. 157-160. See, p. 157.
58. DI, Vol. III, pp. 97-98 & p. 601.
59. Biblioteca Apostolica Vaticana, Borg. Ind. 12, Mss, *Vocabulario Tamulico -Lusitano*, fls. 14-15.
60. Ibid., fl. 15.
61. *Ibid.*
62. *Ibid.*
63. *Ibid.*, fl. 16.
64. *Ibid.*
65. *Ibid.*, fl. 17.
66. *Ibid.*, fl. 18.
67. *Ibid.*, fl. 12.
68. *Ibid.*
69. Ibid., fl.13.
70. *Ibid.*
71. *Ibid.*
72. Dalgado & Antony Xavier Soares, *Portuguese Vocabales in Asiatic Languages*, New Delhi, 1936; Vaiyapuri Pillai, *Tamil Lexicon*, University of Madras, 1982; See also H. Yule and A.C. Burnell, *Hobson-Jobson*, London, 1903. Sebastião Rodolfo Dalgado, *Glossario Luso-Asiatico*, III Vols, (Reprint) New Delhi, 1988.

8

Portuguese Contribution to Tamil Grammar and Lexicography

Although the Portuguese landed in Kappad near Kozhikodu on Sunday, 20 May 1498, their commercial activities extended to the Tamil Coast only after the year 1507. They first came into contact with the *paravas* who were considered outcastes by the highly caste ridden Tamil society and learnt that a highly colloquial form of Tamil was spoken by them. But there was also a highly literary form of Tamil in use among the upper castes which was the legacy of the *Sangam* literature. The first conversion of the people of the Pearl Fishery Coast began only in the year 1536 and so the real missionary efforts in the Tamil Country could have only started after that. When they commenced their missionary activities, they were confronted with very many difficulties especially in the field of language to communicate with the locals. It was necessary for them to master the spoken language, in order to convey the message of Christianity. First they had to master the language and also to preach the tenets of their religion in a language that will be more accessible to the people even in the lowest strata of the Tamil Society. So the second task was to raise the level of colloquial language and give it a literary status. It was this, that prompted them to devote their attention to formulate a new literary form of prose in Tamil which was absent till then.

The earliest phases of the process of modernisation of the Tamil language were thus initiated by the Portuguese missionaries in Tamilnadu as early as in the Sixteenth and Seventeenth Centuries unlike the other languages of South India. Among the studies undertaken by the missionaries, three categories of works such as grammar, dictionaries and writings of Christian doctrine received priority attention as a matter of course. The Luso-Tamil projects started in India by Portuguese on subjects such as Tamil grammar and lexicography. They are available only in manuscript form scattered in various archives in Europe and India.

Tamil is said to be the eldest daughter of the original Dravidian language that was once prevalent in the Peninsular India. In fact the Portuguese traveller Duarte Barbosa in the first decade of the Sixteenth Century had noted that the Tamil spoken in the Coromandel Coast was different from the one that was spoken in the Malabar Coast very much like the Portuguese language generally spoken by the Castillians and others. Duarte Barbosa thought that they were two different dialects of the same language.[1] Further there were variations along caste, class and regional lines in Tamil.

Tamil Grammar in the Pre-Portuguese Period

Tolkaappiyam is the earliest among the Tamil grammatical works now available[2] and it deals with *ezhuthu* (basic sounds and letters) *sol* (words) *porul* (subject matter of poetry) *yappu* (prosody) and *ani* (rhetoric), of the early literary Tamil. It was written after a careful study of the earliest treatises on the model of *Aindra-Vyakarna*. It was first presented in the court of a Pandya king for recognition before the grammarian *Athankottasan*. According to some scholars Tolkaappiyar is reported to have written his Tamil grammar based on the models of Sanskrit *Pratisakhyas*, Yaska's *Nirukta* and Panini's *Siksa,* although he must have known that Tamil was not related to Sanskrit either morphologically or genealogically.[3] There were a number of commentators of Tolkaapiyar's grammar in Tamil of whom mention may be made of Ilampuranar, (probably Tenth Century) otherwise known as *urai aciriyar*. He is said to be the earliest known commentator of *Tolkaappiyam*. Others like Senavarayar, Dheyvachilaiyar and Nachinarkiniyar (whose periods are not exactly known) are the other well known commentators of *Tolkaapiyam*. There is another work of Tamil grammar called *Viracoliyum* by Puthamithiranar (Eleventh Century). Perunthevanar (Eleventh and Twelfth Centuries) made a commentary on *Viracoliyam*. Further Kunavirapandithar, (Thirteenth Century) the author of *Neminatham*, and Bhavananthi (Thirteenth Century), the author of *Nannul* also produced works on Tamil grammar. Mayilainathar (Fourteenth Century) was the earliest commentator of *Nannul*.

Portuguese and the Study of Tamil Language

The Tamil Country, its language, religion and culture almost presented a different spectacle to the Portuguese. Every single element of difference attracted their attention. Portuguese missionaries who had a purpose initially, i.e., they themselves wanted to get well versed in Tamil, so that they could in turn reach out to the people with their message of Christianity. They were thus able to introduce many of the innovations introduced in printing books especially Latin which held sway among the scholars in Europe. Fr. Antonio de Proença (1625-1666), a Portuguese missionary who composed a Tamil-Portuguese dictionary (1679) had noted the existence of high and low Tamil, pure and corrupt Tamil, according to various classes and castes of the Tamil society of that time.[4] He testifies the fact that Tamil *Brahmins* used Sanskrit words even in their ordinary conversations. In his preface to the dictionary he had provided guidelines for the Portuguese readers to read Tamil correctly by giving the transliterations of the Tamil words in Portuguese. As the Tamil alphabets were so perplexing and contrary to Roman alphabet used by the Portuguese with variations in the pronunciation of n's, r's and l's, he has given also a chart of all the Tamil alphabets so as to help learners to read without any difficulty. He mentions the four pronunciations for Xa, Cha, Sa, Ja. and also similarly for other alphabets such as qa/ca; ka/ga; pa/ba; and ta/da in Sanskrit.

It is surprising to know that three Portuguese missionaries had seriously taken the study Tamil grammar in the absence of learning aids to a considerable degree of perfection.

It is perhaps possible that owing to the political disturbances during the Eighteenth Century, Portuguese-Tamil grammar could not have been composed by the missionaries. It is very important to examine how each of these Portuguese missionaries evolved his own method of learning and authoring Tamil grammar by understanding the rich grammatical tradition, since even scholars like K. Meenakshi Sundaram[5] who have made attempts to study the contributions of many European scholars to the study of Tamil, none of them have touched upon the contributions of Portuguese missionaries.

Fr. Henrique Henriques (1520-1600)

Henrique Henriques was born at Villa Vicosa in the diocese of Evora in Portugal. He had his education in the University of Coimbra. On 8 October 1545, at the age of twenty five, he joined the Society of Jesus. Later he left for India and reached Goa on 17 September 1546 and came to the Pearl Fishery Coast and was at Tuticorin in 1547, at Vembar in 1548, at Kanyakumari in 1548. He became the Superior of the Jesuit Mission in the Pearl Fishery Coast in the year 1549 with residence at Punnaikayal from 1550 to 1556. He then moved to Mannar and lived there during 1560-1561 and finally as per records, returned to Punnaikayal and continued to live there until his death on 6 February 1600. His body lies buried at Tuticorin.

Francis Xavier had requested Fr. Henriques in 1548 to learn Tamil and to compose a Tamil grammar on the model of the Latin and Greek grammars.[6] It is noted from the letters of Fr. Henriques written subsequently that he had taken the advice of Fr. Francis Xavier very seriously and was busily engaged in learning Tamil grammar. In 1549 Henriques wrote thus: "When I came to this coast I wanted to learn this language so that I could read it. I determined to learn the language. And so, day and night, though not giving up my visitation of the places in my charge, I did nothing else, and God was pleased to help me. To learn it, I used a grammatical pattern they use in Latin to learn the conjugations. In this way I worked to learn this language. I conjugated the verbs. To find the past-participles, futures, infinitives, subjunctives, etc., it cost me much labour; also to learn the accusatives, genitives, datives and the other cases. I also had to learn which (subject, predicate and object) to put first."[7] Thus to prepare this Tamil grammar, Henriques had drawn the basics from the language spoken by the *paravas.* He structured the spoken Tamil on the grammatical pattern of Latin. When he began to learn Tamil, he wrote it down in Portuguese phonetics.

Fr. Henriques in his letter dated 13 November 1549 to Ignatius of Loyola mentioned that his Tamil grammar had been completed.[8] He had enclosed a rough draft of the grammar along with the letter and awaited decision to know whether or not it could be printed. He expressed his desire to bring out in print the same within two years by which time he could make a perfect grammar with some more additions to it.[9] He also wanted to omit some parts in the manuscript copy of the Tamil grammar he had submitted. He however preferred to send another draft that would be more legible, neat, and complete. He himself thought that the manuscript he had submitted was unsuitable for publication as it stood.[10] Over a period of seventeen years Henriques thus continued his efforts to improve the grammar as evident from his letter dated 24 December 1564 written from Punnaikayal.[11] He had by this time reached the stage when he could state with confidence in his letter written from Punnaikayal dated 31 December 1567 as follows: "I have the feeling that I now have the ability to compose a grammar in any language if I could have an interpreter or two and a scribe in that language"[12] Further he mentions that for his Tamil grammar to be understood more easily, it is necessary to have a knowledge of Latin grammar. Those who do not know Latin should read through with the help of the Portuguese grammar of João de Barros.[13] Fr. Henriques has stated that after working many years on the Tamil grammar, he could achieve some measure of perfection only in the year 1566. He must have thus worked doggedly to accomplish this formidable task.[14]

A Tamil grammar manuscript exists at the *Bibliotheca Nacional de Lisboa*, Portugal. Based on internal and external evidences scholars attribute this manuscript to Fr. Henriques.[15] This manuscript entitled "*A Arte de Lingua Malavar*" has a total of 159 + 1 folios of 213 x 153 cms size. He may have made additions, deletions and rearranged the text. The folios may therefore have been numbered and then renumbered as we notice that folio 146 also bears the new folio number 156 although according to the old folio number, the manuscript ends at fl.150.

Fr.Gasper da Aguilar (1588-1648)

Gasper da Aguilar was born at Lamego in Portugal in 1588. At the age of twenty-two, he joined the Society of Jesus. Later he left Portugal in 1619 and reached Colombo in 1620. He was at Santhome of Mylapore in 1623 and at Kochi in 1627 where he taught grammar and theology in the seminary. He worked as a missionary at Karaithivu in 1628 and was back again at Kochi in 1644. He was dismissed from the Society of Jesus in 1648.

From a record we find that Gasper da Aguilar spoke Tamil very fluently and was therefore sent from Tuticorin to Madurai to hold discussions with Tirumalai Nayak of Madurai on 22 March 1638 regarding the purchase of saltpetre by the Portuguese.[16] It is reported later by Fr. Balthasar da Costa, another Portuguese Jesuit that Fr. Gasper da Aguilar had written a more advanced grammar in Tamil which he found more helpful to learn Tamil.[17]

Philippus Baldaeus (1632-1672) a Dutch missionary who had earlier worked in Tuticorin and Nagapattinam also mentions about Gasper da Aguilar, and the Portuguese-Tamil grammar composed by him available at that time. Baldeaus who wrote a short Tamil grammar in the Dutch language got it printed in 1672 (being the first Tamil grammar to be printed in any European language). He mentions in his introduction that the work of Fr. Gasper da Aguilar was good.[18] It is sad however that an authenticated manuscript copy of Gasper da Aguilar's grammar (cited by Balthasar da Costa and Philippus Baldeaus) could not be located in any of the archives till date.

Fr. Jean Venant Bouchet, a Jesuit in his letter written from Pondicherry to Fr. Pierre du Halde dated 18 December 1714 mentioned that a Tamil grammar manuscript was being sent to the Library of the King of France.[19] We have therefore reasons to believe that the manuscript sent to France could be that of Fr. Gasper da Aguilar. Among the collection of manuscripts now available in the *Bibliotheque Nationale*, Paris, under Tamil manuscripts, (Vide No.188) there is a Tamil grammar in Portuguese. The name of the author and the date is not found mentioned but the text of the manuscript records that the French who were initially in Masulipatnam (in 1672) attempted to learn the Tamil language with the help of this manuscript. Therefore it may possibly be concluded that this Paris manuscript ascribed to Gasper da Aguilar was widely used by the missionaries of that time and might have been sent from Pondicherry to France.

Fr. Balthasar da Costa (1610-1673)

Balthasar da Costa was born in 1610 at Aldea Nova, a parish in the diocese of Guarda in Portugal. He was admitted into the Society of Jesus at Coimbra on 20th June 1627. He professed the vows and came to Goa in 1635. He later reached the Tamil Coast and began his missionary work at Vembar in 1639. He was the one who inaugurated the Apostolate of *pandarasami* in the Madurai Mission in July 1640. He did missionary work at Karur, Tiruchirapalli and Madurai in 1643, at Thanjavur in 1644, at Sathyamangalam and Erode in1644, 1648 and 1653 respectively and once again at Madurai in 1655. He served as the Superior of the Madurai Mission from 1649 to 1656. He wrote the annual letters for the years 1643, 1644-1646, 1648 and 1653. It is reported that he died on 11th April 1673.

Fr.Balthasar da Costa learnt Tamil and had an excellent command over the language.[20] Fr. Balthasar da Costa had composed a Tamil grammar (*Arte Tamulica*) and this manuscript is preserved in the State Central Library of Panjim in Goa (vide Mss. M/49). The title page and the first page of the manuscript are found missing. The manuscript consists of 49 pages in all and it is attached to the Portuguese -Tamil Dictionary compiled by him and therefore must have escaped the attention of scholars for a long time. Balthasar da Costa in his Tamil grammar mentions that his work was mainly based on the earlier grammar of Fr.Gasper da Aguilar. He therefore instructs the learners needing more detailed information to refer to the grammar of Gasper da Aguilar.

In the last page of Balthasar da Costa's grammar manuscript, there is a note of a later date declaring that this particular copy belonged to one Fr. António das Chegas, OESA, an Augustinian monk. It appears that Balthasar da Costa's manuscript of Tamil grammar was used by Fr. Antonio das Chegas who was ordained a priest on 27 December 1787 to learn Tamil. According to a record dated 20 November 1802, (preserved under the collection of Mss. *Monções do Reino* at the Historical Archives of Goa) this Fr. António das Chegas was capable of preaching sermons and giving religious instructions in fluent Tamil to the Catholics in Nagapattinam. We also find that in the year 1806 he was the parish priest at Manapadu and working among the low castes. Later in 1807 he became the parish priest of Periyathalai. Further we find that he was residing at Santhome of Mylapore in 1810. Thus we come to understand that the Tamil grammar of Balthasar da Costa was very popular among the fellow missionaries even after a century.

Portuguese missionaries came to the Tamil Coast in search of souls to start their mission of conversion to strengthen the hands of their nation and the church in addition to attend to the spiritual needs of the Portuguese traders. In the initial years, learning Tamil language became essential. The task before the Portuguese at that time was twofold. One was to learn the spoken language more than the literary form of Tamil, which they could have done by studying the ancient Tamil grammatical works such as *Tolkaapiyam*, *Nannul*, etc. But the Portuguese first learnt the language with the help of *dubashis* (interpreters) and *vathiyars* (teachers) and carried on their work with the help of *upadesiyars* (catechists). The second task was to teach the spoken language to the large number of missionaries who had opted to work among the natives, who were themselves not conversant with the literary forms. In fact there was no prose form of writing, except perhaps in some of the inscriptions, which were themselves not free from flaws and deficiencies as the stone engravers were themselves not literate to any appreciable extent. When the more daunting task came along to teach the language to their own Portuguese missionaries who could in turn teach the tenets of the religion to the natives in their own language, missionaries were driven to learn spoken Tamil, master Tamil grammar and develop Tamil prose. Although it was not found practical to ask every missionary to make his own arrangement to learn the language his own way, but there was no other way in the beginning. These circumstances prompted some of the very ardent missionaries to work on grammars which could be taught in seminaries in Portugal in the beginning and then later in Goa, Kochi and other places in India.

Portuguese missionaries began to work on grammar (to teach those early missionaries on the one hand) to teach the prayers to the local converts in their own language, because the Christian religion laid more stress on "faith" unlike Hinduism where "rituals" held greater sway. When the possibility of printing in Tamil opened up, their efforts were diverted to making the Tamil language suitable for printing. They printed books in Tamil.[21] The first one (among all Indian languages) is entitled "*Cartilha Che conte brevemente ho q todo christao deve aprender pera sua saluacam, a qual rey dom joham terceiro deste nome nosso senhor mandou imprimir e lingua Tamul e Portugues coha declaracam do Tamul por cima vermelho*" (Primer which contains in brief all that a Christian should know for his salvation and which Our Lord the King, Dom John III had ordered to be printed in the Tamil language and in Portuguese with the Tamil meaning printed above in red) containing 38 pages published on 2 February 1554 by Germao Galhardo in Lisbon. In addition to this first Luso-Tamil project undertaken in Portugal, several other tracts in Tamil such as *Doctrina Christam en lingua Malauar Tamul* (1578), *Doctrina Christam* (1579), *Confessionario* (1580), *Flos Sanctorum* (1586) all based on Christian doctrine were published.[22] It may be mentioned here that *Flos Sanctorum* is a translation from Portuguese into Tamil. Thus thanks to their efforts, a more refined but highly simplified form of Tamil prose became accessible to a large number of people even in the lowest rungs of society soon after their conversion and the very introduction of the prayers, the confessional, etc., had its impact among the new converts who were inclined to refine their manner of speech by incorporating many Sanskrit words and Portuguese words in their ordinary conversations. A more detailed study of the changes brought about in the spoken language of the converts seems necessary to analyse the cultural impact of the efforts of the early Portuguese missionaries on the Tamils. Hence for all these reasons, the Portuguese may be regarded both as modernisers of the Tamil language and as having been instrumental for the democratisation of Tamil, in the sense that many more had easy access to a new form of literary Tamil, which eventually gave rise to the sprouting of modern prose literature.

Portuguese missionaries who set themselves to learn Tamil realised soon that Tamil grammar would facilitate in a larger measure to master Tamil quickly and systematically. Hence they began to write down the elements of Tamil grammar in their own language. Printing books in Tamil that dealt with the Christian tenets had been given priority so as to reach the people. As only limited number of copies of Portuguese-Tamil Grammar perhaps were required and that too only for missionaries no attempt was made to print the same. Several manuscript copies of such Portuguese-Tamil grammar were made by the copyists employed for that purpose and they were in private circulation. This writer could in all identify five different manuscripts and would not like to speculate further on the existence of other versions. We shall evaluate these works of the Portuguese missionaries through analysis and also by comparison.

The Portuguese-Tamil grammar of Fr.Henrique Henriques has been written in Portuguese with occasional lapses into Latin. The pronunciation of the words in Tamil is given in the Roman alphabet to which a rendering in Tamil script is frequently added. The grammar begins with a fairly well detailed "Table of Contents" on folios two and three. The page numbers given in the "Contents", do not tally with the actual pagination of the text. This discrepancy could perhaps be attributed to the fact that the grammar may have been in the process of completion. In his introductory notes on folios five and six, he explains the pronunciation of Tamil vowels and consonants. Every page of the manuscript begins with an invocation to *Sesu Maria* (Jesus & Mary). Interestingly in the section on nouns we find the following inscription: "In the name of our Lord Jesus Christ".

The first part of the grammar of Henriques deals with Tamil words and phrases which are given in Latin accompanied by their corresponding Tamil spelling. Although the difference between the short and long vowels in Tamil, contrary to Portuguese pronunciation, is mentioned in the sixth folio, the author of the manuscript had however failed to mark the phonological difference in the text. Further the representation of r (ra) and R (ra) is also arbitrary in the manuscript. Adjectives are explained in fls. 26^{r}-27^{v}. The conjugation of verbs has been dealt with elaborately in fls.37^{r} to 142^{v}. The author has given all the five declensions of the nouns with their variations under the nominative, vocative, accusative, genitive, dative and ablative cases. Syntax is explained in the last nine folios. The Tamil words used in this grammar amounts to 310 in number.[23] In the manuscript we find that no dots (*pulli*) are used over consonants as we know the *pulli* was introduced only later by Fr.Beschi. The manuscript is however incomplete and abruptly ends with fl. 159^v. In the grammar he uses only commonly spoken Tamil words, since the purpose was to teach the missionaries to speak the Tamil language fluently rather than using it for writing.

The manuscript of Portuguese-Tamil grammar of Fr. Henriques has been the subject of study and many have pointed out the merits and defects of this grammar. Henriques had put the pronouns under the category of nouns. Although on folio 5^v, he mentioned that he would distinguish between the long and short vowels by putting some mark over the long vowel, the author had rarely done so. Henriques had just mentioned the verbal compounds but does not explain the difference between them and the simple verbs in folio 48^r and even suggests it as a gerund in folios 48^r, 141^r and 140^v.[24]

Henriques deals with the nouns in the first section of his grammar. The author has identified the five declensions of the noun ending with an, al, am, tay, tu, and ru in relation to the six cases, viz. nominative, vocative, accusative, genitive, dative and ablative. He explains the rules for the declension of nouns in folios 23^v-25^v. He points out (in folio 25^r) that the Tamils are not accustomed to using the plural form unlike the Portuguese. Adjectives are dealt with in folios 26^r-27^v. The author is aware of two categories of verbs which he calls variously as personal and impersonal, rational and irrational, regular and irregular. He gives eleven different variations of the tenses starting from the present tense along with their meanings. He also gives a summary of the rules for the use of cases. He makes a passing reference to the degrees of comparison and how they are formed in Tamil. Thereafter the manuscript very abruptly ends in fl. 159^v. Towards the close, Henriques states that he would like to add a few more things in the text.

The Portuguese-Tamil Grammar of Gasper da Aguilar is written on both sides of the paper. There are fifty-seven sheets. The manuscript begins with Tamil vowels and consonants on folio one and ends on folio 3^r. The Sanskrit alphabets commonly used in Tamil are given on the fourth folio. The declension of nouns start on folio five and all the variations of Tamil vowels and consonants are given on folio seven along with the numerals from one to ten besides 100 and 1000. The author has not used dots over consonants as was the practice at that time. The first declension starts on folio eight with the word *rasa*. For the second declension the word *toppi* is used and its plural form is also given. The word *kambu* is used for the third declension on folio ten. The word *pandam* is used for the fourth declension. Further, adjectives are explained with the use of the word *nallavan* and we find here both the singular and plural forms. The comparative and the superlative degrees are explained on fl 16^{V}. The number names from one to ten find place on folio seventeen. The verbs are explained on folio twenty-four. While the participles find place on folio 45^{V} and the infinitives on folio fifty-two, the prepositions are given on folio 53^{V}. The manuscript finally ends on folio fifty seven. In all, folios 44^{V} and 45 alone are left blank.

Fr. Balthasar da Costa in the first chapter of his Portuguese-Tamil grammar deals with nouns in Tamil. He then proceeds to explain the singular and plural variations for the words such as river-rivers, house-houses. Fr. Costa then explains the declensions, and gives the various forms in respect of six cases such as *avaralaye*, *avarode*, *avaraiparthu*, *avaraikurithu*, *avarukkay* and *avaraikondu*. Further he records that the Tamil *Brahmins* use the word *avargal* as *avaal* and *avaaludaya*. Then he proceeds to discuss the relative pronouns and compare the same with Portuguese and Latin. He maintains that nouns common to all genders always occur before the names. Then Fr. Costa proceeds to deal with the masculine, feminine and neuter genders and explains here the usage of the expression *Devarir sollitru* and points out that the usage occurs only in masculine singular. Chapter two deals with conjugation of verbs beginning with the present tense, singular and plural and uses the example *vichuvathikiran*. He then goes on to explain the negative forms and later the past tense of the same verb. Chapter three deals with the active voice and the passive voice and the word *muhkikiran* (modern usage *mudikiran*) is used as an example. Chapter four deals with joint verbs (*kuttu vinai)*, command verbs (*eval vinai),* and also the combination of both. Chapter five contains auxiliary verbs and irregular verbs. Chapter six deals prepositions, adverbs, interjections, conjunctions and disjunctions.

Some of the salient features of Costa's grammar may be worth mentioning here. Balthasar da Costa explains how a finite verb is changed into a noun in Tamil, such as *visuvasikkrathu*, *visuvasithathu*, *visuvasippathu*, and *visuvasiyathathu*. He also gives a list of expressions in Tamil which were considered *amangalam* (inauspicious) and we may give an example here such as *muhikiran* instead of *mudikiran*. He then refers to irregular verbs and distinguishes the root difference, in additon to finite verbs and verbal nouns. Balthasar da Costa while explaining the prepositions in chapter six, records that the grammar of Gasper da Aguilar, a predecessor, should be consulted for further details.

Efforts by other Europeans such as Karl Theophil Ewald Rhenius who published " A Grammar of the Tamil Language" in Madras in 1836 was also reported to be known to Fr. Amarante.[25] Rhenius states that he had observed shortcomings in the grammar of Ziegenbalg (the Danish missionary) and Beschi (the Italian missionary). Rhenius in the introduction of his work records as follows: "Ziegenbalg and Beschi failed to give us a grammar for learning the pure Tamil but introduced mixed vulgarities with grammatical niceties and left us in want of a regularly digested syntax".[26] While writing the first two chapters on orthography and etymology, Rhenius followed more the fashion of the native Tamil grammarians. The study of Rhenius grammar made Fr. Amarante to compose a very good Tamil grammar in Portuguese by introducing similar features on orthography and etymology in the first and the third lessons besides on syntax at the end of the manuscript.

It may be said that all of these Portuguese missionaries have shown a remarkable degree of individuality in learning Tamil and composing a grammar for the Portuguese audience. Every successive missionary grammarian tried his best to constantly improve the standard of his Tamil knowledge and some times adopted the best portion of the grammar composed by his immediate predecessor. It is to be noted that all these grammarians have examined in detail only on the aspects of grammar such as alphabets (*ezuthu*) words (*sol*) and meanings (*porul*) and they have left out prosody (*yappu*) and rhetorics (*ani*) which they considered not important for their grammatical study. The main reason may be that the Portuguese were interested only in developing Tamil prose and not Tamil poetry for which prosody and rhetorics were chiefly used.

Out of the Portuguese grammarians, Henrique Henriques (16th Century), Balthasar da Costa (17th Century), and Paulo Francisco de Noronha (19th Century), were the three missionaries who had composed Portuguese-Tamil dictionary for the use of Portuguese and Tamil-Portuguese dictionary for the use of Tamils. A general knowledge of Tamil grammar was part of the missionaries' expertise in making dictionaries. The Portuguese-Tamil grammar served as a base for all other French-Tamil grammar composed by missionaries as seen from the manuscripts preserved in the *Bibliothèque Nationale*, Paris. Philippus Baldeaus, the Dutch missionary who wrote in Dutch and published in 1672, the first printed book on Tamil grammar refers in his preface that he used Gasper da Aguilar's Portuguese-Tamil grammar when he began to learn Tamil language and grammar in the Seventeenth Century.

Bartholomaus Ziegenbalg (1683-1719) who published *Grammatica Damulica* (Latin-Tamil grammar) in a press at Halle in Germany in the year 1716 had to a large measure use the Portuguese-Tamil grammar of Fr. Balthasar da Costa (1610-1673) and it is evident from the sixth chapter of Zieganbalg where the description is given on the three tenses, negatives, number, gender, auxiliary verbs and irregular verbs along with the examples cited.

Constanzo Giuseppe Beschi (1680-1747) who wrote *Grammatica Latino-Tamulica ubi de Vulgari Tamulicae* although does not make mention of the Portuguese-Tamil grammar of Fr. Costa in his grammar, we may conclude that he must have extensively used it. We find in his sixth chapter dealing with "syntax" and "irregular verbs" whatever is found in the work of Fr. Balthasar da Costa. The information provided by Beschi includes some suffixes such as, *um, o, a, aiyo, anro, yeen, aakkum, mun, pin, muthi, padi, appuram, appaal, mel, kizh, maathiram, alavu, thanai, varaikkum, mattum, athikam, paarka, kaatilum, udanay, illaamal, allaamal, anri, inri, aanalum, enkil, aam, onril, pola, idaividaamal, illaavittal, ozhiya, thavira, oruppada, orumikka, yerakuraiya, ara, azha, kitta, vilaga, kaduga, muduga* and *mai*. Even some examples of sentences cited by Fr.Costa such as "*Ni visuvaskiraye, appothu avan visuvasithan*", "*Ni visuvasikiraye appothu nan visuvasipaen*", "*Ni visuvaskiraye athukku munay nan visuvasipaen*" had been mentioned by Beschi in his work *Kodunthamizh* under Part 113. Here Fr.Beschi says that some other author (without naming Fr. Costa) had mentioned such usages, but they were not found common among Tamils of his times. Thus we find that Fr. Balthazar da Costa's Portuguese-Tamil grammar had been used by Beschi and Zieganbalg while composing their Latin-Tamil grammars. Thus Portuguese missionaries were the fore-runners among all of the European missionaries and scholars of Tamil language and grammar.

The Portuguese missionaries of the Sixteenth and Seventeenth Centuries in general had desired initially to study the grammatical structures of the Tamil language in its spoken form. Paulo Francisco de Noronha and Benjamin Francisco Amarante, the missionaries of the Eighteenth and Nineteenth Centuries slowly moved to study literary forms and explained Tamil orthography, etymology and syntax in a very detailed manner. They also followed the Latin model as known to them and they did their best by widening the horizon of Tamil grammar. *Nannul* and *Tolkaappiyam*, the traditional Tamil grammars did not help them in any way to compose Portuguese-Tamil grammar. It was only Beschi who learnt directly the essential elements of the classical Tamil language from the traditional Tamil grammatical treatise such as *Nannul* although *Tolkaappiyam* is not cited by him.

A close study of the manuscripts of these Portuguese-Tamil grammars reveals certain similarities. The infinitive verb *visuvasiththal* (to believe) is used for conjugation by Fr. Henrique Henriques in folios 33^r-35^r and the same infinitive is again used by Philippus Baldeaus, the Dutch grammarian in his work from pages 195 to 197. In my opinion this is an important word from the point of view of Christian theology, because the whole edifice of Christianity is built on the bed rock of "faith". This will also perhaps be the most important word in the Tamil Christian vocabulary of any believer of that time. The days of agnosticism were still far away. Similarly the noun *pandam* (commodity) is used in the Lisbon manuscript on folio 17^r and the same noun is again found mentioned in the Paris manuscript in folios 5-6 and this word is an important word from the point of view of the then emerging international trade conducted between Europe and India at that time. So also with the word *rasa* (king) used in the Lisbon manuscript on folio 18^r, and the same noun is again used in the Paris manuscript on fls.6 & 8 which is important from the point of view of the political and diplomatic relations.

While examining the texts of the Tamil grammars in Portuguese composed by these missionaries, we find new Tamil words relating to Christian literature and tenets. For instance, the verb, "to believe" is mainly used for conjugation in all their texts. Other examples of some simple sentences include such as, "If Peter believes in God, I will treat him well", "It is easier to believe in idols than in God", "To believe in idols is as much as to believe in demons" found in the Lisbon manuscript on folios 42^v, 44^r, 44 and 61^r. Similarly in the Mylapore manuscript expressions like "Jesus Save Me", "May the God whom I love and adore save me" had been found.

It may be appropriate to state briefly the processes through which the Portuguese language and grammar evolved and developed to meet the requirements of that period. Archaic Portuguese was much used in speech that consisted of popular Latin usages from the Twelfth Century to the Sixteenth Century. Later Portuguese language entered a definite and regular phase by taking ample and opulent forms which were shaped by the help of the early grammarian Fernão de Oliveira who wrote "*Gramattica da Lingoagem Portuguesa*" in 1536. João de Barros who wrote "*Grammatica da Lingua Portuguesa*" in 1540 was himself known to Fr. Henrique Henriques and therefore he used and mentioned the same salient features while composing the Portuguese-Tamil grammar. It is be noted that the Portuguese language was just then coming of age leaving behind the archaisms of its infancy, Tamil with its age old traditional grammar which had already attained adulthood with its rich vocabulary and literary elegances attracted the attention of the Portuguese prompting them to learn the oriental language with seriousness and dedication. Portuguese missionaries had pointed out that nouns in Portuguese language had no case forms, though nouns were distinguished only between singular and plural which was not the case in Tamil. Further, the second and the third case, fused into a single one in Portuguese language at that time is mentioned while it was not so in classical Latin. Based on their experience with Portuguese language, they pointed out the salient features of Tamil grammar. They informed that all nouns in Tamil denoting inanimate substances, irrational beings are of the neuter gender.

Portuguese missionaries were pioneers in the field of Tamil grammar writing in prose from the mid-Sixteenth Century to the first half of the Eighteenth Century and ushered the Tamil language, the knowledge of which, until then held as the exclusive preserve of the "chosen and priviledged few" into the modern era by triggering the process of its modernisation and accelerating the process of its democratisation. The concept of humanism rising to prominence in Portugal at that time mainly had also an impact in the process of democratisation of Tamil and it began to get into the Tamil stream.

Lexicography in Tamilnadu before the Advent of the Portuguese

In the course of learning Tamil language, Portuguese missionaries attempted to compose bilingual and multilingual dictionaries or vocabularies or glossaries for their use. The purpose and scope of the dictionary, methods or the basic characters of such work, the plan and arrangement, and the sources of the dictionary had varied from individual to individual. Portuguese words borrowed into Tamil, treatment of philology, morphology, etymology of vocabulary, the problems confronted by them in the process are also important in this context. Various Portuguese-Tamil and Tamil-Portuguese dictionaries exist in manuscript form in the various archives and libraries in Europe which were composed during the Sixteenth, Seventeenth and Eighteenth centuries. It may be worthwhile to know at first the history of dictionary making in Tamil language and evolution of Tamil lexicography before the advent of the Portuguese in the Sixteenth century.

The beginnings of Tamil dictionary could be gleaned directly from the classical work of Tolkappiyam, where alphabetical arrangements of words appear not strictly or logically. There is a chapter on qualifying words or qualifiers which deals with lexical matter (Tolkappiyam, Uri-i-iyal, 796). There are also two more chapters, while one deals with particles (Tolkappiyam, itai-iyal, 750) and the other on literary usage with names of masculine gender, feminine gender (Tolkappiyam Marapiyal) which contains matters of lexicographical interest. In another chapter on miscellaneous

(Tolkappiyam, eccaviyal) we find details of the classification of words into four groups, such as common native words, literary words, words of foreign origin (ticai-col) and words of Sanskirt origin (vada-col) (Tolkappiyam Sutra, 928-930) in Tamil language. Thus we find the rough classification of the sources of Tamil vocabulary of the ancient period.[27] We cannot say that there is dictionary in Tolkappiyam, but what we may mention that the seed for the growth of dictionary is present.

Following the age of Tolkappiyar, Tamil country witnessed intense religious propaganda through Buddhism, Jainism, Saivism and Vaishnavism. Sanskrit language at that time had a powerful influence and increased the vocabulary of Tamil. According to the then desired needs, some works of reference such as Tivakaram, a dictionary came to be written in the middle of Eighth century. The author of this work was Tivakarar. It has ten sections and deals with class–vocabularies, divided into sections according to subject matter where we find the names of gods and deities, heavenly bodies, names of ranks, orders of men, parts of the body, names of birds, beasts, insects, plants, trees, places, countries, tools and weapons. In the eleventh part we find one word with many meanings and the twelfth part deals with five sense and seven births. It has approximately 9500 words and there is a reference in this work to the Chalukya rulers.[28]

The next classs-vocabulary in Tamil called Pinkalantai appeared between Eighth and Thirteenth centuries and the author was Pinkalar, son of a certain Tivakarar. It has a vocabulary enlarged in many directions and first found mentioned in Nannul, (vide Sutra 460) a Tamil grammar of the Thirteenth century. Here we have ten parts and the tenth part deals with the eleventh part of Tivarkarar giving details of one word with multiple meanings. The rest nine parts are expanded version of the rest of the things found in the work of Tivakaram. There are approximately 14,700 words in the Pinkalam.

Besides these above works, there has been also many word-books such as the work of Ilampuranar of the Eleventh century, the great commentator on Tolkappiyam where we find a Nikantu Sutra (vide Col-atikaram, 390) of which the source is not yet traced. Similarly Yapperunkala Viruti-rai also gives (vide p.222) the various sources of the word apparently from a sutra, not found in any of the existing Nikantus.[29] Thus works such as Tolkappiyam, Tivakaram, and Pingala Nikantu paved the way for the origin and development of Tamil lexicions. They had Tamil words in alphabetical order and their meanings were also given. Tamil lexicography had thus outgrown the crude form of class-vocabularies.

Cutamani Nikantu, another work was composed in AD 1520 and its author was Mandala Purutan, a Jain. He in his prefatory stanzas made it clear that he was a chieftain of Virai and the disciple of Gunabhadra, a Jain. From a reference in the work to Krishnadevaraya its date may be about AD.1520. This Cutamani Nikantu became famous for it was helpful to memorise easily. Akarathi Nikantu was another important lexicographical work composed by Revana Siddhar of Chidambaram (then known as Puliyur) in AD 1594 (Saka year 1516). The author had arranged Tamil words (A. AA, E, EE,) in alphabetical order. This was the first work to bear the name Akarathi (Dictionary) in Tamil. Reference and the alphabetical arrangement of Tamil words had evolved, though it had not advanced beyond the second letter of the Tamil word. While such was the stage of mono-lingual vocabulary in Tamil, Portuguese began to learn Tamil and they composed bi-lingual dictionary in Tamil. There was no clear distinction between vocabulary arranged alphabetically with definitions of the words and the dictionary arranged alphabetically words of language at that time. We really do not know whether these Tamil lexical works of the natives during the Sixteenth century had any Portuguese influence or impact. It may be surmised that the native contacts with Portuguese missionaries and the linguistic interaction should been minimal, otherwise these sources might have mentioned some details. Further since these works were mostly in poetic form certainly the Portuguese missionaries would not have had any hand in this venture.

Bi-Lingual Lexicography: Description and Evaluation of Tamil-Portuguese Dictionary

Portuguese missionaries who came to spread the Gospel among the Tamils realized the need to speak Tamil.[30] While learning the language, they examined Tamil words and collected them along with the equivalent Portuguese words and meanings composing a Tamil-Portuguese dictionary. This enabled perhaps the new missionaries also to learn Tamil very quickly. They composed Tamil words first in Portuguese alphabetical order and gave the equivalent Portuguese words. We have before us five works.

Fr. Henrique Henriques and his Tamil-Portuguese Dictionary

Henrique Henriques, a Jesuit is the first Portuguese missonary to learn Tamil systematically. He composed a Tamil-Portuguese dictionary, a new manual for scholars, introducing the new discipline of linguistics in Tamil that began in the Sixteenth century. His first bilingual dictionary in Tamil was prepared by him while working among the Paravas on the Pearl Fishery Coast. In a letter sent from the Jesuit College in Goa to Igantius of Loyola in Rome dated 9 September 1549 mention is made of Fr. Henriques learning Tamil which was difficult and his beginning attempts made to compose a Tamil-Portuguese dictionary.[81] After a period of three years. We find that letters dated 27 January 1552, 5th and 6th November 1552 also mention that Henriques has been in the process of composing Tamil-Portuguese dictionary.[82] Here we find in the letter that he himself speaks of his Tamil-Portuguese vocabulary in progress for the use of the Portuguese missionaries compiled by him, which he hoped to bring out soon.[83] The work was in progress in 1558 and also continued even as late as in 1566, and we do not know when exactly he had completed.[84] Finally in the Annual letter of the year 1601 sent to Rome while informing his death in AD.1600, it has been reported that Fr. Henriques had completed earlier the compilation of one Tamil-Portuguese dictionary. No extant copy of this first Tamil-Portuguese dictionary is available anywhere today. We also have no recorded evidence as to suggest whether this dictionary was ever printed, while his other books were printed and circulated at that time to the Tamil world of knowledge.

Fr. Antão de Proença and his Tamil-Portuguese Dictionary

Antão de Proença was born in 1625 at Ramella, a parish in the diocese of Guarda. He joined the Society of Jesus on 13 March 1643 and reached India in 1647. He came to the Madurai Mission in

1653. He became the superior of the mission in 1666. He wrote annual letters of 1655-1656, 1659, 1660, 1662, 1663, 1664 and 1665. He died at Thottiam near Tiruchirapalli on 14 December 1666.

Antão de Proença, compiled a Tamil-Portuguese dictionary. It contains 16546 main entries against which Tamil words and meanings have been given in Portuguese. Words given as subsidiary entries under one main entry have not been counted as separate entries. Hence the total nominal, verbal and adjectival besides composed forms and idioms in the dictionary if counted separately would make a total of more than 16,546 words. He mentions that he had collected Tamil words from "*Flos Sanctorum*", a book of Fr. Henriques and also from the "Jaffnapatanam Vocabulary of Tamil" by Fr. Ignacio Bruno. Words mostly used in poetical works which were abundant in the works of Ignacio Bruno were carefully omitted since they were not much in vogue in the spoken Tamil. Further Proença mentions that he had included however many Sanskrit words in this dictionary since they were commonly used in the ordinary conversation of the Tamil Brahmins. He says that he used these Sanskrit words to help those who would read the books of Fr. Roberto Nobili, in which these Sanskrit words were found numerous.

His Tamil-Portuguese dictionary was the first one to be published by the Jesuit Press at Amabalakadu in Kerala on 30 July 1679, posthumously i.e., thirteen years after his death. The original is now preserved under Mss. Borg. Ind. 12 at the Vatican Library.[35] The view of Gregory James that the manuscripts of dictionary preserved in Goa and Lisbon are of Fr. Proença is therefore incorrect.[36]

There are three copies of Fr. Proenca's Tamil-Portuguese dictionary in France. There is a manuscript copy of Fr. Proenca's Tamil-Portuguese dictionary in the National Library, Paris, France, under Mss. Indien No.221. It has the dimensions of 22 x34 cms, with a total of 197 folios and it was transcribed in the year 1750. This manuscript is written on both sides of the paper and each side of the page is numbered. It is mentioned at folio one, "auctor forte R.P. Hanxleden (Fr. John Ernest Hanxleden, known as Arnos Padre 1681-1732) vide Exam. Historcrit calendre Bibl.Cong. Do Propaganda fide, ouet, P.Paulion (1792) p.55 no. X". It is also recorded in folio two, "Mss. Inde de la Biblt da Roi no. 204." I have compared this manuscript along with the original printed version of the dictionary of 1679 and found that there is no difference.

There is also another copy of Fr. Proença's Tamil-Portuguese dictionary in the same National Library, Paris, France under Mss. Indien, No. 222. It has the dimensions of 23 x 35.2 cms. It is written on both sides of the paper and each side of the page is not numbered. It is in double columns with a total of 111v folios.

There is yet another copy of Tamil-Portuguese dictionary of Fr. Proença under Mss, Indien no.224 preserved at the National Library of Paris, France, entitled "Dictionnaire Tamil- Portugais" which is incomplete. It is recorded that this copy was made during the year 1848-1849 by Mr. Rattinam. It has the dimensions of 21.5 x29.2 cms with a total of 103 folios and it is foliated in Tamil. A total of 5500 words are in Tamil in this dictionary. In folio one, it is mentioned "Copie le Tamil par Rattinam (1848) Le Portugais por invi (1849) sur un manuscrit appartenant a la famille Tiruvengadam, cet original est petit in 4 (vaqeir intrer) et se compose de 280 pagen don't la pra contrint de meme que la 3 de la 4, le commencement de l'ourage; le est comme la copie l' Indique, non termene" La garde de la relievre poste em n. 13 avec la signature Vazadarayar, Collatinni Par moi (1849) E. Ariel, Septembre, 1849". Both sides of the manuscripts have been used for writing and page number is given only on one side. The dictionary is written in Tamil and Portuguese words only till page number eleven, while from page number eleven onwards, only Tamil words are written and the Portuguese words are incomplete. Tamil numerals are written up to folio 101 and later from folio 102 Arabic numerals are given. It is found that folios 11b to 102a do not have the Portuguese equivalents of Tamil entries I have examined this manuscript and learnt that it is a copy of Fr. Proenca's printed dictionary of 1679. The original of this fragment manuscript is even now preserved at the house of Ananda Ranga Pillai in Pondicherry, South India. Mrs & Mr. Ananda Ranga Ravichandar, the descendant of the famous Tamil Diarist, Ananda Ranga Pillai of the Eighteenth Century had been kind enough to permit me to look at this manuscript and use it. In fact it is true that the transcription was made by Rattinam, one of the copyists of Eduardo Ariel, who collected Tamil manuscripts in Pondicherry during the Nineteenth Century.[37] An examination of the manuscript helps us to conclude that it was transcribed in the following manner. First of all, a list of Tamil words was written on loose leaves and their Portuguese equivalents were then added to each and in the process some words copied are left without writing.

Antao de Proença's introduction in the Tamil-Portuguese dictionary is very clear and we find here that as a compiler he was aware of his own limitations. The method followed by him in this dictionary compilation has been explained in the introduction. It is observed that the type used in printing this dictionary is not as clear as that of the book *"Flos Sanctorum"*of Fr. Henriques. The paper is very transparent. The Tamil portions seem to have been made from engraved wooden blocks while the Portuguese portion has been made by using the moveable type. The printer was a Tamil by name Ignacio Aichamoni and the press is called the Tamil Press of the Province of Malabar.[38]

Proença listed lemmata in Tamil script but in Roman ABCD order, according to Portuguese phonological convention. Thus he begins with words in A, B/P, A, C/S in imitation of ABC instead of the Tamil order of independent vowels A, AA, E EE, followed by consonants. Proença has given his explanation and reasons for this order of entry, since he was preparing this vocabulary for the Portuguese missionaries and to facilitate several pronunciations for the same letter. Thus the dictionary work was aimed specifically for Portuguese speakers. On meeting a Tamil word, a Portuguese missionary could immediately look it up according to his perceived relation of sound and symbol, without having to learn the Tamil syllabo-graphemic order. This is thus a learner's dictionary constructed to the needs of the users. Colloquial idiom, a quick reference mechanism, head words with subsidiary entries giving the multiplically incremented forms and a very brief individual Portuguese glosses for the Tamil entries.

The Tamil consonants in this printed dictionary have no dots or pulli. The 'r's do not have the oblique elongations. The long 'e' and 'o' are not distinct from the short 'e' and 'o'. The double loop (kombu) in Tamil has not been introduced. The cacuminal (r) has only one loop instead of the double loop as used in Tamil at present.

Antão Proença mentions the purity and dignity of the Tamil words (*pureza e alteza de palavaras*) and he seems to have had a good understanding of both, high and the low, the pure and the corrupt forms in accordance with the usage of the various classes of people. He had selected and used only such words of those words in the Tamil-Portuguese dictionary as would meet the requirements of the people in all walks of life to learn the Tamil language although it was mainly intended for the use of the Portuguese missionaries.[39]

This Tamil-Portuguese Dictionary of Fr. Antão de Proença had been very useful for the missionaries of later period. Fr. Louis Noel de Bourzes, a French missionary says that he had consulted the dictionary of Fr. Proença for making his Tamil-French Dictionary which he began in the year 1721 and completed the work in 1724. It is found mentioned in the preface of his work by Fr. Bourzes.[40]

Fr. Domingos Madeyra and his Tamil-Portuguese Dictionary

Domingos Madeyra was born in 1685 and he joined the Society of Jesus, later worked in the Madurai Mission and died in 1757. He had composed a Tamil-Portuguese dictionary and it is preserved in the State Central Library in Goa, under Mss Cote M/37 entitled "Vocabulario-Thamulico-Lusitano".[41] It is mentioned here that it was prepared for the use of the missionaries of the Society of Jesus "*para uzo dos Missionarios da Companhia de Jesu*". It records that the work was completed in the year 1750.[42] In the end of the manuscript we find the extracts from the preface to Fr. Beschi's "*Grammatica-Latino-Tamulica*" (1738) followed by a note in Portuguese to the effect that, following the example of Fr. Antão de Proença in his "*Vocabulario Tamulico Lusitano*" (Ambalakadu, 1679), the Latin script order of entries has been preferred to that of the Tamil. The author says that he does not use the order of the Tamil alphabet, because he judges it to be too confusing for the beginners, who, he had heard, to find a word need to read through the whole list of those beginning with the same letter. As they already knew the order of the Portuguese alphabet, they can search and find words quickly.

Fr. João de Sequeira and his Tamil -Portuguese Dictionary

João de Sequeira was the son of Francisco de Negrereiros and Maria de Sequeira, born in Lisbon, baptized in the parish of S.

Nicoalo. He joined the OESA at the age of sixteen on 31 May 1673, Professed on 3 June 1674, Vice-Rector of College of the people (Collegio do Populo de Goa) in 1681, Procurator- General of the congregation in 1684, went to Lisbon and returned to Goa in 1692, went to Bengal in 1696 and returned to Goa, later became novice-master on 21 September 1701, and remained in the Convento da Graça in Goa in 1717. There he died on 14 January 1724. João de Sequeira had compiled a Tamil-Portuguese dictionary. A copy of this dictionary is preserved at the the *Bibliotheque Royale*, Albertine, (Albert Royal Library) in Brussles, Belgium, under Mss. No. 21868. It has 262 folios in total with the dimensions of 12 x 17 cms.

Fr. Paulo Francisco de Noronha and his Tamil-Portuguese Dictionary

There is a Tamil-Portuguese Dictionary (*Vocabulario-Tamuliço em Luzitano*) preserved at the Geographical Society of Lisbon, (*Bibliotheca da Sociedade de Geografia de Lisboa*) Portugal, vide Mss. Reservados 146-(A)-14. This manuscript has 144v folios in total. It has the dimensions of 20 x 16 cms. In the first folio we find "*Ar. Arch. Do Ministerio da marinha e ultramar le a Fevereiro 1887 off.. Jose Joao Per. Borges d' Agor Ennes, Juiz de Ultramar*". At the end it is recorded "*Finis, Perture ao R. Me. Pe. De Noroha da Congregação do Oratorio de Cidade de Goa, Missionario Ilhe de Ceylao, Manar, Pejalle, 8 November 1838.*" Thus it is known that this copy of the dictionary was made at Pesalai near Thalai Mannar in Sri Lanka. A close study of the dictionary reveals that the years mentioned in some of the pages of dictionary such as 1703, 1722, and 1724 (vide fl.89v, fl.141) proves the fact the original was compiled perhaps in the first or second half of the Eighteenth Century.

It seems to me that Antão de Proença compiled his printed dictionary from the manuscript of Fr. Henrique Henriques although no mention is made of it. Proença only admits that he collected words from the Tamil works of Roberto Nobili and Ignacio Bruno and this means that Proença perhaps had added much besides some omissions which were also carried out as mentioned by him. Nevertheless it is true that Proença worked on his dictionary for a long time and produced it. It may be concluded that for many years, Antão de Proença's Tamil-Portuguese dictionary followed the principal tool for many Portuguese missionaries who devoted themselves to learn and study Tamil language. Since three copies of the same are available it is certain. It may also said that among all the five Tamil-Portuguese Dictionaries available today, four dictionaries were compiled by the Jesuits who worked in Tamil Country, while one dictionary was compiled by the Oratorian missionary who worked among the Tamils in Sri Lanka. It is to be noted that Fr. Henrique Henriques and Fr. Paulo Francisco de Noronha had also separtely composed works on Portuguese-Tamil grammar.

Portuguese – Tamil Dictionary

After the arrival of the Portuguese in Tamilnadu, their language spread and it came to be widely understood and spoken along the coastal region. In a letter of St. Francis Xavier written in 1545 from Santhome of Mylapore he mentioned that Portuguese language had spread in the Orient and he said that. "If were to come from our Society, any foreigners who do not know Portuguese, they must first learn it, because otherwise no interpreters will understand them".[43] Those Portuguese missionaries who arrived also found necessary to communicate well in Tamil and so they felt the need to compile a Portuguese-Tamil dictionary for their use. Their work took several years for compiling this Portuguese- Tamil dictionary for they needed a good command and mastery over languages and to judge by the length of years it is not that easy.

Balthazar da Costa and his Portuguese- Tamil Dictionary

Balthazar da Costa who began his missionary work in Tamil Country in 1639 learnt Tamil. He had an excellent command over the language.[44] There was a need to move to learn written Tamil from ordinary spoken Tamil by the Portuguese missionaries at that time. Fr. Costa who began to compose a Portuguese-Tamil Dictionary had completed it in 1670, i.e., three years before his death in 1673. A copy of this Portuguese-Tamil Dictionary exists vide Mss. cote M/ 35 with 340 pages at the State Central Library of Goa, India. It is to be noted that Costa's work comprises two parts, a Portuguese-Tamil Grammar and a Portuguese-Tamil Dictionary.

Balthazar Esteves da Cruz and his Portuguese-Tamil Dictionary

He was another Jesuit and his work entitled *"Vocabulario Lusitano Tamulico"*, exists vide Mss. Cote M/32, numero de ordem 7574, preserved in the State Central Library in Goa. It has 480 folios and at the end of the page it is stated the dictionary work was begun on 29 September 1738.

Onorato de Udine and his Portuguese-Tamil Dictionary

Onarato de Udine was a Capuchin friar who worked in Madras (now Chennai) and he composed a Portuguese-Tamil dictionary in 1793. This manuscript entitled *"Vocabulario das palavars Malabares mais frequenters nos discursos, com a sua explicacao em idioma Portuguez"* consists of five brief thematic Tamil-Portuguese wordlists such as *"as partes do corpo humano, as paixoes do Homem, as tres potencias da alma, Os cinco sentidos and do deo e dos elementos"*.[45] This is preserved in the *Bibliotheca Nazionale Centrale di Roma, Vittorio Emmanule III* (Victor Emmanuel Library of Rome) under Mss. Varia 53(598). It has the dimensions of 22.9 x 19.1 cms. The dictionary commences at folio 85a and ends at folio 118 b. Onarato de Udine has put up three entries for the word arroz, i.e., rice in his dictionary.

Two Anonymous Portuguese-Tamil Dictionaries

There exists a Portuguese-Tamil Dictionary vide Mss. Cote M/33 ordern No. 7573, entitled "Vocabulario Luysitano Tamulico" at the State Central Library, Goa. It has 186 folios, written in two columns with twenty entries per column. Another copy of the same Portuguese-Tamil Dictionary manuscript exists in the same Library vide Mss. Cote M/36, entitled *"Vocabulario Lusitano-Tamulico"*. It has 212 folios, written in two columns with 20 words per column which resembles Mss. Cote M/33 as mentioned above.

There is yet another Portuguese-Tamil dictionary preserved in the National Library of Paris under Mss, Indien No. 223 with a total of 132 folios. It has 23,000 entries. It is written on both sides of the paper. It starts with letter A (Aba do vestido- Vadimbu) and ends in letter Z with the word Zurir (Veesukirathu). There is an inscription at the end entitled "Finis, Laus Deo".[46]

Thus it may be concluded that two Jesuits and a Capuchin who worked in Tamilnadu had compiled the Portuguese-Tamil Dictionaries, besides the anonymous copy. These Portuguese-Tamil dictionaries enabled the output of both a productive and a receptive dictionary i.e., a dictionary geared to the needs of Portuguese users for whom Tamil is a foreign language and one for Tamil users for whom the Portuguese entries and their uses needed extra clarification.

Tri-Lingual- or Multi-Lingual Dictionaries

After many years, some Portuguese missionaries attempted to add words in Singala along with the then existed Portuguese-Tamil dictionary. Some missionaries including those of Italian origin who did work among the Tamils in Tamilnadu began to look for yet another more usable Portuguese-Latin-Tamil dictionary by adding Latin words. We also find an attempt to compile a Danish-Portuguese-Tamil dictionary. Thus each missionary attempted to add Singala, Latin and Danish words to the then existed Portuguese-Tamil dictionary, compiling it in their own way with their own skill in three languages. As a result, the linguistic research on two languages slowly moved into three languages compiling into one single dictionary which is really a welcome feature.

Jacome Gonçalves and his Portuguese-Tamil and Singala Dictionary

Fr. Jacome Gonçalves was born in Goa in 1676. His father was Thomas Gonçalves and his mother name was Maria de Abreu. Jacome Gonçalves studied Latin and humanities in the Jesuit College in Goa. He entered the Oratorian Congregation which was founded in Goa in 1699. (we find a certificate of Dom Gaspar, the Bishop of Mylapore in Goa dated 13 November 1693 for the formation of a community of priests born from Goa and asking the King of Portugal to get it approved from the Holy See) These priests worked in Canara Coast and Ceylon. It was called "Congregation of St. Philip Neri in Rome or Oratorians in Lisbon.[47] As converted Brahmins were permitted to enter into the congregation, Jacome Gonçalves entered the Oratorian order and became the Superior of the Mission and Vicar-General in Ceylon from 1724. Several Tamils lived in Ceylon since the Pearl Fishery Coast had contacts with Ceylon. Manapad was an imporatnt centre which contacts with Jaffna. These priests took care of the Christians of Jaffnapatnam and the Christians of Fishery Coast.[48] Oratorians learnt Tamil from Jesuits to serve in the kingdom of Jaffnapatnam. Gonçalves made a voyage to Ceylon in 1706 along with the other priests such as Joseph de Jesus Maria, Manuel de Miranda and Miguel de Mello.[49] It is mentioned that Fr. Gonçalves was learning Tamil. "O padre Jacome Gonçalves esta muy adiantado na lingoa Tamul e a sabe com fundammento".[50] In his letter from Colombo dated 22 May 1709, it is said that Fr. Gonçalves preached in three kindoms of Ceylon in three languages of Tamil, Portuguese and Singala.[51] Gonçalves wrote a catechism in Tamil and it is mentioned in 1708.[52] Gonçalves worked for thirty three years in Sri Lanka and died on 17 July in 1742.

Jacome Gonçalves compiled a "*Vocabulario Lusitano-Tamulico e Chingalatico* " Portuguese-Tamil-Singala Dictionary in 1735 and it exists at the *Sociedade de Geografia de Lisboa*, under Ms. Reservados, 146-A-17. It has the dimensions of 19 x 15 cms. It is mentioned that (*Vocabulario Portuguez-Tamul e Chingala, Copeado por hum certo Missionario de Ceylao, Padre de Congregação do Oratorio de S. Philippe Neri et Goa o qual foi composto por padre Jacome Gonsalves da mesma congegarcão e superieur que foi et mesma missão et Ceylao*) it was copied by a certain missionary in Ceylon, a priest of the order of the Oratorians of St. Philip Neri in Goa, composed by Fr. Jacome Gonçalves of the same mission in Ceylon. The description of the Tamil alphabets had been given vide folio one to two. In Singala we find details from fl. 2v to 4. Then we have the introduction from folio 5 to 11. The dictionary with the Alphabet starts at folio 12. The dictionary has in total 277v folios. At the end of the manuscript it is recorded "*Finis, Laus Deo et B.V. Maria Angelorum Hominum que Domino*" The appendix begins from folio 278 to 291v where we find *nomes de deos e couzas espiritual and nomes de deos e couzas celastiaes*. The dictionary ends at folio 291v.

Another copy of the same dictionary is now preserved under "*Livro Reservado*" No. 375 at the Overseas Historical Archives of Lisbon, Portugal. It is bound in leather, has the dimensions of 20.5 x16.5 cms with a total of 209v folios. In the manuscript it is recorded that it belonged to "*Bibliotheca S. Benedisch de Singeverga*" the Benedictine Library of Singeverga, a place near Santo Tirso in the north of Portugal. This monastery when closed in 1834, the manuscript found way to the Overseas Historical Archives in Lisbon. This manuscript starts with letter A and ends at Z from folio 1 to 196v. The folios from 197 to 200v had been empty without any writing. There is an appendix which starts from folio 201 with the *nome de deos e cousas especiarais* and ends at folio 209v.

Another copy of the same Portuguese-Tamil-Singala Dictionary (*Vocabulario- Luzitano-Tamulico e Chingalatico*) exists at the *Bibliotheca da Sociedade de Geografia de Lisboa*, (with the seal of the Library for the year 1857) under Mss. Reservados, 146-(A)-16. It has the dimensions of 20 x 16 cms with a total of 163v folios. At the end it is mentioned that "copied according to a desire from a vocabulary of the Venerable Reverend Father de. N.R. Catholic missionary, Islands Caits" (Near Brazil). It was completed on Monday, 9 July 1838.

Yet another copy of the manuscript Portuguese-Tamil-Singala dictionary is preserved in the Archives of the Archbishop of Colombo in Sri Lanka. It is mentioned here that "*Vocabulario ordenado para os que se applicacao ao Tamil, e Chingala comecado pello Portuguez proseguido pello Tamil, e accabdo pello Chingala tresladado pello pe. Euzebio do Rosario da congregacao do Oratorio de Goa no anno de 1772*" this dictionary begins with Portuguese followed by Tamil and ending with Singalese words. It was transcribed by Fr. Euzebio do Rosario who belonged to the order of the Oratorians of Goa in the year 1772. Thus we find that four copies of Portuguese-Tamil-Singala Dictionary of Fr. Jacome Gonçalves available today but the original is lost. This shows that it was very much used by missionaries and it was popular too.

Beschi and his Portuguese-Latin-Tamil Dictionary

Giuseppe Constantino Beschi was born on 8 November 1680 at Casticlione in Italy. He was admitted into the Society of Jesus on 23 October 1698 and he came to India in 1710. He joined the Madurai Mission on 8 May 1711 and served as a missionary at Ezhur and Ayyampatti in 1711, at Kamanayakkanpatti and Gurukalpatti in 1713 and 1715, at Madurai and Marava country in 1715 and 1716, at

Thanjavur, Elakurichi, Kunampatti during 1717 and 1740, at Tiruchirapalli in 1740-1741 at Thuthukudi and Manapadu in 1742-1745. He died on 4 February 1747.

Fr. Beschi was very familiar with languages such as Portuguese, French, Latin and Tamil. It is gleaned from his Latin preface of *Chathur agarathi* where he says that "in the common Tamil dictionary I give explanations to each word in Latin, French and Portuguese" (*Vulgaris, Linguae Lexicon, ubi qualibet lectiones latine, Gallie, ac Lusitane explico*". Beschi had compiled his Portuguese-Latin-Tamil dictionary in 1742.

The original manuscript exists at the Madurai Province Jesuit Archives, Shembaganur, South India. Out of the two manuscripts of Portuguese-Latin-Tamil dictionary, kept there (Under Mss, No.3 and Mss. AS.5) one is appended to the *Chathur agarathi* of Fr. Beschi and it contains 103 pages. Each word is given a number and it has total of 4073 words. In a separate page in the beginning of the dictionary we read as follows: "*A.M.D.G; Vulgaris Tamulicae Linguae Dictionarium Pars Secunda Mque Lusitanis Vocibus Lattine Explicatis Vulgaris Idiomatis Tamulicae Verba Ajunguntur Auctore P. Constantion Josepho Beschio Soc. Jesu Missionario*". There is a preface in Latin followed by the above note.[63]

The Portuguese-Latin-Tamil dictionary copy made later is separately kept where the first and last the page is found missing. But there is a note recording that forty four words in the first page and twenty nine words at the last page are found missing. The dictionary contains 4353 words and meanings as noted by Fr. Leo Besse (1853-1919). This shows that new words have been added to this copy of the dictionary.

There is a difference between the Portuguese-Latin-Tamil dictionary of Fr. Beschi and the other dictionaries composed by him It is to be noted that the Tamil words first appear in alphabetical order in the *Chathur agarathi* and Tamil-Latin dictionary, whereas in the Portuguese-Latin-Tamil dictionary we find the words in Portuguese alphabetical order. Thus first comes, words with beginning such as Aba, Abe, Abo, Abr, Abs, Abu, Ar, At, Ax, Az. Thus words of Ac, Ad, Ag, Ah, Ai, Am, An, Ao, Ap, Ar, At, Ax, and Az had been appearing and it followed by words of Ba, Be, etc., The dictionary finally ends with word of Z. It is found that all Portuguese words did not have the corresponding Latin meanings vide Mss.fl.4 and therefore some Portuguese words had only Tamil corresponding words. A closer examination of the Portuguese-Latin-Tamil dictionary reveals that some meanings are given by making sentences vide Mss. fl. 3, such *as "Licet aspexerim, examina verim omnia, non inveni sic composia" "Accidit it puncto non connigint in an"* as earlier done by Beschi in his Tamil-Latin dictionary. Sometimes Thirukural is also used for explaining meanings in sentences vide Mss.fl.7 such as "Anbukkum undo adaikum Thazhl" "Illaramallathu Nallaramalla". Similarly medical terms are also found at folio.8. Active voice and passive voice had also been given at folio 2. Beschi's Portuguese-Latin-Tamil dictionary gives all the words either decent or less decent and phrases and proverbs as found in the ordinary life of the people which the missionaries will have to hear and understand. This dictionary served to help to find the appropriate Tamil expressions. Beschi in this work had confined himself to just those items of immediate use to missionaries. To cite an example he has mentioned only two varieties of rice such as *arros crus* (raw rice) and *arros cosido* (cooked rice). The Shenbaganur copy of Portuguese-Latin-Tamil dictionary was used by Fr.Ford, a Jesuit of the Madurai Mission who prepared a French-Tamil *dictionary (Petit Dictionnaire Francais-Tamoul)* and published by the South India Times Press at Tiruchirapalli in 1881.

A copy of the Portuguese-Latin-Tamil dictionary of Beschi is preserved at the British Library, London, entitled "*Vulgaris Tamulicae Linguae Dictionarium, Pars Segunda, in qua Lusitanis Vocibus Latinae Explicatis Vulgaris Idiomatis Tamulica Verba Adjunguntar,*" under "Additional manuscripts" No. 26110. It has the dimensions of 17.7 x 22.2 cms with a total of 313 folios. The first part of the work contains Tamil-Latin dictionary and the second part was Portuguese-Latin-Tamil dictionary with three appendices with a total of 311 sheets. At the end of the manuscript it is recorded as follows: "This transcription of the dictionary was completed by me, Paschoal Manoel de Reys, on Thursday noon of 26 February 1750". Another copy of the same Portuguese-Latin-Tamil dictionary of Beschi is available at John Rylands University, Manchester under Mss. no. 11. It has the dimensions of 30 x 24 cms with a total of 114 folios.

Danish-Portuguese-Tamil Dictionary

There is a Danish-Portuguese-Tamil dictionary preserved at the Royal Library of Copenhagen, Denmark. Its author is unknown and it is kept under Ms. Rostg 402. This manuscript has 97 folios. It is possible that those protestant missionaries who lived and preached Gospel at Tharangambadi (Tranquebar) perhaps had attempted to compile this and it was mainly used by them.

Thanks to the lexicographical programme (Tamil-Portuguese/ Portuguese-Tamil) of the Portuguese missionaries new domains of Tamil language use such as journalism and scientific discourse developed in the Nineteenth Century Tamilnadu, replacing Portuguese language as medium of instruction and interaction. Tamil remained a major language and an essential means of access to the Portuguese missionaries. Up-to-date dictionaries were felt as a must for both the Tamils and Portuguese and therefore many missionaries continued to undertake the dictionary work compilation. In due course of time words from some languages such as Singala, Latin and Danish were also came to be added to the then existed Bi-lingual, Portuguese-Tamil dictionaries, paving easy way for making tri-lingual dictionaries. The Tamil-Portuguese/ Portuguese-Tamil dictionaries serve even today as treasure trove of information because they alone contain the database with inter-lingual features where many of the curious mixture of non-existing or obsolete Tamil and Portuguese words. Out of all these dictionaries none was published except that of Fr. Antão de Proença in 1679. Tamil was esteemed by the Portuguese missionaries who sailed to the Cape Comorin and the Coast of Coromandel and they not only compared it with Greek and Latin but even with their own tongue. They pointed out that a general defect of Tamil was that though abundant in nouns it was very poor in verbs. They mentioned that Tamil language was still more barbarous in orthography and pronunciation because they neither separate the word nor the periods by full stops and commas and only in the beginning of their words do they used a vowel. They remarked that unless one learns this form of Tamil from his childhood, he can neither never pronounce the words with the same energy nor can their sound be properly written only with Portuguese letters, because there are numerous l's t's and it is the same with the vowel A.

These Portuguese missionaries had compiled the dictionaries owing to religious demand. They moved from bilingual to trilingual dictionaries also. There are several points of which it may be said that Tamil lexicography which existed in poetry form called *Nikantu* earlier came to be made very easily by Portuguese in separate word form. Then we find that the alphabetical arrangement of the words which were earlier limited in Tamil only to the second letter of the word came to be made from the first letter to the final letter i.e., the whole word, for dictionary entry construction. Easy words and difficult words were thus combined into one and thus Tamil words came in full shape. Portuguese missionaries who came preach the Gospel to Tamils introduced all the colloquial words in spoken language in their dictionaries. They separately identified and showed the roots words of the verbs and showed the difference from them against the other verbs. They also showed the Portuguese words and the Tamil equivalent words in dictionaries. As learners of Tamil, Portuguese compilers also began to act as teachers of their own mother tongue to Tamil speakers. Portuguese missionaries had their own well educated background, partly in the language, classics, rhetorics, grammar, and so they introduced novel purposes to which innovation into Tamil-Portuguese/Portuguese-Tamil dictionary construction was inevitable. Then came with their familiarity with the process of printing press, they had a considerable effect on the structural development of dictionary compilation in Tamil.

To estimate their work of linguistic scholarship at its true wisdom, one has to bear in mind the time when it was undertaken and the circumstances under which they achieved. These Portuguese missionaries were the pioneers in the fullest sense and they had to collect themselves, and copy them at a time in which none of the technical aids we have become dependent on, were at their disposal. The inconsistency in matter of Tamil and Portuguese spelling in the manuscripts is a well known fact and that was the order of the day.

Finally it may be said that the dictionary making was a very difficult work and exercise. Today Portuguese language is not familiar to many Tamil scholars hence they could not understand the glory of the works of the Portuguese. These Portuguese missionaries had freed the Tamils from reading the *Nikantus* composed in the poetry form and made them to learn the language easily. While Samuel Johnson composed the first English Dictionary in 1755, the Portuguese had been the pioneers in making Tamil-Portuguese/ Portuguese-Tamil dictionary and it served as a new manual of scholars and a new discipline of linguistics.

Notes and References

1. Duarte Barbosa, *The Book of Duarte Barbosa*, 2 Vols, (Reprint) Asian Educational Services, New Delhi, 1989, Vol. I, p. 84, p. 340; Vol. II, pp.71-73.
2. D. Albert, *Tolkappiyam: Phonology & Morphology* (An English Translation), Madras, 1985, See, Porul, 549-553.
3. P.S. Subrahmanya Sastri, *History of grammatical theories in Tamil and their relation to the grammatical literature in Sanskrit*, The Madras Law Journal Press, Madras,1934.
4. *Ibid.*
5. K. Meenakshi Sundaram, *The contribution of European scholars to Tamil*, University of Madras, Madras, 1974.
6. Jose Wicki, *Documenta Indica*, Vols. 1-18, Roma, 1948-1988, (hereafter D.I.) Vol. I, pp. 286-288, 488-489.
7. BNL, Mss. Reservados, Codice 3141, fl.155v.
8. Antonio de Silva Rego, *Documentação Para a Historia das Missões do Padroado Portugues do Oriente*, Vols.1-12, Lisboa,1947-1958, Vol. I, ff. 153.
9. Jose Wicki, *op.cit.*, Vol. I, pp. 581-582. See the letter written from Punnaikayal dated 21 November 1549.
10. *Ibid.*, Vol. I, p. 584.
11. *Ibid.*, Vol. VI, p. 396, p.751. See the letter written from Kollam dated 27 January 1566.
12. *Ibid.*, Vol. VII, p. 442.
13. João de Barros, *Grammatica da Lingua Portuguesa*, (ed.,) M.L.C. Buescu, Lisboa, 1971. See also, Telmo Verdelho, *As origens da gramaticografia e da lexicografia Latino-Portuguesas*, Aveiro, 1995.
14. Jose Wicki, *op.cit.*, Vol. VII, p.174. The medieval work of Tamil grammar, i.e. *Nannul* which was written in verse form during the Thirteenth Century was of course available to the Portuguese missionaries for learning the grammatical nuances of the language. But Fr. Henriques tells us that he devised his own method and mastered it by spending

sleepless nights. He began composing a Tamil grammar in 1549 and the book was completed in 1552. Thus he succeeded in simplifying Tamil grammar for the Portuguese to learn the language. This was revised again in 1565. By this time, he improved his vocabulary to more than 2000 words. He said in one of his letters that his command over Latin facilitated him to write Tamil grammar within a given time. This grammar however never got printed. See, DI, Vol. I, p. 285, 287, (31 October 1548); Vol. I, pp. 581-582, (31 October 1548 and 21 November 1549).

15. BNL, Mss. No. 3141, "A Arte da Lingua Malabar". See, Xavier Thaninayagam, "Tamil Manuscripts in European Libraries ", *Tamil Culture*, Vol. III. October, 1954, pp. 210-288. See also, Hans.J.Vermeer & Angelika Morath, *The First European Tamil Grammar*, Heidelberg, 1982. See, Michael Manickam, "*On Describing a Non-Indo-European Language in Traditional Indo-European Grammatical Categories*, Unpublished Master's Thesis, Hartford Seminary Foundation, Hartford, Conn.1968. H. Jeanne, "Father Henriques' Grammar of Spoken Tamil" *Indian Church History Review*, Vol.11, 1977, pp.127-157. Henriques may be described as the first grammarian of modern Tamil. He was also the first lexicographer. All the missionaries who came to the Tamil Coast used his Tamil Grammar book. Henriques claimed that he could construct sentences in Tamil in a very simple manner better than the Tamils. In a letter written to Ignatius of Loyola he said that with God's help he accomplished the task of writing the Tamil Grammar. Further he stated that he worked on the Tamil Grammar so that the priests may learn it easily, as Francis Xavier had commanded him long ago. He worked on the conjugations, declensions and the rules of grammar, so that one could learn Tamil through a teacher or even independently. From the Spanish preface that he wrote to the book *Flos Sanctorum* printed in 1586 we understand that he had already completed writing the Tamil grammar. The only existing manuscript which is preserved in the *Biblioteca Nacional de Lisboã* in Portugal under the title *A Arte de Lingua Malauar* is a copy of the grammar of the Tamil language compiled by this Portuguese missionary. It is gleaned from folio 7v that this first Tamil grammar is based on the model of Latin grammar. The manuscript has 144 folios recto and verso and is written in Portuguese with occasional digressions into Latin. All the pages begin with *Sesu Maria* (Jesus and Mary). The illustration of Tamil words had been found in the Roman alphabet for which the rendering in Tamil script is frequently given. The style of the grammar is personal as spoken directly to a student. The Tamil grammar begins with a detailed table of contents. (BNL, Mss No.3141, fls. 2-3). There is a short

introduction where the author explains the Tamil alphabet about how it is to be pronounced (fls. 5-6). The long and short vowels are distinguished in this grammar book (fl 5v). The section on nouns begins with the caption "In the name of Our Lord Jesus Christ". The treatment of the noun forms are found in the first section of the grammar. The author had devised six cases such as, nominative, vocative, accusative, genitive, dative and ablative. He also proceeds to develop eleven tenses. The pronouns, (fls. 30-31) declensions (fls. 23v -25v) conjugations (fls. 41-42) and infinitives(fls. 33-34) are also found in the grammar book. Fr. Henrique Henriques, the author of the Grammar gives examples such as "*Vai dizer a Pedro q venha logoca*" (Go tell Peter to come soon) and in Tamil "*Pedro quitta poy avoenoei chardinu inge vara cholu*". The grammar book very abruptly ends and it is possible that the work was not completed.

16. IANTT, Mss. *Documentos Remetidos da India*, Livro 44, fl.73; Livro 45, fl.67.
17. State Central Library, Panjim, Goa, Mss. M/49.
18. J.A.B. Van Buiteen and P.C.Ganseh Sundaram, "A 17th Century Dutch Grammar of Tamil", *Bulletin of the Deccan College Research Institute*, Poona, Vol. XIV, No.3. December, 1952, pp.168-182. See also, T.P. Meenakshi Sundaram, "Tamil Letters and sounds of the Seventeenth Century", *Collected papers of Prof. T.P.M* (Sixty-first Birthday Commemoration Volume), Annamalai Nagar, 1961.
19. Archives Parisiensis Societatis Jesu, Lyon, Mss. Index 3.
20. S. Jeyaseela Stephen, *Portuguese in the Tamil Coast*, p. 351.
21. Xavier Thaninayagam, "The first printed books in Tamil" *Tamil Culture*, Vol.VII, No.3, July, pp.288-308. See also "Tamil manuscripts in European libraries" *Tamil Culture*, Vol.III, October, 1954, pp.210-288; Gregory James, *Col Porul: A History of Tamil Dictionaries*, Chennai, 2000.
22. S. Jeyaseela Stephen, *Portuguese in the Tamil Coast: Historical Explorations in Commerce and Culture, 1507-1749*, Navajyothi publishing House, Pondicherry, 1988, pp.330-331, 341-345.
23. Hans.J. Vermeer, *op.cit.*, pp.ix-xx.
24. *Ibid*, p.xix.
25. Karl Theophil Ewald Rhenius, the Swiss (1790-1830) joined the Protestant Mission in 1810 and was ordained a priest in 1812. He left England on 4 February 1814 for his missionary work in South India and reached Madras on 4 July 1814. He spent at first some time in Tranquebar till 1820 and later left for Tirunelveli Mission. He reached Palayamkottai on 7 July 1820 and began his missionary work in the region. He wrote "*A*

Grammar of the Tamil Language with an appendix" and it was printed in Madras in 1836. (294 pp +vii). He died on 5 June 1838. Rhenius held the view that Madurai and Tirunelveli were the seats of the pure Tamil. His grammar consisted of four parts such as orthography, etymology, syntax and appendix. He explains certain peculiar grammatical rules of the English grammar and how they are to be disposed of in Tamil. Rhenius before writing his grammar read many traditional Tamil grammars.

26. C.T.E. Rhenius, *A Grammar of the Tamil Language with an Appendix*, Madras, 1836, Introduction p. III.
27. S. Vaiyapurai Pillai, *History of Tamil Lexicography*, University of Madras, n.d; See also, Sundara Shanmuganar, *Tamil Akarathi Kalai* (Tamil Lexicography), Pondicherry, 1965. See also A.Dhamotharn, *Tamil Dictionaries- A Bibliography*, Wiesbaden, 1978; V. Jayadevan, *Tamil Akarathiiyal Valarchi Varalaru* (History and Development of Tamil Lexiciography), Madras, 1985. V. Veerasami, *Akarathikalai*, (History of Dictionaries) Madras, 1989.
28. The first edition of this work appeared in 1835 undertaken by Thandavaraya Mudaliar.
29. Gregory James, *Tamil Lexicography*, Tubingen, 1991.
30. Municipal Library of O Porto, Portugal, Mss.No. 1135.
31. Raphael Ricci, *Selecate Indicarum Epistoale*, Florence, 1887, p. 120. See also, Joseph Wicki, *Documenta Indica*, 1948, 492 (See the letter of AD.1549)
32. Silva Rego, *op.cit*, Vol. VII, p.204 and Vol. V, p.153.
33. *Documenta Indica*, Vol. XI, document 64, p.16. Rome, 1960.The text runs as follows. "Tinhamos a dias hum vocabulario feito. Este anno passando se trabahou de se acrecentar, e passarao de dois mil vocabulos que sao acrecentados"
34. See the letter of 27 January 1566 in J. Wicki, 1960, D.I, Vl II, 751; See the letter of 1558, in J. Wicki, D.I., 1959: 159.
35. Xavier Thaninayagam, *Tamil-Portuguese Dictionary, AD.1679*, Kuala Lumpur, 1966. See also Edgar C. Knowlton, "Antao de Proenca's Vocabulario Tamulico Lusitano: Indo-Portuguese Elements, *Tamil Culture*, Vol. XI, 1964, pp.135-164. E.C. Knowlton, Portuguese-Tamil Linguistic Contacts, in *Proceedings of the First International-Seminar-Conference of Tamil Studies*, 1966, pp. 607-617.
36. There is a copy of this dictionary exists in the State Central Library, Goa, vide Cote M/34 dated 1670, numero ordem 7578, entitled "*Vocabulario Tamulico-Lusitano*" with 223 folios in two columns.10. The view of Gregory James is incorrect in citing M/34 as copy of Antao de Proenca.

See, Gregory James, *Col- Porul: A History of Tamil Dictionaries*, CREA, Chennai, 2000, p. 598. He is also incorrect in saying that Ms. 146-A-14 of SGL, Lisboa, belongs to the work of Antao de Proenca.

37. See for details, S. Jeyaseela Stephen, *The Diary of Rangappa Thiruvengadam Pillai, 1761-1768., Translated from original Tamil*, Pondicherry, 2001.

38. In the book we find this information "Na imprensa Tamulica da provincia do malabar, Por Igancio Aihamoni impressar della Amabalacatta, em 30 de Julho 1679 annos".

39. Bibliotheca Apostolica Vaticana , Mss, Borg Ind, No. 12. folio 10.

40. BNP, Paris, Mss. Dictionnaire Tamoul et Francais, Mss. Ind. 213. PP.1-2. See also Mss. Ind. 214. See also Gabriel Francis Xavier Raj, *L'apport français a la lexicographie Tamile*, JNU, Ph.D. Dissertation, 1995.

41. See the catalogue of Goa Library of the year 1907, p.131. State Central Library, Panjim, Goa, India, Mss. 37.The prologue of the text runs as follows: "Prologue to the Reader: It is not my intention, gentle missionary reader, to prey on your ... wisdom or to offend the prudence of your judgment, in that you should refrain from critiquing this dictionary which is certainly be deserving of censure, for there one can always find a sufficient reasons for our abilities not to be considered inferior or deserving of criticism. I should like to clarify the motives which have led me to produce this somewhat limited work. For example, I was asked by various Fathers to put together this dictionary, and include in it different things missing from others. I considered that there were no dictionaries in this Province necessary or adequate for the common benefits of the many beginners in the Tamil language, since so many have been written by different authors in the more elevated style, apart from the astuteness and skill of the recent one by the Rev. Fr.Giuseppe Constantino Beschi which, without exaggeration, has no equal either in ordinary Tamil, which is called Kodunthamizh or in elevated Tamil called Senthamizh, used for poetry. It is so fine that it exceeds in quality even those of native pundits, who rightly marvel at seeing such knowledge in a foreigner.

The reason why I dare to undertake this compilation is that I think it is very worthwhile, this is the reason that I have taken up this routine alone. Like a clever bee who gathers from the most fragrant flowers only what she needs to produce the sweet honeycomb for the common good, I have spared no effort in gathering together many grammar rules and proofs of them, in order to assemble something like a tasty honeycomb to facilitate and stimulate the will to study and to use what is contained in this dictionary. Hence I have not been so long-winded as to induce boredom, nor so brief as to omit doubts about obscurities I have not explained. Following the proverb "Verbosity provokes aversion; Brevity invites approbation", I have, in effect adapted it in order to encourage everyone to learn its contents.

In so far as concerns the Grammar, I write nothing, since my age of sixty five does not allow me, and my poor health prevents me from writing it all. I will take it that the grammar of Tamil had already been studied, so I will deal only with the words of the dictionary, including the verbs: to these, I assign the past, future, affirmative, negative, imperative, infinitive and certain participles. These are what is the most necessary for beginners. Indeed, the determination of the past tenses of verbs is extremely troublesome in this language, and only over time are they learned. I confess that although I have served in the Madurai Mission for thirty years, I am still unsure of some of them, but after consulting certain experts, I can fulfill my promise.

By the grace of God, I hope to satisfy all the .... Like the other David, with the help of the words... like pebbles from the sling of eloquence, which guides (them) to the bulls eye of the Goliath of Heathenism. I trust that they achieve this ... where others would surrender, saying Lord, What is that you want me to do? Putting themselves into the hands of the ministers of the vineyard of the Lord, through whose guidance they will be ... like ... so that they would also be qualified to teach others what is necessary for their salvation.

At the end of the dictionary, I add a postscript, in which I put the major part of Fr. Beschi's own introduction, as I think will help significantly in composition, reading and also writing, together ... with of certain ... letters, in which cases we use single or double letters or when we change them into others according to the rules of grammar but preserving the meaning. I hope that in your prayers, I will find relief and after I have completed my life, as determined by the Lord, remember also to help me with your intercessions. Adieu".

42. *Ibid.*

43. Boletim da Filmoteca Ultramarina Portuguesa, No. 17. p. 38.

44. S. Jeyaseela Stephen, *Portuguese in the Tamil Coast, op.cit.*, p.351.

45. This manuscript of Portuguese-Tamil Dictionary is attached to a Grammar of Tamil in Latin composed by Fr. Onarto de Udine. It has been recorded in the manuscript as follows: "Gramatica Tamulica a Fr. Honorato Utinensi Capuccino Missionario Apostolico Madraspatnam in India Orientali exarata anno Domini 1793". It includes several Tamil-Latin wordlists illustrating parts of speech. Although the title is Tamil-Portuguese

dictionary, it is in fact Portuguese-Tamil Dictionary. Fr. Xavier Thaninayagam has mistakenly attributed it to the copy of Fr. Antão de Proença's dictionary, See, Thaninayagam, *op.cit.,* p. 223.

46. BNP, Mss, Indien No. 223.

47. B.A. Mss, 51-VI-25, fl.248-248v.

48. B.A. Mss. Miscelana ultramarina, 51-viii-40-fl.11v.

49. IANTT, Relacao Anno 1706, Livraria Manuscrito, fl.3.

50. IANTT, Manuscrito Livraria, fl.74.

51. BA Mss. 51-IX-2, P. Sebastião de Rego, Cronologia da Congregação do Oratorio de Goa, Livro IV, Capitulo, IX, pp. 448-485.

52. Relação dos Annos 1722-1725, IANTT, Livraria Manuscrito, 636, fl.234.

53. Madurai Province Jesuit Archives, Shembaganur, India, Mss. No. AS. 5. The text of the preface runs as follows: "In this second part, since almost all the people in India knew Portuguese words have been at first given by me. However I do not deny the fact that many people are unable to understand these words. Therefore to remedy the defect, I have added along with Portuguese words the Latin words. Thus Portuguese words alone can be found in alphabetical order and all their meanings can be found in Latin. In order to obtain the fruits of the two, all those evinced interest I could not avoid this double work. As I chose the words as minimum as possible, this work is not a large one. Those words in Portuguese which had multiple meanings had been hot given here. These words which are frequently used, more significant one or two words alone are given. Ordinarily, verbs, nouns are given either before or after. Adjectives and adverbs are separately given either before or after, following the respective words. Hence the dictionary fulfills the purpose all that what is in the mind of one can be understood by the other. So also, all the Portuguese words and their corresponding Tamil words are not given. But those words which are very frequently used alone are given. The structure of the verbs and the conjugations are not given because all the people knew it from part I of the dictionary. The aim of the second part is to enable to help those children who would begin to speak with common words and to proceed to pave way for the difficult words. As a precaution, I removed those awkward words from the first part of the dictionary. This also I have done with a view that it is necessary for a learned man, because we must understand, while others express it. Thus for this brevity, I am sure that no one will find fault with me. Those newcomers should read these cautiously what I have said carefully and keep it in their mind and should use this dictionary. They will feel that there is nothing in this dictionary to make them uninterested".

SECTION-IV

9

Portuguese and the Religious Architecture in the Churches of Tamil Nadu

In the beginning, the places of worship raised by the Portuguese in the Tamil Coast were simple mud wall structures which could not be compared to even ordinary chapels. Moreover it could not be expected of them to build chapels and churches in the initial days of their settlement as their primary concern was to build their own trading factories and forts. As they had come as traders primarily here to trade they did not want to fritter away their wealth by creating permanent assets. Whenever the climate for trade in one place turned out to be unfavourable, they lost no time to move over to another port. The position and status that they enjoyed at the ports as traders was inferior to that of the local citizens like the left hand castes even during the early years of the modern era. The Portuguese authorities created permanent assets only after they could establish themselves firmly at the ports in the Tamil Coast. In these circumstances the Portuguese missionaries here had only a precarious existence. They seem to have been satisfied with these thatched and mud wall structures where they could collect their flock of early Christian converts.

The Portuguese who settled down at Vedalai built a chapel there dedicated to St. Vincent to fulfill their religious duties in 1538. Some Franciscan and Jesuit missionaries were instrumental in building a Chapel dedicated to St. Andrews in 1545 at Melmanakudi. It is said in the documents that the chapel in Vedalai was destroyed by the Vijayanagara army in 1559.[1] In the Jesuit Annual Letter of 1596 written by Fr. Francisco Cabral, the Provincial of Malabar mention is made of chapels built at Vembar and Vaippar. The Jesuit Annual Letter of 1603 mentions a chapel dedicated to the Holy Trinity at Kottar which had developed as a pilgrim site besides a chapel at Kanyakumari in honour of the Blessed Virgin Mary. Fr. Andre Buccerio who had worked for eighteen years (1593-1610) had built this church at Kottar.

There was a church built by Fr. Roberto Nobili in Madurai. We have an excellent description of this church in the account of Fr. Buccerio dated 24 January 1617. "The church built by Fr. Nobili is made of bricks and it consists of three naves separated by rows in black granite with cross beams of the same material. In the sanctuary above the altar there is a painting representing the Saviour with his Apostles. I wish it were better painted. It is partly covered with a cloth of the same colour as the antependium and the Christians, according to their devotion adorn it with leaves and anoint the feet of Our Lord with sweet perfumes. They have however a small picture of the Most Holy Virgin with Child Jesus in her arms. The antependium, the ornaments of the altar and vestments for Holy Mass are exactly the same as that of Fr. Gonçalvo's church. Instead of a wooden bookstand for the Missal, he uses a cushion according to the Italian custom. In the sanctuary there is a curtain of fine white 'vacha' which is drawn when he prepares the chalice or purifies it."[2]

It is further mentioned that the church has one main door and on both sides two windows with iron bars. The portico is covered by a terrace because timber was very expensive in Madurai. The women to keep to one of the three naves, and are separated from the rest by a curtain so as not to be seen by men. Fr. Nobili did not build his church in the same style as the Jesuits had another church in Madurai or those on the Pearl Fishery Coast, but with a terrace and this is not only because timber was expensive, but chiefly to adopt himself to the custom of the country.

In and around Tiruchirapalli four chapels were built between 1647 and 1651. While two of them were located in the town, one was meant for the high caste Christians and the other for the low castes.[3] There was only one small chapel located within the fort of

Pondicherry and that was used by the French and the native Christians. The native Christian women did not take an active participation in the services of the church owing to the native custom.[4] Therefore to solve this problem, Lazaare de Motha, the chief of the Tamil merchants of the French east India Company built a chapel exclusively for the use of the native Christians at Pondicherry in 1684.[5] As Thanappa Mudaliar, the head of the natives, gave the land for the construction of a chapel the Capuchins built it after the name of the benefactor and it was called the chapel of St. Lazar. The consecration of the chapel took place on 15 August 1692 and was attended by François Martin, the then French Governor of Pondicherry. It was located somewhere between the present day Dumas street and the Muslim quarters as seen in the plan of Pondicherry prepared by Nicolas de Fer in 1705. There was another chapel dedicated to St. Louis in the present day Rue Victor de Simonel as per the plan of Pondicherry drawn in 1748.

The Church of Apostle St. Thomas in Santhome of Mylapore

The very first and the earliest religious building activity undertaken by the Portuguese in the Coromandel Coast was to carry out the renovation of what came to be believed as the 'old sepulchre of St. Thomas' and convert it into a chapel. Later this chapel was raised into a church in 1536.[6] As by this time many Portuguese had settled down here and the population had increased, it was felt necessary to erect a portico as large as the size of the church which existed there. Hence the portico was added to the old church to accommodate the members of the congregation. At the same time the old campus wall of the church was also strengthened.[7] In all an amount of 6000 *cruzados* was spent for the construction works.[8] The tomb of St. Thomas in this church of Mylapore became a pilgrim centre visited by the Christians of Kerala who had great devotion towards St. Thomas. This is recorded in a letter of Fr. Francisco Pina written from Santhome on 11 December 1563.[9]

Albert de Mandelslo, the traveller who visited Mylapore in 1638 has mentioned that the Cathedral of Santhome had no steeple. We find that the Cathedral in Mylapore was repaired in 1647 and the expenses incurred for the purpose were met from the royal treasury.[10] According to some French records even the Muslims are said to have had great respect for the Cathedral of St. Thomas and dared not meddle with it.[11] The Cathedral had timber roofing and it was an outstanding specimen of wood work noted for its beauty and boldness of execution.[12] However, on account of the imminent threat of attacks by the Dutch, the Portuguese took all the church ornaments belonging to the Cathedral to Madras for safe custody in 1672.[13] The tomb of St. Thomas was opened on 29 April in 1729 to distribute earth to the pilgrims. It was at this time the Portuguese also found it necessary in order to set up the foundations properly. This information is known from the letter of Dom José Pinheiro, the Bishop of Mylapore written to the Bishop of Verapoly.

Chapels inside the Fort of Santhome

Following the arrival of the various religious congregations in Santhome, many more chapels came to be built by the missionaries. The Dominicans built a chapel dedicated to Our Lady of Rosary in Mylapore in 1635 and the year is found engraved above the gate of the church.

St. Rita's Chapel which is today located within the campus of the Santhome Higher Secondary School was built by the Augustinians. An inscription records that this church was fully renovated in the year 1740 by Friar Gaspar dos Reis, the Vicar. This was probably the original chapel that existed in 1729 as there are some Armenian inscriptions of that year there.[14]

Chapels outside the Fort of Santhome

The Portuguese had also built several chapels just outside the fort of Santhome. The Chapel of *Madre de Deus* (Mother of God) built by the Portuguese was consecrated on 8 September 1576 on the feast day of Our Lady of Nativity.[15] In a letter written by Fr. Andrea Lopez, the Jesuit Provincial of Malabar who visited Mylapore in 1644 it is said "that the number of Christians attending the religious services had exceeded 1700 here... A man by his last will had left to his heirs the obligation of paying certain rent, so that on every Saturday they should send floor-mats to the church, a custom which is kept up even to this day which I saw when I visited".[16]

The chapel of St. Lazar was built by the Portuguese in 1582 on the South-Western side of the Portuguese settlement of

Santhome close to the native quarters. Gaspero Balbi has given a vivid description of this chapel in his travelogue.[17] According to him there were in all four chapels in Santhome, two each constructed by the Franciscans and the Jesuits. There was one chapel of St. Lazar for the natives situated a little further away from the Church of St. Thomas. This chapel of St. Lazar was rebuilt in 1637 by Manuel Madeira, a devout Portuguese at his own expense.[18] Today it is known as the Church of Our Lady of Guidance but the locals call it as *sallazar kovil* (Church of São Lazar).

Further we find another chapel built by the Portuguese called as the Chapel of Our Lady of Rest (*Nossa Senhora de Descanção*) now at St. Mary's Road in Raja Annamalaipuram near Santhome. There are several Portuguese inscriptions of the period between 1688 and 1703 in that church.[19]

The Franciscans had built a chapel dedicated to Our Lady of Light (*Nossa Senhora da Luz*) in Mylapore. It was built through the efforts of one Friar Pedro da Atongia of the Order of St. Francis of Assisi in 1516. In spite of the clarity of the inscription the date remains a matter of controversy among epigraphists.[20]

Churches in the Environs of Mylapore

The Church of Our Lady of Expectations on the hill at St. Thomas Mount was erected in 1547 after replacing the small oratory which could hardly contain eight persons, built by Diogo Fernandez in 1523. The name of *Nossa Senhora da Expectação* written in Portuguese around an arch in front of the sanctuary can be seen even today. Dom Frei Andre, the Bishop of Kochi came to this church in the year 1600 during his fourth pastoral visit to Mylapore.[21] The church was extended by the Armenians in the Eighteenth Century as evident from a tablet[22] in the outer wall: "Coja Safar Zacharias had this porch at the entrance of the church made in the year 1707."

Nuno Alvares de Faria, a Portuguese had obtained the lease of *chinna malai* (Little Mount) near Saidapet in 1545. He cleared the bushes and thickets around the place and several houses came up later. A chapel was built in 1551 by the missionaries and almost thirty years later it was expanded into a church at the expense of Nuno Alvares de Faria.[23] The church, now located close to the newly built big circular church, was named after Our Lady of Health and it is maintained in very good condition.

The Jesuits were given some land to reside and take care of the Christians who lived in *chinna malai* but they handed over the site back to Nuno Alvares de Faria as per the instructions given by their Jesuit Superior General in Rome. Later we find in a letter dated 18 January 1711 written by Fr. Guy Tachard S.J. to Fr. Dar Trevon, the confessor to his Royal Highness, the Duke of Orleans that this parish was given to the Portuguese Jesuits and they had built a small hermitage on top of the hill where Fr.Guy Tachard stayed for two months along with the parish priest.[24]

Churches in the Portuguese Settlements

Among the many churches built by the Portuguese in the various settlements, the one in Devanampattinam was built in the year 1574. Devanampattinam was one of the major settlements of the Portuguese where there were two churches in 1597 serving a flock of 300 Christians.[25] It was the only parish located between Santhome of Mylapore and Nagapattinam.[26]

The next stone church was built at Tuticorin in 1582 dedicated to Our Lady of Mercy (*Nossa Senhora da Piedade*) which required as much as 700 *cruzados* to build. The Feast of Our Lady of Snows was celebrated in this church on 8 September. In 1582 more than 600 Christians received the Holy Communion.[27] There was also a church of St. Peter in Tuticorin and it was looked after by the Jesuits.[28]

The Jesuits in Porto Novo had named the place as Port St. Michael and dedicated the newly built church to Our Lady of Good Hope. Krishnappa Nayak of Gingee also gave a piece of land in 1599 to build a church at Porto Novo. Fr. Alessandro Levanto was entrusted the task of building the church which he accomplished in 1601.[29]

Nagapattinam was one of the important missionary centres where the Portuguese had built five chapels and two oratories by 1606. The grants given to erect the chapels in Nagapattinam are mentioned in a record dated 8 February 1610.[30] There were two different Christian churches outside the town by 1640. One was dedicated to St. Michael and the other to Our Lady of Health (*Nossa*

Senhora da Saude) at Velankanni.[31] The sketch of Nagapattinam drawn by Pero Barreto de Resende in 1635 and the description of the town by António Bocarro (1630) throw considerable light on the extent and character of the port town.[32] The Chapel of *Madre de Deus* (Mother of God) was located on the north-eastern corner of the Portuguese quarters. The chapel of St. Jerome was located on the south, overlooking the river bend. The Jesuit chapel was situated on the south-western part of the settlement. While the chapel of St. Dominic was on the northern side, the chapel of Our Lady of Nazareth was on the west. That the Portuguese settlement of Nagapattinam could have as many as five churches within its confines stands as a sure indication of the zeal of the missionaries as well as the Christian population of the town. The Hindus in the place were more tolerant towards Christians than towards the Muslims even in the aftermath of the Vijayanagara Empire which stood as the bulwark of Hinduism.

Churches in the Native Settlements

According to the evidences available from records, a stone church was built at Manapadu in 1581 in honour of the Holy Cross. The *parava* Christians and Hindus generously contributed as much as one thousand *pardaus* for the construction of this church.[33]

Fr. Nicolas Pimenta who visited Madurai in June 1598 has mentioned the existence of a church here. His letter dated 2 December 1599 written from Goa says "we have in the town (Madurai) a church which is neither beautiful nor rich, nor adorned with towers or gilded pinnacles as are the temples of Idols but it is neat and inspires devotion".

Churches in the other European Settlements

Achyutappa Nayak of Thanjavur desired that a church be built at the port of Tranquebar.[34] The Jesuit Annual letter of 1602 further confirms that a church was built by a native Christian at Tranquebar in 1601. Jón ólaffson, the traveller who visited Tranquebar in 1622 reported that "within the walls right in the middle of the place where roll-calls were held, there was the church - an old building which originally belonged to a Portuguese Papist". The Jesuit Annual Letter of 1623 revealed that the Danes on their arrival were led to this small Roman Catholic Church by a team of Muslims who broke the church open. Nothing is heard about this church when the Danes had developed their settlement. However between 1644 and 1645 we come to know that a large number of Portuguese had migrated to Tranquebar owing to the disturbed conditions that prevailed in Nagapattinam and Sri Lanka. They sought permission from the Danish authorities to build a church and it was constructed near the gate of the town. Further the Lutheran missionary records also mentioned that another Catholic Church was built at the village of Sathankudi located half a mile, west of Tranquebar in 1730. It is said that the church at that place was dedicated to St. Francis Xavier.[35]

A church dedicated to Our Lady of Angels (*Église de Notre Dame de Anges*) was built in 1687 in Pondicherry by the Capuchin missionaries who lived in *Rue des Français* (French Street). This church is today called *Capus kovil* (Church of the Capuchins) in the vernacular. The French had a chapel built within the fort of St. Louis in Pondicherry and it was under the Capuchins as mentioned in the Proceedings dated 17 February 1738. The Jesuits who came from Siam after the revolution began their missionary work in Pondicherry in 1675. The native Christians built in 1691 a fine vaulted church in which the Jesuits in Pondicherry had officiated mass.[36] The Jesuits later began to build a Church and the construction was permitted by the French on 28 May 1728. It was known to the natives as Church of São Paulo (Church of St. Paul) and today called *samba kovil* in the vernacular. The construction works of this Jesuit Church dedicated to Our Lady of Immaculate Conception was also completed in 1791 following the enforcement of the above said rules of 1746.[37]

There was a chapel located at the north-west of the white town of Madras built by Petrus Khwajah Voscan, the famous Armenian merchant. The exact date of construction is unknown. It is learnt that the English in Madras ordered on 18 November 1749 to take this chapel and property from the possession of the Capuchins to whom Petrus Khwajah Voscan had earlier donated. Petrus Voscan therefore raised objection and claimed the ownership of the chapel. Although the matter was pending, Petrus Voscan died on 15 January 1751 and he was buried in the same chapel.[38]

Portuguese Missionaries, Armenian Traders and Religious Architecture

It is clear that Church architecture is different from that of the civil architecture which includes town planning, roads, houses, mansions, palaces besides military architecture such as the Portuguese forts and fortifications which I have appraised else where.[39] The Church architecture in a way shows the religious power of the Portuguese in Tamil country. This ecclesiastical architecture is studied here not only as a manifestation of the artistic genius of the people but also as a very faithful reflection on the cultural life of the Tamil Christians. Under the religious architecture we shall deal herewith construction style of the churches, their renovations and decorations. It is a fact that Tamil country witnessed enormous amount of development of art and architecture under the Pallavas, Cholas and Vijayanagara rulers. As the light shines dimly upon the contribution of the Portuguese towards art and architecture this study is undertaken.

King Dom Manuel in his letter to King Zamorin of Calicut mentioned that "We are sending in this expedition religious persons and men well versed in the Christian faith and religion that they may celebrate the divine worship and administer the sacraments, so that you may be able to see for yourselves what is our religion and faith, which was established by Jesus Christ our Saviour".[40] Further the Christian religious spirit is also gleaned from the answer "*Vimos buscar Cristaos e especiaraia*" (we have come in search of Christians and spices) given by one of the companions of Vasco da Gama to a couple of Muslims who were questioning him about the purpose of their journey to India.

The place of worship of the Christians came to be known as a church a word 'Ecclesia' derived from a Greek root meaning – belonging to the almighty. The first church at Mylapore before the advent of the Portuguese was built by Indians and it was not in European style. It was a spacious one surrounded by a high wall. Marco Polo who visited the church of St. Thomas in Mylapore mentions that there were a number of houses attached to the Church and one of them was a pilgrims's rest-house.[41]

According to the first Portuguese reports of 1517 it is said that the church of St. Thomas at Mylapore was with a dome. In

1523 it was feared that the dome might collapse and it was decided that the grace of the apostle which formed part of the foundation of the dome must be excavated. This was carried out on a Saturday and Sunday in July 1523.[42] There was only one entrance door in front of the church noticed in the two churches built by the Tamils such as St. Thomas Church at Mylapore and at St. Thomas Mount before the coming of the Portuguese.

Churches built in Tamil country did not enjoy the royal patronage by the Kings of Portugal. The Portuguese missionaries did their best through their efforts by collection of funds. Construction of chapels and churches depended on the need of the locality and material available. The technical know-how of the missionaries was an important aspect. The general plan of the church had the sanctum, the altar, and the nave for the congregation. Portugal became the transmitting of the values of Christian civilization. There had been changes found in the construction of churches in the period of the Portuguese expansion in the Tamil coast. The nave and the sanctum came to be clearly separated. The nave was spacious and it was rectangular in shape and had two pillared aisles on either side which was rather a verandah to protect the congregation from the heat and rain. The nave had a main entrance and one side entrances on each side as we find the church of St. Thomas in Mylapore built by Khwajah Safar in 1722 at Pondicherry.[43]

The church of St Thomas in Mylapore was built of stone by the end of the Sixteenth Century and before that it was made of wood.[44] It is also said by François Martin that the Church had timber roofing the most outstanding one because of the beauty of the wood and the boldness in execution. The vault of the church was supported by a single key stone.[45] A benefactor of the church called Vasco Roiz, the Knight of the King of Portugal had made contributions towards the making of the whole façade of the church.[46]

In 1635 Constantino Sardinha Rangal, the Administrator of the Diocese of Mylapore had completed the repair and renovation of the church at St. Thomas Mount with contributions from the people. Khwajah Safar an Armenian had extended and embellished the same church in 1707. A tablet on the outer side of the northern wall of the church bears an inscription that he had the porch at the door of the church made in 1707. The church as it stands today measures 109 by 87 feet and bears the royal arms of Portugal on the façade of the porch that faces the west.

Madre de Deus Church in the Periya Palli Street in Mylapore had an extension of the nave connecting the face of the old church with the gateway in the Seventeenth century. Separating the old nave from the new extension there are a pair of massive wooden doors. These are divided into little squares each containing a lotus. The lotuses are many and are of two types. One has a single row of petals while the other has three rows. The pilasters and arch above are of granite very simple in design. The main altar and its reredos are richly carved. The flowers on the reredos are about 10" across with large protruding centres resembling sunflowers or perhaps Zinnias. Above the reredos the Jesuit monogram I.H.S can be clearly seen. The older portion of the Church of Madre de Deus in Mylapore is vaulted. The walls are enormously thick. Heavy buttress on both sides support the edifice.

The Church in Velankanni was the sailor's chapel measuring 24 ft by 12 ft with windows, roof and tower. Later the church was enlarged to 70 ft by 22 ft without including the little sanctuary and the high altar. The background is inlaid with antique porcelain plates illustrating scenes from Old and New Testament. The high altar is pronounced with a sanctuary proper which is spacious and is enclosed on three sides with fancy rails. Over head there is the dome provided with several skylights which overflowed the church with subdued colour. The whole ceiling is paved with black and white marble slabs. According to records Velankannai became was a separate parish in 1771 from Nagapattinam by the order of the Bishop of Mylapore. Later Fr. Sebastião Xavier de Noronha did improvements to the church. Besides the spires and the long nave mentioned the Church has now two new wings which meet the high altar to the older nave. It has also a large vestry behind the high altar thus completing the four arms of a Latin cross. At the centre thereof, right over the image of Our Lady of Health and the high altar stand an inspiring dome of generous dimensions. Length of the main door on the East to vestry door on the West is 182 ft. From one end of the new wing to the other across the sanctuary it is 112 ft width. Of the new wings sanctuary and vestry are 24 ft and that of the old nave 22 ft. Height of the spires and dome including the crosses are

82 ft and 93 ft respectively. The width of the dome is 24 ft. The dome has eight skylights. In the new wings there are two altars in donated by Messrs. Arulananda Samy Nadar and Ponnu Samy Nadar of Thanajvur.[47] Thus the style from baroque had been changed later into Gothic in this church.

Designs and Styles in Church Construction

The churches built in the Sixteenth Century in Tamil Country originated from Manueline style with long rectangular design. Historians have agreed that the Manueline style is peculiar Portuguese form of flamboyant gothic which acquired its individuality through lavish use of decorative motifs derived from various European and prototypes.[48] Next the churches came to be built by the missionaries in the Mannerist style. Most of these were hall churches. The Chapel of St. Thomas Mount in 1547 was in this style. Mannerism came to an end with the new style known as baroque that spread.

Baroque is a style developed during the late renaissance in reaction from classical forms characterized by elaboration of scrolls, curves, and carved ornament. The word derived from *borroco* in Portuguese meaning an irregular pearl. The most outstanding feature of a baroque was that it was far removed from the classical ideal of the renaissance. During this period emphasis was laid on contrasts of light and shade. Baroque art is emotional and created illusory feelings. The columns in the churches were twisted and often gave a feeling of instability. It came to be known as the art of the counter-reformation. Baroque style of Church construction reached a climax during the pontificate of Pope Urban III. The chapel of St. João de Britto built in Oriyur in 1734 is of Barqoue style. The Portuguese Baroque style derives from the renaissance style which came into Portugal and the most striking characteristic style had been the undulating walls with vertical lines while the plans are round and octagonal.[49]

The Church of Il Gesu, the mother church of the Jesuits was built in Rome in 1568 by the architect Vignola. Copies of the design of Il Gesu Church were carried all over the world by the Jesuits. However, it must be said that the churches of the Jesuits were built in unique style. They were with three naves with some height in rectangular plan. The concave arch, the sinuous lines, and the pillared faced pierced with a window became salient features of Jesuit churches. The missionaries had built churches in an effort to reflect the heavenly glory and divine light that Christianity believed is channelled towards the earth.

The Jesuit Church plan was generally in the form of cross covered by a cupola. The nave was provided with chapels on both sides for individual saints each with its own altar. They made use of barrel vaults to ensure acoustics. The face of the churches was based very much on the design of the triumphal arch. It had a central entrance flanked by two smaller ones. The columns were usually doubled and this gave the building greater richness and a feeling of fullness in the centre. The scrolls, columns, pilasters volutes and other decorations were used in abundance.

Rococo is a type of renaissance ornament combining in profusion rocklike forms, scrolls and crimpled shells, often without organic coherence but presenting a lavish display of decoration. The rococo style created in France in the early Eighteenth Century was a creation against baroque massiveness and is characterized by the delicate asymmetrical ornament capriciously applied without reference to structural requirements to architecture.

The Romanesque architecture also developed with various phases of European architecture that was based on Roman forms usually more specifically labelled as Italian Basque & French Romanesque and German Romanesque. The growing use of the pointed arch and the gothic conception was not one style but rather a group of traditional local styles. The Church of Our Lady of Immaculate Conception in Mission street in Pondicherry was of Franco-Indian Barqoue church. Again the church at Nellithope was also of the same style.

The most important change from Latin to the Romanesque is in respect of the roof. For a wooden roof is after all, something laid on a stone building not structurally but architecturally a part of it. Stucco, the plastering of exterior walls was done for all churches. Some churches in the Seventeenth Century were built adopting strong influence of Italian designs of Sacred Congregation of the Propaganda Fide. These churches were with domes. Some Churches were also built with towers. Most of these churches built were with the design of Latin cross and one tower. Thus Missionaries began to build churches of varied style and design in Tamil country.

Gothic architecture came to be characterised by the structural techniques associated with the pointed and rounded arch, the ribbed vault and the buttress. The slender columns give an impression of spaciousness and lightness. The French missionaries were the first to introduce the trend. Churches constructed were colourful with light filtering through the stained glass imported from France and Europe.

According to Vitruvius the Roman architect the ground plan of a basilica was a parallelogram in which the width was not greater than one half of the length and not less than one third of it. The middle space was separated by columns from a lower portico.[50] There was no basilica built in Tamil Country between the Sixteenth and Nineteenth Centuries. The St. Thomas basilica in Mylapore and basilica of Our Lady in Velankanni came up only in the Twentieth century.

The Roman revival of architecture thus went through four phases. At first it is the renaissance style that we find when the European aesthetic spirit, from being gothic gradually assimilated the ancient idiom and acquired Roman amplitude without losing response and tranquility. Next when renaissance style manipulated the mastered idiom with a high intellectual self consciousness, in which was a strong tension, barely suppressed we find the mannerist style. The third was the baroque style with spirit of rect-linearity that prevailed in these modes in the succeeding stage over mastered by the curve, expressed in spirals and volutes and attended by a greater power over mass and Chiaroscuro. Eventually the control over volumes and contours was realized, with the curves running riot and solid masses being dispersed in elegant foliated sprays which is said to be the Rococo.

As the Catholic Church in Europe had no single special style of her own from apostolic times and used all styles of architectures to decorate the houses of God, the missionaries who came to Tamil country to preach the Gospel did the same. The churches were curio since the untouchables and low caste converts were not accustomed to worship God in temples but saw only the decorated *gopurams* of Tamil temples from far and did not see the images of the Gods physically inside. Although the High castes Hindus were allowed inside the temple for worship yet they did not know best the religion since the Brahmins monopolized the rituals. Knowing these facts fully the missionaries made the new converts to understand their Christian Faith thoroughly through instruction and also provided an opportunity for them to participate in the religious services. The European and Armenian traders generously contributed money for construction of churches.

Structure and Architectural Elements

A church has a sacramental midpoint which is the altar towards which everything converges. The choir is the sanctuary sheltering the altar and the nave is like a path leading from the outer word towards this sanctuary. When the church is divided into the narthex, nave and choir, it bespeaks a hierarchy of approach to the sacred. The light which falls in a church from the windows of the choir and also from the sky-lights of the middle nave accentuates this movement.

The façade is the front elevation of the church and it served the purpose of the gable for the roof of the interior of the Church which slopes in two directions and giving the structure an ornamental face which conceals the tiled roof behind. Water pot (*kalasas*) like structures in single and double were placed as we find in the St. Louis church of the fort of Pondicherry. The whole façade is decorated with the carvings of flowers and other such religious objects.

The beams used in the church are thick and rectangular in size. Arches in the churches were the architectural devices used to span an opening with small stones capable of supporting a super-imposed load usually round. The giant gateway of the entrance to St. Thomas Mount with an arc is very beautiful and it is square. Sacristy and baptistery had been of purely Christian origin while the former usually was a small annex at the side of the sanctum and the latter a chamber inside the nave near the entrance.

Liturgical Architecture in Tamilnadu

Catholic religious architecture is mainly guided by the attitude towards the sacred and it stresses the mystery aspect the veiling.

The divine is to be hidden from the profane. Sanctum is the place of manifestation of the glory of the Risen Christ, so it becomes the most beautiful, highly decorated and well illuminated spot of the church. Sanctum becomes vaulted with decoration in square panels.

Altar is the first place dedicated God. The missionary conducts holy sacrifice of the Mass at the altar. This is the first place of devotion to God where offerings were made and prayers are said for the acceptance. A very big tabernacle was placed on the altar and it was always fixed on a raised platform in the sanctum. On the altar there was normally one decorated cross. Fr. Alvaro Penteado wrote to the King of Portugal in 1517 that the natives had crosses in their churches on the altars as well as engravings but no images or engraved outlines of profiles and faces.

Altar carvings depict various scenes connected with the scripture or life of the particular saint to whom the church is dedicated along the floral design.[51] The Luz church stucco work in the vaulted ceiling of the church before the sanctuary is very beautiful. The angels are carved out in such a way that they seem to be kneeling and worshipping the Lord. The Painting of the last supper is found at the Immaculate Conception at Pondicherry. Fr. Beschi who built the church at Elakurichi and made his altar beautiful.[52] A stylized decoration derived from Portuguese tiles (*azulejos*) is used on the altar at Velankanni Church where religious scenes are found. This shows that part played by the Portuguese sailors in building up the church.

Cross used by the natives prior to the coming of the Portuguese was made of stone in Mylapore. In 1547 when the Portuguese were digging the foundation for an oratory on the alleged site of the martyrdom of St. Thomas they found unexpectedly a cross made of granite. It is mentioned that this cross was of unusual type and was incised beneath an arch around which was there an inscription in unknown letter and unknown tongue.

The type of Cross called the Persian cross was widely used and it was formed by the intersection in the centre and at right angles of the two bars equal in length with inscriptions and are similar in many respects to the Greek crosses. The wings of the Persian crosses end with floral design. The Persian cross at St.

Thomas Mount is carved out from the stone on which wounded St. Thomas fell. It has been said that this stone was sweating blood on 18 December 1558. Friar Domingo Navarrete who visited the Jesuit house at Little Mount also saw two crosses cut in rocks.[53] It has been mentioned that the cross at St. Thomas Mount sweat sometimes every year and at other times every two years. The last recorded sweating was in 1704.

In course of time the missionaries who came in the Sixteenth and seventeenth centuries introduced the Latin cross. This cross is produced by the intersection at right angles of two lines so that one line is longer than the other three which are of equal size. The ends of the Latin crosses are plain. Abbe Caree mentions that he saw a big cross before the door of the church at Aramagon (Durgarjapattinam) on Monday, 10 April 1672 built in the middle of the village. He learnt at that time that the Portuguese missionaries visited and converted people to Christianity.[54]

There were Baptismal fonts or basins used in Churches to carry out the sacrament of baptism. The water used to pour over the head of the baptized person was collected in the basin. These fonts were mainly carved out of granite very beautiful. The baptismal font that has been scooped out of a single stone is preserved in the Santhome Church Museum.

The pulpits were used in churches that were of floral structures carved out in wood and fixed to the walls of the main body of the church to facilitate a commanding position for the missionary to address the worshippers. The pulpit structures find their shape depending on the imagination and skill of the carpenter and architects. The pulpit of the Santhome cathedral is excellent with the Augustinian emblem. The wooden support of the pulpit in the church at St. Thomas Mount bears an inscription in memory of Agha Allaverdi Sarkiis in the year 1721. It may be mentioned here that Agha Gregory Erevan was a noted pearl merchant in Madras who died in 1707 was a relative of the donor. This pulpit is very pretty with eight petals and six petals lotus designs with winged angel heads, a mermaid angel like a naginin swith a cross above the head equal armed crosses with trefoil Relics of Apostle St. Thomas were preserved in the church of Santhome by the Vicar in a well decorated box made of teak wood.

The Portuguese Viceroy Francisco de Tavora, Conde de Alvor in Goa issued an order on 12 May 1683 stating that the venerable relics of St Thomas should be kept in a box with three keys. One of the keys were to be with the Governor, one key with the person in the service of the Treasury (despositario) and the third key with Alvaro Carrilho do Valleė. The Viceroy ordered that all the three persons have to send a copy authenticated of the relics and the relics were to be opened only on certain festivals.[55]

Bells made of metal were rung during the church ceremonies and other functions of the church. Belfry structures are built to accommodate the bells of the church. In *Madre de Deus* church in Mylapore the big bell has an inscription, "In/voce exultation/nis fait a Pondichery en 1755 par Pierre Brunet". We also find in the same bell it is mentioned that this was made by Arulappan son of Thavayan. On the big bell of the Holy Rosary Church in Mylapore it is written "Jaffnapatnam, 1769", perhaps the place of manufacture and the year. Further, on the small bell of the *Madre de Deus* church it is written "voce mea ad dominium" besides a cross below next we find AMDG. AD 1803 made by Arulappan. In the Luz Church on the big bell two lines in Tamil runs "Work done by Arulappan , Anno Domini 1806. In the Holy Rosary Church small bell, two lines in Tamil runs "Made by Xaveri Muthu, son of Arulappa Mestri, Gloria in Excelsis Deo, St. Domingos Church, Santhome, 1829".

Christian Cemetry was always located at some distance away from the church where the dead were buried. In many cases the missionaries were buried inside the church. The cenotaphs and tombstones came into existence when the Portuguese began to bury the dead. J.J Cotton has published the tomb inscriptions of the Madras Presidency.[56] Engravings on tomb stones is another type of architecture that developed. The epigraphy is interesting since the tombs inscriptions record the biographical details with place of origin, length of life, position (civil/ ecclesiastical) of the deceased, laudatory epithets, initials such as RIP, IHS and the cross. These tomb stones are of rectangular and square size with floral designs and logo like the skull, keys and the crown.

Plans of the Churches

The Portuguese in Mylapore decided to build the church according to a new plan whereby the presbytery of the Vicar, the church and the tomb of St. Thomas were separated. They were successful in execution and we find the mention by Francis Xavier who lived there with Fr. Gaspero Coelho the vicar of the church in 1545. When these old buildings had given way the new cathedral was built and it was consecrated on 10 May 1896. Fr. J.J. Pinto the Vicar of the cathedral had prepared three plans to show how things were in 1892. The first plan shows in black the background of the plan of the church, the tomb with no.10, the presbytery as no.20 and the garden no.3 as they were in his opinion in the year 1545. We find the second one with the ground plan of the cathedral and presbytery as they were before the demolition in 1893. The draughtsman M. S.N. Appavu Mudaliar to whom Fr. J.J. Pinto ordered to make four copies of Fr. Pinto's original plans are preserved in the Bishop's House Archives at Mylapore. The draughtsman had forgotten to indicate the position no.4 or the altar of the relics in the church.[57] The ecclesiastical administration of Mylapore remained first under the Diocese of Goa (1533-1557) and later under the Diocese of Cochin (1557-1606). It remained a bastion of Roman Catholicism as an independent diocese (1606-1952) in South India for a long time.

The plan of the church of Our Lady of Angels built by the Capuchins in Pondicherry is also available. This plan was found by me among the unpublished manuscripts of "*Registre du papier terrier de la ville Pondichéry fait un execution de l' ordonnance de M.M. les administrateurs du Roy en datte du 1er Juillet, 1777, Ville Blanche*", preserved in the National Archives of India, Pondicherry.[58] The Capuchins built their church close to the fort at a distance of 100 *toises*. They wanted to raise its height up to forty four feet in the year 1746. It was against all the rules and considered risky for the defence of the fort. Therefore it was forbidden and the Capuchins had to withdraw their idea of building accordingly.[59] The French Governor of Pondicherry had ordered that there should be no building located within a distance of 200 metres around the fort of St. Louis in Pondicherry and no building was allowed to be built more than fifty feet height. The elevation of the Chapel of St. Louis erected inside the fort in Pondicherry in 1722 preserved at the Centre des Archives d' Outre-mer, Aix-en -Provence, France.[60]

Although Tamil country was rich in Hindu religious architecture patronized by the Pallavas, Cholas and Vijayanagara rulers, Portuguese did not follow or accept any of these Hindu styles in worship. Many church buildings came up with new styles that co-existed in France, Portugal and Italy. The Missionaries also felt that the Indian temple models were not fitted for performing Catholic rites and did not adopt the models although temples were very large complexes. The Portuguese followed and introduced only the religious architecture of Europe and built churches for Christian worship. It is to be mentioned here that the Italian Jesuits who were in Madurai had much influence in the court of Tirumalai Nayak and the ruler had taken the help of the Italian architect while constructing his palace in 1636. The influence of the Italian architecture is found in the Mahal of Royal palace even today. It is concluded that four variant styles of architecture such as Renaissance, mannerism, Baroque and Rococo were adopted in the construction of churches in Tamilnadu. We also find three types of churches being built such as the Hall Church, Greek-Cross–Domed church and the Diminuted Sanctuary church by the Portuguese missionaries in this period. We also notice three types of altars such as iconostasis, aedicule retable and trono were in use in the churches of Tamil Country. Some churches had Roman use of arch and pier while some churches had the Manueline portal of main entrance with a Cross. These are the new architectural elements introduced by the Portuguese in the Tamil Coast.

Notes and References

1. Letter of Fr. Henrique Henriques dated 10 January 1574 in J. Wicki, DI. Vol. IX, p.314; See also DI, Vol. X, p. 27.
2. S. Rajamanickam, *Robert de Nobili: The First Oriental Scholar*, Palyamkottai, 1971, p. 26.
3. Bertrand, *op.cit.*. Vol. II, p. 340.
4. Archivio della S. Congregazione di Propaganda Fide (hereafter APF) *Scritture Riferitenei Congressi, Indie Orientali e Cina*, Vol. 7 fl. 206.
5. Archives General of the Capuchin Order, (hereafter AGS) Rome, H, 55 (India) XIIJ.,2; Archivio della S. Congregazione di Porpaganda Fide, (here

after APF), *Scritture Riferite nei Congressi, Indie Orientali e Cina,* fl. 144; 268ss.

6. Edith Timory, - "The Early Church of St Thomas at Mylapore" *Indica,* Vol. 47, (1), pp. 51-54.

7. Correia, *op.cit.,* Vol. II, pp. 787-788.

8. Antonio da Silva Rego, *As Gavetas da Torre do Tombo,* Lisboa, 1948, Vol. II, 712-718. Letter of the Portuguese residents of Santhome of Mylapore to the King of Portugal dated 27 December 1535 in IANTT, Gavetas, XI-8-18; See also, A.M. Mathias Mundadan, "The Portuguese Settlement in Mylapore" *Indian Church History Review,* Vol. III, 1969, p. 111.

9. DI Vol.1, pp. 91-92. The Portuguese church was replaced in 1896 by the present cathedral built in gothic style.

10. MDR, Livro 5, fl. 187.

11. *Memoirs,* p. 118.

12. *Memoirs,* p. 119.

13. *Memoirs,* p. 439.

14. Petrus Voskan gave money for its construction in 1729. Fre Gaspar dos Reis a native of Santhome supervised and finished the church construction in 1740. J,J Cotton, *op.cit.,* Vol. I, p. 154.

15. Paulo da Trinidade, *Conquisto Espiritual do Oriente,* Lisboa, 1962-67, Vol. II, p. 156.

16. ARSI, *Litterae Annuae: Provinciae Malabarensis,* 1644.

17. Samuel Purchas, *op.cit.,* Vol. X, pp. 146-148.

18. *Madras Mail,* Madras, 23 July, 1927. The tomb of Manuel Madeira discovered by Mgr. Texiera along with the inscription is given here.

19. J.J. Cotton, *op.cit.,* Vol. I, p. 158.

20. Love, *Vestiges of old Madras,* London, 1913, Vol. I, p. 289.

21. ARSI, Mss *Goa,* see the report of Bishop of Kochi in AD. 1600.

22. *Ibid.* Petrus Voskan an Armenian had built a flight of 161 stone steps from the base of the hill to the top because thousands of Christian pilgrims visited the church. Voskan also built the chapel of our Lady of Miracles at Verpery and placed it under the control of the Capuchin priests. See, Anne Basil, *Armenian Settlement in India*, Armenian college. Calcutta, 1969, p. 47.

23. DI, Vol. XII, pp. 81-84, Vol. XIV, pp. 213-214, Vol. XV, pp.13,281, 289. The information provided in the Catholic Directory of India that the church was built in 1551 is incorrect.

24. LEC, Vol. XI, Letter dated 18 January 1711 written by Fr. Guy Tachard. to Fr. Dar Trevon.
25. BFUP, Vol. V, pp. 559& 597, (16 January 1585) (23 November 1589) BFUP, Vol. I, p. 299; ARSI, Mss *Goa,* 32, fl. 654^{v}.
26. BFUP, Vol. I, p. 299. See also Fernao Guerriero, (ed.,) A. Veigas, *Relação Anual das Coisas que Fizeram Os Padres da Companhia de Jesus nas Suas Missões India,* III vols, Coimbra, 1930, p.76. The details of Devanampattinam as a mission station under the Jesuits are well known during 1607 and 1608.
27. ARSI, *Litterae Annuae: Provinciae Malabarensis, 1583;* A. Roche, *Fishermen of Coromandel,* New Delhi, 1984, p. 52.
28. HAG, MDR, Livro 1, Codice 7/14/5, fl. 96.
29. ARSI, Mss *Goa,* Letter of Fr. Pimenta in 1598; C.S. Srinivasachari, *History of Gingee and its Rulers,* Annamalai Nagar, 1945, pp. 100-101.
30. IANTT, DRI, Livro 3, fl.77.
31. Pissurlencar, *Assentos do Conselho do Estado,* Vol. III, pp. 655-656; see also Achilles Meersmen, "The Origin of the Shrine and Cult of Our Lady of Vailankanni", *Indian Ecclesiastical Studies,* Vol. I, 1962, p. 67.
32. The work of Pero Barreto Resende entitled *"Livro das Plantas das Fortalezas"* is available in the National Library of Lisbon. It has the map of Nagapattinam and has been published by Antonio de Mariz Carneiro in *"Descrição de fortaleza de Sofala e das mais da India com huma rellaçãm das religioces todas e que ha no mesmo estado 1639"* Codice lluminado 149, Lisboa, 1990. The map of Nagapattinam is No. 44, with the title Negapatão in the Dimensions of 442 X 682 mm. In the Nagapattinam map we find that there were only two temples, one temple has a *nandi* (Sacred cow) and the other temple has a *ther* (car) used for procession. Among the five churches, there were two in the east facing the sea while two other churches were located in the southern side of Nagapattinam. One of the churches was facing the river and the other was situated in the south-west direction in addition to a chapel found in the map. Hence the view of Sanjay Subrahmanyam that there were six churches and three temples in Nagapattinam may be called into question. See, Sanjay Subrahmanyam, *Political Economy... op.cit.,* p. 199.
33. DI, Vol. XII, pp. 717-718. The information provided in the Catholic Directory of India published in 1990 that the church of St James constructed in 1791 and the Holy Spirit Church in 1856 is not correct.
34. DI, Vol. XV, pp. 334-44, 756-759. The Bishop of Mylapore wrote a letter to the King of Portugal about the construction of the fort at Tranquebar by

the Danes vide his letter dated 27 November 1624. See, *Documentos Remettidos da India, Vol. I, 1625-1627,* Centro de Estudos Damaiao Gois, Lisboa, 2000, Doc. No. 695. Further, we find that Fr. Jose da Graça OSA, was ordered to leave Tranquebar by the Danes. See, Silva Rego, *Documentação,* Vol. XI, pp. 227, 616, 666.

35. R. C. Temple, (ed.,) *The Life of the Icelander Jon Olaffson, Traveller to India, 2* Vols, London, 1932, ARSI, *Litterae Annuae Provinciae Malabarensis,1620-1623;* W. Gensichen, " The Churches" in (ed.) Daniel, *New Jerusalem Church Tranquebar, 1718-1968,* Madras, 1968, p. 16.

36. Regarding the Capuchin church See, J. H Cunha Riveira, *A Jurisdisção Diocesana do Bispasdo de S.Thome de Meliapor,* Nova Goa, 1867, p. 19. on the Jesuits church see, MPJA, *Documents Bertrand,* Vol. I, Document No.9, p. 93.

37. *ARP diary,* Vol. V, p.286. This Jesuit Church was located next to Vedapuriswarar temple and there was arose problem and tension between the Hindus and the Catholics. In order to remedy the situation, Dupleix, the then French Governor of Pondicherry requested the Hindus to build the temple at some distance and promised to allot a new site and necessary funds to be spent for the construction of the Vedapuriswarar temple. A Brahmin by name Annapurna Ayyan came forward to help at this time to get the consent of the Hindus to demolish the Vedapuriswarar temple and build it at a different site and further requested the Governor to appoint him as the broker of the French Company. He also promised to give 5000 *varahans* to Dupleix and his wife a sum of 600 varahans for the post. However the temple came to be destroyed and the Hindus were given permission to build a new temple in a new site by the French Governor. See, *ARP diary,* Vol. V, p. 286. The Cathedral in the present shape was later rebuilt and completed on 20 June 1791.

38. Love, *op.cit.,* pp. 425 & 467.

39. See Urbanization of the Portuguese Settlements, in S. Jeyaseela Stephen, *Portuguse in the Tamil coast op.cit.,* pp. 226-275.

40. Fernão Lopez da Catenheda, *Historia op.cit.,* Livro I, Capitulo 35, p. 78.

41. A.C. Moule & P. Pelliot, *Marco Polo: The Description of the World,* London, 1938.

42. ARSI, Mss. Goa, 31: 18-25v. A textual report of the year 1600 differs in some details. See, ARSI, Mss. Goa, 49: fl. 125-128v. See also report in detail by Gaspar Correa, *Lendas da India,* Lisboa, 1858-61, Vol. II, pp. 722-26, 788-79.

43. The Church of St Louis within the fort of Pondicherry was built in 1722. The elevation of the church is available at Centre des Archives d' Outre-

mer, Aix-en -Provence, France, vide Depot des Fortifications des Colonies, Portefeuille 32B, 18. The church was destroyed by the English in 1761.

44. Linschoten, *op.cit.*, Vol. I, p. 89.
45. Lotika Varadarajan, *op.cit.*, Vol. II, p. 119.
46. J.J. Cotton, *List of Inscriptions on Tombs and Monuments*, Madras, 1905.
47. S.R. Santos, *The Shrine Basilica of Our Lady of Health*, Vailankanni, (11th edition), Thanjaviur, 1980.
48. G. Kubler & M. Soria, *Art and Architecture in Spain and Portugal*, Baltimore, 1958, pp. 101-131.
49. Teresa Martins de Caravalho, "A Evoulção de Arte em Portugal", in *Um Patrimonio Artistico*, Lisboa, 1983, pp. 163-174.
50. De Architectura, V, 2 cited in Heras, "Indian Art in Catholic Churches", *The Examiner*, Bombay, 1927, No. 78, pp. 474-475, 488, 501.
51. Letter from Goa dated 22 November 1548 in Silva Rego, *Documentção,* Vol. IV, pp. 128-129. We find that a new painting was required to replace the altarpiece executed locally by the Goanese artists as the first one had detonated on account of the climate.
52. Henry Heras, "The Altar of Father Beschi", *The Examiner*, 1932, No. 83, pp. 494-495.
53. See, *The Travels of Friar Domingo Navarrete, 1618-1688,* (ed.,) J.S. Cummins, II, Vols, London, 1960, Vol. II, pp. 298-99
54. See, *The Travels of Abbe Carre in India and the Near East, 1672 to 1674,* (reprint), Delhi, 1990, Vol. II, pp. 360-361.
55. HAG, Livro de Serviço, fl 25v.
56. J.J Cotton, *List of Inscriptions on Tombs and Monuments*, Madras, 1905.
57. H. Hosten, *Antiquities from Santhome and Mylapore, op.cit.*, p. 163.
58. NAIP, Mss, *Eighteenth Century Documents,* no. 430, ft. 2-2v.
59. NAIP, Mss, *Arrets du Conseil Superior de Pondichery,* dated 12 July 1746.
60. Centre des Archives d' Outre-mer, Aix-en -Provence, France. Depot des Fortifications des Colonies, Portefeuille 32B, 18.

10

Inside the Tamil Church: Ecclesiastical Art, Role of the Portuguese Missionaries and the Armenian Merchants

Paintings in India cover a wide panorama in time and space. In the past, a set of scholars have examined the rock paintings in India and they have produced several good works.[1] Then we find another group of researchers who studied the traditional paintings of India in the various regions covering different historical periods.[2] Thirdly we notice that some scholars have only dealt with the emergence of the various schools of medieval paintings under the patronage of the different rulers and empires in India like the Vijayanagara and the Mughals. They had emphasized mainly on the impact of the Indo-European art and also largely concentrated on the influence of the European motifs and costumes found in the Indian Paintings in the Early modern period.[3] Another team of scholars also analyzed the wall paintings, besides the paper, wood and textiles paintings that well developed under the interest largely evinced and also at the request made by the officers and servants of the European trading companies in India.[4] Culminated from such multiple writings on art history, A.K. Ananda Coomaraswamy published his work and following him several other scholarly works began to appear on the arts of India and the Far East, revealing their symbolism and the metaphysical principles. However, the study of paintings that developed in India and the key role of the Portuguese missionaries and the Armenian traders has not been touched upon till date by researchers.[5] In fact we find some studies limited to the Portuguese art in Goa.[6] Therefore here we shall deal in detail the arrival of the Portuguese in the Tamil Coast and hinterland and the paintings made available in the chapels and churches.

The writings of A.K. Ananda Coomarasamy had unfolded the unbelievable depth of the traditional art of India and also to a larger extent that of medieval Europe. Art is by definition an externalization- should reflect in its own fashion what is most inward in that civilization. The birth of Christian art images sacred and secular, the common language of art, the Christian calligraphy with Latin and Portuguese, art and liturgy have to be studied. The role of Portugal in the formation of Tamil Christian culture was extremely important particularly in the sphere of religion because art became an integral part of Tamils' life from the Sixteenth Century onwards.

In the early phase of the Portuguese expansion in the Sixteenth century paintings and retables were initially exported from Portugal to India at the request of the different religious orders that had no way other than to fill the newly built churches with Christian arts and objects. These painting were sent from Lisbon to Goa in ships and then they were sent to other places such as Kochi (Cochin) and Kollam (Quilon) on the West coast of India where the Portuguese missionaries lived. As early as in the year 1511, we find a list of religious items found in the chapel of the fort of Cochin on 9 September 1511 which includes Christian paintings and art objects.[7] Again we find in a Letter of Fr. Sebastião Pires to the King of Cochin dated 10 January 1522 about the inventory of additional religious paintings, pictures and objects in the same church.[8] Further, we find in a letter written from Goa dated 22 November 1548 wherein we find mention of a new painting which was said to be required in the church to be replaced in the altar which was executed locally by an artist of Goa (name not mentioned in the record) since the previous/earlier first painting had detonated on account of climate.[9] In another letter dated 4 January 1562 we find mention of sincere thanks to the King of Portugal for sending a small retable to the Kollam church.[10] An altar piece was requested by João Perreira from the King of Portugal for the church of St. James College at

Cranganore which was under Frei Vicente. It is stated that Joao Perreira was very particular to have the altar piece with the life of St Thomas the apostle as the Christians in Cranganore were much devoted to St. Thomas.[11] These paintings made and brought from Portugal at that time had a strong Flemish influence and it was chiefly because of the cultural and trade links with Flanders and the family links between the Portuguese court and the court of Burgundy. Another important reason was the fact that the painter Jan van Eyck from Flanders had also remained in Lisbon for a long time and his influence was reflected in these paintings.[12]

The Vicar of Calicut wanted to do an altar piece through the ambassador of the King Zamorin of Calicut. The Portuguese managed to get a local painter. They decided to paint the whole passion of Christ on that altar piece with the help of that painter. The estimated expense for that altar piece was said to be 800 *cruzados*.[13] The demand for many Christian paintings and pictures in India necessitated the Portuguese to employ the local painters in Goa as early as 1548. However at the dawn of the employment of these artists it was instructed and insisted that the (Hindu/Indian) influence should not to be allowed especially with the Hindu motifs. Further, the missionaries also strictly disapproved the non-Christians creating Christian images and paintings.

Prior to the advent of the Portuguese in India, we find that the paintings in India in its extant records could be some what broadly classified into two categories. The first can be said to be Wall Painting *(bhitti-chitra)* and the other can be called miniature, while the former was executed in a kind of tempera on walls in large scale, the latter in gouache in the small format of manuscripts. The fact that Srikumara an eminent painter lived under the patronage of king Devanarayana at the capital town of Ambalapuzha in Travancore during the late Sixteenth century period is an example of the survival of the indigenous tradition of painting in South India.[14] Patronage of the various kings of Vijayanagar had also continued to be extended and the art of painting well flourished in Tamil, Telugu and Kannada country. We shall examine in detail the nature of Christian paintings, the dating of the pictures, the centres or the places where the paintings had flourished, besides who were the painters, why did they paint at all, and how they were appreciated by the people. We shall also analyze the problem of outside influence in these paintings.

In the beginning, we find that the Portuguese missionaries brought Christian pictures engraved for the print sellers of Antwerp. These pictures were very necessary for them to serve as illustrative tools to preach the Gospel. Further these pictures were needed also to be gifted or presented to the Indian rulers in the courts. However particularly after Martin Luther (1483-1546) and the revolt in Wittenberg in 1577 the whole Christian world was shaken by new ideas unthinkable to the previous centuries and periods.[15] The artist in Europe no longer had a clear vision, and also he never accepted the medieval iconography though it was more acceptable only by the Catholics. During this Counter-Reformation period a style called *baroque* appeared. The Society of Jesus which was founded at that time (on 15 April 1539) had played an important role in the spread of the movement of the counter-reformation and also the *baroque* Christian art both in Europe and in India.

The Painting of the Madonna and Infant Jesus in St. Thomas Mount Church

According to records there was a very beautiful painting of the Madonna with the Child Jesus in the Church of St. Thomas Mount. It was in 1559, Ramaraya, the ruler of Vijayanagar had attacked the Portuguese settlement of Mylapore. It is gleaned from the letter of Manoel Nunes written (after the attack of Ramaraya) from Goa to Portugal that the reason for such an attack was a reprisal for the destruction of Hindu deities in a temple by the Portuguese missionaries at Santhome.[16] Ramaraya had taken thirty-one citizens at that time as hostages, also carried away the relics of St. Thomas preserved in Mylapore. The beautiful painting of the Madonna kept in the church of St. Thomas Mount was also taken away by the nayak of Chandragiri. However, the captives paid a ransom of 50,000 *pardaus* and they were later released.[17]

This colour painting of the Madonna and Infant Jesus made on wood was an object of great devotion. The painting of Our Lady is of three spans (each span equal to nine inches) long and two spans broad. It is mentioned that when this coloured painting of Madonna arrived at the court the queen was so frightened in a dream with the apparition of the Virgin Mary. Therefore she compelled the ruler to send back the painting in 1560. It was brought back being respectfully placed in a palanquin and handed over to one of the principal citizen of Santhome called Gil Vaz Palha, a married man living in Santhome for a long time. The painting was installed in the Church of Our Lady of Expectation.[18] The oratory that existed in the hill of St. Thomas Mount was already converted into a church by the Portuguese missionaries in 1547. It must have been one of the oldest Christian paintings in Tamilnadu and we have this being preserved in the church even today.

The painting of Our Lady and the Child Jesus is in half portrait. She is tenderly embracing the child who, half-swathed, raises the right hand in a gracious pose. The virgin wears a long-sleeved red robe with a glided border. A blue veil also with gilded border covers her head and falls down in graceful, undulating folds of either side of the face. The features of both the Madonna and child are refined and pleasing. The expression of the child is charming; that of the Madonna is one of sorrowful beauty. However defects in proportion throughout the picture somewhat detract from its artistic effect. The colours remain fresh and clear although the paint is peeling away and damaging the face of the Madonna. In style it is western and seems to date to the post-renaissance period. This picture of Our Lady painted upon board had been seen by travellers of the Seventeenth century. Friar Domingo Navarrete who visited the church mentions this beautiful painting but says that the colours somewhat decayed and he had touched the painting with his rosary.[19] Another visitor called Ippolito Desideri the Jesuit who visited the church also speaks about this painting in 1726.

Jesuit Missionaries and their Paintings in Tamil Country

Jesuits used sacred pictures in the church and it is a concrete instance of the divine presence revivifying matter. During the time of Francis Xavier a Portuguese was sent to Goa to paint salvation history from creation to the last judgment. These paintings were brought from Goa to Tuticorin in the Tamil coast where they were like a book from which one could learn the Christian faith. It is mentioned that this created a demand for such pictures in other places in the Tamil Coast as well. Owing to the scarcity of Christian paintings in India they used pictures and began to print it. We know that the Jesuits introduced a printing press in Goa in 1556 (but it was closed down in 1683). The first picture printed at Goa in 1558 depicted Jesus Christ on the cross with his mother and St. John sitting on either side. It was particularly distributed to various churches. The print order was said to be less but none has survived today. Many pictures of the crucifixion, the agony of our Lord Jesus Christ and the sorrows of our Blessed Virgin Mary had been also printed in Goa. It is mentioned in the records that the church at Tuticorin had these printed pictures at that time.[20] The synod of Diamper held in 1599 decreed that there should be put up at the high altar of every church the picture of its patron saint and of other saints at the side altars.[21] Therefore sacred paintings and pictures of Christ, Virgin Mary and the saints were prepared.

Fr. Nicholas Pimenta in 1598 came from Rome on an official visit to the various Jesuit residences in India. He desired at that time a mission station to be started at Chandragiri, the capital of King Venkata II, the last ruler of Vijayanagar. Therefore to commence the work immediately, Fr. Francisco Ricci and Fr. D'Sa along with a merchant made journey. At first they reached Chittoor and there they met the Raja of Chittoor. He permitted the Jesuits to build a church at Condur. Later these two Jesuit missionaries along with Fr. Antonio Dubinò proceeded to Chandragiri and they arrived there on 16 August 1599.[22] These priests took several paintings and pictures and they went to show them to the King. They explained to him the things of salvation principally with the help of paintings and showed especially the painting of St. George the martyr on horse back, spearing a dragon. The heading of the painting was written in the language of *Badaga* (Telugu). In the very painting exhibition conducted by the Jesuits to the king they related a summary of St. George's history. It is mentioned by the missionaries that they spoke a great deal on the Christian doctrine and the king was very well satisfied seeing the paintings and pictures.

As the King of Vijayanagar at Chandragiri had expressed a very keen desire to see more Christian paintings the Jesuits desired to appoint Brother Alessandro and Brother Bartolomeo Fontebona who were fine painters. The Italian Jesuit Brother was sent at first to meet the king. The ruler also appreciated his coming to the palace very much since he knew that he had been sent by the Jesuits to show his paintings. As the king was so fond of paintings, he received this brother with great respect and asked him at once whether he had any good paintings to show him. The brother had nothing else at that time of his first visit except the portraits of Ignatius of Loyola, the founder of the Society of Jesus and Fr. Francis Xavier.[23] After seeing these portraits the king was astonished and so he asked the Jesuit brother to paint them in full size. So the brother painted a portrait of Ignatius of Loyola within one and a half hours of time. The king therefore gave a gift of golden cloth costing twenty *cruzados* and sent him back. After a few days, the brother again visited the palace and at that time the king desired the Brother to paint something of Brother's own choice. Then the Brother painted the portrait of the Blessed Virgin Mary with the Child Jesus in the king's presence little by little. The brother also painted a panel of John the Baptist and this panel was done well. Therefore the king ordered it to be hung in a prominent place in the assembly hall opposite to his royal throne. It is mentioned in the Jesuit records that the Brahmins of the court disliked the panel. During the subsequent visit, it is also mentioned that the Jesuit brother had showed the king a book of pictures and the king was very happy to see it. This is a book that contained a set of pictures representing the scenes on the life of our Lord Jesus Christ made by several Flemish painters at the request of Fr. Jerome Nadal a Jesuit in 1567.[24] The king patiently looked at all the pictures, one after another, asking the subject and being very much pleased with the answer and the mysteries of the life of Lord Jesus Christ. Thus the brother also had much explained to the king on this occasion about the tenets of Christianity.

Venkata II, the King of Vijayanagar had later granted the Jesuits a place for building of a church in Chandragiri itself. Soon the missionaries took up the construction of a chapel in the site granted to them close to the royal palace. When it was completed, crowds of Hindus visited and they showed great reverence to all the paintings, pictures and statuettes which the Jesuits had kept there. They also explained to the Hindu visitors the tents of the Christian faith. To the king also, the Jesuits carried away these paintings and pictures kept in the church to show in person. In the letter of Fr. Francis Ricci to Fr. Claudius Aqua Viva in Rome dated 20 October 1601 these details are mentioned.[25] The King of Vijayanagar shifted his capital and he started residing in Vellore in 1606. The Jesuits appointed Fr. Melchior Coutinho and two lay brothers in 1607 to start another mission station there. However, the Jesuits from Vellore and Chandragiri had closed down their mission stations and moved out from there in 1611 owing to some reasons. A Capuchin Missionary namely Fr. Ephraim lived in Madras and he took care of the Portuguese and the native Christians. It is recorded that he displayed an image of Our Lords' body being bought down dead from the cross on Good Friday. This helped the Christians in the service during the Holy Week.[26]

Armenian Traders and their Christian Paintings

Next we find the response of the Armenian traders to supply the Christian paintings to the churches in Tamilnadu. We know that there were many Armenian traders in Madras who settled down under the patronage of the English. According to records the Armenians had formed a settlement in 1666 and conducted trade there. When King of Golconda seized Santhome of Mylapore from the hands of Portuguese in 1662 he had appointed an Armenian named Markur Erezad as the Governor of the place.[27] Among the Armenian traders Khojah Petrus Voskan was one of the rich merchants. Since the Armenians were Christians they often visited the church at St. Thomas Mount. Khojah Petrus Voskan had arranged for a painting to be made on the martyrdom of St. Thomas. This painting on wood is even now fixed high up in the wooden reredos of the altar in the hill Church of St. Thomas Mount. Two circles crown this painting and the name of Petrus Voskan is inscribed as the donor, round the smaller circle. In this painting fixed high up on the main altar in the church the apostle is found praying with folded hands looking at the Cross. The native with a tuft of hair in his head, wearing his sacred thread across the chest, wearing a dhoti, carrying a lance had pierced at the back shoulder of the Apostle. The bleeding is also painted nicely and this painting is of Indian origin made in 1695. This painting represents Apostle

St. Thomas praying before a cross among boulders while a native pierces him from behind with a lance. The painter appears to have followed the belief that the cross above the altar at St. Thomas Mount was carved by St. Thomas or that at any rate he died praying before it. There is another painting in cloth that depicts the martyrdom of St. Thomas.

Similarly, this Thomas Mount hill church has fourteen other paintings made on wood in total. Seven paintings are fixed in the right side and seven in the left side of the wall. There are mainly paintings of the apostles/ disciples of Jesus Christ. Some of the pictures are an improvement on the originals. The arrangement of the pictures on the wall is in the following order from left to right.

St. Peter, holding the keys and a cross,

St. Thaddaeus a book and club,

St. Andrew a book and a cross,

Our Lord,

St. Philip with a book and a cross,

St. James the greater with a pilgrim's staff a guard and a scrip,

St. Mathias with a book and a hat removed,

St. Paul with a book and a sword,

St. Mathew with a book and carpenter's rule,

St. Thomas with a book and a lance,

St. John with a poisoned chalice,

St. Simon with a book and a saw,

St. Bartholomew with a book and some other object,

St. James the lesser with a book and a beam.

Visitors could enjoy even now the sight of twelve exquisite and almost life size paintings of these Apostles that adorn the walls of the church. Their originals were the gift of Petrus Voskan. It is mentioned in the records preserved in the Arch-Bishop's House Archives in Mylapore that these pictures were painted by a Franciscan after the originals that were crumbling to pieces.[28] Names of all the above said fourteen oil paintings depicting the Apostles and Jesus Christ are inscribed in Armenian. It may be said that these paintings are also of Indian origin.

Paintings in the Various Churches of Mylapore Diocese

The Church of St. Thomas in Mylapore had several paintings and pictures. Mir Jumla, the general of Golconda who besieged Santhome of Mylapore in 1646 had occupied the Church but left the paintings in the church without disturbing. The French who later occupied Santhome from 1672 to 1674 had mentioned that in July 1672 when the French went to offer thanks to the Lord for the successful capture of Santhome they found the paintings and pictures in good condition that showed no signs of disarray in the church during the capture and occupation of Santhome by the Abdullah Qutub Shah, the Sultan of Golconda forces.[29]

Again we find in the Church records that the cathedral received a beautiful and large painting representing the taking down of Jesus from the Cross which has been executed for João de Monte, a rich Portuguese merchant of Mylapore. This painting is dated 6 May 1821. According to the parish records it is mentioned that this painting was kept in the Church of Our Lady of Mount Carmel in Kovalam near Mahabalipuram and it was brought to Mylapore.[30] Presently this painting hangs high up near the southern wall of the church near sacristy.

The church of *Madre de Deus* located in the Madha Church Road, Raja Annamalipuram. (which was built by the Portuguese and consecrated on 8 September 1576) has seven paintings on wood which deal with the Stations of the Cross. However dates are not mentioned in the paintings but they these are of Seventeenth century origin.

John Van Linschoten the secretary to the Archbishop of Goa mentions the famous painted cotton textiles and calicoes made in Santhome and Madras.[31] The textile paintings were also used in churches and the Luz Church in Mylapore has eight Armenian paintings on cloth which depict the apostles at their death scene. In this church there is also a painting on glass depicting Our Lady of Dolours pierced with sword. Further, the church has stucco work, paintings in the vaulted ceiling of the church before the sacristy. We find an interesting the painting of the mariners and the light. It represents a sun with six stars round it. Two of which have a triple tail or ray the others hanging only one ray of light.

St. Rita's church located within the premises of the Santhome Higher Secondary School has a painting of St. Rita and it was done by F.X. Correa in 1862. This large oil painting of St. Rita is hanging on the left side of the wall. It represents the Saint amid angels, two nuns of her religious order kneeling beside her.[32]

Portraits

An oil painting representing Dom Frei Manoel de S. Catharina, the 16th Bishop of Cochin, Archbishop of Goa (1780-1812) is preserved in the Bishop's house. It has the inscription in Latin "True likeness of the Most Excellent and Most Reverend Lord, the Lord Frei Emaneol of St. Catherine of the Order of Dicalced Carmelities, Metropolitan Arch-Bishop of Goa, Primate of the East, Visitor General and Apostolic Reformer of all the Religious Bodies in this Portuguese India".[33] Other paintings in the Bishop's House include Dom João Chrysostome de Amorim Pesoa, the Arch-Bishop of Goa ; Dom Ayres de Ornelas, the Arch-Bishop of Goa and Dom Antonio Sebastião Valente, the First Patriarch of Goa. In Ellakurichi church the portrait of Fr. Beschi is also preserved. There is a portrait of Fr. Roberto Nobili done by his contemporary Fr. Balthzar da Costa. It has the inscription in Latin "Fr. Robert de Nobili of the Society of Jesus in this dress and appearance founded, propagated and stabilized the Maduari mission. He died in the College of St. Thomas (Mylapore) on January, 16, 1656 AD when he was about eighty years ago".[34]

Calvin rejected the use of picture and statuettes radically. One sees in Martin Luther reconciliation and even a recommendation of pictorial representations. The Council of Trent reacted to the protestant antipathy to the use of images, relics and other forms of arts sacra by reaffirming its belief in them. Francis Xavier resorted to art as a mission tool. Besides various kinds of paintings, engravings and statuettes of religious icons it came in due course of time to replicate and adapt the grandeur of Mannerist Italy in Tamil Country. The Jesuits gave such importance to the use of art in the propagation of faith. According to Jesuits art like preaching had an extraordinary ability to delight, to teach and to move Hindus at least to respect Christianity and lead the new converts to abandon Hinduism totally. Christian images had also played a mnemonic role and missionaries taught adults and children to use images to store and retrieve information.

Statuettes and Sacred Images

Statuettes made of wood were used in Tamil churches as the icon had been a concrete instance of the divine presence revivifying matter. Thomas Gambo, the Jesuit 1617 mentioned that the image of Our Lady was held in great veneration in Santhome Church at Mylapore. However, it is recorded that St. Francis Xavier used to spend his nights in 1545 before this statuette in prayer and received the divine inspiration to go to the Far East.[35] Today the statuette stands installed in the southern altar on the right side of the church. It is three feet tall and is made of wood as was the custom in those days in Europe. It represents the Blessed Virgin Mary in the sitting posture, with her hands joined in prayer and her eyes piously cast down. She wears a long sleeved robe and a veil over her head falling over her shoulders in the form of a long mantle. Both the mantle and veil are gilded. Her mouth, nose and eyes are finely shaped and are rated as exquisitely beautiful. The high calibre of Portuguese workmanship is evident in this piece of Christian art which seems to have been brought to India from Portugal.

The altar of Our Lady of Rosary chapel in Santhome is located on a high wooden rectangular platform with the usual niche in the centre sheltering the wooden statuette of Our Lady with the Infant Jesus in her left hand and a sceptre in her right hand. The right arm of Infant Jesus is placed around the shoulders of Mother Mary. The Infant Jesus is seen holding an orb on the left palm. The physiognomy, the drapery and general execution of the statuette definitely point to Portuguese craftsmanship in the rococo style as evident from the treatment of the drapery. In a smaller upper niche stands the statuette of St. Dominic with oval shaped carvings representing the fifteen mysteries of the rosary enframing the central niche. The raised shelf for the candle-sticks is also of fine Portuguese workmanship. The writer had seen the altar in the same condition in 1978, but during his visit in 1995, much of the Portuguese trappings had been removed.

The reference to a statuette in *Madre de Deus* church is found in a letter written by Fr. Andrea Lopez, the Jesuit Provincial of

Malabar who visited Mylapore in 1644.[36] "The chapel is well maintained both by the Portuguese and the natives of the land.... There is a beautiful statuette of Our Lady of a good size. It is revered very much even by the non-Christians". The alluringly beautiful wooden statuette of *Madre de Deus* holding Jesus in her left arm is still found in the main altar of the chapel. It is about five feet tall. Above the niche there are two cherubs holding the crown above the head. In the altar there are two rows of twisted columns and we find around it the carved decorative motifs reflecting perhaps the local influence on Christian art.

In the Luz church Our Lady of Light statuette is kept in the main altar in the central niche of a very ornate wooden *reredos* (altar screen) and represents the Madonna holding Infant Jesus in one arm. Above the niche there are two cherubs holding the crown. In a smaller upper niche there is a clothed statue of the Infant Jesus with an Armenian inscription mentioning the name of Khwajah Petrus Voscan the merchant benefactor who had donated this statue.

There is a beautiful statuette of the Blessed Virgin Mary in Little Mount Church holding the Infant Jesus on her left arm. It is three and a half feet tall. The motif of vine leaves and bunches of grapes decorate the background of the altar. Below the altar, the scene of the Last Supper of Jesus Christ is engraved in a very beautiful manner. However there is another statuette of St. Thomas in Little Mount and it is recorded in an inscription there that this statue of St. Thomas was made by António Gonçalves de Athaide at his own cost in the year 1612. In the statue, St. Thomas is shown with a raised right hand in the attitude of benediction and holding a carpenter's square frame in his left hand.[37] Although images of Bronze and stone in worship by Hindus had been very popular in Tamilnadu the Portuguese did not like it but they followed and introduced images made of wood in Christian worship in churches.

Pictures in the Printed Tamil Books

Portuguese used also woodcuts for printing Tamil books. The Christian pictures were printed from the wood blocks appeared in the Tamil books printed by Portuguese. In the book of *Thambiran Vanakkam* a woodcut representing the Trinity in glory and a throng of the elect bearing patrons below is found. Further, Fr. Antão de Proença's Dictionary of 30 July 1679 has fleurem with I.H.S. device. Colophon in the book mentions "*Laus & Gloria Deo & Virgini*". Wooden furniture had been also made in Tamil Country. The Episcopal throne of the Bishop in Mylapore is an example. We also find in Santhome church many tables, cabinets and chest boxes of various designs made for the use of the church and the priests. Three beautifully carved ivory crucifixes are found in St. Rita Church. Cross between the two peacocks in stone had been found from *Madre de Deus* church premises and it is now preserved in St Thomas Cathedral museum. Similarly, the monogram of the Society of Jesus I.H.S in stone was found at the entrance of the *Madre de Deus* church premises.

Many churches contain lofty decorative retables that rise, screen like, behind the main altar to reach the height of the church. The church's brilliant interior combination of wood and gold leaf ornament is characteristic of what has been called the Indian baroque. Pedestal engraved with lotuses, elephants and peacocks and other motifs are found in churches. Pelicans drinking water from a font symbolizes the Eucharist as well as self sacrifice of Christ.

Finally to conclude, it may be said that in the early days of Portuguese trade pictures and paintings came from Europe. By mid-Sixteenth century the Portuguese were using the talents of local artists. The church paintings had important consequences not only on the style of local artists but also on the wall paintings of palaces. An influence of this might be cited where we find in the Thanjavur Palace angels with plaited hair with flowers on head. Similarly painting influences from India were also carried to Portugal in the later period. In a painting of the picture of the Magi in the Cathedral of Evora one of the kings appear in dark colour wearing an elaborate head dress and carries in his hand a coconut as a gift to the Baby Christ. Thus oriental elements came into the paintings in the churches of Portugal.

Notes and References

1. Vishnu S. Wakankar, & Robert R.R. Brooks, *Stone age painting in India*, D.B Taraporavala & Sons, Bombay, 1976; Manoranjan Ghosh, *Rock*

paintings and other antiquities of Pre-historic and late times, Memoirs of the Archaeological Survey of India, No.15, 1932.

2. Dinanath Pathy, *Traditional paintings of Orissa*, Delhi, 1990; C. Sivarama Murthy, South Indian Paintings, New Delhi, 1968.
3. Gauvin Alexander Bailey, *The Jesuits and the Grand Mughal: Renaissance art at the imperial court of India, 1580-1630*, Smithsonian, Washington, 1998; see also, Basil Gray, "The development of painting in India in the 16th century", *Marg,* Vol. VI, No.3, 1953; Moti Chandra, *Technique of Mughal paintings,* Lucknow, 1949.
4. Mildred Archer, *Company paintings in the India Office Library*, London, 1972; John Irwin, "Golconda cotton paintings of early 17th century", *Lalitkala*, No. 5, p.16. We have 141 scaled drawings of on the Meenakshi Sundareswarar Temple and the pillared art of Thirumalai Nayak's Choultry done in 1789 by Adam Blackader, a surgeon who visited Madurai. For details see Blackader, "A description of the great pagoda of Madura, the choultry of Tirumalai naik in a letter from Mr. Adam Blackader surgeon to Sir John Black Bast, PRS, FAS", in *Archaeologia or Miscellaneous Tracts Relating to Antiquities*, London, Vol. X, 1792, pp. 449-459.
5. S. Jeyaseela Stephen, *Portuguese in the Tamil Coast: Historical Explorations in Commerce and Culture, 1507-1749*, Navajyothi Publishers, Pondicherry, 1998.
6. Numerous references to Christian Paintings in the churches of Goa and the gallery portraits of the Viceroys at Panjim have been studied by scholars.
7. Silva Rego, *Documentação para a histroia das missões do padroado Portugues do Oriente*, Lisboa, 1947-1955, Vol.1, p. 124.
8. Ibid, see the Letter of Fr. Sebastião Pires to the King of Cochin dated 10 January 1522, Silva Rego, *Documentação,* vol. I, p. 436
9. Silva Rego *Ibid*, Vol. IV, pp.128-129.
10. Silva Rego, *Ibid*, Vol. IX, p. 25
11. IANTT, CC, Pt. I, Maco 80, doc. 7, fl. 1v.
12. Teresa Martins de Caravalho, "A Evolução de arte em Portugal", in *Um Patrimonio Artistico*, Lisboa, 1983, pp. 163-174.
13. IANTT, CC, Part. I, Maco 19, Doc. 85, fl. 1v.
14. Ashok Bhattacaharya, *Citralaksana: A Treatise on Indian Painting*, Calcutta, 1974.
15. Calvin radically rejected the use of picture and statues in the churches in Europe. Martin Luther recognized and even reconsidered pictorial

representations in Churches. Pictures deserve veneration and the response of the onlooker is directed towards the person represented not towards the picture.

16. S. Jeyaseela Stephen, *Portuguese in the Tamil Coast, op. cit.,* p.302. See also, Joseph Wicki, *Documenta Indica*,(henceforth D.I.) 18 Vols, Rome, 1948-88, See, Vol. IV, p. 491.
17. Joseph Wick, *D.I. op. cit.*, Vol. IV, pp. 368, 491 and Vol. V, p.180.
18. ARSI, Mss. Goa, See, the Report of Dom Frei Andre, the Bishop of Cochin who visited Mylapore for the fourth time in 1600.
19. *Travels of Friar Domingo Navarrete, 1618-1688* (ed.) J.S. Cummins, 2 vols, London, 1960, vol. II, p. 300.
20. Joseph. Wicki, "Jesuiten ler und-bildhaver in Indien in 16 Jahrhundert", in *Neue Zeitscrift fur Missions Wissenchaft*, 1982, pp. 30-38.
21. See, the proceedings of the Synod of Diamper, Accao 8, Decreto, 29; Acção 3, Decreto1, chapter II. For details see, Joseph Thekkadeth, *History of Christianity in India, 1542-1700*, Bangalore,1982.
22. See, Fernão Guerriero, Relaçãm Annual das cousas que fezaram os padres de companhia de Jesus nas partes da India oriental em algumas outras du conquista deste reyno no anno de 606 & 607, Lisboa, 1909, pp. 105-107.
23. *Ibid.*
24. This pictures have been reproduced by Fr. Julio Aleni in Peking in 1635 with a Chinese text of the life of Christ. A copy of 1887 edition Tu-se-We is available in the Arch-Bishop's Library, Wodehouse Road, Fort Bombay. The Jesuits founded a school of painters in Japan in 1583 under the leadership of Giovanni Niccolo.
25. See the Letter of Francis Ricci to Fr. Claudius Aqua Viva dated 20 October 1601, in Henry Heras, *The Aravidu Dynasty of Vijayanagar*, Madras, 1927, pp. 582-583.
26. Nicolau Manucci, *op.cit.*, Vol. III, p. 470.
27. Annie Basil, *Armenian settlements in India*, Armenian College Calcutta, 1969, pp. 44-45.
28. AAMM, Mss. No. 2478.
29. Lotika Varadarajan, *India in the Seventeenth Century: Memoirs of François Martin*, Delhi, 1988, Vol. I, Part I, p.118.
30. AAMM, *João de Monte Papers from Kovalam and Santhome of Mylapore*, Mss. No. 3261.
31. A.C. Burnell & Tiele, *The voyages of Linschoten to the East Indies*, London, 1885, Vol. I, p. 91.

32. The Church also has three beautifully carved ivory crucifixes which I have seen during my field visit.
33. The text runs as follows. "Vera effigies Exami ac Rmi D.D. Fr. Eamano elis a S. Catharina ex ordine Carmeliarum Excalceato rum Archiepiscopi metropolis tani goensis orientisque primates necon omnium regularium corporationum Vizitatoris generalis ac Refor matrosi apostolic hac I Indi Luzitania".
34. The portrait is found in the Portuguese translation of Roberto Nobili's catechism done by Fr. Balthazar da Costa. See Fr. Jean Castets, *Caritas*, July, 1923; see also. Fr. Sauliere, *Caritas,* July, 1966. The inscription in Latin runs as follows: "P/ Robertus de Nobilibus/Societatis IESU/In hoc habitu et specie fundavit/ propagavit et sta/ bilivit/ missionem Madurensem/ obilit in Collegio D.Thomae 16 Januarii/ an.dni 1656/prope/ octogenaris".
35. *Monumenta Xaveriana,* Tome II, pp. 488, 946-948.
36. ARSI, *Litterae Annuae: Provinciae Malabarensis,* 1644.
37. J.J Cotton, *op.cit.,* Vol. I, p. 57.

Conclusion

Portuguese did not know the underpinnings of the traditional Indian society when they came to India in the beginning to spread the Gospel. They started to convert the natives to Christianity with an open mind. How Christian conversion should not be done or how it can be allowed at that time is known from a letter of an Indian *Raja*. It is made evident that conversion meant a break in social structure which would lead to disorder in social relationships which was freely articulated. It was this belief mentioned in the letter of the *Raja* of Cannanore to the King of Portugal dated 6 December 1507 wherein the *Raja* asked that the Hindu slaves should not be converted because the *nayars* had exploited and took immense service besides deriving profits from them.[1] While this being the case in the Malabar Coast, the conversion of João da Cruz, a *chetti* resident of Kayal in the Tamil coast opened the door for the conversion of a large number of *paravas* from the Pearl Fishery region mainly engaged in assisting the Arabs who were having considerable control over the pearl fishery operations. The *paravas* were advised by João da Cruz to seek the protection of the Portuguese by converting themselves to their religion. In fact he took a delegation of the *paravas* in 1532 to Kochi to get them converted to Christianity following the conflict between Muslims and the *paravas*. These conversions took place out of necessity and because of the then prevailing circumstances. Moreover the *paravas* suffered from discrimination and oppression at the hands of both the Arabs and the native merchants. The conversion of *paravas* thus enabled them to get liberated from social oppression and come out of a socially repressive system as humanistic tendencies were still not very much in evidence in the predominantly Hindu society. Thus Parava conversions had been a quest for self respect, dignity and identity. The same is the case with other lower castes in the hinterland of the Tamil country which induced them to get converted to Christianity at a later period. There was apparently no social discrimination in the Christian religion. This change of religion propelled the process of social mobility. A problem faced by the early Christian converts was the persecution they faced from the overzealous protestant Dutch missionaries especially at Tuticorin and Nagapattinam after these Portuguese settlements fell into the hands of the Dutch.

I

In 1545, Francis Xavier wrote that he had converted 10,000 Hindus in a month at Tuticorin.[2] It is humanly impossible and perhaps this is an error of figure. All the more true facts and figures are important in history. As for conversion, the rate of growth had been sometimes rapid and sometimes slow depending generally upon the circumstances. Regarding the statistics we find a missionary mentioning that in 1586 the *Parava* Christians were 55,000 in Tamil country.[3] According to a later report by a missionary in 1644 that there were 26218 Christians in the Pearl Fishery Coast.[4] In the report of year 1646 it is mentioned that during the last forty years, Jesuits have converted only seventy-eight *Brahmins*. Therefore the number of Christians mentioned in 1545 as well as 1586 are not exact figures and the reports of 1644 and 1646 are reasonable, acceptable and definitely authentic.

Five years after the death of Fr. Roberto Nobili, we find Fr. Balthazar da Costa in 1661 had mentioned that there were 30,000 Christians in the Madurai Mission. According to Jesuit records the town of Tuticorin in 1701 had the *Parava* population of three thousand inhabitants.[5] In 1709 there were 1100 Christian converts in Pondicherry.[6] By 1725, there were 3000 Christians converts in the same place.[7] These converts consisted of the low castes, high castes, and the untouchables. In 1712-1713 Fr. Jean Venant Bouchet had converted only one Christian at Ariyankuppam, a village near Pondicherry and later in 1725 the Christian population in that place was nearly 400 and it has increased over a period of twelve years.[8]

Fr. Ducros wrote on 17 October 1725 from Ariyankuppam that from 2 October 1724 to 12 October 1725, he had converted and administered 601 baptisms mainly to the *Sudras* in the region.[9] Thus exact details of conversions are found in individual missionary records. Every Church had the conversion cum baptism register which had the details such as original Hindu name, Christian name after conversion, place of residence, sex, approximate age, date of baptism, caste to which the person belonged, (indicating whether he or she is a slave) and the signature of the priest who gave baptism. The name of the god-parents are not at all mentioned in these registers.[10] In the report of Fr. Paolim we find that the Christian population in 1776 without naming castes and he mentioned that there were 18000 Christians in Madurai and 10,000 in Thanjavur region.[11] The social climate among the caste ridden Tamil society was favourable for conversions to handle different groups of Hindus by different types of missionaries who adopted either the life style of *brahmins* and *pandaraswamis* who concentrated on the conversion of high castes and low castes respectively. Preaching and teaching to the masses was given primary importance by the Jesuits and it is more significant than even listening to confessions or the performance of the spiritual exercises as gleaned from Francis Xavier's letter. In 1542 Xavier had brought out the Short Catechism, the *Doutrina Christiana,* in Portuguese. He felt the need to indigenize and two years later he had translated prayers from Latin to Tamil. He did conversions and gave a detailed explanation of how he did it.[12]

Acculturation, the learning of accepted cultural ways and giving up of old ways by new members of the culture came into existence. The Jesuit missionaries took on the characteristics of the Tamils giving up most of or all of their European cultural ways. In many cases it was the result of the conquest or result of the prolonged contacts between the Luso-Tamil cultures. Acculturation took place as a result of Portuguese influence in the line of colonialism. It involved different stages. In this process there was a host culture and a guest culture. There was a section of missionaries like Fr. Gonçalvo Fernandes in Madurai who opposed the penetration and influence of the Tamil cultural elements just as there will be another section which supported the Tamil culture like Roberto Nobili in spite of differences. The basic reason behind the conflict between cultures was ethnocentrism, the belief that Portuguese ways were superior to Tamils. Jesuits like Roberto Nobili and Baltazar da Costa adopted the method of acculturation in the Seventeenth Century and these missionaries themselves initiated the process of indigenisation of Christianity.

The Dominicans, the Augustinians and the Capuchins mainly attended to the spiritual needs of the European Catholics and the Eurasians. The Franciscans were successful in running hospitals and charitable institutions. The Jesuits took up their apostolate through education by establishing schools, colleges and seminaries, in addition to printing books. The new converts in the Tamil country were so zealous that several of them came forward to be trained as catechists who could instruct the faithful in the absence of the Jesuits in many places. The Jesuits had realised the need for indigenisation of Christian rituals and festivals. They were concerned very much with the material welfare of the Tamils. The poor and the under-privileged groups in the Tamil society found the gospel of Jesus in tune with the activities of the *Padroado* missionaries which offered new and hitherto unprecedented appeal to improve their own economic and social position.

The Portuguese missionaries at first settled down on the port settlements where the Portuguese traders had established their trading factories. Thus Santhome of Mylapore, Devanampattinam, Nagapattinam, Porto Novo, Punnaikayal and Tuticorin became the main centres of missionary activities in the Sixteenth Century while many sub-stations developed at various places in the Seventeenth Century. Regarding the missionary activities on the Pearl Fishery Coast, it may be said that not many conversions had taken place in the littoral extending from the port of Kilakkarai to Rameshwaram, while at the same time the *paravas* who lived in the coastal villages from Vembar to Ovari on the South Eastern Coast embraced Christianity. Periyapattinam and Devanampattinam emerged as the most important mission stations towards the end of the Sixteenth Century. Chaples, churches, schools, seminaries, hospitals, orphanages, sodalities and Holy Houses of Mercy were established in many centres.

Although the Hindu rulers were generally much more tolerant to other religions, they did not stand as mute spectators whenever the Portuguese acted overzealously against the Hindus. The local rulers objected to it and even raided the port settlements. However in the Seventeenth Century the Portuguese missionaries who had taken up residence in the royal courts of Madurai, Chandragiri, etc. converted people and took care of the religious ministrations of the converts in the hinterland. The conversions by the missionaries brought about an increase in the Christian population especially in the Portuguese settlements since natives also migrated towards the ports.

Changes in social characteristics and standards took place in Tamilnadu among the *Paravas*, *Mukkuvars* and *Paraiyar* converts who have embraced Christianity in mass movements more rapidly since their age old social integration was destroyed by individual conversion. It had been found that the way Christian rituals celebrated had either merged with or supplanted the existing rituals. These rituals mirrored the religious and social relationship between the Christian mission and congregation. The products of societal change noticed could be said to be of varied nature such as change by expansion or contraction, change by replacement or substitution, change by incorporation or aggregation, change by addictive or accretionary change besides involuntary change. These changes were made possible and they were brought out because the Portuguese Jesuits as a group or community had a clear policy regarding evangelisation, inculturation and social apostate in Tamil country.

All these changes possessed a morphology or trend. However three types of the morphology of change are found are such as change as smooth and continuous trend, change as a non-linear trend with catastrophic switches and revolutionary movements besides continuity or discontinuity. The influence of Hinduism in the Christian way of life by the *Paravas* was seen by missionaries initially since proper Christian teachings had not been given. In the Sixteenth Century perhaps baptism allowed the change of name was disliked by the Tamil Hindus. Portuguese links only with the maritime communities in Tamilnadu perhaps hindered the growth of expansion of the mission stations interior and other castes in the Sixteenth century. The number of Brahmin converts although increased, was much less, when compared to other castes. The simple reason was that the Brahmins could not obtain any social advancement by becoming Christians. The lower caste converts found it possible to elevate their social status by embracing Christianity. By becoming Christians they could freely enter the church and learn the Holy Scripture which was forbidden fruit to them, a monopoly enjoyed by the Brahmins for down the ages. The Portuguese Jesuit Mission among the Tamils was exclusively for the benefit of men and their family in their spread of Gospel and Christianity. The Jesuits moved from one place to another in search of various castes Hindus in Tamilnadu for conversion and they saw that no elements in the native culture and Hindu religion which they could emulate and much less consider superior to their own Portuguese culture.

The King of Portugal always showed keen interest in the propagation of faith. He commanded the Viceroy of Goa vide his letter issued from Madrid in January 1617 to submit a report on all religious orders at different places in India with details of the various endowments.[13] Further, the Viceroy was also informed through the royal order issued on 8 February 1650 to send a list each year containing the names of all the provincials and major superiors of the religious orders.[14] On 10 March 1687 the King again reminded the Viceroy of Goa about his duty to see that the religious reports are forwarded to him promptly.[15] Substantial funds were allotted for pastoral work by the King of Portugal as the missionaries received generous help when compared to the funds sanctioned by the *Estado da India* for the political consolidation of the Portuguese settlements in India.

As early as in the year 1573 the King of Portugal had come to know about the designs of the Cardinals and the Pope in Rome to establish the Sacred Congregation for the Propagation of Faith, the project of Francis Borgia and adopted by Pope Pius V. The King had taken a definite stand against this project and in his letter dated 11 June 1573 to Don Juan de Zuniga his ambassador in Rome the King had instructed to do all he could to hinder the realization.[16] The King of Portugal was against it because he did not like the Cardinals to meddle with the affairs of the missions in his overseas empire.[17]

However, we find that such attempt had failed and finally the Sacred Congregation for the Propagation of Faith was erected by Pope Gregory XV vide his Bull "*Inscrutabili*" dated 22 June 1622. It was mentioned that the express purpose was to preserve, strengthen and spread the Christian faith. In doing so the Pope opened a new age in the history of the missions.[18] In the first letter dated 15 January 1622 sent by *Monsignor* Francesco Ingoli, the secretary of the Propaganda Fide it is mentioned that their one aim was purely and simply to Christian apostolate.[19]

Given the near identity of the aims pursued by two organizations *Padroado* and Propaganda coincided at least in part it was more or less inevitable that clashes arose between them in the course of time. Diplomatic relations between Rome and Lisbon were broken off for thirty years (1640-1670) for lack of pontifical confirmation and the Bishops of *Padroado* were not replaced.[20] In 1672 the Viceroy of Goa received orders from the King of Portugal to seize any Bishop or missionary sent by the *Propaganda Fide* and dispatch him to Portugal.[21] Pope Clement X took under his protection the Vicar Apostolic and the missionaries working in non-Portuguese territories exempting them from the jurisdiction of the *Padroado* prelates vide his Bull "*Cum ad Aures*" dated 10 November 1673.[22] Pope Innocent XII vide his Bull "*Cum Sicut Acceptimus*" dated 6 February 1697 warned the *Padroado* Bishops and reminded them in virtue of holy obedience not to exercise, under any pretext whatever, any act of jurisdiction in the kingdoms of Bijapur and Golconda besides the Mughal Empire.[23] The Holy See strengthened missionary activity in South India by erecting the Sacred Congregation for the Propagation of Faith, another missionary organ of the Church besides the *padroado*, to accelerate the process of Christianisation of India by the various religious congregations. The *Propaganda Fide* and *Padroado* conflicts did not much affect the apostolic work in Tamil country. Each mission or parish in the Tamil Country had a large number of substations which covered a vast area. Besides cults around many saints, christo-centric and mario-centric devotion also became popular which gave rise to annual festivals celebrated in Indo-Portuguese fashion at various mission stations in the Tamil country dedicated to Jesus and Mary and saints like St. Antony, St. Sebastian, St. James and St. Michael.

There were 320 Jesuits of Portuguese, Italian and French origin who had come to India between 1542 and 1759. Some of them laid down their life as martyrs after their arrival to Tamil Coast within a short duration. Antonio Criminali who came in 1549 lived for nine years. Bro. Luis Mendez arrived in 1552 died after nine years. João de Britto who landed in 1693 died after sixteen years. Fr. Joseph Carvalho died in the jail of Thanjavur in 1701. Many missionaries did not survive long and their life span was perhaps affected by weather and climate besides hard work. Emmanuel Correa landed in 1678 just lived for four years. Antão de Proença came in the year 1666 had lived for nineteen years. Rodriguez de Abreu who landed in 1671 lived for fourteen years. Xavier Maria Borghese lived for twenty-four years preaching the gospel. The next category of priests were some blessed with long life like Andre Freyre with forty years, Roberto Nobili with fifty years, Constantino Beschi with thirty-six years, Balthazar da Costa with thirty-eight years, James Rossi with forty-nine years and Francisco Laynez with thirty six years.[24]

II

Portuguese *casados* had retained and followed all their own customs followed in Portugal. Those Indians married to Portuguese i.e., the *mestiçōes* only began to adopt and mix the Indian and Portuguese manners and customs but they also did not give up the Indian customs in total. There had been an intermingling of customs, manners and ceremonies followed in the Indo-Portuguese families. Some superstitions followed in India were recorded by the Portuguese since they were surprised to see it. It may be said that the Christian and Hindu rituals were not allowed to be mixed for the Portuguese missionaries in India were very strict.

The Portuguese captain of the settlement was initially handling the problems of law and order and later we find that the King of Portugal was compelled to introduce a regular administration of justice through *Relação* (court) and an *Ouvidor* (judge) to control the affairs. The Assembly of the Elders (*Os Eleitos de Povação*) a concept of the Tamil society was established at Nagapattinam and they controlled the social affairs of the Luso-Tamil people and this distinct thread of continuity could be seen here. Blood feud and seeking vengeance was very common. Portuguese women followed a life of luxury and plenty. Some social rejects of the West who were sent out from Portugal as criminals to India and their presence was always destructive to the Indo-Portuguese society as they did not change their way of life. Superstitions occupied also a prominent place and this perhaps was picked up from the Hindu practice. Many Portuguese acculturated and fitted into the Tamil environment and they formed a part of the Indian society. The Portuguese had also followed some evil practices such as robbery, theft, murder in the Tamil Coast. They were not free from love, hate, extravagance and attachment to their material life of the period. This social group had also been accepted by the natives since they contributed to the Indian economy by conducting overseas trade. Some changes such as emergence of new trading groups in the overseas trade of Tamilnadu, with a new settlement pattern in the ports, governed by the Indian rulers and the Indian settlements very near the Portuguese enclaves were administered by the rulers of Vijayanagar Empire. Change of religion took place among those women who got married to Portuguese. Social evils such as sorcery, adultery, slavery, robbery continued in the Luso-Tamil society.

The Indo-Portuguese community was not a homogenous social group and it was considerably stratified in terms of race and status. The *castizos* or the Portuguese of purer blood were less in the Coromandel Coast and the descendants of mixed parentage or the *mestiçōs* were more in number. The wayward life style and lawlessness were found common and it created unusual social pressures. Crimes committed by Portuguese and Indo-Portuguese community could be classified generally into three groups on the basis of their motives, i.e., economic, sexual and miscellaneous. These crimes could also be further classified according to different purposes such as (a) against women (assault and murder) (b) against property (theft and robbery) (c) against public decency or morality (disorderly conduct) (d) against public justice (embezzlement and breach of trust). Blood feud was another practice in society in which the family of a murdered person sought vengeance on the murderer or murderer's family. It is to be mentioned here that good and bad people had existed in that age and society. Various social problems and crimes committed by people had a harmful impact on social interests and detrimental to the well-being of the society of the Sixteenth and Seventeenth centuries in Portuguese India.

III

Although the Portuguese were primarily interested in trade, an appraisal of their cultural influences and efforts in the Tamil Coast should also be considered seriously. Education in the Tamil country had been since Vedic times the preserve of the chosen few among the upper castes, mostly *Brahmins*. Tamil writers were proficient in the production of highly philosophical and literary works which were of little importance to the ordinary folks. The Portuguese missionaries recognized the richness of Tamil literature, the merits and demerits of its diction and grammar. They pointed out the existence of two kinds of Tamil, literary (cultivated dialect) and colloquial Tamil (uncultivated dialect) that were prevalent during the period. The significant contributions made by the Portuguese to Tamil prose, grammar and lexicography in the age of discoveries cannot be underestimated. Religious works in Tamil prose played a prominent part in the development of Tamil Christian devotional literature through translations from Portuguese in the Sixteenth Century. The missionaries seem to have realized the fact that the Tamil language belonged to an independent Dravidian language family. The far-sighted missionaries learnt Tamil after the conversion of the *paravas en masse* on the Pearl Fishery Coast and their conversions was a significant turning point. The Jesuits were altogether successful in their task and they were careful to see that the converts were fully instructed on the Christian tenets in Tamil. Although Inquisition was imposed on the traditional Christians in Goa who were not adhering to the doctrines of the Catholic Church, in the Tamil Coast, Inquisition was not at all evident.

High moral values such as love and charity came to play a key role in the institutionalization of Christianity in the Tamil country. The Holy Houses of Mercy helped arrange the marriage of poor girls and took care of the orphans. Missionaries began to study the Tamil language and literature in depth which they found very highly developed although different from their own language and literature. These missionaries composed works in Tamil both for secular and religious purposes. The Catechism composed by Fr.

Roberto Nobili in Tamil was found fit enough to be rendered it into Portuguese translation by Fr. Baltazar da Costa shows the mastery over Tamil attained by the missionaries. The reformation that took place in Europe shifted the focus from the religious to the laity. Since then the Christian laity came to render greater attention by the Church as a result of reformation which was directly engaged in lifting and the extending the benefits of Christianity to all those formed the Christendom. The shift from leading the monastic way of Christian life to save the soul of the individual to work for the salvation of the community at large in the Tamil Coast by the *Padroado* missionaries led to spread of Christianity and also paved way for cultural interaction and to some extent the assimilation of Christian ethos, at least among the Christian communities in the Tamil country.

The Portuguese were the pioneering modernisers of the Tamil country by introducing the benefits of printing in Tamil and carried out social and cultural reforms in the Tamil Coast. Although their influence was not all pervasive, it was at least very strong among all those who were converted to Christianity. The Portuguese missionaries were responsible to a very large extent in pulling down the barriers of caste although they could not do much to instill the spirit of Christian brotherhood. Knowledge which was the preserve of the *Brahmins* until the arrival of the Portuguese was brought closer to the non-*Brahmins* through the books printed by the Portuguese. The age old myth that the *Brahmins* were the sole repositories of knowledge and wisdom as ordained by the divine was effectively exploded by these Portuguese missionaries.

Portuguese missionaries were pioneers in the field of Tamil grammar writing in prose from the mid-Sixteenth Century to the end of the Eighteenth Century and ushered the Tamil language, the knowledge of which, until then held as the exclusive preserve of the "chosen and privileged few" into the modern era by triggering the process of its modernisation and accelerating the process of its democratisation. The concept of humanism rising to prominence in Portugal at that time mainly had also an impact in the process of democratisation of Tamil and it began to get into the Tamil stream.

To estimate their work of linguistic scholarship at its true wisdom, one has to bear in mind the time when it was undertaken and the circumstances under which they achieved. These Portuguese missionaries were the pioneers in the fullest sense and they had to collect themselves, and copy them at a time in which none of the technical aids we have become dependent on, were at their disposal. The inconsistency in matter of Tamil and Portuguese spelling in the manuscripts is a well known fact and that was the order of the day.

Dictionary making was a very difficult work and exercise. Today Portuguese language is not familiar to many Tamil scholars hence they could not understand the glory of the works of the Portuguese. These Portuguese missionaries had freed the Tamils from reading the *Nikantus* composed in the poetry form and made them to learn the language easily. While Samuel Johnson composed the first English Dictionary in 1755, the Portuguese had been the pioneers in making Tamil-Portuguese/ Portuguese-Tamil dictionary and it served as a new manual of scholars and a new discipline of linguistics.

Although Tamil country was rich in Hindu religious architecture patronized by the Pallavas, Cholas and Vijayanagara rulers Portuguese did not allow, follow or accept any of these Hindu styles in worship. Many church buildings came up with new styles that co-existed in France, Portugal and Italy. The Missionaries also felt that the Indian temple models were not fitted for performing Catholic rites and did not adopt the models although temples were very large complexes. The Portuguese followed and introduced only the religious architecture of Europe and built churches for Christian worship.

In the early days of Portuguese trade pictures and paintings came from Europe. By mid- Sixteenth century the Portuguese were using the talents of local artists. The church paintings had important consequences not only on the style of local artists but also on the wall paintings of palaces. An influence of this might be cited where we find in the Thanjavur Palace angels with plaited hair with flowers on head. Similarly painting influences from India were also carried to Portugal in the later period. In a painting of the picture of the Magi in the Cathedral of Evora one of the kings appear in dark colour wearing an elaborate head dress and carries in his hand a coconut as a gift to the Baby Christ. It may be said that even the last Padroado Bishop of Mylapore was hailing from the city of Evora. Thus perhaps South Indian elements came into the paintings in Portugal.

With the advent of Catholic Christianity in Tamil Country during the Sixteenth century caste and religion in South India began to play a different role. Scholars who began to study the social changes of the early modern age had referred this to the intelligible process in which one can discover significant alterations in the structure and functioning of determinate social system. Continuity and change also went hand in hand. It has been pointed out by M.N. Srinivas that Sankritization was an important feature where in order to raise their social position especially for an upward mobility in the caste hierarchy, members of the lower castes had adopted some customs of the Brahmins and gave up some of their own which were considered impure by the higher castes.[25] Andre Beteille also concurs the same view of M.N Srinivas.[26] Another concept called Westernization was also introduced by M.N. Srinivas and he explained this as the change brought about in Indian society and culture as a result of over 150 years of British rule.[27] It must be said that social changes did not begin to occur in Indian society all on a sudden during the British rule. With the advent of the Portuguese in India during the Sixteenth century socio-cultural changes began to appear. In course of time the Dutch, the French and the Danes also came to India. With the religious conversion activities of these various European missionaries complex and multiple changes were added in culture and society. Hence it is incorrect to begin with British and this can be explained only for the lack of understanding of history by M.N. Srinivas and the colonial process that began. M.N. Srinivas and Andre Beteille have made generalizations that do not hold up when tested against the concrete reality of the life in Tamil country they claim to explain.

With the advent of the Protestant missionaries in Tamil country during the Seventeenth century we find that Catholics being reconverted to Protestantism. The Dutch attempted to reconvert the native Catholic fugitives who moved away from Santhome to Pulicat. We notice the Dutch Minister baptizing forty children in Pulicat during 1615-1616.[28] It is mentioned that Frei João das Chagas the Portuguese missionary was moving from Santhome to Pulicat and he heard confessions during the day and administered baptism in the evening/night for the sons of the mothers being Catholics while the fathers were heretics.[29] The Board of the Directors of the VOC in the Netherlands had instructed in 1617 their factors in India to draw up regulations for propagation of the Calvinist religion. By 1642 the Batavian Code for the East India Company was issued which stipulated that no other religion will be exercised, much less taught than the Reformed Christian religion as it is taught in the public churches of the Netherlands. Violators of the Code were ordered to be put in chains and expelled from the country and receive a punishment involving limb or life. After the occupation of the Portuguese settlements of Tuticorin and Nagapattinam by the Dutch these regulations were faithfully implemented.[30] In 1657 there was auction of fifteen *Paravas* as slaves in punishment for their activities helping the Portuguese and the Catholic Christianity.[31] In the next year the Dutch issued a directive expelling the Catholic priests and outlawed the practice of Roman Catholicism. Baptism according to Catholic rites and meetings of Catholics were prohibited. The numerous Catholic churches were taken over by the Dutch Reformed Church. Rykcloff Van Goens wrote from Tuticorin on 17 March 1658 a letter to the Governor General Joan Maetsycker in Batavia that the Catholics had given much trouble to the Dutch during the siege at Tuticorin. Philip Baldeaus served as the Protestant missionary at Turicorin during 1660-1662 and at Nagapattinam in 1664.[32] After him the missionary work was undertaken by John Kruyf, followed by Nathenaiel de Pape who preached gospel in the surrounding villages of Nagapattinam. Ziegan Balg the Danish protestant missionary arrived at Tranquebar on 9 July 1706. In May 1707 it is reported that five slaves who spoke Portuguese were converted and after examination they were baptized at Zion Church. Later Diogo Savarimuthu a Catholic belonged to the high caste was reconverted as a protestant and he was appointed on 28 December 1733 as the first native protestant preacher.[33] Thus the Dutch and the Danish missionaries mainly attempted to convert the Catholics to Protestantism than making efforts to convert the Hindus. There are fundamental differences between the conversion of the period between 1507 and 1774 and the later period of Nineteenth and Twentieth centuries done by the Catholic missionaries. There were no mass conversions except the *Paravas* in 1537. The Missionaries did not have the concept of liberating the suffering low caste Hindus. Decision to convert the low ranks of society was never the prime target of conversion. Numerous people of high castes and Brahmins had been converted to Catholic Christianity by the Portuguese who were not anti-Brahmins. The priests did not deplore the conversions that become unsuccessful unlike we find in the later period. Most of the converts were the first generation of the Catholics and the missionaries have not paid any sum to the catechumens even to recompense them for the loss of daily wages suffered during the time they were under instruction to become Christians. Money was never paid to the Catholics even during the famine periods. Thus conversions did not advantage the poor at that time. Prohibiting Catholics from joining associations in collaboration of with non-Catholics was strictly adhered to in 1744 by the Pope. This strategy was to maintain a separate identity of the converts so that they do not embrace Hinduism again and they do not also remain ties to their previous world of beliefs. The main anxiety of the missionaries was to create a Christian society in Tamil country with all its institutional paraphernalia based on ideas and beliefs transported from the religious experiences of the Iberian or Mediterranean world. Therefore they made all possible measures were employed to prevent the natives from continuing their heathenish ways. Further, disputes among the high caste and low caste converts regarding the use of space in the church became more serious and numerous because the gap of the converts had widened. In general, the *Padroado* missionaries had not imposed forcible conversion of the natives in Tamil country. The conversion also happened without much opposition from the Hindus. The missionaries in some places like Pondicherry and Thanjavur in their dealings with Hindus were impatient. Apart from this the *Padroado* missionaries seem to have engaged in peaceful or persuasive methods of conversion in Tamil country.

Notes and References

1. Silva Rego, *Documentação op.cit.*, Vol. I, pp. 61-62.
2. Joseph Costelloe, *Letters and Instructions, op.cit.*, Document No. 2, p. 65.

3. Jose Wicki, *Documenta Indica, op.cit.*, Vol. XIV, p. 32.
4. Annual letter of Fr Andre Lopez 1644, in Fr. L.Besse, *La Mission du Maduré*, Trichnopoly, 1914, pp. 30-32 See L. Besse, *op.cit.*, pp. 15-21.
5. MPJA, Jesuit Annual Letter of the Year 1700-1701, p. 5.
6. BNP, *Mss. Nouvelle Acquistion Française*, 9364, Letter de M. Hebert, Governor of Pondicherry dated 12 February 1709. BNP ; Mss.Fr.6231, Mémoires, fl.42.
7. Letter of Fr. Ducros to l'Abbé Ragnet, Directeur de la Compagnie des Indes, written from Ariyankuppam dated 17 October 1725 in *LEC,* tome XIII, pp.335-36.see also, Adrien Launay, *Histoire ...op.cit,* Vol. I, p. xxxii.
8. Letter of Fr. Ducros to l'Abbé Ragnet, 17 October 1725 in *LEC*, tome XIII, p. 336.
9. *Ibid.*
10. MPJA, Louis Facheux, *Baptemes Administres a Pondichery parles Capucins e 1676 a 1693 et par les Jesuites de 1715 a1776*s.
11. See, *Bartolomeu's Voyages to the East India*, London, 1800, p. 65.
12. Joseph Costelloe, *Letters and Instructions, op.cit.*, Document No. 2, p.65. "When I arrived at a pagan village where they had invited me to come in order that they might become Christians, I would have all the men and boys of the village come together in one place. Then beginning with the profession of the Father and of the Son and of the Holy Spirit, I would have them make the sign of the Cross three times and invoke the three Persons by confessing one sole God. And after this I would recite the *Confiteor,* and then the Creed, Commandments, Our Father, Hail Mary, and the *Salve Regina,* in their language which I had learnt two years ago by-heart. After putting on a surplice, I would recite the prayers in a loud voice in the order I have indicated. As I pronounced them, all, both young and old, would repeat them after me. After I had finished the prayers, I would give them an explanation of the articles of the faith and of the commandments of the Law in their own language. After this I would have all of them ask God our Lord for pardon in public for their past life, and this in a loud voice in the presence of other pagans who did not wish to become Christians in order to confound the wicked and console the good. All the pagans were astonished at hearing the law of God, and they were confounded at seeing how they had".
13. IANTT, DRI, Vol. I, fl. 95.
14. AHU, Codice 208, fl. 148v.
15. AHU, *Caixa da India* 34, (1688-89).
16. Josef Metzler, "Wegbereiter und Vorlaufer der Kongregation", *Sacrae Congregationis de Propaganda Fide Memoria Rerum*, Vol. I, pp. 77f.

17. Leon Loptegui, "San Francisco de Borja y el plan Missional de San Pio V", *Arquivum Historicum Societatis Jesu*, (henceforth AHSI) Vol. XI, 1942, pp. 1-26.
18. See, *Collectanea Sacrae Congregationis de Propaganda Fide*, II Vols, Rome, 1907, Vol. I, pp. 3f.
19. *Ibid.*, Vol. I, n. 2.
20. The details of the appointments of the Bishops of Mylapore diocese during 1718, 1780, 1782 and 1805 had been found in Archivio Secreto Vaticano, *Processus Consistorialis*, Vol. 107, fls. 387-396v; Vol. 132, fls. 475-499; Vol. 146, fls. 278-288v; Vol. 182, fl. 238-259; Vol.188, fl. 230-241v; Vol. 224, fl. 205-212. They contain the inquiry report, qualities and character of the bishops before appointments.
21. M D' Sa, *History of the Church in India, op.cit.*, Vol. II, p. vi.
22. Levi Maria Jordão Paiva, *Bullarium Patronatus Portugallie Regum in Eccelsiis Africae, Asiae et Oceanie, Olisipone*, Lisboa, 1870, Vol. II, p. 132. Also, see the Bull "*Sollictudo Pastoralis*" dated 22 December 1673 in connection with the earlier Bull, see, Vol. II, p. 136.
23. *Ibid.*, Vol. II, p. 211.
24. For details. See, S. Jeyaseela Stephen, *Letters of the Portuguese Jesuits from Tamil Countryside, 1668-1688*, Pondicherry, 2001.
25. M.N. Srinivas, *Social Change in Modern India*, California, 1966, p.7. With regard to Sanskritization several questions can be raised. Can a person raise his / her social position in India at that time by merely following the customs of the Brahmins? What attempts and efforts did the Brahmins make to prevent others from following such customs? Did the Brahmins ever make complaints and protest against such activities? Did all castes accept Brahmins as superior at that time? In what sense and at what level superiority was subscribed? It must have been confined only to the level of the performance of rituals in temples and in matters of Hindu religion on the whole. How shall we explain to the fact that every caste had claimed superiority over the other in the medieval period demanding privileges as found in inscriptions? How did the social privileges come in the way of religion? Sanskrit was not spoken by all and we are sure that Brahmins themselves did not speak in Sanskrit as the Portuguese missionaries mention that they spoke in respective languages such as Tamil. How is the term Sanskritization acceptable while referring to social changes? What was special and so unique of the customs of the Brahmins? Does the use of Sanskrit signify Sanskritization? Does Sanskrit indicate level of higher learning in Tamil society at that time?

26. Andre Beteille, *Castes Old and New: Essays in Social Structure and Social Stratification*, Bombay, 1969, p. 158.
27. M. N. Srinivas, "A Note on Sanskritization and Westernization" in *Caste in Modern India and Other Essays*, London, 1962, p. 55.
28. Tapan Raychaudhuri, *Jan Company in Coromandel*, The Hague, 1962, p. 206
29. Silva Rego, *Documentação, op.cit.*, vol. XI, p. 223.
30. See the excerpt from the Batavian code for the VOC quoted in Baldeaus, *op.cit.*, p. XVIII.
31. Tikiri Abyesinge, *Portuguese Rule in Ceylon, 1594-1612*, Colombo, 1962, p. 43.
32. Baldeaus mentions that the Portuguese were permitted to depart with their goods, families and church-ornaments in certain ships arranged for that purpose by the Dutch Company. He says that he preached the first sermon on the 18th both in Dutch and Portuguese and administered the holy sacrament to twenty persons and baptism to several children. See, Philip Baldeaus, *A Description of the East India Coasts of Malabar and Coromandel and also of the Isle of Ceylon with their Adjacent Kingdom and Provinces*, Reprint, New Delhi, 2000, p. 651.
33. Fred Fenger, *History of Tranquebar Mission*, Tranquebar, 1863, pp. 24, 35 & 64.

Appendix 1

Source: ANTT, *Gavetas,* **XI-8-18.**

Your Majesty,

We the residents of this settlement of the Blessed Apostle St. Thomas have the honour of letting Your Majesty know that last year the Municipality of Cochin sent us here an extract from Your Majesty's letter to it. In it you were speaking of the affairs of this holy house of St. Thomas and its residents. You also found fault with us for not furnishing information about it and ourselves to you.

Through Martim Affonso de Mello, the residents of the place wrote and sent a letter giving you an account of the condition in which the holy house of St. Thomas was and of how they were commencing to repair it. In the course of the year 1532 those who, at that time, were responsible for the restoration of the holy house also wrote to you that the house was completed. Over and above this, those who were here at the time did the same thing through Jorge d' Azambuja. No reply was received, except this chapter from your letter to Cochin, which was despatched to us here by the Municipality of Cochin.(fl.1^v) We feel that your silence is due to the fact that there is no one over there (in Lisbon) who takes an interest in the matter rather than because you do not desire to give alms to the holy house or to favour us who live in it.

In the extract of your letter, you have stated that you would be delighted if you could be kept informed on matters concerning the Holy Apostle. This we shall do every year just as we are now doing. These details are meant to inform you how this holy house came into existence, how the settlement began to be populated, how it is administered and how divine services are conducted.

We beg to inform Your Majesty that when Dom Duarte de Menezes was Governor of these regions, one Manuel de Frias was sent here by his orders. He started doing work on the holy house which, with the body of the church and the precincts, was for the most part in a state of complete ruin and neglect. The bigger chapel together with its dome was intact, being as the Blessed Apostle had built it. The chapel which stands at the gospel side of the altar was also intact. In this chapel was discovered the tomb. This chapel had suffered no damage or subsidence, as was the case with the other chapels. This House was being looked after by a Muslim who used to light the chapel with an oil lamp. He became blind and it was the Holy Apostle who restored his sight. Today he is still a hale and hearty man of about ninety years who, inspite of his age, comes to the holy house to pay his reverence there.

The discovery of the tomb was made in the following manner. In order to get to the basement of the bigger chapel to make the necessary repairs, the workmen began to dig a big trench.(fl.2) While excavating at a depth of three spans, they came upon a tomb which was neatly faced with tiles on all sides. A well trowelled, very strong layer of mortar, three spans by three, surmounted the sepulchre, which itself was twenty spans deep. Underneath this layer of mortar there were found two stone slabs which covered the legth of the grave, and below them was found a skeleton, the bones of which, through the ravages of time, had crumbled. With the skeleton there was an iron spear-head, having a wooden shaft in its socket. The people say that with this spear-head, the apostle was pierced and met with his death.

All the elderly people of the land whether *brahmins,* Hindus or Muslims vouched and asserted that these were the bones of the Blessed Apostle and added that when the Christians came to the spot to remove his body they would not show them his true tomb but pointed out another which was the tomb of a disciple of his. The Christians took away from the false tomb shown to them the body found therein, imagining that they were removing the body of St. Thomas.

The true relics of St Thomas were removed in a very respectful manner with the help of priests and laymen who had made their confession for the occasion. The relics were put in a coffer, together with the iron spear-head found in the grave. The coffer is on an altar built in the chapel where the tomb was found. From inquiries made here, all of us are firmly convinced that, that was the very body of the Blessed Apostle.(fl.2^{v}) Also the fact that this tomb is different from all other tombs which were found in this place, lends further credence to the belief. These other tombs belonged to five of his disciples, and one was that of a king who became a Christian and who, as long as he lived, gave all revenues derived from the sea and the land in order to put up the holy house.

Of all this and of the many miracles wrought by the Blessed Saint, an inquiry was held here as Your Majesty enjoined. Miguel Ferreira sent the findings of the inquiry to Nuno da Cunha, the Governor at that time. We do not know whether the letter was forwarded on to Your Majesty. We have a copy of it here and if necessary we shall send it to you.

Immediately after the work in the holy house was completed, some Portuguese men who had married Indian maids and had children came to live in the service of the Lord God in this holy house. They organised a confraternity of the Holy Apostle which was approved by the Vicar General of that time and all his sucessors till now have approved of this confraternity. It was instituted in order that the alms that would be offered to Blessed St. Thomas might be handled by no one except the administrators appointed for this purpose. In this manner the confraternity functions today. It is run by the leading persons here who do this work out of devotion and to honour the Apostle. Later two other confraternities were started, one of Our Lady of the Rosary and the other of the people of God, for whom holy masses are said weekly.

The settlement here began to develop in such a way that the very honourable men of the locality and among them are we your servants, married daughters of the Portuguese.(fl.3) Many of us have built ourselves multi-storied houses of lime and stone. At present we are sixty men with our wives and children living here. A company of married Armenians who lead good Christian lives have also been living with us.

None of us here receive any pay or maintenance from Your Majesty, yet, whenever our services are needed, we are ready to serve Your Majesty in India with our personal services and goods; the only exceptions to this are those who are very old and the sick. We participated in the expedition to Diu with Nuno da Cunha and on other occasions. We have also rendered our services when needed. All of us men who live here have served Your Majesty for many years in your fleets which have their base in these waters.

This holy house was built through alms given for this purpose by the devotees and the members of the confraternity of the Apostle St. Thomas. The receipts and disbursement books show that from the alms received, the sum of five (fl.3^{v}) to six thousand *cruzados* was paid for the work done.

In this holy house there are at present four priests with the Vicar of the house. Besides there are others who always help to celebrate mass. At all Sunday masses and on feast days prayers are offered for yourmajesty and your royal domain. The divine offices are held here so solemnly and devoutly that in no other church are they done so perfectly.

This holy house possesses many rich vestments and frontals which are used for feasts, or even on ordinary days, during the whole year. There are also organs to play music and to help in the solemn celebration of the holy mass. There is everything that is necessary, also more than necessary and that on a lavish scale, as if it were a church with huge revenues which indeed it is not. All this comes from alms contributed by the members of the confraternity of St. Thomas and other devotees. All these expenses together with many other alms to the poor are met by this confraternity.

In this settlement 1800 indigenous people have become Christians, their names have been entered in the register of this holy house which the Vicar keeps. The non-Christians themselves have great respect and veneration towards this holy house as is shown when they celebrate their own feasts for they come to pay obeisance also to the holy house and they bow down before, their idols with great humility at the door of the house of the Apostle. They tell us that their ancestors always did the same thing. Even to this day when their wives are pregnant or their children became sick they come to the house of the Apostle to take some oil from his lamp or some soil from his grave so that with these they believe that their children may recover from their illness and their wives have safe deliveries. We ourselves are true witnesses of this fact occurring in our own times.

We ask Your Majesty to consider the great service to God done in this Holy House through the celebration of the holy sacraments, through the praise given to the name of God and through many other good works done in it; to consider also the many years of service to Your Majesty in your fleets by all of us who live here; and therefore to do us the favour of a royal writ, so that we may live in this settlement with our wives and children without being forced to go away against our will, for most of us are aged and poor, and have suffered heavy losses in goods. We shall pray to the Lord God, as we do here and now, that he may grant Your Majesty many days of life for his holy service and to the blessed Apostle St. Thomas that he may ever be at your help.

Written in this settlement on the 27th day of December, 1535

Signed by

Jorge Diaz Pacanha
Duarte Ferreira
Braz Alvares
Diogo Goterrez
Joham Lobo
Antrique de Vasconcelos
Baltesar Rodriguez
Gaspar Rodriguez
Antonio Vaz
Jorge de Goes
Rodrigo de Sela
Pero Anes Palha
Jeronimo Gomez de Gouvea
Tristam Vaz
Bastiam Rodriguez
Ruy Vaz
Diogo Fernandez
João Afooso
Jeronimo Vaz
Gonçalo Teixeira

(fl.4) To his Majesty from the house of the Apostle at Santhome

Appendix 2

(Translated from Italian)

Source: APF, Scritture Riferite nei Congressi, Indie Orientali e Cina, vol. 7. fl. 268.

I, the undersigned Lazzaro de Motta, do hereby voluntarily donate to the Reverend Fathers Capuchin French Missionaries, the Church of St. Peter in the town of Pondicherry where the Royal French Company has a factory, governed by the Director General François Martin. The church which I had built for the glory of God, for the benefit of my soul and also for the consolation of the Gentiles, who have embraced our Holy Faith by the zeal and exemplary life of the said missionaries, I give over to them. With this Church I hand over to them all its dependencies etc. This is my wish that all remain in their possession for ever and that they are at liberty to use it for divine service. I sign this gift deed with my own hand in the proper manner.

signed Lazzaro de Motta

Appendix 3

Source: MPJA, Litterae Annuae Missionis Madurensis, 1694.

My dear Father,

Through Rangapppan, my catechist, you must have learnt of what has happened in my prison up to my departure for Ramanathapuram. On 28 January, I was obliged to appear before a tribunal. I was told that sentence of death was pronounced against me. I was taken to the place where I was to be made the target and all was prepared. When the Raja, fearing an uprising, gave the order to separate me from my dear children, the other confessors of Jesus Christ in order to hand me over to his brother (Vrenjadevan) Ranganathadevan. He charged him to execute me without delay. On the last day of January I reached the palace of Udayarthevar. The journey was full of hardships. Udayarthevar sent for me on the same day. I had a long conversation with him about religious matters. Then I was brought back to prison, where I find myself still, and in constant expectation of death, which I shall endure for God. The hope of obtaining this happiness led twice to India in the mission and in the Marava Country. Indeed, to secure such happiness has cost me much, but the reward which I hope from God are worth all these, and still greater pains. The crime, of which I am accused is none other than that I preach the true religion of God and of no account must the idols be worshipped. What an honour to suffer death for such a crime! It fills me with joy and consolation in the Lord. I have the soldiers always near and consequently I cannot write much. Goodbye, God be with you, my Father! I beg your blessing and recommend myself to your Holy Masses.

From the prison at Oriyur, 3 February 1693.

Your humble servant in Christ

João de Britto

Appendix 4

Source: AAMM, Mss **2889, Doc. 41, fl.6.**

Most Holy Father,

I humbly prostrate at the feet of Your Holiness. Please allow me to say that the Church in the East Indies is in such a state that in order to preserve it in the midst of the persecutions, besides the blindness of the gentiles which is every day carrying on against our holy religion, it needs the immediate protection of the Church triumphant, and of those in particular, who while on earth were her teachers of the true faith.

In my Diocese of Mylapore, wherein the area of Malabar is found, the fame is universal of the virtues of the Venerable João de Britto of the Society of Jesus, of which I myself am a witness. I was his companion in the Mission of Malabar. All these Christian communities committed to my care by Apostolic dispensation also acknowledge him as a glorious martyr of Christ. Indeed after preaching the Gospel of Christ in this area, he suffered immense tribulations. Going over the lands of his neophytes, he converted many thousands of pagans to our holy religion. He drew upon himself the hatred of the *brahmins* because the temples of their idols were deserted. He was laden with irons almost twenty five years ago and was sentenced by the *Raja* of the Maravas to be beheaded in odium of the faith. Most Holy Father, no one among these neophytes doubts the cause of his martyrdom. So much so that soon after his death they proclaimed him a matryr everywhere. In order that the relics of this most valiant soldier of Christ should not fall into the hands of the gentiles some of the Christians risked their lives by daring to bring them away from the place of execution at night. They brought them to me as a precious keep, which ought to be preserved until such time as the Holy Church should allow them to be publicly venerated.

Most Holy Father, I could mention many of the deeds full of sanctity and virtue that he performed while he was alive, having had to work with him as a missionary for many years in Malabar. I opine that he can be numbered not only among the list of martyrs, but also among the confessors. However, in order not to go beyond the limits of a simple letter, only one thing I shall assert here to Your Holiness, viz, the fame of his sanctity, martyrdom and miracles increases and spreads day by day. In my diocese all the Christians of various regions unanimously desire nothing so much as that Your Holiness places the Venerable João de Britto among the list of the martyrs of the Church. It seems just that the request of so many Malabar Christians be attended to by Your Holiness. Their most praiseworthy desire is to see that their Father and teacher given by heaven to them is honoured by means of public cult. He deserves it so well of Malabar and of the universal church for having shed his blood for the Catholic Faith. I write to you because the people ask me that this request of theirs should be brought to the feet of Your Holiness through me. By doing so, my pastoral solicitude in spreading more and more our Holy Faith in this Church of Meliapor (Mylapore) impels me, because of the intimate friendship of such a notable companion in the ministry during life. While kissing the feet of Your Holiness, I add my own prayer to theirs with as much earnestness as possible and instantly request Your Holiness to grant to such a perfect Missionary and most valiant Martyr the honours of public cult. I hope that these prayers on behalf of him who for many years walked the whole of Malabar as a simple Missionary, and who after being laden with irons more than once endured much for the exaltation of the faith will not go unnoticed by Your Holiness. May God preserve for many years the spread of the Universal Church.

Pondicherry, 2 February 1712.

Most Humble and Devoted son in Christ

Francisco Laynez, Bishop of Mylapore.

Glossary

Alvara	- Decree of the Portuguese King or Viceroy valid for a limited period.
Ashrafis	- Xerafin or ashrafi was the silver currency of Goa.
Adhikari	- Native nomenclature for an officer.
Câmara Municipal	- Municipal Council.
Capitão-mor	- Captain-major.
Carta Regia	- Royal letter.
Casado	- A married Portuguese settler.
Cavaleiro	- Knight.
Chackram	- Fanam of base gold. It was equal to 25 reis.
Chank	- Mother of pearl.
Conselho do Estado	- State Council.
Cruzado	- A coin that had a cross of the order of Christ in the obverse. It was a Portuguese coin usually of silver with a fixed value of 400 reis.
Degredado	- Condemned by common law, exile.
Desembargadores	- Judges.
Diziam de Pescado	- Tithe on fishing.
Estado da Índia	- State of India, the Portuguese empire East of the Cape of Good Hope to the region of Japan.
Fanam	- A tiny gold or silver coin used in the Coromandel of different and fluctuating values called as panam in Tamil, equal to 25 reis. It is also known as fanão and its

	value varied from 10 reis to 29 in Nagapattinam. In Pulicat 10 fanams were equivalent to one pardão de fanões.
Farman	- Royal order or decree.
Faujdhar	- Army Commander ; military governor of a province.
Feitor	- Factor, known as a person in-charge of a trading factory; A commercial agent, the executive head of a factory.
Feitoria	- Crown trading post or an agency in an Asian port.
Fidalgo	- Petty nobleman or a Portuguese gentleman, literally "son of a somebody".
Inam	- Grant of rent free land.
Jagir	- An assignment of land under the Mughals made in return for service usually military.
	- A temporary revenue assignment for three years.
Juiz	- Judge or a magistrate.
Juiz da Fazenda	- A treasury inspector.
Juiz de alfândega	- Customs appraiser.
Mestiço	- Eurasian, of mixed blood between Portuguese merchants and local women.
Nau or Não	- Ship used for trade with three decks and three masts.
Navio	- Larger ship.
Nayaka	- Chief or leader in the Vijayanagar period it usually meant a chief of a territory.
Ola	- Literally a palmyra leaf, hence the leaf on which a deed or document is written.
Ordinaria	- An allowance paid to the Catholic clergy.
Ouvidor	- Judge with appellate jurisdiction.
Ovuidor Geral	- Senior Crown Judge or Superior Crown magistrate in a High Court.
Padroado Real	- The Portuguese royal patronage to religious missions.
Pagodas	- Varahan or huns called as pardão d'ouro. It was equal to 370 reis. Gold coin with the image of Vishnu.

Parau	- Small galley with twenty or thirty rows of oarsmen.
Pardão, Pardau	- Used to denote an Indo - Portuguese coin equivalent in value to 360 reis.
Povação	- Village or settlement.
Provedor	- Hospital administrator.
Provedor dos defunctos	- Purveyor of the estates of the deceased.
Reis, Real	- Portuguese monetary unit of the smallest denomination.
Relação	- High court, the tribunal of Justice at second instance.
Santa Casa da Misericórdia	- Holy House of Mercy, a charitable institution run by a brotherhood.
Senado da Câmara	- Senate House.
Tanga	- Silver coin valued at 60 reis. It was used in Goa derived from South Indian coin. Sometimes it meant a copper coin during pre-Portuguese period.
Topasses	- Artillery men.
Varahan	- Gold coin synonymous with pagoda.
Vedor da Fazenda	- Comptroller of revenue. Chief financial official.
Vereador	- Aldermen or Muncipal Councillor.
Xerafim	- Standard silver coin of Portuguese India valued at 300 reis. The word xerafins derived from Persian ashrafi which meant gold coin weighing 150 grains.

Select Bibliography

PRIMARY SOURCES

I. ARCHIVAL SOURCES

PORTUGAL

1. **ARQUIVO HISTÕRICO ULTRAMARINO, Lisboã**

   Caixa da India, 34 (1688-89)

   Codice 208.

   Mss, Documentos Avulos, Maço 8.

2. **INSTIUTO ARQUIVO NACIONAIS/ TORRE DO TOMBO, Lisboã**

   Corpo Cronolõgico

   (Followed by Part, Maço and Document Number)

   I -6-82, I-019-85, I-37-84, I-80-7, Ia- 83-90, III- 9-94

   Casa Forte:

   Mss. No. 48.

   Chancelarias Reais:

   D. Joao IV, Liv,17.

   D. Filippe II, Liv, 35.

   Colleção Jesuitica :

   Livro 28.

   Manuscritos da Livraria:

   No. 636

   Gavetas:

   XI-8-19

   Documentos Remetidos da India:

   Livro 1, 3, 6, 7, 44, 45, 54 & 57.

3. **BIBLIOTECA DA AJUDA, Lisboã**
Codice Jesuitas na Asia, 49-IV-50, 49-VI-12, 50-VI-21, 51-VI-25 and 51-IX-2.
Mss. Miscelana Ultramarina, 51-VIII-40.

4. **BIBLIOTECA NACIONAL, Lisboã**
Mss. Reservados, No. 3141.
Mss. Codice 1783 and 1976.
Mss. Iluminado, No. 140 and 149.
Mss. Fundo Geral, Codice 7638.

5. **BIBLIOTECA MUNICIPAL DE O PORTO, Porto**
Mss. No.1135.

6. **BIBLIOTECA SOCIEDADE DE GEOGRAFIA DE LISBOA, Lisboã**
Ms. 146-A-14.

ITALY

7. **ARCHIVIO DELLA S. CONGREGAZIONAE DI PROPAGANDA FIDE, Rome**
Acta, Vols, 73, 80, 88.
Scritture Riferite nei Congressi Indie Orientali e Cina, Vols.7, 8.

8. **ARCHIVIO SECRETO VATICANO, Vatican City**
Processus Consistorialis, Vol. 107, 132, 146, 182, 188 &. 224.

9. **ARCHIVES GENERAL OF THE CAPUCHIN ORDER, Rome**
H, 55 (India) XIII.

10. **ARCHIVUM ROMANUM SOCIETATIS JESU, Rome**
Mss Goa, Vol. No. 12, 13-II, 14, 17, 31, 32, 33, 37, 38, 48, 49, 51, 53, 54, 54a and 56.
Mss. Goa, Malabarica, 55.
Mss. Litterae Annuae Provinciae Malabarensis, 1582, 1583,1602, 1603-1680.

Mss. Gall, 118.
Catalogi Trien Cochin et Malabar, Goa. Vol. 29.

11. **BIBLIOTECA APOSTOLICA VATICANA, Vatican City**
Bon Compagni Section E6, Mss. Lettre di Roberto Nobili.
Borg. Ind. 12, Mss. *Vocabulario Tamulico -Lusitano.*

FRANCE

12. **ARCHIVES DES MISSIONS ETRANGÉRES DE PARIS, Paris**
Mss. Inde, Vol. 993 & 995.

13. **ARCHIVES PARISIENSIS SOCIEATATIS JESU, Lyon**
Mss. Index, 3.

14. **ARCHIVES NATIONALES, Paris**
Mss. Serie, T. 1169.

15. **CENTRE DES ARCHIVES D'OUTRE-MER, Aix-en-Provence**
Depot des Fortifications des Colonies, Portefeuille 32B, 18.

16. **BIBLIOTHEQUE NATIONALE, Paris**
Mss. Mss. Indien, No. 213, 214, 221 and 223.
Mss. Français, 6231.
Mss, Nouvelle Acquisition Française, 9225 and 9364.

17. **BIBLIOTHÉQUE FRANCISCAINE PROVINCIALS, Paris**
Mss. 43, Memorabilia 29.
Mss. 192.

SPAIN

18. **ARCHIVO GENERAL DE SIMANCAS, Valladolid**
Secretarias Provinciales, Libro No. 1494, 1551.

THE NETHERLANDS

19:. **NAATIONAL ARCHIEF, The Hague**
Bataviaasch Uitgaand Breidboek, VOC 879 and 882.
Overgekomen Brieven en Papieren VOC, 1143 and 1231.

BELGIUM

20. **BIBLIOTHEQUE ROYALE ALBERTINE, Brussels**
Mss. No. 21868.

UNITED KINGDOM

21. **BRITISH LIBRARY, London** (Manuscript Room)
Additional Manuscripts, 9853.
Mss. Tamil B.3 No. 3101.

22. **BODLEIAN LIBRARY, Oxford**
Mss. Vet. Tam. F.1.

INDIA

23. **ARCHIVES OF THE ARCHDIOCESE OF MADRAS-MYLAPORE, Santhome**
Mss. Bundle No. 8, & 5110.
Mss. No. 2348, 2478, 2889 & 2940.
Mss. No. 3261, João de Monte Papers from Kovalam and Santhome of Mylapore.

24. **ARCHIVES DE L'ARCHEVÉCHÉ DE PONDICHERY - CUDDALORE, Pondicherry**
Manuscrits et Divers Documents Imprimes: Armorie, 1-6, Chemise, I.B. (18 Siecle, 1704-1799).

25. **MADURAI PROVINCE JESUIT ARCHIVES, Shenbaganur**
Mss. No. AS. 5 Tamil & Old Mss. 225/5 Tamil
Mss. Baptemés Indiens Administrés par les RR G.P.Capucins, 20 March 1677.

Mss. Baptemes Administres a Pondichery par les Capucins e 1676 a 1693

Mss, Lieux d' Origine des Chretiens Baptises a Pondichery par les Jesuits de 1715 a 1777.

Mss. Resume du Diarium Marave.

Litterae Annuae Provinciae Malabarensis, VI Vols. See the years 1582, 1600, 1601, 1608-1609.

Litterae Annuae Provinciae Madurensis, XXI Vols. See the years 1644, 1648, 1666, 1676, 1678, 1681, 1683, 1688, 1692, 1701, 1708, 1709, 1711, 1712, 1714, 1730, 1731, 1732, 1734 & 1736.

Annual Letters of the Madurai Mission, (typescript) Loyola College, Madras, 1910.

Documents Bertrand, Vols. I, II & III.

Leon Besse, Mss, Histoire de la Province du Malabar, (typescripts) II vols.

Jean Castets, L' Ancienne Mission du Madure des Origines et Ses Histoire, (typescript) Vol. I.

26. **HISTORICAL ARCHIVES, Panaji, Goa**

Mss. Monçoes do Reino: Livro 1, (1565); 3B, (1589-94); 10, (1604-1609); 12, (1613-1617); 19D, (1634-35) & 30, (1680-86)

Livro de Servico, Vol. I.

27. **NATIONAL ARCHIVES OF INDIA, Pondicherry**

Registre de Deliberations du Conseil de la Compagnie, Vol. I.

Eighteenth Century Documents, No. 430.

Mss. Arrets du Conseil Supérieur de Pondichery, 1746.

28. **STATE CENTRAL LIBRARY, Panaji, Goa**

Mss. No. 37.

Cote M/34 & Cote M/49.

II. PRINTED SOURCES
(IN PORTUGUESE)

Albuquerue, Affonso de, *Cartas de Affonso de Albuquerque,* 7 Vols., Lisboã, 1884-1935, (ed.,) Raymundo Antonio de Bulhão Pato.

Baião, Antonio, *Historia quninhista in edito do segundo cerco do Dio, llustrado com a correspondencia original Tambem, in edita de D. João de Castro, D. João de Mascarenhas e outras,* Coimbra, 1925.

Barros, João de, *Da Asia,* I to IV, 8 Vols. (1777-78), Lisboa, 1973.

Basilio de Sa, Artur, *Documentação para a Historia das Missões do Padroado Portugues do Oriente: Insul India,* 5 Vols., Lisboa, 1954-58.

Biker, J.F. J., *Coleção de Tratado e Concertos do pazes que o Estado da India Portuguesa fez com os reis e Senhores em que teve relações nas partes da Asia e Africa oriental desde o principio da conquista ate ao fim do seculo XVIII,* Vols. 1-14, Lisboa, 1881-87.

Bocarro, Antonio, *Decada 13, da Historia da India,* Lisboa, 2 Vols, 1876.

Castanheda, Fernão Lopes de, *Historia do Descobrimento e Conquista da India pelos Portugueses,* 9 books in 2 Vols., reprint, Porto, 1975.

Coelho Ramos, *Alguns documentos da Torre do tombo a cerca das navegações e Conquistas Portuguesa,* Lisboa,1892.

Correia, Gaspar, *Lendas da India,* 4 vols, reprint, Porto, 1975.

Cortesão, Armando and Luis de Albuquerque (eds.), *Obras Completas de D. João de Castro,* Vol. III, Coimbra, 1976.

Couto, Diogo do, *Decada da Asia,* IV to XII, Lisboa, 1777-78.

Diario da Viagem de Vasco da Gama, 2 Vols, Porto, 1945.

Documentos Remetidos da India ou Livros das Monções, Vols.I-V (ed.) R.A. de Bulhão Pato, Lisboa, 1880-1935, Vl to X (ed.) Antonio da Silva Rego, Lisboã, 1974-1982.

Figueira, Christovão Suarez de, *Historia y Anal Relacion de las Cosas que Hizieron los Padres de la Companhia de Jesus por las Artes de Oriente y Otras en la Propagacion del Santo Evanglico los Anos Passados de 607y 608,* Madrid, 1913.

Goncalves, Sebastião, P. *Primeira parte da Historia dos religiosos da Companhia de Jesus,* Atlantida-Coimbra, 1962.

Guerreiro, Fernão, *Relaçam Anual das Coisas que Fezeram Os Padres da Companhia de Jesus Nas Partes da India Oriental & em Alguas Outras da Conquista Deste Reyno no Anno de 606 & 607 do Proceso de Conversão & Christandade da Quellas*

Partes Tirada das Cartas dos Mesmos Padres Que da la Vierao Pelo Padre Ferão Guerriero da Companhia de Jesu Natural de Almodura de Portugal, 2 vols, Lisboa, 1909.

———, (ed.) A. Veigas, *Relação Anual das Coisas que Fizeram Os Padres da Companhia de Jesus nas Suas Missões India,* vol 3, Coimbra, 1930.

Lima Felner, Rodrigo José de (ed.) *Subsidios para a Historia da India Portugueza,* Lisboa, 1868.

Luz, Mendez da, "Livro das Cidades e fortalezas que o Coroa de Portugal tem nas partes da India, e das capitanias e mais Cargos que nelas ha, e da importancia deles" in the Boletim da Bibliotheca *Universidade de Coimbra,* Vol. XXI, 1953, pp 1-144 (reprinted in *Studia,* no. 6, July 1960)

Orta, Garcia de, *Colloquies on the Simple Drugs of India,* Dehradun, 1979.

Paiva Manso, Levi Maria Jordão, Viconde de, *Bullarium Patronatus Portugallie Regum in Ecclesiis Africae, Asiae atque Oceaniae, Bullas brevia, epistoals decreta acta que Sanctae Sedis ab Alexandre III adhoc a que tempus ampletens,* tomo I, (1400-1600), Lisboa, 1868; tomo II, (1601-1700), Lisboa, 1870.

Pereira, Bragança, *Arquivo Portugues Oriental,* 11 Vols., Bastora, Goa,1936-40.

Pissurlencar, Panduranga S.S. *Regimentos das Fortalezas da India,* Bastora, Goa, 1951.

———, *Assentos do Conselho do Estado,* (1618-1750), 5 vols, Goa, 1953-57.

Queyroz, Fernão de, *The Temporal and Spiritual Conquest of Ceylon,* S.G. Pereira (tr.), Colombo, 1930.

Ribandeneira, Marcelo de, *Historia de las islas del archipelgo y reyno delagran China tartaria Cochinchina, malaca, s'tam, camboxa y Iappon,* Barcelona, 1601.

Rivara, Cunha, J.H. *Archivo Portuguez - Oriental,* 6 Fasciculos in 9 vols, Goa, 1857-76.

Sanceau, Elaine, *Cartas de D. João de Castro,* Lisboã, 1954.

———, *Colecao de Sao Lourenço,* 3 Vols., Lisboã, 1973-83. (Documentacao Ultramarina Portuguesa, Vols. VI-VIII).

Schurhammer, Georg & E.A. Voretzsch, *Ceylon Zurr Zeit des Konigs Bhuvaneka Baku und Franz Xaviers, 1539-1552, 2* Vols, Leipzig, 1928.

———, *Epistolae S. Francisci Xaverii alia que eius scripta,* Rome, 1944.

———, "Uma Relação in Edita de Padre Manuel Barradas, S.I. Sobre S.Francisco Xavier", *Studia* II, Lisboa, 1958, pp. 43-90.

Silva Rego, Antonio, *Documentação para a Historia das Missões do Padroado Portugues do Oriente,* Vol. 1-12, Lisboa, 1947-58.

———, (ed.), *As Gavetas da Torre do Tombo,* Vols. 1-12, Lisboa, 1960-77.

———, *Documentação Ultramarina Portuguesa,* 5 vols, Lisboa, 1960-67.

Trinidade, Paulo da, *Conquisto Espiritual do Oriente,* II.vols, Lisboa, 1962-67.

Wicki, Jose and J. Gomes, *Documenta Indica,* Vols. 1-18, Roma, 1948-88.

———, "Duas relações sobre a situação da India Portuguesa nos annos 1568 e 1569", *Studia,* Vol.8, 1961 pp. 133-220.

(IN DUTCH)

Dagh-Register Gehouden int Casteel Batavia van het Passerende doer leer Plaetse als over geheel Nederlandts Indie, (1624-1682), 31 Vols, The Hague & Batavia, 1887-1931, various editors.

Heeres, J.E, and F.W. Stapel, *Corpus Dipolomaticum Neerlando-Indicum,* 6 Vols, The Hague, 1907-1953.

(IN ENGLISH)

Danvers F.C and W. Foster, *Letters received by the English East India Company from its Servants in the East (1602-1617),* 6 vols, London, 1896-1902.

Fawcett, C. *The English Factories in India* (new series) 1670-1684, 4 vols, Oxford,1936-1945.

Foster, William, *English Factories in India: A Calendar of Documents in the India office, British Museum and Public Relations Office, 1618-1619,* Vols. 1-13, Oxford, 1906-1967.

Records of Fort St George: *Diary and Consultation book,* 1672-81,1686-94,1696-1746. 1749-56, Madras, 1910-50.

(IN FRENCH)

Diagou, Gnanou., *Arrets du Conseil superiéur de Pondichery,* 8 Vols, Paris, 1935-1941.

Gaudart Edmond, *Procés-verbaux des deliberations du Conseil superiéur de Pondichery du 1er fevrier 1701 au 31 decembre 1739,* 3 vols, Pondichery, 1913-15.

Lettres Édifiantes et Curieuses Ecrites des Missions Etrangèrs par Quelques Missionaires de la Compagnie de Jesus, Paris, 1717-1810.

Martineau, Alfred, *Memoirs de François Martin,* 2 Vols, Paris, 1932.

Varadarajan, Lotika, *India in the Seventeenth Century: Memoirs of François Martin,* Delhi, 1980.

(IN TAMIL)

Cartilha em Tamul e Portuguesa: Imprensa em 1554 Almeida, Fernando de (ed.) (Ministerio da Edução Nacional, Direção-Geraldo Superior do Ensino Superior e da Belas - Artes), Lisboa, 1970.

Henrique Henriques, *Tambiran Vanakkam,* A.D. 1578, (ed.) S. Rajamanickam, *Vanakkam,* Tuticorin, 1963.

———, *Kirisitiyani Vanakkam,* A.D. 1579. (ed.) S. Rajamanickam. *Vanakkam,* Tuticorin, 1963.

———, *Flos Sanctorum,* (ed.) S. Rajamanickam, *Adiyar Varalaru,* Tuticorin, 1967.

Price, Frederick, K. Rangachari & Dodwell. H, *The Private Diary of Ananda Ranga Pillai, 1736-1761,* 12 vols, (reprint) New Delhi, 1985.

Proenca Antao, *Tamil-Portuguese Dictionary, AD 1679,* (ed.) Xavier Thaninayagam, Kuala Lumpur, 1966.

Veermeer, Hans. J & Angelika Morath, A *Sumario de Arte Malavar: The First European Tamil Grammar,* Heidelberg, 1982.

III. EPIGRAPHICAL SOURCES

Aiyar, K.R. Srinivasa, *Inscriptions in the Pudukottai State,* Pudukottai, 1929.

Annual Report on Epigraphy (including Indian and South Indian Epigraphy) from 1881 to 1990.

Butterworth, Alan and Veugopal Chetty, A *Collection of the Inscriptions on Copper Plates and Stones in the Nellore District,* 3 vols, Madras, 1905.

Epigraphia Indica, Vol. 1-12, Mysore, 1900-1978.

Sastry, Sadhu Subramanya, *Tirumalai-Tirupati Devasthanam Epigraphical Series,* 6 vols, Madras, 1931-38.

South Indian Inscriptions, Texts (Publication of the Archaeological Survey of India) Vols. 1-16, Madras, New Delhi, 1890-1990.

Srinivasan, P.R. & Marie Louise Reiniche, *Tiruvannamalai: A Saiva Sacred Complex of South India,* Vol.11: (Inscriptions), Pondicherry, 1990.

Subramaniam, T.N. *South Indian Temple Inscriptions,* (Madras Government Oriental Series), III vols, Madras, 1954-1957.

IV. TRAVELOGUES

Balbi, Gaspero, "The voyage of Gasparo Balbi", in Samuel Purchas, *His Pilgrims,* Vol. X, Glasgow, 1905.

Baldeaus, Philip, A True *and Exact Description of the Most Celebrated East India Coasts of Malabar and Coromandel as well as of the Isle of Ceylon with their Adjacent Kingdom and Provinces,* 1672, London,1703; Reprint, New Delhi, 2000.

Barbosa, Duarte, *The Book of Duarte Barbosa,* 2 Vols., New Delhi, 1989.

Carre, Abbe, *The Travels of Abbe Carre in India and the Near East, 1672 to 1674,* (reprint), II Vols, Delhi, 1990.

Federici, Caesar de, "The travels of Caesar de Federici" in Purchas, *His Pilgrims,* Vol.X, Glasgow, 1905.

Fitch, Robert, "The voyage of Robert Fitch", in Purchas, *His Pilgrims,* Vol. X, Glasgow, 1905.

Foster, William, *Early Travels in India,* London, 1820.

Fryer, John., *A New Account of the East Indies and Persia: Being Nine Years Travels, (1672-1681,* (ed. Crooke, W.C.) London, 1698, (rpt) Nedeln, 1967.

Linschoten, John Van, *The Voyages of John Van Linschoten to the East Indies,* 2 Vols., London, 1885.

Lockman, John (ed.,) *Travels of the Jesuits into Various Parts of the World: Compiled from their Letters, Now First Attempted in English,* 2 vols. London, 1743.

Major, R.H. (ed), *India in the 15th Century: Being a Collection of Narratives of Voyages to India in the Century Preceding the Portuguese Discovery of the Cape of Good Hope from Latin, Persian, Russian and Italian sources*, London, 1857.

Mandelso, John Albert, (ed.) John Davis, *The Voyage and Travels of John Albert Mandelso 1669*, London, 1910.

Manucci, Nicolao, (ed.) William Irvine, *Storia do Mogor*, 1653-1708, 4 Vols, New Delhi, 1981.

Navarette, Friar Domingo, *The Travels of Friar Domingo Navarrete, 1618-1688*, (ed.,) J.S. Cummins, II, Vols, London, 1960.

Nieuhoff, John., *Zee en Lant Reize Door Verscheide Gewesten Van Ost-Indien*, Amsterdam, 1682.

Pires, Tome, *The Suma Oriental of Tome Pires and the Book of Rodrigues*, 2 Vols., New Delhi, 1990.

Polo, Marco, (ed.,) Moule, A.C and P. Pelliot, *Marco Polo, The Description of the World*, London, 1938.

Purchas, Samuel, *His Pilgrims*, Glasgow, Vol. X, 1905.

Temple R. (ed.) *The Life of the Icelander Jon Olaffson, Traveller to India*, 2 Vols, London, 1932.

Texeira, Pedro, *The Travels of Pedro Texeira*, (trans.,) W.F. Sinclair, London, 1902.

V. THESES AND DISSERTATIONS

Fernando, Venantius *"The Impact of the Portuguese Padroado on the Indian Pearl Fishery Coast: Guidelines for Renewal and practical Indigenisation of the Church"*, Unpublished Dissertation in the Faculty of Missiology, Urban University, Rome, 1977.

Gnanapragasam, V.M, *Contributions of Fr. Beschi to Tamil*, Ph.D. Dissertation, University of Madras, 1965.

Manickam, Michael, *"On Describing a Non-Indo-European Language in Traditional Indo-European Grammatical Categories*, Unpublished Master's Thesis, Hartford Seminary Foundation, Hartford, Conn.1968.

Mosse, David, *Caste, Christianity and Ideology: A Study of Social Organization and Religion in Rural Ramand*, D.Phil. Thesis, University of Oxford, 1986.

Rajamani, S. Maria, *A Critical Study of the Foreign Catholic Missionary Contributions to Tamil Language and Literature in the XVIth Century,* Ph.D. Thesis, Madurai Kamaraj University, 1972.

SECONDARY WORKS

Aiyar, R, Sathiyanatha, *History of the Nayaks of Madura,* Oxford, 1924.

Arokiaswamy, M., "The Capuchins in Madras" in *Journal of Indian History,* Trivandrum, Vol. 37, 1959, pp. 103-108.

———, "The Origin of the Vellalars" *Journal of Indian History,* Vol. XXXIII, 1955, pp.25-29; See also, Vol. XXXIV, 1956, pp. 191-193.

Arokiasamy, Susai, *Dharma, Hindu & Christian According to Robert de Nobili: Analysis of its Meaning and its use in Hinduism and Christianity,* Documenta Missionalia 19, Roma, 1986.

Arumairaj, M., *Historical Setting in the Jesuit Letters: Tamilaham in 17th Century AD,* Madras, 1984.

Basil, Anne., *Armenian Settlements in India,* Armenian College, Calcutta, 1969.

Bayly, Susan, *Saints, Gods & Kings: Muslims and Christians in South Indian Society, 1700-1900,* Cambridge, 1989.

Bertrand, J. *La Mission du Madure,* IV vols, Paris, 1847-1854.

———, *Memoirs Historiques Sur les Missions,* Paris, 1862.

——., *Excerpta e Catalogis Provincae Malabaricae,* Trichy, 1910-1911,

Besse, L., *La Mission du Madure,* Trichnopoly, 1914.

———-, *Father Beschi of the Society of Jesus: His Times and His Writings,* Trichnopoly. 1918.

Boxer, C.R. "A Note on the Portuguese Missionary Methods in the East, 16th-18th Century", *Ceylon Historical Journal,* Vol. X, 1961, pp. 77-90.

Britto, Fernão Perreira de, *Historia do Nascimento, Vida e Martyrio do Venaeravel P. João de Britto,* Coimbra, 1722.

Brown, Judith M., & Robert Erick Frykenberg, (eds.,) *Christians, Cultural Interactions and India's Religious Traditions,* Michigan, 2002.

Bugge, Henriette, *Mission and Tamil Society: Social and Religious Change in South India, 1840-1900,* London, 1994.

Buiteen, J.A.B. Van and P.C.Ganseh Sundaram, "A 17th Century Dutch Grammar of Tamil", *Bulletin of the Deccan College Research Institute*, Poona, Vol. XIV, No.3. December, 1952, pp.168-182.

Burguiere, Andre, "The Fate of History of Mentalites in the Annales", *Society for Comparative Study of History and Society*, 24, 1982, pp. 424-437.

Carvalho, Teresa Martins de., "A Evoulção de Arte em Portugal", in *Um Patrimonio Artistico*, Lisboa, 1983, pp. 163-174.

Celestine, Peter, *Early Capuchin Missions in India,* Sahidabad, 1982.

Chandler, J., *History of the Jesuit Mission in Madura: South India in the 17th and 18th Centuries,* Madras, 1907.

Chetty, Simon Cassie, *The Castes, Customs, Manners and Literature of the Tamils,* (reprint) Delhi, 1988.

Coleridge, James, *The Life and Letters of St. Francis Xavier,* London, 1881.

Cotton, J.J, *List of Inscriptions on Tombs or Monuments,* Madras, 1905.

Cunha Rivara, J.H. *A Jurisdiçõo Diocesano do Bispado de Mylapore as Possessoes Francezas Inglezas,* Nova Goa, 1867.

Dalgado, Sebastião, R., & Antony Xavier Soares, *Portuguese Vocabales in Asiatic Languages,* New Delhi, 1936.

De Melo, Carlos Merces *The Recruitment and Formation of the Native Clergy in India*, Lisbon, 1955.

D'Sa, M. *History of the Catholic Church in India, Vol. 1, AD 52-1652,* Bombay, 1910; *Vol. II, 1652 -1924*, Bombay, 1924.

De Silva, Chandra Richard, "The Portuguese and Pearl Fishing off South India and Sri Lanka" *South Asia,* Vol. IX, No. l, 1979, pp.14-28.

Devi, Konduri Sarojini, *Religion in Vijayanagara Empire*, New Delhi, 1990.

Dewald, Jonathan, "Roger Chartier and the Fate of Cultural History", *French Historical Studies*, 21 (2) 1998, pp. 221-240.

D'Orsey, Alex, J.D, *Portuguese Discoveries, Dependencies and Missions in Asia and Africa*, London, 1893.

Ferroli, D., *The Jesuits in Malabar,* II vols, Bangalore, 1951.

Foucault, Michel, *The History of Sexuality,* Vol. I, (trs.,) by Robert Hurlay, New York, 1978. Michel Foucault, *The Use of Pleasure: The History of Sexuality,* Vol. II, (trs.,) by Robert Hurlay, New York, 1985.

Frykenberg, Robert Eric., On the Study of Conversion Movements: A Review Article and a Theoretical Note", in *IESHR,* Vol. 17, No.1, 1988, p. 121-123.

Geertz, Clifford, *The Interpretation of Culture: Selected Essays,* New York, 1973.

Ginzburg, Carlo, "Micro History, Two or Three Things that I Know about it", (trs.,) John & Anne C. Tedeschi, *Critical Inquiry,* Vol. No. 20 1993, pp. 10-35.

Gnanapragasam, V.M. "Tamil in the Early Madurai Mission", *Caritas* Dindigul, July, 1963, pp. 141-146.

———, " Father Beschi: The Missionary", *Studia Missionalia,* Vol. 13, 1963, pp. 169-180.

——, "Some Salient Features of Fr. Beschi's Latin Commentary on Tirukkural", *Proceedings of the First International Seminar-Conference on Tamil Studies,* Kuala Lumpur, 1968, pp 580-586.

Gomez G. Rodeles & S. Cardon, "Early Jesuit Presence in India" *Journal of the Royal Asiatic Society of Bengal,* Vol. IX, pp. 149-168.

Grafe, Hugald, *Tamilnadu in the 19th and 20th Centuries: History of Christianity in India,* Vol. IV, *Pt.2,* Bangalore, 1990.

Hambye, E.R., *History of Christianity in India: Eighteenth Century,* Bangalore, 1997.

Heras, Henry, "Venkatapatidevaraya I and the Portuguese" *Quarterly Journal of the Mythic Society,* Vol. XIV, 1923-24, pp. 312-317.

————, "Jesuit Influence in the Court of Vijayanagara" *Quarterly Journal of the Mythic Society,* Vol. XIV, 1923-24, p. 135-140.

————, "Early Relations between Vijayanagara and Portugal", *Quarterly Journal of Mythic Society,* Vol. XXVI, 1925-26, pp. 63-74.

————, *The Aravidu Dynasty of Vijayanagara,* Madras, 1927.

——, "Indian Art in Catholic Churches", *The Examiner*, Bombay, 1927, No.78, pp 474- 501.

——, "The Altar of Father Beschi", *The Examiner*, 1932, No. 83, pp. 494-495.

————, "Two Missionary Methods in the Nation of Ancient Civilization", in *Studia Missionalia,* Rome, Vol.6, 1951, pp. 181-184.

Hosten, Henry, "Two Portuguese Inscriptions in the Kapaleeswarar Temple, Mailapur, (Madras)" in *Journal of the Asiatic Society of Bengal,* New Series, Vol. IX, No. 4,1913, pp. 169-171.

———, *Antiquities from Santhome and Mylapore,* Calcutta, 1936.

Houpert, Joseph. C., *A South Indian Mission: The Madurai Catholic Mission from 1535 -1935*, Trichy, 1937.

Houtart Francois & Genevieve Lemercinier, *Genesis and Institutionalisation of the Indian Catholicism*, Louvain-la Neuve, 1981.

Jackson, William J., *Vijayanagara Visions: Religious Experience and Cultural Creativity in a South Indian Empire,* OUP., Delhi, 2007.

Jaiswal, Suvira, *Caste: Origin, Function and Dimension of Change*, Delhi, 1998.

James, Gregory, *Tamil Lexicography*, Tubingen, 1991.

———, *Col- Porul: A History of Tamil Dictionaries*, CREA, Chennai, 2000.

Jeanne, H., "Father Henriques' Grammar of Spoken Tamil" *Indian Church History Review*, Vol.11, 1977, pp.127-157.

Karashima, Noborou., "Nayak's rule in North and South Arcot districts in South India during the Sixteenth Century", *Acta Asiatica*, 48, Tokyo, 1985, pp.1-26.

——, "The Kammalars of Sixteenth Century in South Arcot District in South India", K.V. Ramesh, S.P. Tewari arid M.J. Sharma, *Dr. G.S. Gai Felicitation Volume*, Delhi, 1990, pp. 205-8.

——, "The Uprising of the Valangai and Idangai Groups: Conflict in Agrarian Society" *Toward a New Formation*, Delhi, 1992, pp. 141-158.

Khadirvel, S. *A History of the Maravas*, 1700-1802, Madurai, 1977.

Knowlton, Edgar C, " Antão de Proenca's Vocabulario Tamulico-Lusitano: Indo-Portuguese Elements", *Tamil Culture*, Vol. XI, 1964, pp.135-164.

———, "Portuguese-Tamil Linguistic Contacts" in *Proceedings of the First International Seminar- Conference of Tamil Studies*, Kuala Lumpur, 1966, pp. 607-617.

Krishnaswami, A., *Tamil Country under Vijayanagara*, Annamalai Nagar, 1964.

Kubler G., & M. Soria, Art and Architecture in Spain and Portugal, Baltimore, 1958.

Launy, Adrien, Histoire de la Mission de L'Inde: Pondichery Maissour, Coimbatour, IV Vols, Paris, 1898.

Lionel, Caplan, "Class and Christianity in South India", *Modern Asian Studies*, Vol. 14, 1980, pp, 645-71.

Lopez, Fernando Felix, Missões Franciscans na India Oriental em 1595 Casa Pessoal e Legislacdo, 1953.

Love, Henry Davidson, Vestiges of Old Madras, 1640-1800: Traced from the East India Company's Records Preserved at Fort St. George and the India Office and from other Sources, III Vols, London, 1913, (reprint) Delhi, 1988.

Magnusson, Sigurdur Gylfi, "The Significance of History: Social History, and Micro History within the Post-Modernist State of Knowledge", *Journal of Social History*, Vol. No. 36, 2003, pp. 701-735.

Mallampalli, Chandra, *Christians and Public Life in Colonial South India, 1863-1937*, London, 2006.

Manickam, S., "The Politico-Economic Impact of the Religious Conversions of the Paravas in the Gulf of Mannar, 1 537-1552 ". *Tamil Civilization*, Vol. I, No. 1, pp. 57-73.

Marx, Karl, *Articles on India*, Bombay, 1945.

Mathew, K.S., "Indian Ocean and Cultural Interaction" *Indica*, Vol.35, No.2, 1998, pp.97-133.

Mcpherson, Kenneth, "Processes of cultural interaction in the Indian Ocean: An Historical Perspective", *The Great Circle*, Vol.6, No.2, 1984, pp.78-92.

Meersman, Achilles. *The Franciscans in Tamilnad*, Schoneck Beckenried, 1962.

——, "The Origin of the Shrine and Cult of Our Lady of Vailankanni", *Indian Ecclesiastical Studies,* Vol. I, 1962, pp. 60-67.

———, "The Catholic Church in Tranquebar and Tanjore", *Indian Church History Review,* Vol. I, 1967, pp. 94-95.

Mosse, David, "Catholic Saints and the Hindu Village Pantheon in Rural Tamilnadu", *Man*, 29, 1994, pp. 301-302.

More, J.B. P. "Hindu-Christian Interaction in Pondicherry, 1700-1900" in *Contributions to Indian Sociology*, New Series 32, 1, 1998, pp.98-121.

Mundadan, Mathias, "The Portuguese Settlement in Mylapore", *Indian Church History Review,* Vol. III, 1969, pp. 103-114.

Muthuraj, J. Gnana Selvam, "A survey of the Tamil Christian Writings in European Libraries", *Journal of the Royal Asiatic Society of Great Britain and Ireland*, London, No. 2, 1985, pp. 181-190.

Narayanan, M.G.S. & Veluthat Kesavan, 'Bhakti Movement in South India' in S.C. Mallik, (ed.,) *Indian Movements: Some Aspects of Dissent, Protest and Reform*, Simla, 1978.

Nazareth, Casimiro de., *Mitras Lusitanas no Oriente,* II. vols, Lisboa, 1913.

Nevett, A., *John de Britto and His Times*, Anand, 1980.

Norbert, Wolf, "Capuchin Missions in South India: 17th and 18th Centuries, in *Round Table of Franciscan Research,* Vol. 26, 1961, pp.11-18.

Oddie, G.A., "Protestant Missions, Caste and Social Changes in India, 1850-1914", in *IESHR*, Vol.6. 1969, pp.259-291.

Pandian, J, *Caste, Nationalism and Ethnicity, An interpretation of Tamil Cultural History and Social Order*, Bombay, 1987.

Pillai, K.K., "Were the Pallavas Brahmanas?" *Journal of Oriental Research*, Silver Jubilee Volume, 1975, pp. 242-245.

Pillei, Muthusami, "A Brief Sketch of the Life and Writings of Fr. C.J. Beschi, Veeramamuni", *Madras Journal of Literature and Science*, 11, 27, 1840, pp. 250-300.

Plattner, Felix Alfred, *The Catholic Church in India: Yesterday and Today*, Bangalore, 1964.

Rajamanickam, S., *The First Oriental Scholar,* Tirunelveli, 1972.

———, *Robert de Nobili on Indian Customs,* Palayamkottai, 1972.

———, "De Nobili in the Madurai Jail: A Letter to Sebastian de Maya" Indian Church History Review, Vol. 18, No. 2, 1984.

Ramaswamy, Vijaya, "Artisans in Vijayanagar Society", *Indian Economic and Social History Review* XXIII (4), 1985, pp.417-43.

Roche, Patrick, A., *Fishermen of the Coromandel,* New Delhi, 1984.

Santos, S.R., *The Shrine Basilica of Our Lady of Health,* Vailankanni, (11th edition), Thanjavur, 1980.

Sauliere, A., "Extracts from Some Jesuit Annual Letters: Malabar and the Fishery Coast Translated from Latin " in *The Indian Athenaeum,* Calcutta, Vol.1, No.2, August, 1923, pp. 55-58.

———, "The Annual Letter of 1582", in *The Indian Athenaeum* Vol. I, No.3, September, 1923, pp. 11-16.

———, "Fr. Roberto de Nobili S.J: The First European Indologist", *Indica,* (Commemoration Volume), Bombay, 1953, pp. 272-276.

———, (Revised by S.Rajamanickam) *His Star in the East,* Anand, 1995.

Schurhammer, Georg, "Iniqitembrane and Bete Perumal Chera and Pandya Kings in South India ", *Journal of the Bombay Historical Society,* Vol. 3, 1930, pp. 1-40.

——, "Festas em Goa no Ano 1624" in *Boletim do Institute Vasco da Gama,* Vol.69, 1952, p. 36.

———, *St. Francis Xavier: His Life, His Times,* Rome, 1977.

Sebastian, Joe., *The Jesuit Carnatic Mission,* Hyderabad, 2004.

Seggiano, Ignazio Da, "Documenti Inediti sull Apostolato del Minori Cappuccini nel Vicino Oriente, (1623-1683)" in *Collectanea Francescana,* Roma, Vol. 23, 1953, pp. 301-317.

Soares, Aloysious, *Catholic Church in India: A Historical Sketch,* Bombay, 1904.

Srinivasachari, C.S. A *History of Gingee and its Rulers,* Annamalai Nagar, 1943.

Stein, Burton, Brahmana and Peasant in Early South Indian Society, *The Adyar Library Bulletin,* Vol. XXXI-XXXII, Madras, 1967-68, pp. 229-269.

Stephen. S. Jeyaseela, "Socio-Economic Role of Dubash Pedro Kanakaraya Mudaliar in the French Colony of Pondicherry,

1711-1746: A Study in Resilience" *Revue Historique de Pondichéry*, vol. XVIII, 1995, pp. 15-32.

———, "Indo-Portuguese Archives at Santhome of Mylapore in South India: An Exploratory Study of its Records", *Itihas*, XXII, January-December, 1996, pp. 55-89.

———, "Urbanism and the Chequered Existence of the Indo-French Town of Pondicherry" *Revue Historique de Pondichéry*, Vol. XIX, 1996, pp. 29-64.

———, *The Coromandel Coast and its Hinterland: Economy, Society and Political System, 1500-1600*, New Delhi, 1997.

———, *Portuguese in the Tamil Coast: Historical Explorations in Commerce and Culture, 1507-1749*, Navajyothi Publishing House, Pondicherry, 1998

———, *Muthu Vijaya Thiruvengadam Pillai Naatkurippu, 1794-1795*, (The Diary of Muthu Vijaya Thiruvengadam Pillai) Pondicherry, 1999.

———, *The Diary of Rangappa Thiruvengadam Pillai, 1760-1766*, (in original Tamil, Critical introduction and edited with Historical Notes) 2 vols, Pondicherry Institute of Linguistics and Culture, Pondicherry, 2000.

———, *The Diary of Rangappa Thiruvengadam Pillai, 1761-1768, Translated from Original Tamil*, Institute for Indo-European Studies, Pondicherry, 2000.

———, Portuguese Tamil Grammar: Modernization and Democratization of Tamil, Institute for Indo-European Studies, Pondicherry, 2001.

———, *Letters of the Portuguese Jesuits from Tamil Countryside, 1666-1688*, Pondicherry, 2001.

———, "Societal Changes: Portuguese and the Native Christians in Tamil Country, Cir AD 1537-1759", in K.S. Mathew, Teotonio Rosario, Desouza and Pius Malekandathil, (eds.,) *Portuguese and the Socio-Cultural Changes in India, 1500-1800*, Tellicherry, 2002, pp.479-513.

—, "Social Life of the Portuguese and the Luso-Tamils in Mylapore and Nagapattinam during the 16th & 17th centuries, *Bharta Vidya*, Vol. II, 2003, pp.7-14.

——, *Literature, Caste and Society: The Masks and Veils*, Kalpaz Publications, Delhi, 2006.

Stephen, Neill, *A History of Christianity, 1707-1850*, Vol. II, Cambridge, 1985.

Sundaram, Meenakshi T.P & M. Shanmugam Pillai, "Portuguese influence revealed by the Tamil words", *Journal of the Annamalai University,* Vol. 16, no. 3, 1951, pp. 11-25.

———, "Tamil Letters and sounds of the Seventeenth Century", *Collected papers of Prof. T.P.M* (Sixty-first Birthday Commemoration Volume), Annamalai Nagar, 1961.

Sundaram K. Meenakshi, *The contribution of European scholars to Tamil*, University of Madras, Madras, 1974.

Thamby, K. Siva, "Early South Indian Society and Economy: The Tinai Concept", *Social Scientist*, Vol. 29, 1974, pp. 20-37.

Thaninayagam, Xavier., "Tamil Manuscripts in European Libraries", *Tamil Culture,* Vol. III. October, 1954, pp. 210-288.

———, "The First Printed Books in Tamil" *Tamil Culture,* Vol. VII, No.3, July, 1958, pp. 288-308.

Thekkedath, Joseph., *The Troubled Days of Francis Garcia S.J: Archbishop of Cranganore, 1641-1659*, Rome, 1972.

———, *History of Christianity in India: From the Mid 16th Century to the End of 17th Century, 1542-1700,* Bangalore, 1982.

Timory, Edith.," The Early Church of St Thomas at Mylapore" *Indica,* Vol. 47, No. 1, pp. 51-54.

Vermeer J. Hans & Angelika Morath, *The First European Tamil Grammar*, Heidelberg, 1982.

Victor, Henry, " Tamil Translation of the Bible by the Danish Halle Mission of the 18th Century", *Indian Church History Review,* Vol. XVI, No. 1, June, 1982, pp. 72-85.

Vishwanathan, Gauri., *Outside the Fold: Conversion, Modernity and Belief*, New Delhi, 2001.

Vriddhagirisan, *The Nayaks of Tanjore,* Annamalai Nagar, 1942.

Whiteway, R.S., *The Rise of Portuguese Power in India,* London, 1899.

Wicki, Joseph, "Duas Relações Sobre a Situação da India Portuguesa nos annos 1568-1569" in *Studia,* Vol. XVIII, 1961, pp 151-153.

——, "Life of P. Henrique Henriques S.J. (1520-1600)" *Studia Missionalia,* Vol. XIII, 1963, pp. 157-160.

———, "The Confraternity of the Charity of Fr. Henriques", *Indian Church History Review,* Vol.1, 1967, pp. 3-8.

———, "Six Unpublished Letters of Fr. Roberto Nobili Existing in the Vatican Library", *Proceedings of the Second International Seminar-Conference on Tamil Studies,* Madras, 1969, Vol. II, pp. 295-297.

———, "Jesuit Residence of St. John in Santhome Mylapore 1549-1598", in Anand Amaladas, (ed.) *Jesuit Presence in Indian History,* Anand, 1988, pp.54-61.

Williams, Raymond, "Base and Superstructure in Marxist Cultural Theory", *New Left Review*, No. 82, 1973, pp.3-16.

Winius, George Davison, "The Shadow Empire of Goa in the Bay of Bengal" in *Itinerario,* VII, (2) 1983, p. 92.

Zupanaov, Ines G., *Disputed Mission, Jesuit Experiments and Brahmanical Knowledge in Seventeenth Century India*, Delhi, 2001.

Index

A

B

N

T